45.00

D1715195

S. L. Frank

S. L. Frank

*The Life and Work of
A Russian Philosopher*

1877–1950

Philip Boobbyer

OHIO UNIVERSITY PRESS
ATHENS

Ohio University Press, Athens, Ohio 45701
©1995 by Philip Boobbyer
Printed in the United States of America
All rights reserved

99   98   97   96   95   5   4   3   2   1

Ohio University Press books are printed on acid-free paper ∞

Library of Congress Cataloging-in-Publication Data

Boobbyer, Philip.
    S. L. Frank : the life and work of a Russian philosopher,
1877–1950 / Philip Boobbyer.
        p.   cm.
    Includes bibliographical references and index.
    ISBN 0–8214–1110–1
    1. Frank, S. L. (Semen Liudvigovich), 1877–1950.   2. Philosophers
—Russia—Biography.   I. Title.   II. Semen Liudvigovich
Frank.
B4238.F73B66   1995
197—dc20
[B]   94–34209
                                                                 CIP

Contents

Acknowledgments

I FIRST BECAME interested in Semyon Frank in 1987 while I was doing a Master's degree at Georgetown University, and I wrote my thesis on his political philosophy. After returning to Britain, I entered the Government Department at the London School of Economics and Political Science (LSE) to write a more comprehensive doctoral thesis on Frank's life and work. I completed that in the summer of 1992, and after a few changes, that has become the book which is published here.

I am extremely grateful for the help and advice of many people. I would particularly like to thank Professor Dominic Lieven, my supervisor at the LSE, whose original idea it was to write the Ph.D.; Professor Janet Coleman and Rt. Reverend Rowan Williams, who read some of the philosophical chapters; Dr. Philip Swoboda, whose own Ph.D. on Frank was so stimulating and who kindly read my work and offered some useful suggestions; Frank's daughter and son, Natalia Norman and Vasilii Frank, for giving extensive interviews, allowing me access to some of their family papers, and making available their photographs; Aleksandr Frank, also for making available his family photograph archive; Aleksandr and Natalia Solzhenitsyn, for giving me access to their archive; Iurii Senokosov, with whose assistance I was able to spend three months based at the Institute of Philosophy in Moscow in 1991, and whose continual encouragement has been invaluable; Albert Sobolev, for his assistance while I was based at the Institute of Philosophy; Dr. Stephen Carter and Professor Geoffrey Hosking, my Ph.D. examiners, for their advice and encouragement; Irina Alberti, for her advice and help; Nikita Struve, for making available Frank's letters to his father; Modest Kolerov, for his help, advice, and teamwork; Aleksei Garponenkov, for showing me his notes from the Saratov archives; Gabriel Superfin, for his archival advice and locating the Frank letters in the British Museum; and Dr. Michael Hughes, for reading my manuscript and his comments. I would also like to thank Natalia Afanas'eva, Professor David Goldfrank, Boris Jakim, Richard Kindersley, Irina Kirillova, Vadim Kozevoi, and Professor Valerii Petrochenkov for their generous help at different times. I also extend thanks to Ellen Scarufi of the Columbia University Bakhmeteff Archive, Natalia Chekmareva of the Russian State Historical Archive of St. Petersburg, and Zinaida Peregudova of the State Archive of the Russian Federation for their helpful assistance.

I am grateful to the Economic and Social Research Council for funding my research; the British Council for arranging my study visit to Moscow; and Elsie Hayter and Gérard d'Hautville for their financial assistance at the beginning of my Ph.D. work. I am also grateful to Alan Channer for his help in preparing the photographs.

Finally I would like to express my great appreciation to Leif Hovelson and Bryan Hamlin for their encouragement; Mrs. Carol Dunbar for her care and hospitality when I was in Washington, D.C.; John and Elizabeth Lester, whose home in London provided such a good atmosphere for writing a Ph.D.; and most of all, my parents, for their love and support over these last years.

Philip Boobbyer, London

Out of the depths have I cried unto thee, O Lord.
—Psalm 130

Introduction

THERE ARE MANY reasons for writing a biography of Semyon Frank. Quite apart from his philosophy, he lived a remarkable life. Born in Moscow in 1877, he was exiled from Soviet Russia in 1922 and died in London in 1950. The son of a Jewish doctor, he became a revolutionary Social Democrat in his teens and finished his life as a Neoplatonist Christian. One of the Russian revisionist Marxists, he was then involved in the Kadet Party during the 1905 revolution before breaking with active political activity and turning to philosophy. He lived in Petrograd through the First World War until September 1917, after which he went to Saratov, where he experienced the chaos of the Russian Civil War. Living in Germany after his exile, he witnessed the rise of Hitler in Berlin, left for France in a hurry in 1937, and spent part of the war hiding from the Gestapo in the Grenoble mountains. It was a life that encompassed a lot of history.

Yet along with this, Frank was arguably Russia's greatest twentieth-century philosopher. Indeed, V. V. Zen'kovskii, the historian of Russian philosophy, considered Frank "in strength of philosophic vision . . . the most outstanding among Russian philosophers generally— not merely among those who share his ideas." For its lucidity, conciseness, systematic character, and unity, Zen'kovskii considered Frank's system "the highest achievement . . . of Russian philosophy."[1] Doubtless, Zen'kovskii's assessment is disputable, but his remarks emphasize Frank's stature in the Russian tradition. In the style of German idealism, Frank constructed a comprehensive philosophical system, which he believed offered a coherent alternative to materialism. He was deeply worried by the implications of epistemological relativism and constructed a system of metaphysics designed to link epistemology and ontology, to bridge the gulf between throught and being. In addition, he attempted to express the idea of a personal

God in philosophical language. His system also embraced social philosophy, anthropology, and ethics.

Russian philosophy has its own character and traditions. It is almost always engaged with "ultimate questions" and is consequently very interdisciplinary. In this sense, Frank's work was typically Russian. For him, philosophy always had a religious dimension. At the same time, Frank's work, like the work of his contemporaries Nikolai Berdiaev and Nikolai Losskii, was rooted in the broader European philosophical discourse of the late nineteenth and early twentieth centuries. The issues Frank chose to raise in his thought were often very Russian, but it was Europeans who excercized the greatest influence over him. As a philosopher, he was a European Russian.

In regard to his political and social thought, Frank is often associated with the Russian liberal intellectual Petr Struve and the religious philosophers Berdiaev and Sergei Bulgakov. These men, who had all been Marxists in the 1890s, after 1900 moved in the direction of German idealism and Christianity, then broke with the revolutionary movement altogether. Frank is often best remembered for his biting essay "The Ethic of Nihilism," which appeared in their famous critique of the Russian revolutionary intelligentsia in the collection of essays *Landmarks* (*Vekhi*) of 1909.

Nevertheless, Frank's significance in this sphere goes far beyond his contribution to *Landmarks*. Especially in emigration, he developed a coherent "liberal conservative" political philosophy. In this he must be bracketed with Struve, who was probably the most important of the Russian twentieth-century liberal conservative thinkers. The political realism of Frank and Struve rested on a belief that political reforms are never effective without an accompanying cultural transformation. Inspired by Struve, and on the basis of his own metaphysical ideas, Frank constructed a political philosophy that combined a vision of absolute values with the demands of a pluralist society. Issues relating to the state, law, human rights, and social change all received serious attention within the framework of his political thought. In addition, in response to the various crises caused by Bolshevism and Nazism, Frank developed the politics of what he later termed *Christian realism*. This was a bold attempt to apply spiritual values in the political arena. It suggests that, in Frank's thought at least, Russia does possess elements of a middle-ground Christian democratic political tradition.

Religious ideas were, of course, central to Frank's thought. The historian of Russian religious thought, N. M. Zernov, put Berdiaev, Bulgakov, Struve, and Frank at the center of "the Russian religious renaissance of the twentieth century."[2] Their break with Marxism and positivism, he believed, was representative of a broader return to

Christianity, which began among certain sections of the Russian intelligentsia before the revolution and developed powerfully in emigration. For his part, Frank is undoubtedly a very interesting figure from a religious and theological perspective. A Jewish convert to Russian Orthodoxy, his Christian beliefs were of a universalist, nondogmatic kind. Having been a Marxist socialist, his spiritual ideas were constructed in direct response to the challenge of secular ideology. Living a life of perpetual difficulty, his religion was an attempt to cope with a chaotic and evil world where on the face of it a divine order was lacking.

In 1922 Lenin ordered the exile from the Soviet Union of more than two hundred of the "bourgeois professors." Frank was among this group, which included Russia's foremost philosophers, historians, and theologians and represented the cutting edge of the intellectual opposition to Bolshevism. The ironic result was that Russian intellectual life was able to continue and even flourish in emigration. Admittedly, these Russian thinkers lived in obscurity, often poverty, and very few were really accepted into Western intellectual circles. Nevertheless, as they had hoped would happen, they were able to keep alive the old Russian intellectual heritage. With the collapse of the Soviet Union, they have become very important. Russia has never welcomed Western ideas and values unconditionally, and the discomfort caused by Westernization is no less strong in the post-Soviet world than it was in pre-Soviet times. In this sense, Frank and those of his colleagues who knew and respected both Russia and the West are particularly important. They represent an authentic, moderate Russian tradition which can now, as it were, replant itself in Russian soil. Their style of thought may have dated in some ways, but many of their concerns remain relevant to any era.

Zen'kovskii, Losskii, and F. C. Copleston, in their histories of Russian philosophy, offer useful introductions to Frank's ideas but tell us little about what lay behind them. There are two, more detailed studies of selected aspects of Frank's thought in German—R. Tannert's *Zur Theorie des Wissens: Ein Neuansatz nach S. L. Frank 1877–1950* and R. Gläser's *Die Frage nach Gott in der Philosophie S. L. Franks*—but again, they are written for philosophical rather than historical audiences. Philip Swoboda's recent doctoral dissertation on Frank's metaphysics from 1902 to 1915 is excellent, and I have benefited greatly from it; in particular, his examination of the influence of Kant, neo-Kantianism, and Fichte on Frank. There is also a doctoral dissertation on Frank's social and political thought by M. M. Boll. However, a clear need for a full historical biography of Frank remains.

In writing this book, I have had access to a lot of Frank's unpublished letters. Many of them—for example, his correspondence with his wife, Tatiana Sergeevna, Berdiaev, and the Swiss psychiatrist Ludwig Binswanger—were written in emigration. Other important sources for the emigration period include his recently discovered and now published correspondence with Struve of 1922–25, his wartime notebooks, and his numerous unpublished manuscripts. For those readers who already know something of Frank's life in Russia, this emigration experience will perhaps be of most interest. New material that I have used from Frank's life in Russia includes the previously unknown police files on his activities as a radical student in the 1890s and two fascinating collections of letters, both now published: Frank's correspondence with Struve of 1901–5; and his letters about *Landmarks* to its editor, M. O. Gershenzon. The result of all this is that I have been able to produce a detailed picture of Frank's life and the thinking that lay behind his philosophical vision.

Frank once wrote that "all philosophy is nothing but confession— confession of what one believes and loves, what stirs in the soul, what one is supported by and what one lives by."[3] Frank's ideas undoubtedly grew out of his experience and personality. In itself, that is not surprising; one would expect it of any thinker. In addition, it does not tell us whether his philosophy is great philosophy. Nevertheless, I have deliberately included a lot of material in this book that relates to Frank's personal life and the life of his family. Apart from a desire to put together the sources of his ideas, there are a number of reasons for this. First, this is the first biography of Frank, and I wanted to include the material simply so that readers could have access to it. Second, Frank was much respected by his contemporaries. He was a man of great integrity, and that in itself is worth studying. Third, I wanted to give an intimate as well as intellectual picture of one of Russia's foremost twentieth-century thinkers. Finally, I wished to put Frank's life in the perspective of the social history of the Russian professoriate and emigration.

Frank's son Viktor wrote that his father in a sense "defined the spiritual character of a whole generation of Russians, especially in emigration."[4] Both in Russia and emigration, Frank's life is a window to Russian twentieth-century history. I hope readers will find it as interesting as I have.

1

Early Years

SEMYON FRANK was born in Moscow on 16 January 1877. His parents lived on Piatnitskaia Street, just south of the Moscow River, but they soon moved north of the river to the Miasniki district, and it was there that Frank grew up. In March 1882 his father, Liudvig Semyonovich, died of leukemia after a long illness. Frank, who was too young to be deeply affected by his death, had few memories of his father, just the picture of tiptoeing in to see him when he was dying.[1]

Liudvig Semyonovich Frank was born in 1844 in the western region of Russia. It seems that his father was the manager of an estate in Lithuania and that further back, the family may have been descended from the Jewish community that had fled Spain at the end of the fifteenth century.[2] Liudvig Semyonovich had many brothers and sisters, a number of whom died of consumption. Joseph, the oldest, was a wandering adventurer who lived for a time in Bulgaria. Another brother, Sigismund, was a chemist who worked in Moscow. Liudvig Semyonovich went to Vilnius University, but his studies were interrupted by the Polish rebellion of 1863.

Many of the Polish rebels escaped into the surrounding forests and from there exerted moral and sometimes physical pressure on the young people of Vilnius to join them. Consequently Liudvig Semyonovich's father sent him away to Moscow, where he entered the Medical Faculty at Moscow University, becoming a full doctor in 1872. He stayed on in Moscow and worked in the Medical Department of the Ministry of Internal Affairs. After his father died, his mother, Felitsia (born Frenkel), and sisters, Teofiliia and Eva, came to join him. He worked as a military doctor in the Turkish war of 1877, for which he received personal noble status, the Order of St. Stanislas, third class. His exploits included going out to help the wounded under enemy fire and looking after the children of people exiled to Siberia.[3] It was the

1

only such decoration given to a Jew for services in the war, and nobility was extremely rare among the Jewish population. It meant that Semyon Liudvigovich, as his son, was officially titled "honorary citizen."

Felitsia Frank lived to a great age, dying in Warsaw in the early 1900s. She lived with her daughters in Moscow, spoke French and German, had a great interest in the histories of Europe's leading families, played the piano, and was generally well educated. Her room was crammed with furniture and trinkets in the rococo style, and Frank later commented that its effect on him was "the first artistic impression of my childhood, a childhood which was generally poor in artistic impressions."[4]

Frank's mother's family came from Germany—her father, Moisei Mironovich Rossiianskii, from Kovno, and his wife, Sara Dobriner, from Tilsit. Rozaliia Moiseevna, Frank's mother, born in January 1856, was their only child. In the mid-1860s, they moved to Moscow where Moisei Rossiianskii was one of the pillars of the local Jewish community. Rozaliia went to the First Moscow Women's Gymnasium where she received a typical Russian bourgeois education, which would have involved compulsory classes in a variety of subjects from religion and Russian literature to needlework and gymnastics.[5] She married Frank's father when she was 18 and bore him three children: Sofia, Semyon, and Mikhail. She was practical rather than intellectual, but according to Frank's half brother, Lev Zak, who was born after she remarried in 1891, Frank owed his intellectual abilities primarily to her: "Mother was a passionate person . . . exceptionally good but subject to fits of anger, which blinded her. . . . It always seemed to me that mother was filled with an exceptional fund of potential talent, which was only felt but never found creative expression. I think that Senia's [Semyon Liudvigovich's] talent and quality—the depth of his philosophical thought, and the enormous memory which enabled him to possess great erudition, [and] all his intellectual ability—was inherited by him from his mother, the more so because his father's sister and two of his brothers, whom we knew, gave no sense that they were people with any kind of intellectual gifts."[6]

Frank had a tranquil and serious temperament. While Sofia and Mikhail played games, he would sit on a footstool and read. He was inclined to be so serious that the family later joked that he used to meditate as a baby. He was also very determined. Sofia described him as "always stubborn."[7]

After Liudvig Frank's death, Rozaliia's father became the main influence on Frank. He lived with the Franks in various places in the Miasniki district, and from 1889 they lived with him in a detached house he had bought on Krivoi Street. Moisei Rossiianskii spoke bad Russian and could not write in the language at all. Like most Jews from the western region, he had a thorough grounding in Jewish theology through the Bible and the Talmud and was well informed on nine-teenth-century political history. By profession, he was a tea dealer and acted as a middleman between Chinese tea companies and Moscow traders. According to Frank, he had no formal education but had a huge number of Jewish religious books, great intellectual breadth, and a real devotion to Jewish traditions. He was Frank's first intellec-tual mentor, the inspiration for his earliest religious feelings:

> My grandfather was my first educator. He forced me to study the an-cient Jewish language . . . and to read the Bible in it. He took me to the synagogue (on the big Jewish festivals—he did not observe the Sabbath and all the complex details of the ceremonial law), where I received my first religious impressions which were to last my whole life (these along with the religious impressions of Russian Orthodoxy, through my nan-nies and the surrounding Russian milieu). The blessed feeling with which I kissed the cover of the Bible when they brought round the "scrolls of the law" in the synagogue, in a genetically-psychological sense became the foundation of a religious feeling which defined my whole life (with the exception of my unbelieving youth, approximately when I was be-tween 16 and 30). My grandfather's stories about the history of the Jew-ish people and Europe became the first foundation of my intellectual outlook.[8]

Frank's half brother, Lev, records that on his deathbed in 1891, his grandfather expressed the desire for Frank to take up the study of the Bible and the Talmud. Although at that time Frank lost his religious beliefs, he later said that his commitment to religious philosophy was a fulfilment of that wish.[9]

During Frank's childhood, the Jewish population of Moscow in-creased considerably, peaking at 26,000 in 1889 before falling sharply in 1891–92, because of a mass expulsion of Jews.[10] Frank's father, as a doctor, was not socially typical of the Jewish population, which con-sisted mainly of mechanics, distillers, and craftsmen, who played an important role in Moscow commercial life.[11] In addition, the Franks felt fully integrated into the life of the Russian intelligentsia. They were quite wealthy and were able to afford Russian nannies and a German nursery governess. Rozaliia Moiseevna was on occasions able to go away to Carlsbad for cures. In a way, it was a European upbring-ing rather than specifically Russian or Jewish. The German influence was considerable. Frank grew up bilingual in Russian and German, and some of his mother's family still lived in Germany.

The last decades of the nineteenth century were difficult for Jews in Russia. In the 1880s there was a quota system for Jews entering schools and universities; Jews were excluded from the bar; Jewish doctors were excluded from employment with public authorities; and Jews lost their franchise rights in the *zemstva* (district councils). The process reached a climax in the winter of 1891–92 when the government evicted thousands of Jewish artisans from Moscow and moved Jews from territory on the western frontiers into the interior. In spite of all this, there is no evidence to suggest that the Franks were seriously affected. In spite of the fact that in St. Petersburg and Moscow only 3 percent of gymnasium students and 2 percent of university students could be Jewish,[12] Frank went to school and university in Moscow without apparent difficulty and was soon followed by his brother, Mikhail.

Moscow itself was expanding rapidly, and the population reached almost a million by 1897. Through its textiles, the Moscow area was the biggest industrial region in the empire. It was also the center of Russia's vast tea trade, so Frank, through his grandfather, must have grown up with an awareness of Moscow commercial life. He would also have been aware of the changing urban environment. The family lived in the area around Pokrovka and Maroseika streets in the Miasniki district, which was located to the north and east of Chinatown and the Kremlin. Although it was not as important industrially as the outer ring of Moscow, it saw considerable industrial expansion in the 1870s and 1880s.[13]

In the autumn of 1886, before he was 10, Frank entered the Lazarevskii Institute of Oriental Languages in Moscow. He went straight into the second class, which suggests that he may have had academic tuition at home. The school, founded in 1815 for Armenians, had prepared clerks for the Asiatic reaches of the empire. By the time Frank went there, it had become more general, and its classes were conducted according to the model of the classical high schools.[14] There is no evidence to suggest that Frank studied any of the oriental languages. There were 246 pupils for the school year 1886–87, of whom 12 were Jewish. It was a school with a cosmopolitan flavor. The number of Russian Orthodox was 72, and the majority, belonging to the Armeno-Grigorian tradition, numbered 156.[15] Frank studied there for nearly six years.

In the spring of 1891 his mother married again. Her husband was a former radical populist who had been exiled to Siberia, Vasilii Ivanovich Zak. Along with Sofia and Mikhail, they moved to Nizhnii Novgorod, a city famous for its fair and with a growing commercial base. Sometime after, Sofia married a very wealthy Jewish businessman, Abram L'vovich Zhivotovskii, and moved out of the intelligentsia world she had grown up in. Frank stayed in Moscow, living with his grandfather until he died in December 1891. He lived another year with relatives in Moscow, but because his right of residence depended on his living in the parental home, he had to leave, and he followed the family to Nizhnii Novgorod. The Franks lived in Kanavino, which was at the center of the town's economic and industrial life and the location of the fair.[16]

V. I. Zak was the next great influence on Frank after his grandfather. Born around 1854 in Moscow, he worked as an assistant chemist in a Moscow pharmacy and attended classes at Moscow University as an occasional student. In the late 1870s, he got involved with the populists. He was arrested in 1878 when the police intercepted mail to him about the importation of radical propaganda for the St. Petersburg workers, and he was sent under police surveillance to eastern Siberia. He settled in Irkutsk, where he worked in a chemist shop. He attempted to escape from Irkutsk with another revolutionary and onetime follower of the anarchist Mikhail Bakunin, Nadezhda Smetskaia, but they were caught, and he was sent farther away, to Verkhoiansk in the Iakutsk region. In 1882, Zak and a group of friends tried to escape by boat down the Iana River into the Arctic Ocean, but they were caught, and Zak was transferred again to another settlement in the region. He eventually finished his term of exile in 1884.[17]

Zak's radicalism was formed in the 1870s, the age of P. L. Lavrov and N. K. Mikhailovskii and the "going to the people." His friends, to whom he introduced Frank in Nizhnii Novgorod, and the philosophy they espoused belonged to this earlier generation of idealistic populists. Zak's appearance in the Frank family led to "endless conversations on political themes,"[18] and his experience and beliefs deeply affected Frank. He recalled later: "The first 'serious' book which I read on his recommendation were some essays by Mikhailovskii (*What is Progress?* etc.); then I read Dobroliubov, Pisarev, Lavrov and others." According to Frank, the overall influence of these ideas was not deep, and they did not fit his mentality. "Rather," he wrote, "it was simply the general atmosphere of ideological search that affected me, . . . and strengthened my consciousness of the importance of having a world-outlook."[19]

The passionate desire to have a complete picture of the world was typical of the Russian intelligentsia. Nikolai Losskii, the famous philosopher and contemporary of Frank, who was also attracted by radical ideas in his youth, recalled reading the same authors and wrote: "Like many of the 'Russian lads' whom Dostoevskii speaks about, I wanted to have a distinctively formulated worldview."[20]

These "populist" writers differed considerably in their beliefs. N. A.

Dobroliubov and D. I. Pisarev were committed materialists; Mikhailovskii, with his "subjective method in sociology," and Lavrov stressed the role of the individual in creating history. Taken as a whole, they offered a combination of passionate ethical concern and deep secularism. They lived in the shadow of English utilitarianism, and positivism dominated their world.

Although there is probably some substance to Frank's assertion that he was never really attracted by populist ideas, his whole outlook changed. The religious faith of his grandfather disappeared and was replaced by an interest in the social sciences and political economy. Whether Frank lost his religious faith with a struggle is hard to tell. It may have been like Sergei Bulgakov, who also lost his faith and later refound it. Bulgakov later wrote that he lost his belief in God almost without a struggle: "I was helpless in the face of unbelief, and in my naivity thought . . . that it was the only possible and sound form of worldview for 'clever' people. I had nothing with which to oppose and defend myself against nihilism."[21] Bulgakov also pointed out that the process of becoming an *intelligent* was part of a growing sense of the incongruities of contemporary Russian life. This was how Losskii saw it: "It is not surprising that young people who began to reflect on questions of justice, immediately fell into the position of conspirators, forming secret groups, and were doomed to fall under biassed influences and get a tendentious interpretation of social phenomena."[22]

The focus for the liberal and populist intelligentsia in Nizhnii Novgorod was the home of S. Ia. Elpat'evskii (1854–1933), to whom Zak introduced Frank. Elpat'evskii had started his studies at seminary but then left to read medicine at Moscow University. He was arrested and repeatedly exiled for his activities in the revolutionary movement but eventually settled in Nizhnii Novgorod, where he pursued his medical practice. Frank made good friends of the Elpat'evskii family. When crossing the river back to Kanavino became difficult because of ice drifting, he would stay in the town, sometimes with the Elpat'evskiis. Liudmila Elpat'evskii, their daughter, recalled Frank in those early days: "Senia was a very fine pianist for his age and would often accompany me on the piano, and we thought that he would turn into a remarkable scholar because he struck us with his mature mind and comprehensive knowledge."[23]

The Nizhnii Novgorod intelligentsia of the early 1890s was lively. Many returning exiles used to pass through the town, and in the months after the famine of 1891–92 whole groups of students who had been exiled from St. Petersburg and Moscow began to accumulate there.[24] The famous writer V. G. Korolenko, who had been involved with the "going to the people" movement of the mid-1870s and was later exiled to Iakutsk for refusing to swear allegiance to Alexander III, had settled in Nizhnii Novgorod. At the Elpat'evskii home, Frank met Korolenko and his friend N. F. Annenskii, both involved with the populist journal *Russian Wealth* (*Russkoe bogatstvo*), and through them he also met the aging populist Gleb Uspenskii. It was a politically active set of people. Korolenko and Annenskii were the official exponents in Nizhnii Novgorod of the People's Rights Party, a short-lived populist political group set up in 1893 under the veteran revolutionary Mark Natanson whose members were to play a major role in the 1905 revolution.[25] There were debates at the Elpat'evskii home, which Frank attended. Elpat'evskii's intellectual milieu was clearly associated with *Russian Wealth* at this time, and although Frank moved toward Marxism rather than populism, he must have felt at home with these people. In 1898, his first major article on Marxist theory was published in *Russian Wealth.* Later in life, Frank recalled belonging to a Korolenko circle in Nizhnii Novgorod.[26] Whether this was at the Elpat'evskii home or another venue is not clear, but it is an indication of the extent of his involvement in populist discussion.

The great issue of the early 1890s was the 1891–92 famine. In the summer of 1891 there were serious crop failures all along the Volga. The situation was made worse in 1892 by an outbreak of cholera and typhus that claimed 400,000 lives. Many of the *zemstva* were directly involved in famine relief, and in subsequent years there was anger among members of the *zemstva* that the government did not respond to their useful work by giving them more responsibility. The relationship between *zemstvo* and government in Nizhnii Novgorod was complicated by the fact that during the famine the governor of the region tried to bypass the *zemstvo* by setting up an alternative food supply commission in spite of the fact that the statistical department of the *zemstvo*, headed by Annenskii, was one of the best in the country.[27]

The famine sparked a controversy. "No underground organization could have aroused the political consciousness of the Russian intelligentsia the way the famine did."[28] The populist response, articulated by Mikhailovskii, V. P. Vorontsov, and N. F. Danielson in *Russian Wealth*, was to blame capitalism for the famine. Among the Marxists, however, Peter Struve, who was to become Frank's closest friend, saw the famine as a clear indication that class differentiation had triumphed in the villages. With the promise of a new landless proletariat, he welcomed a new era of capitalism in Russia. Plekhanov and Lenin took similar positions. This cold-blooded response shocked people and intensified the Marxist-populist debate. In Nizhnii Novgorod, the debate was intense, and it turned into a generational as well as ideological struggle. From the summer of 1891, Marxist thought began to exercise a strong pull on a new generation of students. In Nizhnii Novgorod they were grouped around an older Marxist, P. N. Skvortsov, and various university and high school students. They went into open debate with the populist camp focused around Elpat'evskii. One of those involved, S. N. Mitskevich, who was at that time a student at Moscow University and was to be involved in the founding of the Moscow Workers' Union, recalled the heat of the debate: "The polemic was heated. The question was how to relate to the famine, and how the famine would affect the future of Russian capitalism. . . . The populists accused the Marxists of welcoming the famine, of a heartless attitude to the hungry, said that the Marxists should go and help the factory owners and kulaks to deprive the people of their land . . . . [The Marxists] did not stop accusing the populists of utopianism, petty-bourgeois attitudes, starry-eyed idealism etc. The basic theme of these arguments was also the question of the role of the individual in history, of the laws of the historical process."[29]

The local schools were affected by Marxist influence. Mitskevich relates that almost all the capable and lively young people in the upper classes of the Nizhnii schools were subject to Marxist influence in the years 1891–93: "[The students] read and studied a lot; in particular they with great enthusiasm studied the Russian economy through the *zemstvo* statistical handbooks, studied and criticized the populist books and essays."[30] Three of the most influential figures in the schools were I. P. Goldenberg, M. A. Silvin, and A. A. Vaneev—all were subsequently to work with the St. Petersburg Social-Democrats. In his memoir, Silvin states that there was little teacher-pupil antagonism at the local gymnasium and that the atmosphere there was good. However, he became attracted by Marxism because it offered a challenge for life: "Tolstoianism and its teaching about individual primitive work and non-resistance to evil offered no way out. In the fiction writers— Korolenko, Chekhov and others, we found human ideas which struck a chord in our mentality, but their works lacked a challenge to a living activity, to a struggle for a different life."[31] Silvin and the other high school students organized various Marxist groups and met together in a central circle to plan their activities and prepare topics for discussion. Students used to sell photographic pictures of Marx, Engels, Plekhanov, Lavrov, and Chernyshevskii to the town intelligentsia and had contacts with local factories.

Frank entered the local gymnasium in the autumn of 1892. He did very well academically, got top marks in all his subjects, and left the school with a gold medal.[32] As in all the gymnasiums, there was great emphasis on the classics; upwards of 30 percent of school time was spent on Latin and Greek.[33] There was also an emphasis on Russian language and literature and mathematics. In later life Frank was always to stress the value of a classical education.[34]

Frank also got involved with one of Silvin's Marxist groups. In his autobiographical memoir, Frank states that he belonged to a small intellectual circle of about six students, under whose influence he read the first two volumes of *Capital*.[35] This was either the Silvin group or one of its affiliates. The only other well-known figure in this group was A. M. Nikitin, later a Menshevik who was to be the minister of posts and telegraph in both Kerenskii's coalition governments. Frank's brother, Mikhail, three years his junior, also encountered revolutionary ideas at the gymnasium, but the details are vague.[36] Silvin recalled that the circle read lithographed copies of works by V. O. Kliuchevskii and G. V. Plekhanov and discussed Marx, Engels, and Lassalle.[37] It is not clear whether Frank's Marxist activity extended to agitational work while still in Nizhnii Novgorod, but he was a known figure in the Marxist camp, and his involvement in the Nizhnii Marxist milieu is mentioned in the memoirs of two contemporary radicals—Mitskevich[38] and M. G. Grigor'ev.[39]

Frank was simultaneously involved, then, in one populist group under Korolenko and one Marxist group under Silvin. The former group may have represented his parents' generation and a broader intellectual community in the town, while the latter was a student body with more agitational interests. In that atmosphere Frank would have been aware of the tensions within radical circles. Grigor'ev states that "the Marxists of that time had contact with Elpat'evskii least of all,"[40] so Frank almost certainly found himself in the middle of these disputes. Silvin had a reputation as a fierce proponent of Marxism against all forms of populism.[41]

Frank was drawn to Marxism by its intellectual breadth. It answered the need that he, Losskii, and many others felt for a complete explanation of the universe. "Marxism attracted me," he wrote later, "because of its scientific form, specifically as 'scientific' socialism. I was attracted by the idea that the life of human society, if studied in the way natural science studies nature, can be known through natural laws. When I consequently read in Spinoza's *Ethics* the phrase: 'I will talk about human passions and vices as if they were lines, planes and bodies,' I found there expression of the same cherished mood which I felt on studying Marx's theory. It is natural that I also accepted the revolutionary and ethical tendency of Marxism, although my soul did not lie in that direction."[42]

In addition to its "scientific" quality, Frank found in Marxism a system of beliefs that claimed to explain everything. This suited his mentality, and unites his Marxist period with the philosophy that followed it. "I was always a monist," he wrote later, "always conscious of multiplicity as subject to unity. . . . I was a 'Platonist,' accepting the reality of general principles and forces. I am inclined to see the inner, spiritual, 'other' world in its opposition to the outer-empirical world." Later in life, Frank characterized himself as a dreamer.[43] He meant that he was always concerned with the divine foundation of things. Frank's seriousness as a person, the early religious influence of his grandfather, and the Marxist monism that followed it suggest that he was already dreaming in these early years.

The only source of personal information that relates to this time comes from Lev Zak, who although born in 1891, gives a very good idea of Frank's personality in the 1890s—his love of music, his seriousness, and a certain personal magnetism:

> I see Senia now at the dacha in Chernii near Nizhnii, still a schoolboy, with his trousers tucked right up, dragging a net into the water with Misha and the other village kids—Misha and Senia very much loved fishing at that time—and now at the piano in our drawing room in Kanavino. Senia played the piano a lot in his youth. . . . He had enough [technique] to pick out the notes and play quite difficult pieces, but never had any pretensions to be a real performer. Almost every evening I fell asleep in the children's room to the sounds of Beethoven and Chopin, which floated in from the drawing room. . . . Often, Senia sat me on his knee and we sang children's songs together. . . . But during childhood the singing was the only moment when I did anything with Senia, generally I interested him less than Misha or Sonia. . . . I think that at that time children did not interest Senia, and even when he was younger he was not inclined to play. . . . Nevertheless . . . every time he returned home after a long absence, it was a great celebration for me.[44]

2

Marxism

THE FIRST MARXIST circle in Moscow had been founded in 1893 by Mits-kevich, but it had collapsed in December 1894 when he and the rest of the group were arrested. In April 1894 a number of radical groups came together to form the Central Workers' Union. Frank must have arrived in Moscow sometime in the spring because he was involved with one of these groups, which used to meet on the edge of Moscow and discuss the development of agitation among workers and the creation of circles for propaganda. On 30 April, they organized a se-cret meeting of workers from all parts of the city, which was attended by over two hundred people. This, followed by a subsequent attempt to issue a proclamation to the workers of Moscow, resulted in wide-spread arrests. Apparently, Frank avoided arrest because he was away with two other members of the group gathering information about a strike in Iaroslavl.[1]

In June 1894 Frank registered at the Law Faculty at Moscow Uni-versity. Instead of going to lectures, he participated in Social-Demo-cratic debating circles and conspiratorial activities. He used to change into civilian clothes so that the formal dress of the student would not draw attention, then go off to the Sokolniki district in the northern part of Moscow to propagandize the workers.

The revolutionary milieu Frank participated in was an extension of the group in Nizhnii Novgorod. Frank wrote that in his first two years at university it was the group from his school gymnasium that domi-nated his life.[2] There were two leading figures in it, M. N. Kotov[3] and M. F. Vladimirskii, probably heading different factions, but they were both members of the Silvin circle from Nizhnii Novgorod.

The Vladimirskii group, although short of money and literature, began to organize workers' groups and find members of the intelli-gentsia to help with the educational work. One of the leaflets they

11

produced called for a shorter working day.⁴ Some of the workers' circles underwent systematic training, presumably in revolutionary methods and ideas, and there were a couple of discussion groups that raised issues about everyday working life. They tried to attract as many workers as possible into these informal groups, and they would pick out the best for more formal, organized work. By that method they built up a small group of workers who in January 1896 united with another group to form the Moscow Workers' Union that led the Moscow workers movement in 1896–7.⁵

The full nature of Frank's involvement in the underground activity at this time is not clear. He was known to the Moscow police for his activities in the Kotov circle, but he was certainly not in a leading position in any of these groups. During the year 1895–96, he had begun to have doubts about what he was doing. At the end of the academic year, he went back to Nizhnii Novgorod. Exams finished before the end of May that year because the authorities wanted to get students out of Moscow before the coronation of Nicholas II. Witte had chosen Nizhnii Novgorod as the site of the all-Russian exhibition that took place at that time and Frank saw Nicholas II there with the tsarina for the first and only time. On his return to Moscow in the autumn, Frank's disillusionment with underground political activity came to a head, and he left the group. Once again he may have avoided arrest, for in December three members of the Vladimirskii group were among those arrested in a police crackdown.

Frank was a typical absent-minded intellectual. His room in Moscow was totally disorganized and heaped up with books and dust.⁶ His health was never strong, and remained a problem throughout his life. At one point, when it was fashionable to go cycling, he tried it but gave up, complaining that it was like running uphill. He was told by a doctor that he had a heart too small for his height.⁷ All this points to a serious, delicate person.

Frank's break with this radical group caused him great anguish:

The "workers" . . . and the social reality in which the revolutionary had to operate did not imprint itself on me in a distinct way. I acted rather like one hypnotized, as if in a dream. . . . I was irritated by the premature, categorical, juvenile opinions and ignorance which lay behind them. And when I was on my own, I caught myself thinking about everything but revolution and practical revolutionary activity. This feeling of dissatisfaction was such that . . . I immediately and thoroughly broke with my colleagues although I was called a "traitor" and "deserter" for it (because it was assumed that any courageous person had to be a revolutionary and to leave the group could be explained only by cowardice). At that time, I was spiritually so lacking in independence that neither I nor anyone else could explain my real motives. I explained that I was disillusioned with the revolutionary worldview and that I could not do practical work until I had checked the assumptions of that worldview. In fact, this was the rebellion of my being against a mentality and activity which did not fit it. And it was also a passionate hunger for pure, disinterested, theoretical knowledge.

[Participating in the underground work of the Social-Democratic movement] I felt that I was beginning to suffocate in that atmosphere of sectarian faith; in the autumn of 1896, after a time of hesitation and tortuous, dramatic explanations with colleagues, I left the revolutionary Marxist movement, and began to seriously study political economy, so that, although I did not stop being a socialist, I came to realize the shakiness and lack of originality of Marx's theory of value.[8]

In spite of what he says here, Frank did not break with Marxism or radical circles at this time. He broke with the people associated with the Silvin group from Nizhnii Novgorod. His social milieu started to broaden, and he began to use his mind. His comment that he was so lacking in spiritual independence that he could not understand himself is helpful. It indicates that his Marxism was not the result of a personal crisis or encounter with authority. Unlike with the execution of Lenin's brother, for example, there was no personal tragedy that solidified his commitment to the revolutionary movement. He absorbed his Marxism at school, and only in 1896 did he realize that the underground mentality was not his. The current revolutionary mood was well expressed in a popular contemporary pamphlet by A. Kremer and Iu. Martov that called on the agitator "to immerse himself constantly in the mass, to listen, to pick on the appropriate point, to take the pulse of the crowd."[9] This did not suit Frank's tranquil temperament, and thus it is not surprising that he did not respond to the atmosphere of conspiracy. The break with this revolutionary circle was an important moment. It was an affirmation of Frank's independence that he later described as a turning point in his life.[10]

After 1896 Frank got more involved in university life. Although he had entered the Law Faculty because of his interest in radical ideas, his first impressions of the lectures had not been good. This seems to have changed. In the second year, Frank studied the history of the philosophy of law, a course that involved an introduction to Hellenistic ideas and Heraclitus, in whom Frank was to have a lifelong interest. He also went to the lectures of the legal philosopher P. I. Novgorodtsev, with whom he was to have considerable contact in subsequent years and whose political lectures were very popular. In Silvin's circle, Frank had read a lithographed copy of Kliuchevskii's course on Russian history, and now in Moscow Frank went to Kliuchevskii's lectures in the Historico-Philological Faculty.[11]

However, by far the most important influence on Frank at this time was A. I. Chuprov, a leading exponent of liberal populist ideas, who was professor of political economy and statistics at Moscow University from 1878 to 1899. Frank described him as a "remarkable lecturer and even more remarkable man." Frank joined a circle of students who would gather in Chuprov's flat to talk over questions of political economy. The flat, always swarming with people asking for help, became a kind of club. Chuprov's angle was very different from the certainties of the political underground. He was a patient man who could handle strong opinions with a certain detachment and would occasionally "shyly express doubt whether the evolution of socialism out of capitalism was scientifically proven."[12]

Frank's break of 1896 can be interpreted, in part at least, as a movement away from the Social-Democratic Marxism of Plekhanov toward what he called a "general ideological trend in Russian social thought," the successor to the Russian "Westernizer" tradition whose main representative was Peter Struve. Struve's *Critical Remarks on the Question of Economic Development in Russia* had appeared at the end of 1894 and caused enormous interest with its conclusion: "Let us recognise our backwardness and go over to the school of capitalism." With Plekhanov in emigration, Struve became the leading Marxist thinker in Russia, but while committed to an essentially economic interpretation of history, he adorned his work with a range of quotations from German neo-Kantian philosophers. Frank was impressed by the breadth of his approach and later commented that his references to such diverse sources stimulated him to reflect on more serious philosophical issues. Under the overall influence of Struve, Frank was to become one of the "Legal Marxists." They were a loose group of writers, consisting of Struve, Frank, Bulgakov, Berdiaev, and M. I. Tugan-Baranovskii, who looked at Marxist theories from a theoretical rather than a political angle.[13]

In 1896 Struve wrote an article on the German neo-Kantian philosopher Rudolf Stammler. Stammler had just published a book, *Economics and Law*, in which he cast doubt on the validity of Marx's sociological ideas. According to Marx, the superstructure of society— its ideas and legal institutions—depend on the economic base. Stammler accepted this but stated that the superstructure's dependence on the base was not total and that it was not always clear which caused the other. He believed that there would be merit in studying society from the legal (superstructural) as well as the economic point of view. He believed that human aspirations were an important feature of society, as well as social conditions.[14] In a polemic that also featured Bulgakov, Struve reacted positively to Stammler, arguing that necessity and freedom formed two orientations of consciousness: "Logically, of course, the whole future is as predetermined as the past is determined. But, in that predetermined future in which our actions participate, there is always a blank spot which volition and free activity can colour according to their desires."[15]

Frank was struck by Struve's response to Stammler: "If you remember that the idea of subjecting the social ideal to the immanent course of social development was a basic dogma of Marxist 'scientific socialism' and that from this position Russian Marxists fought a furious battle with Mikhailovskii's so-called 'subjective method in sociology,' then you can understand the importance of P.B's philosophical piece."[16]

The chance to meet Struve soon came through a close publishing friend of Frank's, M. I. Vodovozova.[17] In 1895, Vodovozova and her husband set up a publishing house for social and economic literature that played a significant role in the development of Marxist ideas in the 1890s, their publications including Bulgakov's *On Markets in Capitalist Production* and Lenin's *The Development of Capitalism in Russia*. In 1897, she was on the editorial board of the Russian Marxist journal *New Word* (*Novoe slovo*). Frank started to work for her, translating books on economics and political science.[18] Also through her, he met a whole circle of Marxist literary figures.

Vodovozova was at the center of discussions relating to the creation of the new Marxist newspaper *The Beginning* (*Nachalo*). Frank was involved and was known by the police to be the author of a letter that requested help with the journal.[19] The impetus behind *The Beginning* came partly from the police informer M. I. Gurovich. There were a number of editorial meetings and luxurious dinners with Gurovich, after which it was decided to invite Struve down from St. Petersburg for discussions. One evening in the autumn of 1898 Frank met Struve in Vodovozova's flat.

Frank remembered the meeting with Struve ever afterward: "I remember the spiritual grace in his character and, with all his outer untidiness and indiscipline, the dull color and fine features of his face, and the manner of speaking which was so typical for him." They met again shortly afterward for a discussion. Frank had two questions on his mind that he asked Struve about. The first related to the revolutionary milieu Frank had just broken with. What should one's attitude to the revolutionary movement be? Struve stated that it was possible to continue to participate in revolutionary work and to retain independence of mind. The second question related to the famine of 1891–92. Social-Democrats had faced the dilemma of whether to support aid to the starving peasantry when they regarded the famine itself as a healthy sign of class struggle. Frank asked Struve whether it was right to feed the peasantry in such circumstances, a question he had previously found "complicated and confused." He was struck and impressed by Struve's simple reply that "when it comes to feeding hungry people, there is no need to get intellectual about it."[20]

Frank described Struve's answer to this second question as "the first of his clear, simple, sharp formulas which in later times so often answered my doubts and were my guiding ideas." When he met Struve, Frank was unclear about what he believed in: "At that time, in spite of all my wide reading in the area of theoretical knowledge, I was still a complete fledgling chicken, fairly helpless in deciding the morality of social questions." In this situation, Struve became for Frank, seven years his junior, his intellectual mentor and was to remain so for the next ten years.[21]

Their mentalities suited each other. They both had serious academic minds. Frank, apparently, had an intellectual magnetism about him from a very early age, which meant that even his mother had a certain awe of him.[22] He had also just published his first major article, an attempt to graft Austrian "psychological" value theory onto Marx's labor theory of value. Struve was a great contrast to the aggressive student world Frank knew. At the end of 1898, Frank attended a crowded gathering at the Moscow Juridical Society at which Struve outlined his ideas on the serf economy. His speech was very theoretical and disappointing to those who wanted a controversial discussion.[23] This style, academic rather than political, would have appealed to Frank, for whom the pursuit of "disinterested, theoretical knowledge" was becoming the aim and calling of his life.

The Beginning appeared in 1899 in St. Petersburg under an editorial group that included Struve, Tugan-Baranovskii, and a future associate of Frank, V. Ia. Bogucharskii. Frank wrote some reviews of books on economics in issues 4 and 5 of *The Beginning*,[24] but the journal was soon closed down by the authorities. Frank also wrote some reviews in the journal *The Divine World* (*Mir bozhii*) at this time.[25]

Frank's work for *The Beginning* was part of his continuing involvement with revolutionary activities. Frank's most detailed memories of the 1890s are in his reminiscences of Struve and this means that the influence of Struve on him in the 1890s is probably overplayed. In later life Frank undoubtedly belittled the importance of his Marxist phase; to his family, he referred to it as part of his youthful immaturity.[26] In his memoir he described the break with the revolutionary group of 1896 as a key moment. However, in 1899 he was arrested for his part in the student demonstrations of that year and the police files of the period indicate that he remained involved in radical circles in these years. Frank was known to the police for his friendship with Vodovozova, involvement with *The Beginning,* and his friendship with a member of the Kiev Union for the Struggle for the Liberation of the Working Class, Natan Vigdorchik.[27] More important, however, he was known to the police as one of the leaders in Moscow of another group of students, the Nizhnii Novgorod Circle (*Kruzhok Nizhegorodtsev*). Elpat'evskii's son Vladimir Sergeevich (who was on the organizing committee behind the student unrest of 1899 in St. Petersburg) was closely involved in this and in October 1897, in a letter intercepted by the police, stated that "[Frank] is not attending the university, having decided to stay an extra year. He is giving lectures to the girls of last year, in a society called 'Emancipation of Women.' . . . [Frank] is putting a lot of hope on these girls."[28]

That year, Frank shared a flat with three other members of the Nizhnii Novgorod Circle—V. A. Kilchevskii, G. A. Liven, and A. V. Romanychev. Also living in the flat were two sisters, Aglaida and Emilia Orlova. They all aroused the suspicions of the police by gathering every evening for discussions.[29]

In early 1898 Frank was involved in the preparations for a radical gathering of students in which members of the Nizhnii Novgorod Circle and members of a "Women's Union"[30] were present. Various figures were arrested, including Kilchevskii, who was exiled from Moscow for two years.[31]

In 1899 the Nizhnii Novgorod Circle was fully involved in the student unrest that broke out in February. The government had given a warning to the students of St. Petersburg University that they would not tolerate demonstrations on 8 February, a traditional day for celebration. The warning was disregarded, and there was a demonstration that resulted in police dispersion of students. A mass rally of university students then decided to boycott the university, and within ten days all the higher schools in Moscow and St. Petersburg had to close. By the end of March, the strike had spread as far as Warsaw and Riga.

In Moscow, the government reacted quickly and decisively. On 15 February, the leaders of the Nizhnii Novgorod Circle were arrested, including Mikhail Frank, and his future brother-in-law, P. M. Gratsionov, and another prominent activist, A. I. Iaroshevich. In following up these arrests, the police discovered that the "centre of gravity of their enquiry was the flat of the Frank brothers." In their view, "All the threads of the matter were in the hands of the older Frank, while Iaroshevich and his comrades were the executive organ."[32] The police thus concluded that Frank was one of the guiding minds behind the student unrest.

Frank was arrested on 31 March and released on 7 April. The police in their report referred to his "extensive links in revolutionary circles and extremely harmful activity":

> Being by inclination a convinced Marxist, Frank has tirelessly preached Social-Democratic and generally radical ideas, both through his work in the legal and non-legal press and in oral propaganda among his friends, from whom he organized a self-education circle, which he led. Separately from this, Frank until very recently was the head of a large circle of Nizhnii Novgorod students whose agitation greatly promoted the latest student unrest and whose representatives were on the executive committee and which independently published proclamations. . . .
>
> One of these proclamations, entitled "From a group of Moscow writers and thinkers" was put together by Frank himself and given to the Executive Committee for distribution, on the eve of his arrest. In this hectographed proclamation, it is said, amongst other things: "The tyranny of the university administration has crossed all boundaries . . . and human dignity demands a categorical and unconditional refusal to sit exams." Not limited by this, Frank openly agitated among the students, arranging gatherings, one of which took place, under his chairmanship, on Prechistenskii Boulevard.

The police also stated that the Orlova sisters had, on Frank's initiative, arranged "readings and gatherings." This was probably another reference to the women's group. They also noted Frank's connection with Vodovozova and Vigdorchik. On the basis of all these things, they exiled him from all university cities for two years.[33] Whether the police considered Frank as dangerous as their report suggests is doubtful. At any rate, 840 Moscow students were expelled from the university, while only 199 were simply exiled.[34]

The experience in prison left no lasting affect on Frank. He appears to have spent his time working out how to communicate with the other students by knocking on walls.[35] However, one event at this time did mark Frank deeply. His close friend G. A. Liven, who was also arrested, attempted suicide by pouring gasoline on his bed and trying to set himself afire on 5 April; he died a day later. Students expressed their anger by gathering in large numbers at the funeral. Frank was among the mourners and took some of Liven's possessions back with him to Nizhnii Novgorod afterward.[36] Before he died, Liven had time to tell the police that he was unfit for life because he could not conquer the habit of masturbation and that he had deceived his parents all his life.[37] It appears that he had suffered pangs of guilt at an inability to be a revolutionary. Frank described the events later in emigration:

> In one innocent revolutionary circle in Moscow there took part a quiet, well-educated, shy young man who came from a Russified German gentry family. When the circle was arrested and it became clear to all that nothing drastic would happen to the participants and that the whole matter would finish with expulsion from university and exile from Moscow, this young man, unexpectedly for all, killed himself in prison and in a terrible way which witnessed to an exceptional degree of emotional despair: firstly, he swallowed some splinters of glass and then pouring petrol over his bed, set fire to himself and died after terrible agonies. Before his death, he confessed he had been tormented by his inability to be a real revolutionary, by his inner aversion to [revolutionary] activity and by an insuperable desire for an ordinary worldly life; he confessed to being a person unfit for anything and had come to a decision to do away with himself. His death stunned us, but we lay the blame for it on the "despotism" of the hated regime; we made . . . the funeral into an anti-government demonstration and reassured ourselves in the consciousness of our own revolutionary virtue. But when now, after all that has happened, I remember this event, I feel the blood of this innocent victim on myself; I feel myself the moral participant in all the murders and evil acts which are committed in abundance in the name of revolution. Because surely we ourselves, the ideological servants of duty, sentenced this innocent young human soul to death by our moral demand for a revolutionary mode of thought and revolutionary heroism; we, although we did not see it, forced it, by our tyrannical, merciless demand for revolutionary service, on one who was not fitted for it.[38]

In this description of the event Frank neither mentions Liven by name nor states that the victim was a very close friend of his. Nevertheless, it is difficult to avoid the conclusion that Liven's suicide was as important in Frank's life as the earlier events of 1896. Frank's later moral philosophy, articulated, for example, in his *Collapse of the Idols* of 1924, is about a morality of salvation rather than judgment, and Liven's experience as well as his own surely form the background to it. In 1896, he had been unable to cope with a sense of being a person at war with himself. This is the focus of his description of Liven.

From Moscow, Frank went back to Nizhnii Novgorod, and from there he went to Berlin and stayed in Germany for the next two years. He took some classes at Berlin University, went to the lectures of the German neo-Kantian George Simmel, and studied the work of two other neo-Kantian philosophers, Wilhelm Windelband and Alois Riehl. Struve and his wife Nina came to Berlin at the end of 1899. At this time Frank also met his relatives from his mother's family.

In the spring of 1900 Struve published some articles in the journal *Life* (*Zhizn'*) that Frank found very interesting. Struve's central concern was Marx's labor theory of value. According to Marx's theory, there are two kinds of capital in a capitalist economy: fixed and variable. The fixed capital is the machinery and buildings, the variable capital the labor. From the labor put into a product, the capitalist gets more value for the product in subsequent exchange than he paid the worker in the first place. Consequently, surplus value is created through the exploitation of labor. Surplus value is therefore a product of variable rather than fixed capital. With the mechanization of industry and the consequent decline in the percentage of labor input, the rate of profit should fall. Marx's theory, however, did not convince everyone. The organic composition of capital—the ratio of fixed to variable capital—did not always seem to affect the rate of profit. Struve concluded in *Life* that surplus value is the product of fixed as well as variable capital, and this, if true, seriously undermined all of Marx's economic theories.[39]

The main concern of Frank's writing was the theory of value. He had already published an article in *Russian Wealth* entitled "The Psychological Tendency in the Theory of Value," and while in Berlin, he wrote his first major work, *Marx's Theory of Value and Its Significance*, published in 1900 by Vodovozova in St. Petersburg. The article in *Russian Wealth* had attempted a form of reconciliation between Marx's labor theory and the new Austrian school of economics that stressed the subjective influence of supply and demand on value. Frank argued that the subjective whims of the consumer and the accompanying fluctuations in supply and demand were useful explanations for price fluctuation in a primitive economy but that the labor theory remained the best overall measure of value. Labor value was the equilibrium to which prices always strive.[40]

While Frank remained basically committed to Marx's labor theory of value in 1898, by 1900 he stood in a position of "friendly neutrality."[41] *Marx's Theory of Value and Its Significance* was an attempt to unite Marx's theory of value with the subjective school. Labor, Frank now declared, was important, but not the only factor for all products in exchange. Objects found in nature or antiques, for example, could be priced by their rarity rather than labor cost. Much better in assessing value, he argued, was supply and demand. Having defended Marx's labor theory two years before, Frank had abandoned it as a measure of exchange value by 1900. However, he wanted to save the labor theory of value, and *Marx's Theory of Value* was an attempt to put it on a different footing altogether. His basic argument was that although exchange value is not based on labor value, there is a way that it can be so if the whole of an economy is taken together. Society as a whole can also be analyzed as a united subject. If society is the subject, then the labor expended within the society to meet its different needs will again have an equivalence to the demand. In this ideal sense, the total subjective value, "the social subjective value," is equivalent to the labor expended to meet the demand.

Frank's argument requires a leap of the imagination. He was not describing a real society. The evaluation of products from the point of view of the interests of society as a whole did not involve evaluation of a definite reality because society did not yet act as a whole. Frank was talking about a potential wholeness rather than a factual one. Yet although only a potential reality, it was still, in Frank's words, "a *real psychological fact*, which in certain conditions—i.e., when society is given the opportunity to consciously act on the economic relations of its members—acquires practical significance." Frank was striving after an ideal vision of society, what the economist J. K. Rodbertus called a "great national-economic idea" that would acquire importance only in the future.[42]

Frank's writings on Marx provide a useful historical insight into the concerns of the "Legal Marxists" and the process they underwent in their abandonment of Marxism, and they also display an eye for detail and a capacity for argument typical of Frank's later writing. Yet the idea of "social subjective value" does not appear to have much practical significance. As Struve said in a generally positive review of the book, Frank's conclusions were of questionable importance: "It is surprising how the sharp critical insight of the author does not see the obvious strangeness of his arguments. The labor theory is a 'real psychological fact,' but the presence of this 'real fact' is determined in conditions which do not exist in economic reality."[43]

More interesting than Frank's actual theories were his comments on methodology. In *Russian Wealth*, he stated that in the science of political economy the desire for economic advantage is presumed to be the main motive for all economic activity. Frank agreed with that approach, but only as a "model" that "partly corresponds to actuality."[44] In the foreword to *Marx's Theory of Value*, he was sharply critical of the division of political science into Marxist and bourgeois schools and critical of the "dogmatic worshipping of [Marx] which takes the place of evaluation and creative work."[45] These points reveal, first, the beginnings of Frank's general skepticism about the very subject of political economy. Political economy was valid, but it was one angle on things; it could no longer provide for Frank the all-embracing vision he hoped to find. Second, it reveals an unhappiness with committed schools of thought. In one sense, all of Frank's thought until his death in 1950 was concerned with reconciling opposites, bridging different schools of thought. This was part of what he called his monism. *Marx's Theory of Value* was his first attempt at a unifying, whole picture.

Frank's monograph on Marx also touched on the subject of "social psychology," a theme on which he was to write an extended essay in 1905. He suggested that it would be valuable to study the process whereby individual opinion becomes objectivized as collective or social value.[46] This was the direction in which Frank's study of society was to move; he was increasingly interested in the relationship between the individual and the collective consciousness.

Frank went back to Russia in 1901. He stopped in Munich to see his brother, Mikhail, who was studying there after his own exile. Struve was also there and came to see him off at the station with a small suitcase that had an illegal collection of the Social-Democratic organ *The Spark (Iskra)* hidden in a double bottom, and he asked Frank to take it to a conspiratorial address in Moscow. Frank refused: "I was confused by this unexpected assignment: having already broken some time before with Social-Democratic work, and feeling no sympathy for its ideas or methods, I immediately decided in my soul not to carry out this dangerous task, but I admit, I did not have the courage to say this openly to P.B., but only expressed hesitation."[47] Struve noticed the hesitation and suggested that instead Frank take the suitcase to the head of the Viennese Social-Democrats, Viktor Adler. That is what he did, taking the opportunity to have a good discussion with Adler about the German revisionist Marxist Eduard Bernstein.[48] It was a notable episode, revealing both Frank's indecisiveness and his deep desire to break with illegal activity.

On reaching home and being banned from taking his university exams in Moscow, he took them instead at Kazan University and graduated in the spring with a first-class diploma. He was "very satisfactory" in every subject except police law, which was only "satisfactory."[49] His student years were over. His Marxist period had basically run its course.

3

Idealism

FRANK'S INTEREST in philosophy had first been aroused by reading Spinoza's *Ethics* and Kuno Fischer's *History of Modern Philosophy* while he was at high school. He commented that Spinoza had a long-term influence on his philosophical thought and that "in 'the intellectual love of God,' in contemplative pantheism, in the mystical feeling of the divine total-unity . . . I felt early on something which touched the deep essence of my personality."[1] Then, in 1896, Frank attended a meeting of the Moscow Psychological Society in honour of the 300th birthday of Descartes. The speakers were N. Ia. Grot, president of the society and professor of philosophy at Moscow University, and L. M. Lopatin. Frank was intrigued and described the occasion as the "first push" on the road of his philosophical career.[2]

Grot was a close friend of the Russian philosopher Vladimir Solov'ev and in 1890 founded the first Russian philosophical journal, *Questions of Philosophy and Psychology* (*Voprosy filosofii i psikhologii*) to combat the positivism of the intelligentsia and offer a focus for idealist and religious writing. Grot was part of a wider circle of philosophers who set the stage for the movement from Marxism to idealism, which was then made famous by the Legal Marxists after 1900. These included A. I. Vvedenskii (1856–1925), who in 1890 gained the chair of philosophy in St. Petersburg and was the first avowed Kantian to become a professor in Russia; P. I. Novgorodtsev (1863–1924), one of Frank's lecturers in the Law Faculty at Moscow University, who specialized in theories of natural law; and the princes Sergei (1862–1905) and Evgenii (1863–1920) Trubetskoi, both of whom were interested in Christian metaphysics and influenced by Solov'ev.[3]

The Legal Marxists were not only influenced by a cautious but growing interest in idealism in Russia itself. The German neo-Kantian movement, which opened up a belief in moral values as an independent sphere of life, was possibly even more important. There were two aspects to Kant's thought of great influence: first, his critical method, which outlined the categories of thought and forms of intuition that render knowledge possible; second, his idealism, which was constructed around the moral "categorical imperative" whereby people have an obligation to act according to moral principles that can be universally applied. The central importance of these ideas for Russian thought was that they justified human freedom and allowed for the influence of individuals as well as social forces in history. Frank first read Kant when he was at university and of the neo-Kantians was especially influenced by Windelband and Simmel, whose ideas he had encountered in Berlin. The theories of Windelband, whose *Preludes* Frank translated into Russian in 1903, emphasized the difference between the natural and social sciences: whereas the former are positivist, the latter allow for the presence of moral purpose in history. Simmel's ideas about "objective motives"—ideal moral goods that are neither altruistic nor egotistic—which he outlined in his *The Philosophy of Money* of 1900, played an important role in Frank's ideas about morality as he outlined them in his contribution to a collection of essays of 1902, *Problems of Idealism (Problemy idealizma).*[4]

In 1900 Berdiaev published *Subjectivism and Individualism in Social Philosophy* in which he attempted to graft the transcendental Kantian categories onto Marxist theories and reconcile human freedom with the march of historical materialism and the victory of the working class.[5] The obvious contradiction between believing in real freedoms at the same time as the inevitable victory of the progressive class soon led Berdiaev away from materialism altogether to a personalist view of history. Struve wrote an introduction to Berdiaev's book that was also significant. He came out in favor of some kind of spiritual life, absolute moral principles, and what he called Christian-democrat morality. Bulgakov was also moving in a religious direction. At the beginning of 1902 he published an essay on Ivan Karamazov in which he criticized the atheistic moralism of Nietzsche and referred positively to Solov'ev.[6]

These were the influences, then, that acted on Frank at the turn of the century. However, the most important immediate influence on Frank's mind was not philosophical but emotional. Having taken his degree at Kazan, he joined his mother on an estate in the Crimea for the summer, then spent the winter in Yalta, where he met literary figures like Maksim Gor'kii, Anton Chekhov, and Konstantin Bal'mont, and some of Tolstoi's family.[7] He was unhappy. He had got into a difficult love affair that had begun in the summer of 1900 in Germany and was to last until the end of 1907.[8] The woman was Fania El'iashevich, the wife of the economist Vasilii El'iashevich. When they first met is not clear, but the El'iasheviches had visited Frank when he was in Berlin, and the relationship must have started at that time. It was an unusual situation because Frank remained friendly with Vasilii while he was close to Fania.[9] In a letter during the Second World War, Frank described the relationship: "In my early years, I wasted many years on a meaningless romance, without having the excuse that I was really infatuated, for I felt clearly that I was on the wrong path, and could not get up the courage to do the right thing."[10] Frank's future wife, Tatiana Sergeevna Bartseva, also described something of this relationship: "Semyon Liudvigovich loved for eight years of his life this lady. . . . He said to me later that this love was artificial, or rather concocted out of his need to love, but [it] only tormented him, proving that it was not a real love."[11]

Whatever the accuracy of these reminiscences, the relationship caused Frank great anguish. It gave him, he wrote later, a sense of the meaning of suffering and an awareness of the spiritual life. It was in this context that by chance he came across a copy of Friedrich Nietzsche's *Thus Spake Zarathustra*. It affected him very deeply: "I was stunned—not by Nietzsche's teaching—but by the atmosphere there of the deep nature of the spiritual life and the spiritual struggle which blew through the book. From that moment on, I sensed the reality of the spirit, the reality of the depth within my own soul, and without making any particular decisions my inner fate was decided."[12]

Nietzsche was very popular in Russia at that time, and Frank was not alone in reading him in a spiritual way. Berdiaev, for example, also read him in a semi-Christian light. Nevertheless, it is perhaps surprising that Nietzsche should have been the one to awaken Frank's sense of the spiritual. A couple of years later, Lev Zak recalled that Frank "started to talk to me about Raskolnikov, as a forerunner of Nietzsche, about the idea that 'everything is permitted,' and how such an idea and its practical consequences are not compatible with the human conscience."[13] In 1904 Frank bracketed Nietzsche with the German philosopher of individualism Max Stirner, describing him as an immoral thinker who lacked training in Kantian idealism.[14] Yet in spite of Frank's comment that he was not attracted by Nietzsche's teaching, he was certainly interested by certain parts of it. The reason was that Nietzsche's ethical teaching offered a solution to some of Frank's deepest moral dilemmas.

During the winter of 1901–2 Frank received an invitation to contribute to a proposed collection of essays on idealism. The project was initiated by Novgorodtsev and Struve, who wanted to produce something to combat positivist ideas. On Struve's suggestion, Novgorodtsev invited Frank to participate. The other contributers were Berdiaev, Bulgakov, S. A. Askol'dov, B. A. Kistiakovskii, A. S. Lappo-Danilevskii, S. F. Oldenburg, Sergei and Evgenii Trubetskoi, and D. E. Zhukovskii. The collection, which came out in November 1902, entitled *Problems of Idealism*, was a landmark in Russian intellectual history since it offered clear evidence of a move in some circles away from a rigidly positivist view of the world. Frank's essay, "Fr.Nietzsche and the Ethic of 'Love for the Faraway'," which he later described as "spiritually very immature," was an attempt to combine Nietzsche's ethics with political and ethical radicalism.[15]

Frank's essay was about two strands of morality, described by Nietzsche as "love of one's neighbour" (*liubov' k blizhnemu*) and "love of the faraway" (*liubov' k dal'nemu*). According to Frank's interpretation of Nietzsche, the first is utilitarian. Utilitarianism advocates a relative morality that in itself has no value but gains its importance from the goal attained. Once the goal has been attained, however, the morality is dropped: "Spiritual purity and loftiness, heroism, the absence of egotistic motives are in the ethic of utilitarianism simply a mechanistic means which is brought into play for the achievement of human happiness but then becomes unnecessary at the moment of achieving the aim, and as such is thrown to the side." The second kind of morality focuses not on happiness but the "*higher meaning of life*": "Heroism and spiritual greatness are devoted not to the establishment of the kingdom of happy pigmies . . . but to the strengthening and development in man of everything morally great, to the raising of his spiritual stature, to the creation of the 'superman.'"[16] The focus of the two moralities is different; the first is concerned with immediate happiness, the second with overall meaning.

One example, quoted by Frank, that Nietzsche used to illustrate these different moralities was the relative attitudes displayed by the sister and the doctor of an ill man. The former will be sentimental about the suffering, displaying "love of one's neighbour," while the latter, in being honest about the disease and choosing to be cruel now so that health can come later, displays "love of the faraway."[17]

Along with this "love of the faraway," Frank, apparently under the influence of Simmel, proposed a "love of things and phantoms" (*liubov' k veshcham i prizrakam*)—objective ideals such as truth, justice, and beauty to which humanity may strive.[18] In the end, he suggested that these high ideals, while still remaining distant from man, are in some way rooted in human nature.

In this regard, one aspect of Frank's essay is especially illuminating. The utilitarian morality was typical, he argued, of the populist mentality whereby absolute spiritual and legal values were expendable in the face of the immediate challenge to change the economic and political world to favor the peasant. In this situation, the material happiness of the greatest number was more important than moral values. However, Frank stated, there are moral obligations that, even in a revolutionary situation, can never be cast aside. These, he believed, had not received adequate attention: "We hear much about self-sacrifice, about renouncing one's personal interests for the sake of a neighbour, about the deep moral obligations which require a person to give everything away to others and to demand nothing for himself but, as before, we hear very little about the rights of man, about those of his interests which he *has no right* to sacrifice, about his obligation to remove all barriers which lie in the way of the establishment of these sacred rights, about socially moral activity which is founded not on the sacrifice of one's 'I', but, on the contrary, on the affirmation and development of the deepest, most sacred and most human sides of that 'I.'" This kind of morality is an absolute morality that although demanding, is not in opposition to human nature. It is an egotistical morality, but not in the traditional sense of the word; rather, it is a morality "immanent" in the human person.[19] Thus, Frank came to defend Nietzsche's egotism and the superman by arguing that a love for high ideals involves simply being true to one's real self.

In the light of his break with Social Democracy, it is obvious why Frank was attracted by Nietzsche. The idea of being true to one's self relates to his break with the revolutionary tradition, and his own sense of personal liberation from a falsely imposed duty. His friend Liven had not felt mentally suited to revolutionary activity. It was not so much laziness or cowardice but a reaction against a dogmatic morality imposed from outside. Now, in Nietzsche, Frank found an absolute moral belief that yet seemed natural.

Frank described his Nietzschean thought as a kind of radical individualism. "Struggle and creativity," he wrote, "must be dedicated *to the creation of conditions for the free development of all the spiritual capabilities of man and for the free satisfaction of his spiritual demands.*"[20] He characterized Nietzsche's philosophy as "*idealistic radicalism*, that is radicalism in the name of the moral rights of the individual."[21] In this way, Nietzsche offered Frank the basis for a new moral philosophy that did not lead to an abandonment of the revolutionary cause. It also, in its defense of certain kinds of subjective aspirations, "licensed Frank to pursue his theoretical interests undisturbed by the qualms which had assailed him in the 1890s as to the ethical legitimacy of the scholar's calling."[22]

In addition, Frank found a vision of the human person that was startlingly different from what he had known before. The utilitarian ethic allowed no room for heroes; Nietzsche's philosophy and artistic genius painted a world fit for heroes to live in.[23] The Legal Marxists had partly broken with Marxism because in their view it paid insufficient attention to the individual. Now Frank discovered a philosophy that affirmed everything about the creativeness of the individual. In this sense, the insight Frank gained from reading Nietzsche was a poetic insight as well as a strictly philosophical conclusion.

Frank's critique of populist ethics suggests that on a personal, as opposed to theoretical level, his break with Marxism was not a break with Marxism specifically but a break with the whole ethical worldview of the revolutionary movement. This may go some way to explaining Frank's later statement in *Landmarks* that all the revolutionary movements, in spite of their differences, could be labeled populist. Frank's personal break with Marxism was, at a profounder level, a break with populist utilitarianism.

It would be wrong to interpret Frank's reading of Nietzsche in a Christian light. His religious conversion came later, although he commented that the seeds of it were to be found at this time. Looking back in 1935, Frank declared that Nietzsche opened him to a spiritual, metaphysical approach to the world; it marked his break with the scientific positivism of the Russian intelligentsia:

> I became an "idealist," not in the Kantian sense, but as an idealist-metaphysical carrier of a certain spiritual experience, which opened the way to the invisible, inner reality of being. I became a "philosopher," although in subsequent years I constantly digressed from this sphere of being, to participate in politics, society and outer being. This revolution acquired its philosophical formulation much later . . . when I conceived and wrote the main work of my life *The Object of Knowledge*, and the final religious or religious-philosophical formulation, still later. But the foundation of my spiritual being was set in place or, rather, consciously revealed itself to me in the winter of 1901–02.[24]

In spite of Frank's assertion that he discovered a metaphysical outlook through reading Nietzsche, he did not express it in those terms at that time. In fact, his contemporary writing was strangely hostile to metaphysics. In December 1901 he wrote to Struve: "I could not subscribe to metaphysical idealism or at least to recognizing that it is a compulsory position."[25]

In the spring of 1903 Frank went to Germany to help Struve with *Liberation* (*Osvobozhdenie*), the journal of the liberation movement he was then editing in Stuttgart. The two men continued their theoretical discussions, particularly about metaphysics, and under Struve's influence, Frank read R. H. Lotze's *Logic and Metaphysics*. According to Frank's biography of Struve, the two men differed strongly in their approach to metaphysics. Struve believed in a metaphysical view of man founded on a perception of the inner spiritual reality of the individual, while Frank was then under the influence of Kant and Fichte and saw the "I" as simply a "transcendental concept."[26]

This antipathy toward metaphysics seems to have been partly political and directed at the potential conservatism of Hegel. This is how it appears in a long article, "On Critical Idealism," that Frank published in *The Divine World* in 1904. This was a strong defense of Kantian criticism, built around the Fichtean idea that the world is a system of consciousness. It was an attack on what Frank called materialist metaphysics. Kant had posited the existence of a metaphysical sphere of reality about which nothing could be known. However, the Kantian revolution, Frank argued, had been completed by Fichte and neo-Kantians such as W. Schuppe (whose *Epistemological Logic* he had just read),[27] who had turned the noumenal sphere into a universal consciousness that embraced everything. Instead, they interpreted reality not as something of which the mind tries to acquire knowledge but as immanent to a system of consciousness. Reality, Frank wrote, is a "constituent part of *the system of consciousness.*" Consciousness should not be considered as part of the objective world, as Hegel and Schelling considered it, but as preceding reality. Reality takes its place as one of the aspects of the spiritual life of consciousness: "The whole should be characterized not as a cosmos [*mirozdanie*] but as spiritual life [*dukhovnaia zhizn'*]." The whole is a "system of consciousness or integral spiritual life."[28]

The problem with metaphysics, Frank wrote to Struve, was that it operated with a region of the world beyond or outside knowledge altogether. To make a statement about a metaphysical world simply could not make sense. More important, however, Frank argued that both positivism and metaphysics were flawed in their concepts of *being*. Neither made an adequate distinction between reality and morality, as in the Kantian system. For the positivist, there was only material reality. In metaphysics, the visible reality was just the cover for an absolute ideal world existing behind it and forming it. This led from the worshiping of the ideal behind reality to the idolization of reality itself. The result was the Hegelian idolatry of the "world soul" or Marx's belief in the "evolution of the means of production." On the other hand, the great value of critical idealism, in Frank's view, was that it preserved the distinction between the real and the moral. As soon as morality was deduced from reality, dogmatism would result.[29]

Frank's argument was directed at all utopian doctrines. The kingdom of reality, he said, is indifferent to the idea of goodness, and goodness will never be fully incarnated in it. However, moral life is an essential part of the free inner life of the consciousness of each person. Each person should fight for the incarnation of the good in the real, but not make his battle dependent on a successful outcome. The good is something to be fought for, whatever the result.[30]

Frank offered two aspects of individuality: the empirical individual, made up of his psychic life and confined to one specific body and life, and the transcendental "I," the carrier of the consciousness of which reality is just one aspect and of which each empirical personality forms a part. This transcendental "I" stands outside time and space because these are simply aspects of the life of the consciousness of which it is a carrier. The empirical individual is the only means for the expression of the transcendental subject in the world, and for this reason each individual is of equal moral value. The consequence of this is that there is no longer an opposition, so typical of Russian populist thought, between egotism and altruism. In serving both the needs of himself and of other empirical individuals, a person is serving the needs of the same transcendental "I." Self-perfection becomes a legitimate moral aim.[31]

Frank certainly regarded this Fichtean position as complementary to what he had learned from Nietzsche, and in effect it provided a philosophical underpinning to his Nietzschean ideas. In 1905, in a review of a new collection of Fichte's essays, Frank stated that "in Fichte, Kant's doctrinaire morality of the categorical imperative and of universally-valid norms, which slights the living personality, is transformed into a profession of humane individualism which says, 'Be what you are,' and already sounds like a promising prelude to the moral designs of Nietzsche."[32]

Frank's attack on metaphysics must be understood essentially as an attack on a materialist form of metaphysics that makes of empirical reality an idol because it reflects the absolute ideal world behind it. Solov'ev, in Frank's view, had fallen victim to this weakness because he assigned the Kingdom of God a place in the hierarchy of being along with the mineral, organic, animal and human kingdoms.[33] Of course, in a sense, his own concept of the transcendental "I" contained a strong metaphysical element. Indeed it could be argued that Frank's position was really a form of metaphysical idealism that he declined to recognize as such, presenting his position as a version of transcendental idealism.[34]

Frank's attempt to construct a system of consciousness contained certain seed ideas that were to be of great importance in his mature metaphysical system as it developed after 1908. He wrote of "regions which are given to us, not as real objects, to be assimilated by merely rational cognition, but as integral experiences of the spirit."[35] In discussing the relationship between individuals and the absolute, Frank referred to some kind of mutual understanding between people that occurs "intuitively, by means of a union with the spiritual life of the other individual and his experience." Elsewhere, he stated that it is not enough to try to understand rationally the idealist philosophy he had put forward but also "necessary to become intuitively aware of it and experience it."[36] These were the first cornerstones in Frank's construction of a nonrational philosophy of knowledge.

In the summer of 1902 Frank received an invitation to go to Germany to help Struve with *Liberation*, the new journal of the radical liberal opposition.[37] However, in the autumn, while he was in Moscow, he was offered a job at the newly founded Faculty of Economics of the Polytechnical Institute in St. Petersburg, the first separate Faculty of Economics in a Russian institution of higher learning.[38] The dean, A. S. Posnikov, a populist economist, had been impressed by Frank's writing on Marx's theory of value. However, Frank turned the job down because it was conditional on his converting to Christianity. He spent the winter of 1902–03 in St. Petersburg and Tsarskoe Tselo before leaving for Germany in the spring.[39]

Frank first went to stay with the Struves in Gaisberg, a working-class suburb of Stuttgart. They lived in a comfortable, spacious farmhouse. There was a Russian nanny for the family and a secretary for the paper. Zhukovskii, who had contributed to and published *Problems of Idealism*, was among those who financed the project, and the Struves were well off. Ariadna Tyrkova, an activist who was later arrested for doing courier work for Struve, wrote: "They refused nothing either to themselves or their close friends. They were not threatened by anything. They did not need to go looking for money for life or for the work. They were supplied by like-minded people living in Russia, with whom it was easy and safe to maintain contact."[40]

The atmosphere of the Struve household provided what Frank called that "unforgettable, distinctive, spiritual delight typical of a Russian intelligentsia family." The atmosphere was intoxicating: "I can remember [the dinner table and] supper with lively conversation, P.B's study overloaded with books and papers, the humble, almost dingy furnishing of the flat and the atmosphere of constant intellectual combustion, ideological vigour and unceasing editorial worries . . . . I was accustomed and inclined by temperament to peace and quiet, and my head span from the whirlwind of conversations, debates . . . and the perpetual chaos of editorial affairs."[41] Frank lived on the ground floor and every morning he was woken by the third son, Konstantin, who could not yet say his name properly and called him "Nłunich," which became his nickname to the Struves.

Frank decided not to live permanently with the Struves. Instead, he went to Munich and came to Stuttgart once a month. His times in Stuttgart were like "reassuring but . . . tormentingly hot baths."[42] Struve could be despotically demanding as an editor. He valued Frank and demanded an enormous amount of work from him as a duty. On one occasion, just after the commencement of the Russo-Japanese War, Struve rang Frank in Munich and ordered him to come to Stuttgart immediately. He was met at the station and handed a collection of articles on the war from the European press and taken straight to a café to do a review of them. Frank could not work under this kind of pressure. It may be that his health was not up to it. The situation was made more difficult because the Struves suggested that Frank's refusal to work full time on *Liberation* indicated a lack of civic duty.[43] This troubled Frank, although in the end he seems to have learned not to be dominated.[44] In Munich he was in isolation, and he did a lot of philosophical work, including his translation of Windelband's *Preludes* published in Russia by Zhukovskii.

In the summer of 1904 Frank went to a sanatorium in Alpirsbach in the Schwarzwald Mountains to stay with the Struves. The two men talked extensively, this time about spiritual as opposed to political or philosophical matters. Struve quoted Goethe, for whose work Frank was to develop a great love, that one's life should be like an artistic creation. Struve's interest in spiritual matters attracted Frank more than his political and academic views. It was a contrast to the typical Russian *intelligent*, who according to Frank regarded spirituality as a bourgeois luxury.[45] Also in the summer of 1904 Frank went on a trip through northern Italy, visiting Milan, Verona, Lake Garda, and Venice, where he spent a month.[46]

The relationship between Frank and Struve was like teacher and pupil. "I remember," Frank wrote, "how flattered I felt when [Struve] said . . . that I had 'good ideas.'"[47] In a letter of June 1903 he compared the effect of Struve's friendship for him to that of a man for his beloved and declared that it inspired him and was "the condition of a bold and energetic life." To Nina Struve in August 1903 he stated: "[My] interest in life usually [sinks] when I am alone." Frank became very close to Nina Struve. In October 1905 he wrote to her that her friendship was "one of the most precious blessings of [my] life."[48]

In these years Frank was unquestionably lonely. He tried to see this positively in the spring of 1903 when he wrote to Struve that any great original writer "*must be lonely.*" A couple of months later, he described his loneliness in greater detail and related his moral philosophy to it:

By nature, by health and the circumstances of my life, I am without a natural sense of joy, am inclined to hypochondria, and to a pessimistic mode of thinking. Life seems to me a very doleful and stupid affair, which only makes sense if you deny what makes up its true existence and turn your spiritual gaze on some kind of beyond [*jenseits*]—on certain higher values, thought, moral principles etc. If I do not want to die, I live and work purely as Pushkin said: "I want to live, think and suffer." And this is the basis of my stoic, moral philosophy. Among the few, true blessings of life, I consider friendship one of the first—it gives a deep sense of satisfaction, but is so hard to find.[49]

The link that Frank thus made between his moral philosophy and his personal sense of isolation indicates how much his philosophical journey was a personal quest for a meaning to life rather than a detached analysis of it. His philosophy was, at a deep level, his belief.

4

Politics

ON HIS ARRIVAL in Germany, Frank discussed politics as well as meta-physics with Struve, and this, he wrote, greatly "broadened [my] polit-ical education," especially his knowledge of recent Russian politics. He read Aleksandr Herzen's essays in *The Bell* (*Kolokol*), his corre-spondence with Ivan Turgenev and the historian K. D. Kavelin, and the essays of the Ukrainian liberal M. P. Dragomanov. He also got for the first time a detailed picture of the events surrounding the assassina-tion of Alexander II and was struck by Struve's opinion, so different from the prevailing radical viewpoint, that the assassination and con-sequent collapse of the Loris-Melikov constitution was a tragic catas-trophe.[1] In the years following, Frank, like Struve himself, slowly but steadily reassessed the Russian revolutionary tradition. Initially, how-ever, both men were at the center of the growing liberation movement.

Frank was present at a three-day meeting at Schaffhausen, Swit-zerland, in July 1903 where the Union of Liberation, which was to play an important role in the 1905 revolution, was first conceived. Before the conference, Struve gathered a group of like-minded intelligentsia radicals for a meeting in Stuttgart. This group consisted of Struve, Frank, Berdiaev, (whom Frank now met for the first time), Bulgakov, Bogucharskii, Kistiakovskii, E. D. Kuskova, and S. N. Prokopovich. For conspiratorial purposes, each day was spent in a different mountain town nearby, and the purpose of their discussions was to prepare the ground for the forthcoming gathering. At the conference itself, they were joined by *zemstvo* radicals such as N. N. L'vov, I. I. Petrunkevich, V. I. Vernadskii, and Zhukovskii and representatives of academic liberal-constitutionalist circles, including Novgorodtsev, V. V. Vodo-vozov, I. M. Grevs, (professor of history at St. Petersburg University), and S. A. Kotliarevskii, (professor of law at Moscow University).[2]

The meeting at Schaffhausen came to two important conclusions.

34

The first was to organize a broad coalition of different currents. This was in keeping with Struve's original vision for *Liberation*, which he envisaged not as the organ for a party but the base for a broad liberal-democratic movement.[3] The second was to open the party to those further on the left. According to Frank, the moderates easily gave way to the radicals. One of the issues of concern was whether to strike out immediately for complete change or to be more cautious. L'vov put forward the thesis "All for the people, but not all through the people," but according to Frank, this was drowned out by "declarations of devotion to democratic principles." Struve defended the idea of single-chamber government.[4] The conference made a decision to set up in different Russian cities "Unions of Liberation," which would call for universal suffrage and land reform. The general aim was to mobilize public opinion in the fight against autocracy. So from the autumn of that year local Unions of Liberation were founded in St. Petersburg, Moscow, Kiev, Odessa, and other cities. In addition, the conference agreed its support for *Liberation*.[5] It was a preliminary meeting. Important liberal figures such as Pavel Miliukov, who was on a lecture tour of the United States, did not attend, and the Union of Liberation proper was launched in January 1904 in St. Petersburg.

At this time, Frank's political credo was a form of liberalism. In June 1903 he wrote to Struve that there was no current difference between advocating Western and national values: "The Russian national-historical task now—is the realization of European ideals. Hegel would say that the European 'spirit' has moved to Russia and must reveal itself in her. In practice that means the need to indicate the inappropriateness of any negative approach to the true bases of political liberalism."[6] As Frank's writing of 1904–6 would reveal, this meant the rule of law, separation of powers, and certain property rights. Behind it was also the radical individualism of Frank's Nietzschean thought and a continuing assumption about the rightness of much of the revolutionary tradition. This would have been his position at Schaffhausen.

Frank worked as a journalist on *Liberation* and the accompanying two collections of *Notebooks of Liberation* (*Knizhki Osvobozhdeniia*) on and off from 1903 to 1905. He wrote very little, contributing nine articles in total, two of them book reviews. He wrote two articles in 1903. In the first, "The Russian Autocracy and Italian Public Opinion," he criticized an invitation by the Italian government for the tsar to visit Italy and declared that Nicholas II did not represent the Russian nation, only "the gendarmes and the cossacks."[7] In the same article, he referred positively to the action of revolutionary France in planting freedom and equality across Europe. In the second, "The Serbian or the German Way?" he discussed the recent assassination of the king of Serbia, Aleksandr Obrenovic, and he made a distinction between the assassin in Serbia and the ordinary student assassin in Russia. The former he condemned as a barbarian, but the latter he admired: "Overcoming his in-built aversion to violence, [the student], in an impulse of heroic ecstasy and hopeless unbelief in the possibility of other means, kills an enemy of the people, and with that gives himself over to death and desecration."[8]

Frank's radical instincts also came out during the Russo-Japanese War. He related that Struve "trembled with joy" on hearing of the sinking of the Russian fleet in Tsushima Strait and that he shared Struve's defeatist mentality.[9] He was also highly critical of what he saw as the duplicity of the Russian government in its failure to accept the inadequacy of its war policies.[10]

The first Congress of the Union of Liberation of January 1904 set up a council of ten, eight of whose members had been at Schaffhausen. Frank stayed in Germany before returning to Russia in the autumn of 1904, in time to attend the secret Second Congress of the Union of Liberation in St. Petersburg (20–22 October). Struve had just published a pamphlet on the Russo-Japanese War in which he urged the Russian people to go to patriotic meetings and shout their support for the army and freedom at the same time. He hoped thereby to link the patriotic feelings created by the war with the liberation movement.[11] Frank arrived in St. Petersburg as Struve's representative and had to encounter the considerable opposition that Struve's pamphlet had engendered. There followed in November and December a campaign of banquets in different cities with the purpose of rousing public opinion to demand a constitution based on universal suffrage. Frank had an operation to remove a swelling on his leg in November that rendered him immobile just as this was getting under way.[12]

As Struve's representative, he would regularly receive envelopes of copies of *Liberation*, which were printed on cigarette paper for distribution in Russia. Sometimes there were messages in the *Liberation* postbox entitled "Runner," a nickname given to him for his practice of walking fast and overtaking people in the street.[13] On one occasion he received a message sewn up in a tie and along with it a box of chocolates from Nina Struve. Frank wrote replies in distorted handwriting, most of them of a political nature.

At this time Frank became involved with another important intellectual current. In 1901, the symbolist poets Dmitri Merezhkovskii and Zinaida Gippius and the religious thinker V. V. Rozanov had started to organize meetings on religious philosophy. They were to prove the preliminary for the later Moscow Religious-Philosophical Society of

1905–14 and the St. Petersburg Religious-Philosophical Society of 1907–17. They also set up a journal, *New Way* (*Novyi put'*), to express their ideas. Berdiaev and Bulgakov, both with increasingly strong religious views, joined the journal, as did Losskii, whose famous *Foundations of Intuitivism* first appeared in installments in the course of 1904 in *Questions of Philosophy and Psychology*. In the autumn of 1904 Frank also joined *New Way* as a coeditor and contributor, although he did not at that time sympathize with the religious ideas of Bulgakov and Berdiaev.[14] Frank contributed one essay to the journal, "The State and the Individual," which presented an argument for a society based on firm legal principles that would be at the foundation of rather than the product of government activity. *New Way* was soon discontinued after an argument among the editors. Merezhkovskii and Gippius resigned, leaving the journal to continue under another name, *Questions of Life* (*Voprosy zhizni*). Losskii took over as the nominal editor. Frank contributed a number of book reviews and a longer article on social psychology, "The Problem of Power."

In the spring of 1905 Frank went back to Germany. He was considering writing a book on social psychology (an idea that was never realized—"The Problem of Power" was the sole fruit of this project), and registered for the summer term at Heidelberg. At the same time he wrote to Struve to say that he was uncertain about continuing his work for *Liberation*, partly because of a growing sense of uncertainty about the primary importance of politics: "This winter I got such a surfeit of politics. I realized how unfit I am for this field, and how disinclined. So much so that I suffered the strongest reaction against it— I don't know how long it will last. Whoever believes politics to be an absolute will condemn me for distancing myself at the most crucial moment. But I cannot remake myself. . . . I am passionately drawn to pure academic, abstract politico-philosophical work. . . . The one thing that makes this abandonment of politics difficult for me is my friendship with you and wish to help you."[15]

However, Frank also doubted the correctness of Struve's line in *Liberation* and felt that the liberation movement had failed to diagnose the fact that after the shooting of worker demonstrators on "Bloody Sunday" (9 January 1905), the situation in Russia required an armed resistance movement. At the same time, while Frank believed that some kind of violent mass movement was needed, he did not feel morally able to participate in it:

It is my deepest conviction, from 9 January onwards and increasing with time, that preparation for armed resistance has become the one real and necessary issue. I am not talking specifically about an uprising, for which the means are perhaps not yet there; but after the ideological means have been exhausted, it only remains to carry on the battle by force—in the form either of a mass movement or of individual terror. . . . Meanwhile neither I nor most of the liberation movement are capable of this. However much I long for political freedom, I cannot kill people for it, nor call for death, nor—being absolutely honest—die myself as cannon-fodder. In such a situation I consider it personally the most honourable thing to retire. . . . The unification of the intelligentsia, through professional unions, into one union, which has already been accomplished, is a useful thing. But this force can have real significance only after a mass of blood has flown on the streets of Petersburg, and—not being a Social-Democrat—I somehow instinctively feel an element of immorality in this activity, made fruitful by alien blood. Whoever wants to be an activist now, must essentially approach the position of the Socialist-Revolutionaries and not deviate from their tactics. At the Liberation Congress in Moscow there was a lot of useless talk about the new "revolutionary" tactic, seeing the latter in propaganda among the forces, people etc. In itself it drew no objections, but its inadequacy was clearly felt. Now there is only one revolutionary tactic—a fight with weapons in the hands or preparation for it. If I were to write for *Liberation*, then I would write *only* about that—but I cannot write about it, because myself I am neither capable nor in a condition to shoot people or throw bombs.[16]

Frank, then, faced a moral conflict between his political goals and his moral convictions or instincts. The ranks of the Socialist-Revolutionaries had been greatly increased since Bloody Sunday, and they were responsible for the assassination of Grand Duke Sergei Aleksandrovich in February 1905. Frank was evidently persuaded by their program of mass action and terror, yet his moral instincts precluded a commitment to it. His head and heart were in conflict.

Frank returned to Germany in the spring of 1905 and worked in Heidelberg in conditions of "absolute loneliness,"[17] apart from a brief visit to Paris to help Struve with *Liberation*. At the end of the semester, he went on holiday with the Struves and the Tyrkova-Williamses in the fishing village of St. Cast on the Brittany coast. They took a dacha, had long philosophical conversations, and sat on the beach reading aloud the novels of Anatole France.[18] In the autumn, they went back to Paris, where Struve continued his editorial work.

Frank then heard from his mother that his stepfather was ill and returned to Moscow to help out with the chemist shop they had newly acquired there. He was just in time for the October Manifesto and for the first Kadet Party Congress of 12–18 October, where he represented Struve. He was much involved with the party, although in the elections for the Central Committee he received just one vote.[19] Frank joined in the euphoria that gripped Moscow at this time. Lev Zak recalls that he "used to return home, very excited, bringing the latest news and the latest rumors."[20] He wrote to Struve just after the Congress and reported the euphoric atmosphere that reigned in Moscow on the day following the October Manifesto and even asserted that the political maturity of some of the workers suggested that the Social-Democrats would have to change or disappear. In his view, Russia was now divided between the opposition forces on one side, including both liberals and revolutionaries, and the forces of extreme reaction, such as the Black Hundreds, on the other. Consequently, Frank expressed himself depressed by attacks on the Left in recent issues of *Liberation*; in the atmosphere of the time, it was simply the wrong tactic. The Kadets should be open to the Left, ready to welcome the masses and crowds.[21]

Frank's political views were a mixture of tactical demands and principled statements. While calling for an alliance with the Left, he also believed that the Kadet Party was becoming dangerously unprincipled. He expressed his concern to Struve in a letter written on the day after the Party Congress:

> I spoke with many members of the Party, and it turned out that apart from Kotliarevskii, only one other man, [A. M.] Koliubakin, values political liberalism as a philosophical principle of the rights of the individual. *I did not find* other adherents. I was condemned as a Tolstoian, was told of the complete fruitlessness of my point of view, as a denial of violence. The other day at a gathering of 10–15 of the most prominent members of the Party (Kokoshkin, Mandelstam, Vinaver, Prokopovich and many others), it was admitted that we differ from the extreme parties only *tactically*, and not in principle. I protested, and only Koliubakin supported me, but for the others my words sounded like Chinese grammar. The same thing happened at the Congress itself. When the point was being discussed about the inviolability of the individual and his abode, Maklakov, generally a very reasonable and thinking person, said that we would soon be in power and thus it would be disadvantageous to us to limit that power![22]

Frank grew increasingly disillusioned with events. In November he wrote to Nina Struve that political life was being dictated by deep and dark instincts in the population and not by any rational will. On one occasion that particularly disgusted him he was present at a gathering of the Union of Writers where all those attending were against a strike by typesetters because it would harm rather than help the revolutionary cause but all voted their sympathy for it.[23] In this situation he believed that he and Struve, in holding to a belief of their own, stood alone. He observed that the moderate right wing forces "in the depths of the soul consider themselves morally inferior to those on the Left and give in to them. Thus their tactics are unprincipled."[24] Frank declared that only the instinct that prevents a sailor deserting a sinking ship prevented him from abandoning the Kadet Party at that point.[25]

This sense of caution also revealed itself in Frank's attitude to Miliukov. After the October Manifesto of 1905, Miliukov declared: "We have won a victory, but in essence nothing has changed; our battle and political line remains unchanged."[26] This attitude was very different from Struve's, who welcomed the changes, imperfect as they were, and viewed them as a basis for some kind of cooperation with the government. In a letter to Nina Struve, Frank welcomed Struve's position:

> P.B. is absolutely right in saying that the constitutionalists, instead of voting various cheap resolutions about distrust and demanding a Constituent Assembly, should have given Witte a set of conditions, and supported him on those conditions. Witte would certainly have gone along with it because he is helpless. But no one thought of it . . . since to criticize, sulk, prepare resolutions is more comfortable . . . than to take serious responsibility and risk one's popularity. . . . With sadness I state (and am sure that in the history books of 100 years time, it will be written) that the intelligentsia has not been on top of the situation, and partly for convenience and partly in its stubborness has betrayed and is betraying Russia at the most dangerous moment.[27]

Frank was particularly critical of Miliukov for his inflexibility in this matter.[28] Although both he and Struve were on the list of contributors to Miliukov's newspaper *Speech* (*Rech'*), he expressed to Nina his "great satisfaction" that Struve was not to be seriously involved with it.[29]

Nevertheless, Frank's position was more ambiguous. In 1944, writing of the conflict within the party, he revealed that he had not been entirely sure of himself:

> Notwithstanding all my political inexperience and inability, [Miliukov's] declaration confused and depressed me: I vaguely sensed that there was something not right, specifically that this huge turn-around of principle which had just happened was indecent. Miliukov's approach coincided with the general mood of the intelligentsia: it was considered good to viciously blame the government just as before—in spite of its liberal course—to maintain contact with the revolutionaries. P.B., on the other hand, immediately took a completely opposite point of view; he declared that with the introduction of a constitutional system, however imperfect it might be, the methods of political struggle not only had to change radically, since they had become open and legal, but the opportunity had

also opened up for the positive cooperation of the liberal layers of society with the government in the matter of reform. I myself did not immediately adopt this position, the only correct one, as I now recognize, and stood further to the left.[30]

In December 1905 in an exchange of articles he had with the liberal theorist A. A. Kaufman, Frank revealed that he remained committed to a revolutionary position. Kaufman had argued that the Social-Democrats, calling for an immediate eight-hour day, were much more likely to appeal to the workers than the Kadets, who wanted a gradual introduction of the change. In the long term the Kadet approach would catch on, even if not in the immediate moment.[31] Frank reacted by saying that criticism of the revolutionaries should be no excuse for passivity; the Kadets should also be willing to express their message to meet the mood of the audience: "One should openly stand on the soil of an all-national revolution . . . and not retreat from the revolutionary struggle in tranquil contemplation of general principles."[32]

Frank's writing of the autumn of 1905, then, was a combination of strong moral principle with a commitment to revolution and a sense of tactics. His position was not clear and points to inner confusion. It involved a confusion of aim: should political or moral principles be primary? It was a tension that was to remain in Frank's thought until the dissolution of the First Duma.

Frank's actual involvement in the political scene declined after Struve returned to Russia. He wrote later: "I myself, not being a practical politician in any way, and feeling no calling or desire to get involved in practical activity, was orientated to this side of P.B.'s life only in a general way."[33] Back in October Frank had written to the Struves of his dream to found a journal "for the propaganda of *our* ideas."[34] This soon became a reality. Struve's hesitation about the Kadet Party meant that although he joined its Central Committee in January 1906, he was a reluctant recruit. He decided to set up his own journal, *Polar Star* (*Poliarnaia zvezda*), which got its name from previous journals produced by the Decembrists and Herzen. Frank joined him. The first issue came out at the end of 1905. Struve's editorial in the first edition disclaimed any intention for the journal to advocate a party position, setting itself instead the broader task to fight for the Russian nation to be founded on principles of freedom, equality, and social justice.[35]

Frank lived near the Struves on Fonarnyi Street, but he simply slept at home and spent all day with them. Struve was often out, so much of the editorial work on *Polar Star* was left to him, and he had the two rooms set aside for editorial purposes almost at his own disposal.

Frank's political ideology of 1904–6 was what he called *humanist individualism,*[36] and it was an ideology that belonged very much with his Kanto-Fichtean defense of the individual. Frank's article on social psychology, "The Problem of Power," was typical of this outlook and gives a picture of Frank as a humanist with a broadly rationalist outlook. He declared that sociology serves to explain the relationships between people in general, and psychology the mentality of individuals. Social psychology should aim to link these two disciplines. This was not a new discipline. Frank referred to the work of his former mentor, George Simmel, and to the French sociologist Gabriel Tarde, who had originally coined the term "social psychology."[37] It was an idea perfectly suited to Frank's mentality. He liked trying to reconcile disciplines and opposites, as his first attempt to reconcile the Marxist and Austrian schools of economics had shown.

Frank's basic argument was that interpersonal relationships can become so strong that they appear to have an objective existence. On a broader scale, the power of a state depends on the accumulation and "objectivization" of such relationships on a national scale and over a long period. Power becomes impersonal, irrational, and controlling. It is then preserved by what he called irrational public opinion. The goal of any enlightened political struggle must be to rationalize this irrational element: "Society must be organized so that this irrationality to as great as possible an extent is balanced out and rendered harmless by the law of reasonable, voluntary agreement and free, planned cooperation of people."[38] While disputing the "social contract" view of the origins of state power, Frank defended Rousseau's and the Enlightenment's call for a rationalization of the political system. "[Power]," he wrote, "must be placed in direct, conscious dependence on public opinion and public will. . . . It is from here that come the demands of liberal-democratic political philosophy."[39] Finally, the rational alternative to the irrational power structures should be based on the autonomy of the individual, whether that autonomy is defended on logical or spiritual grounds.[40]

These comments suggest that Frank, in spite of his "conversion" in reading Nietzsche, was still an adherent of the rational worldview. Eighteenth-century French thought, to which he was later very hostile, held the key to political reform, as he saw it. While this was to change, his emphasis on the social psychology of a nation and its vital relationship with political power and structures was to remain lifelong. Frank was always interested in social as well as individual consciousness.

Frank's article in *New Way* in late 1904 was very much in this style. Writing on the fortieth anniversary of Alexander II's judicial reforms, Frank argued for a set of inalienable principles that would underlie the creation of governments and the existence of the state and that could never be tampered with by the state itself. He had in mind something like the American Constitution. Once the set of principles had been introduced, they could have a long-term influence on the social consciousness of the population.[41]

Frank repeated this kind of argument in one of his articles for *Polar Star*, "A Proposal for a Declaration of Rights." In this case he argued for a system of natural law (*estestvennoe pravo*) that could never be altered and proposed his own "constitutive law on the eternal and inalienable rights of Russian citizens." His plan for a declaration of rights was not a new one. As a basis for his program, he used another proposed declaration of rights, which had been put together by various *zemstvo* representatives and academics.[42] In addition, he declared his debt to Western European constitutions, in particular the Belgian.[43] In this he was also not alone. Miliukov called the Belgian Constitution a "classical example" of a parliamentary monarchy in November 1905.[44] Frank believed his own declaration was interesting for two reasons. He came out first against the death penalty and second against compulsory military service, arguing for alternative forms of service for conscientious objectors.

One aspect of Frank's draft is revealing. He declared in his article 6 that the dwelling of every individual is inviolable. But there was no reference to protection of private property outside that limit or to economic freedoms in general. At this time, Frank did not believe that there need be any conflict between liberalism and socialism. This was the thesis he put forward in his first article for *Polar Star*, "Politics and Ideas," in which he argued for individual freedom and for some form of popular control over the economy. By "socialism," Frank meant the absence of exploitation in a society and a buttress against pure individualism. However, he was clearly uncertain how to bring about this socialist society, commenting, "Socialism is the great *problem* of our time."[45] Possibly Frank remained unclear about how to balance economic freedom and social justice.

When he was with Struve in Paris in September 1905, the two men had conceived the idea for a book on the philosophy of culture. They were to write out their ideas, compare notes, then produce a final draft. The unifying idea behind this was an interest in what was vaguely called spiritual culture.[46] In the end, they managed only the introduction, and most of that was written by Frank,[47] but it was published in two sections in *Polar Star* and was the only piece of writing that Frank valued from his work on the journal.

In the first part, Frank and Struve attacked what they saw as the intelligentsia's view of culture. That view was typified by two kinds of populism: utilitarianism, as represented by Pisarev, and asceticism, as advocated by Tolstoi. Utilitarianism, they argued, denies moral values in the name of the material; asceticism denies the material world for the sake of the moral. Utilitarianism denies the divine spirit in man in the name of his earthly aspirations and needs; asceticism denies man's earthly abode in the name of his divine existence. "Both," they wrote, "are opposed, at least in principle, to the idea of godmanhood, the idea of the incarnation of absolute values of the spirit in earthly life. . . . Neither achieves or allows for the higher unity of the transcendent with the empirical."[48]

Frank's view was that culture is meant to be the sum and repository of all values: "Culture is the totality of absolute values, created and being created by humanity, and forming its spiritual-social being. In the consciousness of humanity there lives a row of eternal ideals—truth, goodness, beauty, holiness—moving it to scientific, artistic, moral and religious creativity."[49] Its essence is a "humanism" big enough to embrace the many values and beliefs of all mankind, whether Christian, atheist, or pagan. Such a culture preaches "breadth and patience, freedom and sincerity."[50]

In the second part, the two men declared their belief that the creativity of the individual is at the center of all cultural life. There is no creator of spiritual values apart from the individual; every individual contains something holy, and although everyone has different talents, all are morally equal. It is the task of the individual to create culture and of culture to protect the independence of the individual. When woven together, these two elements form an "inwardly-harmonious, cultural-philosophical worldview, which could be called *humanist individualism*."[51]

Of all Frank's writings in *Polar Star* and its sequel *Freedom and Culture* (*Svoboda i kul'tura*), these joint essays on culture were the most interesting, and they paved the way for the more extensive attack on the intelligentsia in *Landmarks*. The two articles appeared at the end of December 1905. Their concern was with values as opposed to political power. Superficially, Frank was concerned with revolution, but at a deeper level he was more concerned with values, and for him, these two realms had begun to diverge.

Frank and Struve put forward an interesting argument regarding the use of violence in politics. In spite of an obvious aversion to violence, they declared that in some circumstances the spilling of blood, while remaining a moral sin, becomes a moral obligation. The individual must decide when such occasions occur, utilizing his "moral tact."[52] This argument was to reappear in Frank's later thought.

Polar Star came to an end in March after an article that urged the Kadets to work on stripping Nicholas II of all the powers the constitution had left him.[53] The article was declared seditious, and the journal was closed. Almost immediately, a successor, *Freedom and Culture*, was set up with Frank as the editor in close association with Struve. Frank did most of the work for this, since Struve was trying to launch his own newspaper, *The Duma* (*Duma*). Writers included Berdiaev, Bulgakov, A. S. Izgoev (Lande), Kistiakovskii, A. A. Kizevetter, Kotliarevskii, Merezhkovskii, and Rozanov.

After the March elections to the First Duma, Frank wrote a euphoric article for *Freedom and Culture* in which he welcomed the elections and the victory for the Kadets with great enthusiasm. He hailed "the epoch of the *triumph and flowering of democracy in Russia*"[54] and forecast that Russia, lacking the great bourgeois and conservative traditions of the West, would quickly advance to being the most advanced democratic country in the world. The key to this great event had been, in his view, the unity effected between the people and the intelligentsia, which had been made possible by the Kadet Party's nonfactional spirit.[55] These comments indicate the importance Frank attached to the 1905 revolution and his emotional commitment to it. Here his enthusiasm for the Kadet cause is clear.

On 27 April the Duma met for the first time. On 6 May the Kadets introduced a land law that supported expropriation of lands belonging to gentry, church, and state, leaving peasant holdings intact. This was eventually to lead to the dissolution of the First Duma on 6 July. By late May, Struve's highly positive attitude to political developments had changed completely, and he accused the intelligentsia of an insane commitment to the class struggle and utopian values.[56] Frank's last article for *Freedom and Culture* appeared on 7 May. It seems to have had no connection with the land bill and dealt with the mood of the country, not of the Duma, but there was already a note of caution, which shows how much the atmosphere had changed in a month. Frank called for a more mature attitude to power. Russians, he wrote, usually go to one of two extremes: rejecting all power or living in subservience to it. Some expected the Duma to bring about immediate improvements in their situations; others opposed it, being against all forms of power. There needed to be a middle way. The Russian people should understand that popular government "is not power-from-above" but "power-as-organization, power-as-self-government." It is vital, Frank wrote, that "the whole of society and the whole nation *take up one common task along with the government.*"[57]

Frank was looking for a new attitude to power in the population. It was one thing to change the political structures of a nation, but it was another to acquire the kind of cultural maturity that can go with them. A belief in the need for this mature attitude to power was the source of his growing evolutionary, as opposed to revolutionary, approach to politics.

Freedom and Culture closed down after eight issues. Its publishers were apparently unhappy that Struve did not spend much time on it, and there was also a decline in sales.[58] On the other side, Struve claimed that the financial backing for the enterprise was unreliable.[59] The publishers, it seems, tried to continue the journal under another editor, and Struve and Frank had it in mind to found another journal.[60] Nothing came of this, however, and *Freedom and Culture* came to an end not long before the disbandment of the First Duma.

After the dissolution of the Duma, the Kadet and Trudovik deputies went to Finland and issued the Vyborg Manifesto in which they called upon the people to refuse to pay taxes or do military service until the government reconstituted the Duma. Struve was very angry and saw the manifesto as a symbol of the Kadet failure to follow a moderate line.

For Frank, the experience of 1905–6 left him disgusted with the revolution and with politics itself, and July 1906 marked the end of his direct links with the political scene. The reason was almost certainly his sense, expressed in his earlier letters to Struve, that the political intelligentsia did not know how to work positively with government concessions. However, he did not express this at the time and did not unleash his full invective against the intelligentsia until his article in *Landmarks* in 1909.

At the same time, Frank was simply not at home in politics. In future years he was to write many articles and books on social and political philosophy, but he was not a political animal and did not have a party political mind. In addition, he may not have been happy with his political writing; writing in 1935, he commented that he was never original in his political thought.[61] Nor was he socially at home in the political arena. In November 1905 he was alone in St. Petersburg without Struve, and he wrote to Nina: "I am alone here . . . since I have almost no personal friends, and now any contact in the political sphere leads only to the deepest gloom."[62]

Frank's writing on culture and the evolutionary elements in his thought were the seeds of a growing political conservatism. The causes of this were personal as much as external. According to Zak, Frank's conservatism was not so much the fruit of his political experiences as "a reflection of his love for calm and his attachment to the 'classical' forms of social life."[63] This points to a deeper factor at work. As with reading Nietzsche, it was not just a matter of intellect; it was a matter of Frank feeling comfortable with certain ideas, having a sense that they rang true to his own nature. So his political evolution was not just about the conclusions he drew from the outer world but also about his inner world and his relationship with different ideas.

5

Independence

FRANK MOVED IN with the Struves in the autumn of 1906 and lived with them for almost two years. They lived on Tavricheskaia Street in the house of Tolstoi's son Lev L'vovich, and after that they took two adjacent apartments on Tver Street, Nina Alexandrovna moving into one with the children and Frank and Struve into the other. Frank and Struve's flat was chaotic. The two of them lived like students, with "small studies, a mass of books and broken sofas."[1] Frank's closeness to Struve was such that one of their friends ironically called it "symbiosis."[2]

Frank was Struve's closest confidant. According to his memoirs, Struve had two passionate infatuations for women, apart from his wife, between the years 1905 and 1917, and it was to him that Struve turned for consolation during what Frank called the "paroxysms of grief and despair which sometimes seized him in the course of these dramatic experiences."[3]

Frank was also a mediator between the two Struves in political arguments. Nina was more radical than her husband and was concerned by her husband's move to the right, so Frank, from early 1906, acted as a peacemaker in their discussions.

At the end of 1906, Struve accepted an offer to go and work on *Russian Thought* (*Russkaia mysl'*), a declining literary and political journal that had been founded in the 1890s and had just been bought by A. A. Kizevetter, a professor of Russian history at Moscow University. Until 1910, when Struve became the sole editor and publisher of the journal, the editorial work was done in Moscow, and Struve would travel monthly for editorial meetings. Frank joined Struve in the enterprise, and from 1907 onward edited the philosophical section, from the autumn of 1914 the literary section as well, at which time he also formally joined the editorial board. It seems that the basic editorial

48

work was done by Struve, Frank, and A. S. Izgoev, a close friend who had been a member of the Union of Liberation.[4]

After the failure of the 1905 revolution, Struve moved to the right. He was disillusioned with the liberal intelligentsia and started to put his hope in the government bureaucracy. He was impressed with Stolypin and was in regular contact with him. This move to the right meant that he associated with a loosely defined group of intellectuals and politicians who can best be described as "national liberal." Basically, they advocated reform, but within the context of the traditions of Russia and the Russian Empire. Among this group were Prince E. Trubetskoi, who was editor of *Moscow Weekly* (*Moskovskii ezhenedel'-nik*) from 1907, and Kotliarevskii, a colleague on the journal. Both these men were well-known figures at the editorial offices of *Russian Thought.* E. Trubetskoi's brother Prince G. N. Trubetskoi, who was later director of the Near Eastern Division of the Ministry of Foreign Affairs, was also a regular visitor of the offices of *Russian Thought* and became a good friend of Frank's. Frank seems to have naturally fitted into this social setting. He was later invited to edit the book-review section of *Moscow Weekly*, but declined because of his philosophical preoccupations.[5]

However, probably through Struve again, Frank now became associated with a broader academic community. In January 1906 Frank found a job giving lecture courses at Mme Stoiunina's gymnasium for girls.[6] Then in the autumn for the following two years he got a job lecturing at the newly opened Historico-Philological and Law Higher Evening Classes founded by the historians I. M. Grevs and M. A. D'iakonov. These offered university teaching for people who could not go to university, and they took place in the building of Mme Stoiunina's gymnasium. Frank lectured on "basic problems of philosophy" in 1906–8 and "the logic of the social sciences" in 1907–8. In the former, he lectured on epistemology, ethics, and the philosophy of religion, and in the concluding part of the course focused almost entirely on the individual: the idea of the individual in modern philosophy; the evolution of individualism; the individual in relation to the world, society, moral law, and the meaning of life.[7]

Other lecturers at these evening classes in 1906–8 included El'iashevich, Izgoev, L. P. Karsavin, A. V. Kartashev, Kaufman, Kotliarevskii, I. I. Lapshin, Losskii, Novgorodtsev, G. Shtilman and Struve. Many of these had written for *Polar Star* and *Freedom and Culture* and were on the faculty of the Bestuzhev Courses, which offered the equivalent of a university education for women, where Frank also taught from 1907 to 1917. Although they were not a clearly defined "set" of people, many had come into contact with Struve and had common intellectual interests and objectives. Again, many of these figures were either to emigrate after the October revolution or be exiled from the Soviet Union in 1922. Their appearance here, as a community of lecturers, indicates the formation of a certain milieu. If Frank ever belonged to a particular social group, it was to this one, and thus 1906 was the year when his life began to acquire a certain social stability.

It was through the evening classes at Mme Stoiunina's gymnasium that Frank met his wife, Tatiana Sergeevna Bartseva. In his memoir he recalls that it was at this time that he really established his own independence:

> It was in the spring of 1908 that my two years of living with the Struves came to an end and at the same time the special period of my relationship with Struve. By that time, the epoch which the Germans call *Lehr-und-Wanderjahre* [the years of study and wandering] came to an end— the epoch of youth, study, ideological ferment, and the search for one's inner and outer road in life. In the summer of that year I got married, and returning to Petersburg after a summer trip abroad finally chose as my calling philosophical work and an academic career leading to a professorship. I began systematically to fill in the gaps in my philosophical education, little by little preparing myself for my Master's exam. At the same time, the epoch of my intellectual and spiritual formation came to an end; specifically by this time, I had finally clarified to myself the bases of my own philosophical worldview.[8]

Struve and Frank went on holiday together to Germany at Easter 1907; they stayed in Berlin and met with George Simmel. This time Simmel disappointed Frank for having a "naively-romantic attitude to Russia" involving, like the populists, the belief that Russia could somehow miss the bourgeois stage in history.[9] They then went on to Grefenburg, a town in Austrian Silesia, and had long walks in the mountains and conversations on many general themes. Frank stayed on in Germany for part of the summer with the El'iasheviches. He then spent the remainder of the summer on an estate in Chernigov Province before returning to St. Petersburg for the winter of 1907–8. The relationship between Frank and Fania El'iashevich, however close, continued well into the autumn. At that point, he started to get to know Tatiana Bartseva, and their relationship moved swiftly from friendship to romance.

Tatiana Bartseva was ten years younger than Frank and came from a Russian Orthodox background. She was born in Moscow, but then the family moved to Saratov. Her father, Sergei Ivanovich Bartsev, was the director of a big shipping firm on the Volga, Eastern Society (*Vostochnoe Obshchestvo*), and they lived in a house belonging to the company. Tatiana had a sister, Maria, and two brothers—Sergei, an engineer in naval construction, and Nikolai. Her parents were not officially married because her father had earlier been a revolutionary and had married someone to give her a different name but had never lived with her. When he met Tatiana's mother, the other woman would not agree to a divorce, so they could never marry. It was a great shock to Tatiana when she read on her school report that she was the daughter of S. I. Bartsev and the maiden (*devitsa*) Filipova. In spite of this, they were a happy family and much respected in Saratov.

At the age of sixteen or seventeen, Tatiana apparently became a populist and went to the country to look after peasant children and open some crèches. When she finished school, she was sent to Paris. Her initial purpose was to study medicine, but she got involved in a Russian revolutionary circle in exile. She was persuaded to get some practical experience, so she gave up her medical studies to learn massage. Her parents became concerned and called her back to Russia.[10]

Tatiana was exceptionally beautiful, and many young men wanted to marry her. In Saratov, one of those to pay her court was the well-known artist A. I. Savinov, who painted a magnificent portrait of her.[11] The chance arose to go to St. Petersburg to enroll in the evening courses at Mme Stoiunina's gymnasium, and her parents, after some persuasion, let her go.

Tatiana was delighted by the classes. Her lecturers included Kotliarevskii, Lapshin, Losskii, Struve, and Frank. Apparently she was struck by Frank from the moment she saw him: "I was immediately struck by Frank's face—it was almost as if someone had given me a push. He was young, tall, slim, with thick dark hair, and what particularly struck me were his eyes which were huge, short-sighted, and a little prominent. He wore glasses. And when he read anything, anyone listening to him knew and could feel that he was not simply reading, but in some special way putting into his lectures not only his ideas, but certain 'feelings,' not in a sentimental sense, but in the sense of something which penetrated his whole being. He read quietly, calmly, not raising his voice, evenly and persuasively."[12]

The attraction was mutual, although Tatiana had the impression that Frank paid her no attention. She did not miss any of his lectures, although there is some evidence that she did not find them easy to understand.[13] This would not be surprising because she did not have a philosophical mind. On one occasion Tatiana went up to him and with great embarrassment asked him what books she should read. Among those he recommended were Merezhkovskii's *Eternal Travellers*, and Windelband's *Preludes*.

In the autumn of 1907 Tatiana again enrolled for Frank's evening class. She then wrote him a letter with various questions about the meaning of life. He replied that he had little time to answer her questions and that her handwriting was like "Egyptian hieroglyphics."[14] This was the beginning of their relationship.

Frank broke off the relationship with Fania El'iashevich and declared his love for Tatiana in early December in a special suite at the well-known Palkin restaurant. In subsequent months he would go to her room and read her poems by V. Briusov, A. Fet, and Pushkin. In May he wrote to her in Saratov asking her to meet him in Moscow. Initially, her mother would not allow it. However, they had a lawyer in whom Tatiana confided that she wanted to go to Moscow to see Frank. He knew of Frank's fame and gave her 25 rubles to go.

When she finally found Frank in the crowd at the station, he said that he had arranged for her to stay with his mother, "as his bride." This was the first time that marriage had been mentioned. The fact that Frank came from a Jewish background added to the newness of it: "I was frightened by the new atmosphere. . . . I had never been closely acquainted with Jewish families."[15] Sofia and Mikhail were in St. Petersburg, so the family in Moscow consisted of Frank's mother, stepfather, and Lev. Lev later wrote that the family was charmed, and amazed that such a clever grown-up man would marry such a young girl.

She stayed with the Franks for a few days, and they agreed that he would go to Saratov and that they would get married. She was treated as if she were the same age as Lev, who was then 16—that is, they were sent off to the cinema together and given money. When she bought some flowers for Rozaliia Moiseevna, she was told she should not waste money like that. Before departing, Rozaliia told Tatiana that she was giving away her greatest treasure and that Tatiana was terribly young to bear the responsibility of looking after her son. Struve sent telegrams with similar ideas. The differences between the two of them were obvious: "Senia was already very serious, almost elderly . . . but Tanya was an extremely young, lively girl, who as you can expect, was interested in and dreamed about clothes. . . . At the time my mother and father were really shocked by her frivolity, which came out in her expressed desire to have a new umbrella or that kind of thing."[16] In her memoir, Tatiana refers to the differences between the two families—"[They were] totally different circles, [and] families"— and she refers to many difficulties and misunderstandings.[17]

As personalities, the two were very different. She was energetic, enthusiastic, impulsive, intolerant, and kind. She easily made friends and enjoyed actively doing things for others. Frank had to adjust to a new pace of life. He wrote later in emigration that "before marriage, I got used to a hermit-like attitude of mind."[18] Apart from finances, Tatiana took over running his life. Although they discussed his work and philosophical questions together, she was not philosophically educated or specially interested in the intellectual world. Nevertheless, they seemed to understand each other very well.

The fact that she was a Christian and not a Jew "confused Frank's mother."[19] She had been very worried that Frank would remain a bachelor forever and was very pleased that he was marrying at all, but she found it difficult that he chose to marry a gentile. Previously Mikhail had upset her very much by marrying an Orthodox woman when he was only 19 and converting to Christianity. As Lev Zak explained, "Our parents were not believing Jews, but you have to know the position of Jews in Russia at that time and the role played by the Orthodox Church in government anti-Semitism, along with understanding the ancient roots of the Jewish psychology, to understand the blow a son delivered to his parents when he did not marry a Jew."[20] The blow was softened by the news that Tatiana would convert to Lutheranism. It was forbidden for a member of the Orthodox Church to marry a Jew, but marriages between Jews and Protestants were permitted.

Apparently, Tatiana's parents did not mind Frank's Jewishness, probably because of their revolutionary past. At one point Frank wrote suggesting that they go away to Finland and get married quietly there not to create fuss, but Tatiana's father would not hear of it. Frank came to Saratov in June 1908, and there he met Tatiana's father for the first time. The ceremony took place in a Lutheran church, and Tatiana's parents did not attend the service itself. Frank wanted as few people as possible at the reception, so they invited just relatives, witnesses, and a few very close friends of Tatiana's father. This latter detail is typical of Frank: he was always an exceptionally private man. For the honeymoon, they took a boat down the Volga and then went to Grefenburg, the health resort in Austria.[21]

The dowry was probably not great. Immediately after the honeymoon Tatiana went back to Saratov to see her mother, who had to "make the dowry." In her memoir she wrote that her parents did everything they could and ordered a fur coat with a sable collar and cuffs, and a hat. During the postrevolutionary period from 1919 to 1921 when the Franks lived on the Volga during the famine, they survived partly by exchanging Tatiana's jewelery and cutlery.[22] This suggests that she had at least some private wealth. It is not known whether Frank received anything, although his mother and stepfather had been wealthy enough to have a dacha near Nizhnii Novgorod.[23]

Frank supported himself. From Saratov in 1909 he wrote to his friend M. O. Gershenzon urgently asking for some of the royalties from *Landmarks*, the collection of essays to which he had contributed: "My financial affairs have become so complicated that I cannot leave here without [250 rubles]."[24] Clearly he could not rely on family money to get him out of difficulties. His money came from his writings, his work on *Russian Thought*, and his teaching. Apart from the Bestuzhev Courses and the evening classes at Mme Stoiunina's gymnasium, he taught from 1907 at the Froebel Courses and the Psycho-Neurological Institute and later at St. Petersburg University (1912–17), the Polytechnical Institute (1914–17), the Raevskii Women's Courses, and the Lesgaft Higher Courses.[25]

Between 1909 and 1917, the Franks lived at five different addresses.[26] They were reasonably well off. Tatiana loved entertaining, although she did not cook. They had four children: Viktor was born in 1909, Aleksei in 1910, Natalia in 1912, and Vasilii in 1920. There were German governesses for the boys; apparently the Germans were the cheapest, followed by the French and then the English. They did not live in. There was also an Estonian nanny and a maid.[27] All this was customary for such a family in those days, and this indicates that the Franks belonged to a milieu with high expectations, even if they were not very wealthy.

In 1910 the Franks spent the summer with a large group of intelligentsia friends in Tver Province on the estate of I. I. Petrunkevich. Others there included the Struves, Mme Stoiunina, and her son-in-law Losskii.[28] The gathering—and such gatherings were typical for Russian intelligentsia families during the summer—reveals the extent to which these families formed a real community. Losskii referred on this occasion to a play acted by the young people and produced by Lev Zak. Frank was known for having a good baritone voice and a wide repertoire of children's songs he was ready to perform on such occasions.[29]

Sometime after the marriage, Frank's mother fell ill and died. Frank came when she was already dying, and she said to him that she had "often suffered from, as it seemed to her, his indifference to her, and little [outer] manifestation of love [to her]." These words were to torment him for the rest of his life; he felt he was a "great sinner." Before his exile in 1922, Frank took a little sack of earth from his mother's grave and kept it with him throughout his life; it was placed in his coffin when he died in 1950.[30]

Frank's marriage affected him deeply. Although he never stated it specifically, it probably influenced his philosophical and religious thought profoundly. In later life, he often used romantic imagery to illustrate spiritual truths, and this suggests the power of his emotional experience.

Also in 1908, Frank put in place the foundations of his own philosophical worldview, foundations that would be the base for all his subsequent thought. Although his marriage signified the end of an era in his relationship with Struve, Frank was nevertheless indebted to Struve for the development of his philosophical ideas. In contrast to his own monistic, Platonist attitude to the world, Frank described Struve as a pluralist and Aristotelian, one who saw the concrete reality of the world and saw the spiritual world as immanent in that reality. In his memoirs of Struve, Frank declared himself indebted to his whole spiritual perspective on the world: "Contact with [Struve's] intellectual, spiritual mentality helped me gradually overcome the one-sidedness of a detached spiritualism and on my journey to search for and find the link between the inner and the outer, the world of the spirit and the world of empirical reality."[31]

Frank wrote that Struve's mind was characterized by the quality of "objectivism," which gave his thought a "true, philosophical pathos." This was a feature for which both men much admired Goethe, whose works Frank discovered under Struve's influence. Frank wrote later that his encounter with Goethe's thought was from 1908 onward "the main event of [my] spiritual life."[32] It certainly effected a revolution. Writing about Friedrich Schiller in 1905, Frank stated that "the . . . subjectivism of Schiller, which corresponds to the Kanto-Fichtean philosophy [is a real] contrast to the . . . objectivism of Goethe, the abstract correlation of which is Spinoza's system."[33] With the discovery of Goethe, Frank abandoned the former subjectivist position and embraced the latter "objectivism." This means that he came to see the world as a system of being rather than consciousness.

This objectivism, Frank wrote in 1910 in an essay on Goethe's epistemology, "demands of the researcher a loving involvement in the object, a pure disinterested contemplation which does not add anything to the picture of being, does not bring to it any prejudiced ideas, opinions or wishes, but perceives it humbly and truly, as it meets our gaze."[34] It was a kind of empirical cognition that unlike a logical analysis that divides things up to understand them, takes things in their wholeness, as they appear in nature. It prefers the concrete to the abstract, the dynamic and the living to the dead and divided. It is as much an artistic as a philosophical approach, and Frank much admired Goethe for his ability to synthesize the intellectual and the artistic.[35]

Frank believed that Goethe had managed to overcome the gulf be-

tween the universe and the individual. His philosophy linked the plurality of the world with a unifying source and provided a balance
between the universalism of Spinoza and the individualism of Leibniz: "The world is neither a limitless unity, nor an uncoordinated plurality; however difficult it would be for abstract logical analysis to link
and balance within it the contradictory categories of unity and plurality, a disinterested and comprehensive concrete *clarification* of Being
always gives a picture of the *unity of plurality,* of the fusion of the separate, of a universal linkage of distinct elements."[36] Such an approach
provided, in Frank's view, a theoretical framework for a political philosophy that combined "democratic universalism" with "aristocratic
individualism," a perfect balance, then, between the community and
the individual.

Goethe had also found a unifying element in the subjective and objective worlds. The "objective gaze" was not dry and abstract but dynamic and even creative. And this same dynamism was present in the
world of matter. So Goethe had come to the Spinozistic position of believing that the "order and connection of ideas is the same as the order
and connection of things."[37]

Frank found, then, in Goethe a sense of the living wholeness of the
cosmos, a "spiritual universality."[38] In his view, the abstract correlative
of this was not so much Spinoza but "vitalistic evolutionism,"[39] and he
found the expression of this in the German philosopher and psychologist William Stern, whose *Person and Thing* appeared in Russia in
March 1907. Frank wrote a substantial article about this work, which
appeared in *Russian Thought* in November 1908 also under the title
"Person and Thing." This essay focused on the relationship between the
individual and matter and offered an alternative to the mechanistic
and determinist view of both evolution and history. This latter view of
history, represented by among others Charles Darwin and Herbert
Spencer, was in Frank's view "beginning little by little to break loose
and crack" and was being challenged by two movements: energeti-
cism, threatening the view that all phenomena are simply motions of
material particles, and neovitalism, introducing into natural science
teleological ideas and attacking the relegation of the organic to the inorganic.[40] Stern's book, along with Henri Bergson's *Creative Evolution,* which appeared in Paris in 1907, gave Frank the foundation for
an essentially spiritualized view of matter and the objective world.
Whereas in 1904 Frank regarded reality as a facet of consciousness,
he now saw it as real and existing, although spiritually part of a cosmic
Being.

Stern's philosophy was built around the idea that substance is creative and not lifeless. It is self-preserving and self-creating. The obvious

example of this kind of substance is the individual, who not only adapts to his environment but also expands, develops, and grows, thus mastering the environment. The individual creates as well as responds, so introduces the volitional as well as the mechanistic principle into the world. The matter that makes up the constituent parts of each individual is subject to that individual. However, the inert matter in the world belongs not to individual people but to the supreme individual Substance. So the world itself is a complex unity made up of lesser substances, individuals, and inert matter that forms a direct part of the supreme Substance.

Thus, Stern's system provided a philosophical defense of the Goethean approach to the world. The analytical view, with which it competed, divided the world into its constituent parts but could not put them together again. It could analyze the bits but not the whole. The key to understanding the universe was to approach it from this synthesizing point of view. It meant that the philosopher had to abandon his attachment to an exclusively logical view of the world. This demanded a new form of epistemology.

Frank thus believed that the new epistemology had to be nonrational: "Life and reality—outside of which there would be no world at all—turn out to be here something irrational and in principle unfathomable [*nepostizhym*] for the abstract thinker. This pointer has, in our view, immense philosophical value." It pointed the way, in Frank's view, to a whole review of abstract knowledge.[41]

Thus, on reading Stern, Frank set himself a major task: to defend and ground a nonrational epistemology. The modern mind had divided nature and culture, matter and mind, and had posited a dualist universe. The task, which Frank lauded Stern for embarking upon, was to overcome this dualism. The task was "the construction of a complete philosophical synthesis, in which being and value, nature and culture, the cosmic and the human must find a new reconciliation."[42]

This desire for a complete monistic system was probably the reason for Frank's abandonment of the Kanto-Fichtean worldview, which made material reality subject to mind. Frank wanted a system which would unite the two and in Goethe and Stern found an approach that accepted both matter and mind and saw them as rooted in a higher dynamic reality. In contrast to Spinoza's pantheism, it was always intended to be a panentheism in which plurality, while rooted in unity, was nevertheless preserved. Frank also found that this objectivism offered a philosophy of *life*. In his brief autobiography, Frank declared that in spite of his encounter with neo-Kantianism while he was in Berlin, "[my] soul never lay in Kantianism; it was . . . a purely intellectual construction, which inwardly never satisfied [me]."[43] By contrast, Frank discovered in Goethe a living philosophy that was not a purely intellectual, logical construction.

Another reason for Frank's abandonment of the Kanto-Fichtean position was its potential for skepticism. A couple of years later in early 1910, on the invitation of E. Trubetskoi and M. K. Morozova, a well-known patron of the arts in Moscow, Frank gave a talk at the Moscow Religious-Philosophical Society on pragmatism. He argued that American pragmatism, in judging the truth of a belief by its fruits, was a logical development from empiricism and the ultimate step in skepticism. The philosophy of pragmatism destroyed not only the possibility of acquiring true knowledge but the very existence of true knowledge. Pragmatism, in Frank's interpretation, declared that beyond the boundaries of empirical data there is no ideal reality that our concepts of reality might resemble; on the contrary, these images are essentially what we call reality; we live in a world created and tirelessly being created by ourselves. Consequently, the world is plastic, subject to some extent to our wishes and demands. Truth or reality becomes a product of the will. At the hands of pragmatism, philosophy is turned into an aspect of psychology: "Truth, the ideal of cognition, is simply *our relation* to our thoughts." Thus, pragmatism is the gateway to skepticism. Pragmatism, Frank wrote, is "the most radical of all possible forms of scepticism." It is the final word in subjectivism in the moral framework whose great representatives were Epicurus, Hobbes, Spinoza, Bentham, and Stirner.[44]

Here Frank clearly revealed the nature of the revolution in his thought. In 1904 Frank praised the abolition of objective reality brought about by what he called the Kanto-Fichtean philosophy. Now, however, he turned not only against Fichte but Kant as well. It is true, he wrote, that Kant accepted the existence of the thing-in-itself, but he also said that it could not be known by us. Thus he was a forerunner of this new pragmatic subjectivism: "The idea that cognition is not the resemblance of ideas to the object of cognition, but on the contrary, the subjection of the object to the knowing subject, contains in embryo the essence or at least one of the essential essences of pragmatism. Because what is put forward here is a denial of truth as an absolute superhuman and transsubjective ideal . . . and an attempt is made to define the purpose of knowledge immanently, that is from the subjective conditions, forms and laws of the human spirit. Kant is the greatest . . . creator of the philosophy of subjectivism."[45]

Frank wanted to establish the possibility of knowledge of the outside world, to offer a realist as well as idealist philosophy. He was suspicious of all theories through which philosophy might eventually turn into a branch of psychology. So, on another front, in 1909, in editing the Russian translation of Edmund Husserl's *Logical Investigations,* he paid tribute to the author's success in establishing the character of logical laws in distinction from the process of psychological reflection.[46] Frank linked Kantian thought to the denial of a reality outside the mind and saw in it the seeds of psychologism. His Goethean position offered the existence of an outside reality without making the mind totally dependent on it.

The year 1908 was thus a crucial year in Frank's life. His wanderings had come to an end. Having left the Struves and married, he had found emotional independence. His ability to support the family that soon followed indicates financial independence. Finally, he had acquired the foundations of his own worldview and therefore some intellectual independence and maturity.[47]

6

Landmarks

FRANK'S DEBT TO Struve was as great in the political sphere as in the philosophical. Here, he wrote, Struve was his "true master." Indeed, it was through Struve that he had come into contact with the political world. That contact continued after 1905, although to a lesser extent. In the years 1906–8, Frank would have been aware of all the major political events and discussions of the time. For example, he was a witness to a number of telephone calls between Struve and Stolypin when Struve tried to effect a reconciliation between the Kadets and the government.[1]

The quality Frank learned from Struve in politics was that same "objectivism" they had both found in Goethe—a quality of political realism that would see social life as it really is. Struve, Frank declared, "taught people even in politics always to think according to the essence of things." He went as far as to say that some kind of "Goethean" objectivism had been the basis for his and Struve's Marxism: "One could say that all P.B.'s Marxism in his early years (and also my own) was determined by just that moment of 'Goethean' objectivism in Marx, his subjection of the moral-political ideal to some kind of immanently objective, as it were, cosmic source of social being."[2]

This realism and objectivism was related in Frank's mind to what he called a *state consciousness*. This involved a sense of respect for and responsibility to the state and was the primary political quality he learned from Struve:

> One might say that Struve always discussed politics, not from below, but from above, not as a member of an enslaved society, but as a potential participant in positive state construction. . . . Even when he was still a radical and a socialist, he was not a "rebel," but had a consciousness of himself as one working with the state, who was as it were just temporarily and accidentally in opposition. This of course is the only healthy and

60

fruitful political consciousness. And somehow this consciousness found an immediate echo in my soul and helped cure me of the vicious orientation of a feeble radical sulkiness and criticism. Not having myself a calling to political activity, I simply intellectually felt that this position was the only adequate one for an understanding of the genuine essence of state life. This state consciousness assumes a mature realism in evaluating the present and the possible future, assumes an immediate sense of the principle of hierarchy in state life—an understanding that in any social system (even a democratic one) a rational minority with experience in state affairs is called to genuinely define the state-social life.[3]

This state consciousness was to be the basis for Frank's political thought in the long term. He had already acquired something of this approach in 1905 and 1906. However, he did not move to the right as quickly as Struve. Indeed, as he wrote, he had been required in 1906–8 to act as a mediator between Struve and his more radical wife in political matters. Nevertheless, Struve's liberal conservatism, with its emphatic belief in the importance of the state and government institutions, was to establish itself as Frank's political creed.

This respect for the state, according to Frank, offered a profound contrast to the whole attitude of the Russian radical intelligentsia. "Radical public opinion," he wrote, "felt itself oppressed by authority and completely alienated from it. State power was 'they,' a strange and inaccessible compound of court and bureaucracy, pictured as a group of corrupt and mentally limited rulers over the real 'national and public' Russia. To 'them' were opposed 'we,' 'society,' 'the people,' and above all the 'caste' of the intelligentsia, concerned for the welfare of the people and devoted to its service, but by reason of its lack of rights capable only of criticizing government power, of arousing oppositional feelings, and secretly preparing a revolt."[4]

This sense of the irresponsibility of the Russian radical intelligentsia became very strong in Frank after 1906. Reflecting on the collapse of the First Duma and the failure of the constitutional experiment at that time, he and Struve blamed not the government but the inability of the intelligentsia to work with government reform. It was perhaps this profound hostility to the Russian intelligentsia's moral and political outlook that was the defining feature of *Landmarks*, which came out in March 1909.

In October 1908, the publicist M. O. Gershenzon wrote to Frank suggesting that they might collaborate on producing a collection of essays about the Russian intelligentsia, and in subsequent months they corresponded about the aims of such a collection and contributors. Frank strongly advocated the inclusion of Berdiaev and was in close contact with Struve to encourage him to contribute.[5] Two of Gershenzon's suggestions he strongly objected to: R. V. Ivanov-Razumnik, a critic whose philosophy Frank regarded as partly nihilist,[6] and the publicist and philosopher L. E. Gavrilovich, whom he did not consider a profound enough writer. Instead of the latter, he suggested Izgoev, who indeed wrote an article. Frank also wondered whether Iu. I. Aikhenval'd or A. G. Gornvel'd, both literary specialists, might write on the intelligentsia and aesthetics. His idea for the title was "At the Crossroads."[7] In the end there were seven contributors: Berdiaev, Bulgakov, Gershenzon, Izgoev, Kistiakovskii, Struve, and Frank. Excepting Gershenzon and Izgoev, the contributors had all been present at the Schaffhausen conference of 1903 and contributed to *Problems of Idealism.* The collection must be seen as part of a broader trend away from positivism in which Struve had been a defining influence.

The hostility of *Landmarks* toward the mentality of the Russian intelligentsia focused on its antipathy toward three things: spiritual life, economic productivity, and state and legal institutions. In addition, the authors collectively had a deep belief in the importance of absolute moral and religious values. Gershenzon wrote that all the contributors were united in a common cause: "They support a common platform— the theoretical and practical preeminence of spiritual life over the external forms of community; in the sense that the individual's inner life is the sole creative force of human existence and that it, and not any self-sufficient principle of a political order, is the only basis for any social construction."[8]

The moral and spiritual perspective was indeed strong in almost all the contributions. Bulgakov, for example, contrasted the secular, maximalist revolutionary heroism, typical of the Russian intelligentsia with a Christian heroism based on humility, personal service, and penance. In addition, he argued that Western political freedoms had grown from religious roots but that Russian revolutionaries wanted such freedoms without working from the foundations. Berdiaev criticized the intelligentsia for making truth subject to revolutionary aims: philosophy was important only to the extent that it was useful, that it in some way served the revolutionary struggle. Izgoev linked the fanaticism of Russian youth to the sexual immorality of Russian society. Behind the grandiose radicalism of the Russian student lay a profound moral decadence. Struve reviewed the history of the intelligentsia back to the Time of Troubles in the seventeenth century and accused the intelligentsia of having all the trappings of a religious belief without its content.

At the same time, there were considerable differences between the *Landmarks* contributors. For example, Gershenzon's statement about a belief in the "preeminence" of spiritual values was not completely true. Kistiakovskii's essay, "In Defence of Law," was about the need for the discipline of legal culture and institutions as well as moral values. Kistiakovskii, Izgoev, Struve, and Frank were all associated with the Kadets, even if Frank had ceased political activity. Berdiaev and Bulgakov were much more involved with contemporary religious and mystical ideas. Frank regarded Gershenzon as an odd man out among the group, describing him as a kind of "Tolstoian populist" who wanted Russia to return to the organic wholeness of her former spiritual culture. Whereas he, Frank declared later, wanted the Russian intelligentsia to abandon its complex, even luxurious culture, the rest of the contributors attacked the intelligentsia for its intellectual dogmatism.[9]

However, it would be wrong to look for agreeement on all issues among the writers of *Landmarks*. Frank foresaw the potential dilemma their differences would pose when in a letter to Gershenzon he declared: "The main *inner* difficulty of our undertaking is that, in my view, criticism is fruitful only in combination with a clear indication of a new ideal, and in this, the positive aspect, there is no hope of unanimity among the contributors."[10] It was the weakness of *Landmarks* that while it provided a sharp and prophetic diagnosis of the failings of the intelligentsia, it did not have a clear and unambiguous solution to the problems of Russian society.

Frank's essay in *Landmarks*, "The Ethic of Nihilism," was built around the moral philosophy he had been developing since his critique of utilitarianism in *Problems of Idealism*. Frank had not abandoned the lessons he had learned from Nietzsche.[11] In 1906 he wrote an essay on Tolstoian morality in which he defended a moral humanism based on the value of remaining true to oneself: in Fichte's formula, "Be as you are."[12] However, by 1909 he saw man as occupying a humbler position in the universe. While the Nietzschean moral teaching denied the existence of fixed rules of behavior, his philosophy now affirmed the presence of universal obligations. In one definition of "objectivism," for example, Frank linked a disinterested contemplation of reality with "a consciousness of some higher meaning of reality . . . and the duty of the individual in some sense to subject himself to it."[13] In the debate on pragmatism that followed Frank's presentation to the Moscow Religious-Philosophical Society in 1910, he stated that "religion is not humanist, but superhumanist and in this sense decisively contradicts pragmatic humanism."[14] Frank now understood humanism in a Feuerbachian sense: man is God. His new position, which involved not a break with the previous one but the development of its religious foundations, was what he termed *religious hu-*

manism, and this is what he called for at the end of his essay in *Landmarks.*[15]

"The Ethic of Nihilism," contained perhaps the most biting criticism of the intelligentsia in the collection. His intention was to lay bare the basic structure of the nihilistic mentality. The immediate prelude to his essay was an anti-utopian essay he wrote in 1907, "The Philosophical Presuppositions of Despotism." His basic point in that essay was that despotism becomes a reality when earthly and heavenly ideals get mixed up. As soon as someone believes that someone or some institution is the incarnation of the absolute ideal, differing opinions are no longer permitted. Hatred of sin becomes hatred of the sinner, and any means are justified to deal with it. Frank's idea of democracy was founded on a recognition of this. "Democracy," he wrote, "depends . . . on a denial of any infallibility . . . ; against all infallibility it juxtaposes the right of every individual to participate in decisions about social well-being."[16]

Frank's ideas were not exclusively his own. Quite apart from the influence of Struve, his arguments against socialism, for example, which were so strong in *Landmarks,* had been put forward in 1906 by Berdiaev in an article, "The Religion of Socialism." Berdiaev's essay contained almost every point that Frank made in *Landmarks.*[17] Moreover, this was a popular theme among Russian thinkers at that time, even among socialists. In 1908, A. V. Lunacharskii started publishing his *Religion and Socialism* in which he argued that socialism was indeed becoming a new religious faith. It would be wrong, therefore, to see "The Ethic of Nihilism" as an original work. The value of the essay was its clarity in setting out certain ideas.

The context for Frank's essay, as for his fellow contributors, was the failure of the 1905 revolution and the subsequent soul-searching of the Russian intelligentsia. The intelligentsia, Frank believed, had proved itself so incapable of mature leadership that the time had come for a review of its most basic assumptions. Frank's essay attempted to be such a review; it was an attempt to "clarify and evaluate critically the intelligentsia's *moral* outlook." While on the one hand it is not possible to divide the human soul into parts, Frank believed that the moral illness was such that "one must attempt to anatomize it mentally and penetrate it to its roots."[18] His essay, then, was a description of the inner structures of the intelligentsia's moral outlook.

Frank characterized the moral outlook of the Russian *intelligent* as "nihilistic moralism." This creed was based, on the one hand, on a belief that there are no objective moral values in the world, that all religious and aesthetic ideas must be subject to the satisfaction of the material needs of the majority, and on the other hand, a passionate moral commitment to the satisfaction of those needs:

> *Nihilistic moralism* is the fundamental and most profound feature of the Russian *intelligent*'s spiritual physiognomy. The rejection of objective values gives rise to the deification of one's fellow man's (the people's) subjective interests, whence follows his recognition of service to the people as man's highest and sole mission, and this in turn leads to the ascetic hatred for everything that impedes or even simply does not facilitate the realization of that mission. Life has no objective or intrinsic meaning whatsoever; the sole good in it is material security and the satisfaction of subjective requirements. Therefore man is obligated to dedicate all his powers to improving the lot of the majority. Everything that distracts him from this is evil and must be ruthlessly extirpated. . . . Nihilism and moralism; the lack of faith and fanatic severity of moral requirements.[19]

This nihilistic moralism was founded, in Frank's view, on a utilitarian view of culture. The European concept of culture, which was founded on "the perfection of political, social and colloquial forms of communication [and] the progress of morality, religion, science and art" was exchanged for a utilitarian view of culture: "When people speak about culture here, they have in mind either railroads, sewer systems, or paved roads, or the development of a national education system, or the perfection of the political mechanism; it is always something useful, some kind of *means* for the realization of another end." According to Frank, the Russian intelligentsia was incapable of believing in spiritual values for their own sake. Consequently, culture had become "an unnecessary and morally inadmissable aristocratic indulgence."[20]

The basis for this utilitarianism was populism. Populism, taken as a broad spiritual current, could be considered, in Frank's view, the underlying worldview of all the Russian intelligentsia, even the Marxists: "One would think Marxism struggles against populism; and in fact with the appearance of Marxism, motifs alien to the intelligentsia consciousness were heard for the first time—respect for culture and raising productivity (material, as well as spiritual). . . . But these motifs did not dominate intelligentsia thought for long; the victorious and all-consuming populist spirit swallowed up and assimilated Marxist theory. At the present time, the distinction between admitted populists and populists who profess Marxism at most comes down to a distinction in political programme and sociological theory, and not one of cultural and philosophical principles."[21]

Populism, for Frank, could be divided into two kinds: the genuine

aspiration to serve the material needs of individuals and the maximalist desire to answer the problems of mankind as a whole. In Frank's
view, the latter maximalist form of populism had become the domi-
nant strain. He saw the roots of the populist worldview in the rational
optimism of the eighteenth century. Evil came to be identified with
individuals or classes. If the oppressors were eliminated and the popu-
lace reeducated, the earthly paradise could be established: "[This kind
of] social optimism rests on the *mechanistic-rationalistic theory of
happiness*. From this viewpoint, the problem of human happiness is a
problem of society's external organization, and since happiness is guaranteed by material blessings, it is a question of *distribution*. In order to
guarantee mankind's prosperity, one has only to take these blessings
away from those in unjust control of them and ensure against a minority ever having the opportunity to take control of them again. Such
is the uncomplicated but powerful train of thought that unites nihilistic moralism with the *religion of socialism*."[22]

However, on the basis of this populism that focused on answering
all man's needs, this socialist love for man quickly became distorted:

> A socialist is not an altruist. True, he also strives for human happiness,
> however, he loves not living people but only his *idea*—the idea of happi-
> ness for all mankind. Sacrificing himself for the sake of this idea, he
> does not hesitate to sacrifice other people for it. Among his contempo-
> raries he sees either merely the victims of the world's evil he dreams of
> eradicating or the perpetrators of that evil. He pities the former, but he
> cannot help them directly since his activities must benefit only their re-
> mote descendants; consequently, there is no genuine concern for them.
> The latter he despises, and he regards the task at hand and the funda-
> mental means for realizing his ideal in the struggle against them. This
> feeling of hatred for the enemies of the people forms the concrete and
> active psychological foundation of his life. Thus the great love of man-
> kind of the future gives birth to a great hatred for people; the passion for
> organizing an earthly paradise becomes a passion for destruction; and
> the faithful populist-socialist becomes the *revolutionary*.[23]

Eventually, hatred takes control of the soul and starts to destroy the
spiritual core of the personality.

These facets of the *intelligent'*s outlook made his worldview a fruitless one. He was motivated by hate, not by love. This was an aspect of
Frank's definition of "the religion of socialism": the socialist was fired
by a desire to redistribute wealth rather than the desire to create it. In
fact, he was even suspicious of wealth. It is necessary, Frank believed,
to love wealth in order to create it, but the intelligentsia had become
deeply suspicious of wealth: "In its soul, love for the *poor* has become

love for *poverty*. It dreams of feeding all the poor, but its deepest, unrealized metaphysical instinct resists the dissemination of true wealth in the world."[24]

The result of all this was a contradictory mentality that lay at the root of the Russian *intelligent*'s fanaticism:

> We can define the classic Russian *intelligent* as a *militant monk of the nihilistic religion of earthly contentment*. If there are contradictions in this combination of features, they are the dynamic contradictions of the intelligentsia soul. By his outlook and way of life the *intelligent* is, above all else, a monk. He shuns reality, avoids the world, and lives outside genuine, historical, everyday life, in a world of phantoms, daydreams and pious faith. . . .
>
> But having isolated himself in his own monastery, the *intelligent* is not indifferent to the world; on the contrary, he wants to rule the world from his monastery and proselytize it. He is a militant monk, a monk-revolutionary. . . . [The intelligentsia's] political activity has a goal not so much of bringing about some kind of objectively useful, in the worldly sense, reform, as of liquidating the enemies of the faith and forcibly converting the world.
>
> . . . The content of this faith is an idolatry founded on religious unbelief, of earthly material contentment. . . . A handful of monks, alien to and contemptuous of the world, declare war on the world in order to forcibly do it a great favour and gratify its earthly, material needs.[25]

At the end of his essay, Frank very briefly summarized his alternative to this revolutionary mentality: "We must pass from unproductive, anti-cultural *nihilistic moralism* to the creative and constructive culture of *religious humanism*."[26]

Frank's thinking had clearly changed since 1905. No longer did he think of uniting the socialist and the liberal strands of the opposition movement. Now he was totally in opposition to "the religion of socialism." In another contemporary essay he made a clear distinction between socialism as a practical sociopolitical system and socialism as a religion.[27] Whenever he attacked socialism in his subsequent life, he meant the latter: a creed, based on eighteenth- and nineteenth-century rationalism and romanticism, that aimed to convert the world, eradicate evil, and create heaven on earth. From his essay in *Landmarks*, it is clear that he thought the intelligentsia had embraced this latter form of it.

In this connection, Frank's comments on Marxism were also very sharp, indicating that much of his former respect for Marxist doctrine had disappeared: "It is highly characteristic of [our] philosophical senselessness that of all the formulations of socialism which could have dominated our minds, we accepted the teachings of Marx, a system which despite all the breadth of its scientific structure, is not only lacking in any philosophical foundation whatsoever, but even rejects it on principle."[28] On Lenin, Frank was equally scathing. In reviewing his book *Materialism and Empirio-Criticism*, which offered a sharp attack on various forms of idealism, Frank accused the author of extreme dogmatism, compared the book to the literature of the extreme Right, and stated that a "more disgusting combination of abstract conceptions and abusive epithets it is difficult to imagine, . . . [and] its approach to philosophical problems witnesses to the inner insolvency of the position of the author."[29]

Frank's essay in *Landmarks* shows his social and political writing at its boldest and most forceful. Its power is partly due to certain typical stylistic features of his social and political writing. He takes words like "moralism," "nihilism," "utilitarianism," and "populism" and uses them as hooks on which to hang his analysis. His use of the words is an important clue to his whole mentality. These key words become the building blocks of his argument. It is a method he used throughout his life and indicates a mind with a passion for order.

This style of analysis, which was so important to his attempt to dissect the structure of a mentality, finds an echo in another essay he wrote at this time for the neo-Kantian journal *Logos*. In "Nature and Culture," he divided philosophy since Aristotle into those writers who emphasized the dominance of nature over culture and those who held the opposite view. The former, "physiocrats," he again subdivided into Epicureans and Stoics; the latter, "noocrats," into rationalists and religious people. Thus he divided the whole history of philosophy into four categories. Of course, he stressed, no one thinker represented only one category; the categories were present to a greater or lesser extent in all thinkers.[30] Taking Frank's equally ordered description of the revolutionary as the "militant monk of the nihilistic religion of earthly happiness," it seems likely that these characteristics of the revolutionary are built out of at least similar philosophical building blocks. The Epicurean searches for earthly happiness; the revolutionary rationalist becomes the militant monk. The parallel does not fit perfectly between the essays, but it confirms the structural foundation for Frank's analysis and how he attempted to fulfill his atomistic description of the intelligentsia's moralism.

Landmarks was, in Frank's words, a "noisy, sensational success"[31] and was greeted by a storm of controversy. In 1909–10 over two hundred articles and books appeared in response to it, including ones from all the different political parties. Lenin described it as an "encyclopedia of liberal renegacy."[32] Miliukov, who was so incensed that he went on a lecture tour to attack it, wrote a long critique in the Kadet response to it, *The Intelligentsia in Russia* of 1910. He stated that the basic message of the book was that politics as a whole was to blame because it placed social values above the ethical and religious.[33] He made a similar point in his memoirs where he declared that the authors of *Landmarks* "had a hostile attitude to the 'formalism' of strict parliamentary forms." "They were ready," he wrote, "to return to the old formula: 'not institutions, but people,' 'not politics, but morality.' Since the time of Karamzin, this suspicious formula had concealed reactionary tendencies within it."[34] Kistiakovskii and Struve excepted, it could certainly be argued that some of these authors did not think in a political way.

The philosopher A. F. Losev, who knew Frank and other members of the *Landmarks* group, offered toward the end of his life a similar observation about the collection. He said that "it feels like a work of literature. . . . Now we have to construct life not according to literature, but another way."[35] The weakness of *Landmarks* was the lack of practical answers. The diagnosis was very sharp, but it was not clear what precisely it meant to rebuild a society on moral and spiritual foundations. There was, in fact, a lack of reality in Frank's thinking on the subject of practical politics. In his earlier essay on despotism, he came out in favor of the vote for all in a political system. This, he said vaguely, should be understood not only in a narrow technical sense but also in a wider philosophical sense.[36] Frank was always suspicious of those who were interested more in the forms of political life than the spirit of it. With that, he was also suspicious of party politics or more precisely, "the domination of slavish conservatism and party thinking."[37] This is all very well in theory, but his interest in both universal suffrage and the nonparty spirit suggests a certain lack of realism.

In spite of all this, *Landmarks* was not really an attack on politics itself or indeed an attack on party politics; it was a review of the moral and political assumptions of the Russian intelligentsia. Frank, for example, specifically stated that his essay was about morality. The intelligentsia, in his thought, identified evil with the "system." He, on the other hand, viewed individuals as the primary source of good and evil and consequently believed that society was in need of an ethical and cultural change of a much deeper order. In this sense, Frank's essay, like the essays of his colleagues, had profound political implications. These ideas assumed that an evolutionary approach to social change was far preferable to a revolutionary one, and this implied that it was best to work with the state as far as possible. Frank and his colleagues were thus rejecting much of the Russian intelligentsia's traditional discourse about politics and revolution.

Another criticism of *Landmarks* was that its concept of the intelligentsia was ill-defined. Surely its authors were members or products of this caste they were trying to denigrate.[38] This, of course, was true, and it was a point the authors were aware of. Frank, it should be said, was always describing the model *intelligent*, the ideal representative of this revolutionary worldview. That not everyone fitted in to it he would have been the first to admit. The criticism is a valid one, but it is peripheral.

One of the most astute critics of Frank was the well-known liberal publicist S. V. Lur'e. He took Frank to task for two things: an idolization of culture and a vague attitude to religion.[39] There was some truth in both statements. Frank's concept of culture could be interpreted as a kind of religion. His basic concept of culture was that it was the sum of all religious, artistic, and material values. In an article of 1910, "Capitalism and Culture," Frank argued that material wealth could lay the basis for spiritual progress and did not necessarily lead to "Americanism." In defending capitalism's contribution to material culture, he nevertheless argued that "a genuinely convincing 'justification' of capitalism cannot be simply economic; it must depend on a religious-philosophical idea of culture, as the totality of historically established objective and absolute values."[40] Looked at like this, culture could easily become a God.

In regard to Frank's vagueness about religion, that was due more to the target of the essay than a general lack of clarity. Frank's concept of religious humanism was part of a broader aim of reconciling the absolute demands of the spiritual world with the realities of human life. Frank had already rejected any metaphysical attempts to identify the ideal world with some aspect of reality because of the inherent dangers of dogmatism resulting from such a view. In 1910, in a review of a collection of essays by Berdiaev, *The Spiritual Crisis of the Intelligentsia*, he emphasized this point. Berdiaev had declared that God's will rather than the people's will was the best defense of the rights of the individual and had argued in favor not of an ideal constitutional democracy but "the organic ideal of free theocracy." Although Frank still admired Berdiaev's thought, he felt that this position offered a dangerous confusion of the absolute and relative worlds. In his lack of clarity, Berdiaev was even revealing features typical of the Russian *intelligent*.[41] The attempt to link God and man without confusing the two was to be central to all of Frank's ideas.

There were public discussions of *Landmarks*, and one of these took place at the St. Petersburg Religious-Philosophical Society in April 1909. There were so many people at the debate that they had to move the location from the Polish Club to the room of a large newspaper auditorium. There, Merezhkovskii, supported by his wife Gippius and D. V. Filosofov, led the attack on the publication, trying to prove that it was reactionary. This, of course, illustrated the very point that the authors of *Landmarks* wished to make: the seeming inability of the Russian intelligentsia to see things outside a Left and Right context. Struve and Frank represented *Landmarks* at the gathering, and according to Frank, in spite of the general hostility to them, did very well. In describing the debate in the newspaper *The Word (Slovo)*, Frank stated: "We are searching for a new road which is not confined to the old, customary line 'from right to left and left to right.'"[42]

Landmarks touched a deep chord in many Russian thinkers. One liberal, I. V. Gessen, wrote later: "For the first time, I realized that our epoch was coming to an end; I saw that *Landmarks* had coined the slogans of the future, which were supported by modern knowledge; even science was moving towards metaphysics."[43] Just as Frank's thinking reflected many of the concerns of his fellow revisionists, so their religious concerns reflected a deeper trend in society. There were probably many others who could have contributed to the collection. Losskii relates that Bulgakov invited him to participate in *Landmarks* but that he refused.[44] Writing in 1944, Frank noted this same broad trend and suggested that it had long-term importance: "*Landmarks* did achieve one object; the book helped break through the solid wall of censorship enforced by public opinion which forbade anyone to speak except with deep reverence about the sacred tradition of radicalism. It could not, however, influence the course of Russian political life. The ideas it expressed were drowned in the rising waves of the revolution, yet it had helped to promote the initial unanimous and energetic resistance of the intelligentsia to the Bolsheviks, and to stimulate the spiritual revival and penitence which accompanied this movement."[45]

Landmarks was also to inspire a collection of essays, *From the Depths*, written in 1918 about the Russian revolution, to which Frank contributed, and found echoes in a much later collection of 1973, *From Under the Rubble*, in which Solzhenitsyn, its editor, wrote: "Even after sixty years [*Landmarks*'] testimony has not lost its brightness; [it] today still seems to us to have been a vision of future."[46]

7

Conversion to Orthodoxy

FRANK DESCRIBED HIS reading of Nietzsche as a great spiritual turning point in his life. According to the religious historian A. V. Kartashev, a good friend of Frank, Frank considered himself a Christian even before 1905.[1] Nevertheless, unlike Sergei Bulgakov, his break with Marxism did not result in a sudden formal conversion to Russian Orthodoxy and an obviously religious worldview, and there is very little of a serious religious nature in Frank's writing until 1906.

At this point, Frank was broadly in favor of religion but hostile to anything that might lead to dogmatism and warned against those who simply exchanged the dogmas of Marxism for the dogmas of the Orthodox Church.[2] This, as he expressed it to Gershenzon in 1908, had been a point he had wanted Bulgakov to tackle in *Landmarks*. He strongly disputed Merezhkovskii's concept of a new religious consciousness that would combine a belief in God with a belief in revolution: "Merezhkovskii thinks that you only have to put Christ in the place of Marx and the kingdom of God in the place of socialism in order for the reform of the intelligentsia's worldview . . . to be complete. . . . But against this, it is exceptionally important for us to stress the need for an inner, cultural-moral, religious reeducation of the intelligentsia."[3]

In 1906 Frank stated that there were two kinds of religious faith: "[There is] the belief in *authority* and the belief in the *rights of a free conscience*. Speaking philosophically, there lies an unconquerable abyss between these two points. The former denies any validity to independent thought and a free conscience, the second denies all rights of authority and confesses the unrestricted freedom of personal spiritual creativity. The first seeks for God in texts, canons and statutes; the second seeks for and finds him only in an immediate . . . experience of the spirit. You can make a choice between these two kinds of belief, but you cannot join them together."[4] In his lectures of 1906–7

72

Frank also distinguished between the religion of fear and the religion of love.[5]

The St. Petersburg Religious-Philosophical Society, founded in 1907, included among its members the religious thinkers Berdiaev, V. F. Ern, Filosofov, Gippius, Kartashev, Merezhkovskii, Rozanov, and a priest, K. M. Aggeev, pure philosophers like Vvedenskii and political thinkers like Struve. Frank was at the first meeting in October 1907 and was among the organizers.[6] In his introductory speech, Kartashev referred to Frank as "an ideologue of individualism, [and] a philosopher-agnostic." Frank was seen as a representative of the nonreligious wing of the society, in contrast to those members of the Orthodox establishment.[7] Askol'dov gave the main speech, "On the Old and New Religious Consciousness," and in the discussion that followed Frank expressed his concerns about all forms of dogmatic religion but nevertheless stated that he "[accepted] religion"; he saw the essence of Christianity as the replacement of the rigorism of the moral law with the moral code of Christ.[8]

Frank's religion, then, was experience-centred. While disputing the pragmatism of William James, for example, he was impressed by the radical empiricism of his *Varieties of Religious Experience.*[9] He had little time for the church. When he went to Germany at Easter in 1907 with Struve, the two of them were "indifferent to the activity of the church."[10] His experience of Marxist dogma clearly made him forever suspicious of rules that seemed to act against human nature, and his critique of religious dogma, which was later softened but never fully abandoned, was part of that reaction.

Although Frank was numbered among the organizers of the St. Petersburg Religious-Philosophical Society, he states in his memoir of Struve that it was from the autumn of 1908 onward that he used to go to the meetings of the society.[11] He had stated that his era of unbelief ended when he was about 30, which was in 1907, and it was during the summer of 1908 that his long-term worldview was beginning to form. If it is possible to pinpoint any moment for a strengthening of his religious convictions, it would thus be in these two years. Certainly there was a major change around this time, for Frank's "humanist individualism" of 1906 had turned by early 1909 into "religious humanism."

In his memoir of Struve, Frank records an event in late 1910 that reveals a move to a more formal framework for religion. In November 1910 Russia went into mourning at the death of Tolstoi. Frank said later that there was a feeling that something had collapsed in the nation with his death.[12] This was one of the events that played a role in Frank's baptism into the Orthodox Church in 1912. There was a gathering of the St. Petersburg Religious-Philosophical Society on 16 November 1910 to commemorate the death of Tolstoi at which Frank, Struve, and Gippius gave talks. Frank lamented the passing of Tolstoi. Although he indicated many intellectual differences with Tolstoi, he praised his relentless pursuit of truth, described him as a prophet, and stated that his death might mark "the beginning of a radical spiritual transformation in the consciousness of society."[13] The meeting was followed by prayers, which were something new for the society:

> On the suggestion of the Merezhkovskiis, an unusual decision was taken . . . : after the speeches, the gathering would close with a prayer. It was arranged that the Old Believer Bishop Mikhail . . . would be the last to speak and that he would then finish his speech with a spontaneous prayer for the rest of Tolstoi's soul; this was to be a signal for the gathering to rise and then some specially invited choir would sing "the precepts of blessedness." This was the first attempt to move the religiously-interested intelligentsia from religious-philosophical discussions to participation in some kind of non-confessional church worship. In this decision, in spite of a certain artificiality, there was something which corresponded to the general mood of shock at the death of Tolstoi. I remember, for example, at the educational courses of the Froebel Society, some girls also, after my lecture on Tolstoi, on their own initiative, sang a requiem prayer. . . . The unexpected religious singing was received by our very varied gathering with a certain puzzlement, but it seemed to have an effect. In the wider intelligentsia circles it was met with mockery. I tell this episode in such detail because I think that for P.B., as for some of the other participants in the gathering, it was an expression of a dim but growing aspiration for a church framework for our religious search.[14]

The impression is that in spite of Frank's suspicion of dogma, he too felt pulled toward a framework whereby he could interpret his experience. One imagines that the peace and harmony offered by the Orthodox liturgy also had an effect.

In 1910 Frank had chosen a spiritual director, K. M. Aggeev, who was the priest of the church attached to the Larinskii Gymnasium on Vasilievskii Island. He was a popular preacher in St. Petersburg and one of the few members of the St. Petersburg Religious-Philosophical Society who came from the church. He was an advocate of church reform—for example, believing that the Orthodox Church was too closely tied with the Russian state—and he had some sympathy with those, like Merezhkovskii and Gippius, who called for a religious revolution.[15]

Frank had plenty of opportunity to get to know Aggeev, for they moved in the same academic circles. Aggeev had done editorial work with *Questions of Life* and had taught at the Bestuzhev Courses, the Froebel Courses, and the Psycho-Neurological Institute. Frank had chosen him to baptize his first son, Viktor. Then he made the decision to convert to Orthodoxy. Aggeev baptized him at his church at the Larinskii Gymnasium on 3 May 1912.[16] Tatiana recalled the event in her memoirs:

[Semyon Liudvigovich said] that he was inwardly ready to accept Christianity and that he wanted to be baptized—it was so precious a thing for him that he wanted to be alone—this corresponded with my own plans—I had long decided that I would go to stay with mother . . . we arranged that he would send me a telegram when his movement to Christianity had been completed. And I received his telegram and was with him in spirit all the time. Before taking this step, we had gone together to visit the Struves to tell them, as his closest friends, about his decision. There was a long and difficult conversation with Nina Alexandrovna Struve who was at that time very radical and atheist—she gloomily said that it was a betrayal of his people etc—she could not conceive of other motives—i.e. religious, which moved Semyon's conscience. Petr B. even then understood Semyon and as it were inwardly blessed him.[17]

It is interesting that Nina Struve should accuse Frank of betraying his people. It was quite common for Jews to convert to Orthodoxy, not out of conviction but because it would further personal advancement. Evidently she accused Frank of doing it for this reason. Frank was certainly open to the charge. To get a job teaching at St. Petersburg University, he needed to be Orthodox, and three weeks later he applied to become a private docent there, beginning his curriculum vitae with the phrase "Semyon Liudvigovich Frank, an Orthodox believer."[18] It is possible that Frank was encouraged to convert to Orthodoxy by the prospect of a job, and indeed his job application was accepted. However, Frank's motives were not fundamentally utilitarian. His Christian beliefs were real if not at the time wholly Orthodox, and it was not in character to put career before conviction. He had already turned down such an opportunity in 1902.

Apparently sometime after the conversion, Frank met Hermann Cohen, the famous neo-Kantian philosopher from Marburg, who was also Jewish. Cohen had the view that the Kantian concepts of duty and the categorical imperative had much in common with the duty of the Old Testament and that Lutheranism was very close to Judaism. Cohen gave a talk,[19] and Frank went up to converse with him afterwards. Cohen discovered that Frank was a baptized Jew, declared his dislike of such people, and walked off.[20]

In an essay on Cohen's religious philosophy, Frank contrasted what he saw as the abstraction of Judaism with the concreteness of Christianity. Commenting on the apocalyptic nature of Judaism, he wrote:

> Although in the concrete religious consciousness of Judaism, this striving for the future was linked . . . with a religious evaluation of the past, that is with faith in a revelation which has already happened, nevertheless the tense loyalty to the observation of the purity and greatness of the Future easily led psychologically to a denial of the past and the real . . . for the sake of the purity of a dream which is abstracted from all living spirituality; here religion easily passes or can pass into a rationalist moralism, a passionate emphasis on the transcendent nature of Divinity to all established, empirical reality,—in a denial of His concreteness. The relation between Judaism and Christianity, and the whole world tragedy of the Judaic religious consciousness perhaps could be explained . . . from this point of view.[21]

Apart from the general critique of Judaism contained here, the phrases "tense loyalty" and "rationalist moralism" suggest that Frank's break with Judaism stemmed from the same source, at least in part, as his break with the revolutionary movement. Frank hated obligation without life, ethics without an ontological root in human nature. Christianity offered grace as well as duty. In regard to what he called the "transcendent" quality of Jewish religion, Frank later wrote that Judaism is really a religion of unbelief. In a lecture he gave in emigration, he said that for the Jews, God's "immanentness is transferred to the future." Real belief is replaced by a belief in progress, and in this Judaism and socialism belong together.[22]

Over twenty years later, Frank explained in an essay, "The Religious Tragedy of the Jews," how difficult it is for a Jew to convert to Christianity:

> Throughout the history of Christianity, Judaism has faced a terrible alternative—a real religious antinomy: either to give up its nationality (of which the only basis is the belief of the Old Testament) and to prepare the chosen people of Israel for the prophetic promise of a definite calling—or to deny the Messiah and God's greatest revelation revealed by him. The positive solution to this antinomy is made impossible because of the following circumstance: since the Christian church has become the ruling church in both the state and the world, and, at the same time, Judaism has been persecuted for its belief, every conversion to Christianity inevitably seems like a betrayal of the people and its belief, rewarded by earthly advantage.[23]

It would seem that Nina Struve's reaction to Frank's decision to convert reflected this. The Jewish religion and nationality were so linked that to convert from the religion meant to betray the nation.

Frank always stressed that he was not converting away from Judaism, just taking a step on from it: "I believe that in a general sense, turning to Christianity and losing my link with Judaism, I nevertheless remained true to the testament of my grandfather, because I remained true to the religious foundations which he implanted in me. . . . I always thought of my Christianity as a building on an Old Testament foundation, as a natural development from the religious life of my childhood."[24] Nevertheless, it would be true to say that in spite of his Jewishness, Frank was never a religious Jew except in his earliest years. His difficulty was not breaking with a religious tradition. If there was a difficulty, it would have been this sense of betraying his nation. Then again, he had never lived in the Russian Jewish community; his social and intellectual milieu was that of the broader Russian intelligentsia. His parents were no longer alive, and he had no community to break away from. This must have made things easier.[25]

In his essay "The Religious Tragedy of the Jews," Frank stated that any impartial observer could not fail to see that God's revelation was at its greatest in the history of Judaism in the person of Christ. This, however, may be the reason of hindsight. Frank's writing of the period contains almost nothing about the person of Christ. However, the reason for Frank's conversion must have been that at heart he became a Christian. It is doubtful that he felt at this time a particular attachment to the Orthodox Church. Writing previously on Tolstoi's moral philosophy, he had expressed admiration for his religious outlook: "[Tolstoi's] new religiosity is primarily individualistic, it searches and finds God not in the organization of the church, not in old books and outward wonders, but only in the great mystery of the God-conscious human soul."[26] So, even with his acceptance of Orthodoxy, his religious and philosophical thought of the time was experience-centered, and he remained suspicious of dogma. On one occasion, when he was in Marburg in Germany in 1913, he came out of the old Gothic cathedral and announced to Lev Zak: "All the same, a bright Greek temple is closer to me in spirit."[27] It shows the extent to which his religious conversion was a broad rather than precise one.

One notable factor, although perhaps not surprising in view of Frank's Jewish background, is the sparsity of Russian sources in his religious reading. It is true that he was acquainted with Solov'ev by this time and that he much admired Tiutchev. But his conversion was not a "Russian" conversion. His reading was consistently European, often German, and usually philosophical. So his intellectual encounter with religious experience was not tinged with nationalism or a Slavophile enthusiasm for Russian roots. In fact, Frank had a dispute in *Russian Thought* in 1910 with the nationalist philosopher V. F. Ern. Ern had criticized Western thought for its rationalism and attacked the neo-Kantian journal *Logos* for its advocacy of a false Western "logos." Frank replied by stating that no nationalism was needed in philosophy and that Russian philosophy had been degraded by its anti-rationalism.[28]

Tatiana would certainly not have opposed Frank's conversion, although there is no evidence to suggest that she influenced him. They had obviously discussed religious matters together, and in spite of Tatiana's conversion to Lutheranism, she was, or at least became, a religious woman. In one of her memoirs she recalls an early religious experience of her own: "We lived beside a large convent, and, making friends with the nuns, I used to spend all my time there. All the convent services became a necessity for me, especially Passion week. The memory of the Passion entered my soul forever."[29] Tatiana's faith was an emotional one, very different from her husband's. She was probably enthusiastic about Viktor being baptized into the Orthodox Church.

What kind of religion, then, did Frank believe in? Miliukov, in his long essay in *Landmarks*, borrowed from William James his three characteristics of the religious mind: first, the believer believes that the visible world is a part of and dependent on a great spiritual absolute; second, the aim of our life is union with this spiritual absolute; and finally, prayer and inner communication with the spirit of this absolute is the process whereby spiritual energy is transferred from one world to the other. Applying these criteria to the authors of *Landmarks*, he concluded that only Bulgakov could be called religious. Regarding Frank, he certainly fulfilled the first two criteria, but the third was more doubtful. However, with his description of the prayer at the Religious-Philosophical Society's meeting following Tolstoi's death, it would be fair to say that Frank was also, if just tentatively, embarking on the journey of the third.

In a short essay on Konstantin Leont'ev, Frank expressed admiration for Oscar Wilde's prison confession *De Profundis*. Wilde, he wrote, had broken with moralistic religion and found a religious experience based on a "feeling of universal aesthetic harmony."[30] An idea of harmony is perhaps the best description of Frank's religious intuition. It may, in fact, be the key to understanding the very nature of his mind. This becomes clear in one of his longer essays written at this time. He had done a translation of F. Schleiermacher's lectures on religion and monologues for *Russian Thought* and in his introduction paid particular attention to his interest in feeling and religion. "Feeling," he wrote, "being in opposition to theoretical knowledge is, along with it, a higher knowledge, and one can even say that 'all knowledge is a memory,' a memory of that primary unity, which is given in and through feeling. Feeling, or which is the same thing, religious intuition."[31] Clearly, Frank's concept of religion was related to a feeling about a "primary unity." It involved a feeling of harmony.

Frank called religious feeling "higher knowledge." It was evidently the same higher knowledge for which he praised Goethe: an immediate as opposed to analytical apprehension of reality. Evidently, Frank's sense of a religious harmony was little different from his philosophical idea of it. Again in his essay on Schleiermacher, he declared that whereas the foundation for the thought of Descartes and Fichte had been *Cogito ergo sum* (I think, therefore I am), the foundation for Schleiermacher was *Sum in infinito, ergo scio et ago* (I am in infinity, therefore I know and act).[32]

This kind of writing is difficult to define as either religious or philosophical. Frank himself confirmed this in a subsequent lecture course on philosophy: "[Theoretical and practical philosophy] come together into a whole philosophical system, which is always . . . *religious philosophy.*"[33]

The sense of religious and philosophical harmony was also a poetic feeling. In an article of 1913, Frank expressed great admiration for the poetry of Tiutchev. He liked "not his description of the outer form of things, but his penetration into their cosmic depth." Poetry more than prose, Frank wrote, gives a full and concrete expression of being.[34] Frank's subsequent interest in mysticism and his admiration for poets who were best able to express their mystical experiences, like Goethe, Tiutchev, Pushkin, and Rilke, points to a sense that his own religious experience was a poetic discovery of the harmony of the world.

In the same article, Frank praised Tiutchev's pantheism. There was much that was pantheistic about Frank's religion, as there was to be a strong pantheistic tendency in his philosophy. Here again, Frank's religion and philosophy merge. However, Frank called Tiutchev's approach "dualistic pantheism."[35] He meant by that the same plurality-in-unity he found in Stern.

Frank's comment on Schleiermacher that feeling and religious intuition are the same suggests that his conversion to Orthodoxy involved some kind of "feelings" of his own. He had come to feel that Orthodoxy was right, or more probably that Christianity generally was correct. That still does not explain why he would suddenly convert. The reminiscences of his wife indicate that the decision was long thought over, but there is no direct reference in Frank's writing to a direct encounter with a personal God at this time. IIis God was a God of harmony and unity. This would go some way to explaining his evident attraction to pantheism, the pantheism of Spinoza and Goethe, and the strangely impersonal concepts of God that occasionally appear in his writing. In one place, for example, he says that "religion is primarily a mood; it gives an absolute foundation for our ideal evaluations."[36]

Frank was officially given a post as private docent in the Philosophy Department of St. Petersburg University on 31 May 1912. The other permanent teachers in the department were Vvedenskii, Lapshin, and Losskii, and the four of them also made up the faculty of the Bestuzhev Courses.

Frank's philosophical interests were increasingly focused on the problems of epistemology. His work at the Bestuzhev Courses had included two seminars on theories of cognition (1908–9, and 1911–12) as well as lectures on German idealism after Kant (1910–11). In preparing his Master's thesis, he began to synthesize his ideas into one philosophical system, and with this work in mind, he took his family to Germany from May 1913 to August 1914 to gather material. Frank's faculty financed the trip to the tune of 2,000 roubles per year with money from the Ministry of Education.[37] Initially they were in the small university town of Marburg where Frank worked in the library, in the winter of 1913–14 in Munich, and finally on the outskirts of Munich in Herrsching.

Struve visited the Franks twice, first in the summer of 1913, then in the winter of 1913–14. They spent Russian New Year together in Munich along with El'iashevich, who was then a colleague of Struve at the Polytechnical Institute. They went to the PrinzRegenten opera and saw one of the first performances of Strauss's *Der Rosenkavalier*, conducted by the famous Bruno Walter.[38] Struve was very keen to go on holiday with Frank, and they eventually settled on a small town in the hills of the Austrian Tyrol called Kufstein. There they spent three days in the isolation of a provincial hotel, having long conversations by the dining-room fire and wandering off around the snowy streets.

The holiday was one of the high points of their friendship, for they revealed to each other the most intimate details of their lives:

> In a friendship between women these kind of intimate confessions are an ordinary thing: they are proffered easily, without a special tension, and often they do not even witness to a really deep relationship; but in friendship between grown-up men this kind of communication is a rare thing; in this case open confessions are given with difficulty; not only is

an unconditional mutual moral trust demanded, but also certainty in a genuine intimate understanding, in a certain deep inner consonance of souls. And in a friendship between men, such rare moments of complete intimacy remain unforgettable landmarks in life's journey and become the firm foundations for a life-long spiritual closeness. It was this kind of happiness, comparable only with the emotional happiness in the erotic love of a man and a woman, which I experienced in those days in Kufstein. It was given to me to get to know P.B. from a new angle—to look into the depth of his heart, to get to know the youthful purity, the youthful passion of soul of this apparently absent-minded academic and activist who was indifferent to himself and burdened by social worries.[39]

After drinking a toast to "brotherhood," they both returned to Munich refreshed; Struve went back to St. Petersburg fairly soon afterward.

Frank worked incessantly and had the habit of getting totally absorbed by his philosophical interests, to the exclusion of all else. He managed to complete his work before war broke out. At the station in Munich there was a large angry anti-Russian demonstration, but they managed to get out to Switzerland, then on to Italy, to Greece, and by ship to Odessa. Frank went to St. Petersburg, found a flat, and the rest of the family joined him from Saratov. Frank called this flight home his "first experience of being a refugee."[40] He was certainly lucky, for he had the manuscript of his Master's thesis, *The Object of Knowledge*, with him in his bag when they crossed into Switzerland. At the checkpoint, the guard ordered him to open the bag. The manuscript, being in a foreign script, might easily have aroused suspicion, but someone called out to the guard at that very moment, and he waved them through without checking the bag.[41]

8

The Object of Knowledge

IN AN ESSAY on Bergson in 1912, Frank wrote that "the philosopher is always led by a primary intuition, and never starts from some ready-made, already existing ideas: rather he only arrives at the latter."[1] Following Bergson, Frank did not believe in philosophy as a purely rational discipline. There was no isolated Cartesian mind that could unravel the mysteries of the world through pure reason. Nor was a philosopher born into the history of thought and simply destined to continue with the development of ideas as handed down to him. However, in emphasis at least, Frank distanced himself from Bergson regarding the distinction between intuition and reason. The two were not abstractly divisible, he argued, with rational thought simply a construction around an intuitive core; rather, the two were interrelated. An individual has his peculiar outlook that is in its turn modified by polemic in the world. He explained this to Gershenzon in 1912:

> [Bergson's] separation of the intuitive foundation from the outer logical form of a system, in spite of its undoubted truth and importance, *suffers from the one-sidedness of abstract definitions.* Just as a plant is not the root alone, but the root and the flower, so the *essence* of a philosophical worldview is not only its intuitive core, but rather the intuition flowing into a defined, abstract form. This form is not something only external—in its turn it is capable . . . of influencing the intuitive base. Spinoza had his pantheism, of course, before any acquaintance with Descartes—simply had it in his blood; and yet the later, rationalistic form of his system made the intuition more complex and refined it, gave it a certain new tone. This relation is like that between the inner character of a person and the influence of his outer surroundings: it would be stupid to think of the individual as a "product of his environment," and of course it is an undoubted fact that as a man he grows from *within* from a distinct spiritual physiognomy, that is from the particular nature of his en-

telechy, his seed, and yet the individual, as a whole, carries the mark of his age and environment.[2]

These thoughts are of great importance. They display Frank's concern for a synthesis between intuition and reason. At the same time, they reveal Frank's inner preference for intuition. For his language makes it clear that for him the inner man is more significant than the outer environment. This preference for the inner intuition, within the context of an attempt to create a fusion, is the mark of all of Frank's philosophical thought. The letter also displays the duality that was to become central to Frank's philosophy: the differing influences of the inner world and the outer environment.

Frank's experience fits in with his descriptions. It could well be argued that in his Marxist period Frank was led by outside pressures. His break with Marxism, however, was a personal response. He was attracted by Marxism because of its attempt to paint an integrated picture of the world. He rejected it because it did not harmonise with his inner feelings. The nature of his ideas reflected his cultural milieu; his motivations, however, were his own.

Losskii, whose *Foundations of Intuitivism* was the first step in the development of Russian intuitivism, relates that he got his first inspiration while traveling through St. Petersburg in a carriage. It was a misty autumn day, and he was reflecting that if consciousness has access only to what is immanent to it, then it has access only to its own mental life. Losskii explained that while he was looking at the gloomy street in front of him, "a thought suddenly flashed at [me]: 'Everything is immanent in everything else'." He wrote: "I immediately sensed that the enigma was solved, and that the working out of this idea would give an answer to all the questions worrying me. . . . From that moment, the idea of an all-penetrating world-unity became my leading thought."[3]

This story concerns not simply an intuition but a kind of philosophical revelation. This sense of the inspirational nature of philosophy is also present in Frank's experience. Recalling reading Nietzsche, Frank wrote: "The foundation of my spiritual being was set in place, or more accurately, revealed itself consciously to me, in the winter of 1901–2."[4] The key word here is "revealed itself" (*otkrylsia*), for it implies a deeper layer of being that wells up in the depths of a man and is an active as opposed to passive feature of life. However, like Losskii, Frank had a specific moment of inspiration, which he described to his son Viktor just a few months before his death in 1950: "Father said, 'I had one real philosophical revelation. It was in Munich in 1913, when I was writing *The Object of Knowledge*. I had reached a certain boundary and got into a dead end. I gave up writing and wandered around the room thinking for a whole week. Then there was a flowing of blood to the head, and I decided to leave everything and rest. And then in the night a voice said to me: "Can't you understand a simple thing? Why start from consciousness? Start from being!"' I [said] to him, '*Sum, ergo cogito,*' and he replied, 'No, rather, *Cogito ergo est esse absolutum.*'"[5]

This description of this moment of inspiration provides an excellent setting for the main themes of *The Object of Knowledge*. The context of Frank's philosophical discourse is the traditional battle in European philosophy between idealism and empiricism. If the world is simply a part of consciousness, its objective and transcendent significance is abolished. There is no world apart from mind. If, however, mind is simply an extension of the material world and a result of physiological processes, then in turn there is no freedom of thought but only mechanism. Within this context, Frank argues in *The Object of Knowledge* that behind the conflict between being and consciousness, the two coincide. There is no division between the two. If being or consciousness is expanded to take into account all of reality, then behind the words "being" and "consciousness" there is no discernible difference. The words can be exchanged for each other. The ideas turn out to be part of an interlinked succession of thoughts: "the object in itself—the object of knowledge—the known object—knowledge of the object—the objectivity of knowledge—the objective moment of consciousness." Essentially, knowledge and object are unthinkable without each other. Thus, Frank believed, the division between idealism and empiricism is shown to be an abstraction that does not correspond to reality.[6]

The key to Frank's attempt to bridge the division between being and consciousness is in his dream. This he explained in more detail in *The Object of Knowledge*. Descartes's great contribution was not the deduction of his own existence from his thought; it was the revelation that consciousness belongs to being. There *is* thought.[7] If thought is part of being, then it is possible to say that the two worlds of ideas and matter belong to an all-embracing being, as Frank said in his explanation of the dream, to absolute being or as he called it, "total-unity." This, in Bergson's language, is Frank's primary philosophical intuition. *The Object of Knowledge* was an attempt to give this concept of total-unity a full philosophical explanation; as he stated it, it is the "basic task" of philosophical enlightenment to explain the existence of super-temporal total-unity as the reality of genuine being.[8]

An essential part of Frank's religious consciousness at the time of his conversion was a sense of the harmony of the world. This sense is at the heart of his philosophical thought. *The Object of Knowledge* is full of the idea that everything finite is rooted in the infinite: "Every finite amount is a piece of an infinitely great whole."[9] Every individual thing, although appearing separate from other things, belongs to the realm of being. The subject is no exception. Every person necessarily belongs to this absolute, all-embracing being. Everything, then, is interconnected. There is a complete system. It is a monistic vision because it sees everything rooted in an absolute, but it is also dualistic because a division remains between what is infinite and what is finite.

In Frank's discussion of Bergson, he isolates intuition and reason as two correlative moments in the philosophical mind. These two moments relate to the dualistic aspect of his philosophy. It is the rational, logical mind that deals with the world of distinct objects. It deals with knowledge about the world. However, intuitive knowledge is based on the fact that every person is rooted in being and has this in common with all objects. In an almost mystical sense, each person already possesses the being of the object he rationally analyzes. Thus, because both the subject and the object are rooted in the same absolute being, immediate, intuitive, living knowledge is possible. So there are two kinds of knowledge:

> Knowledge is necessarily knowledge about an object, that is the disclosure for our consciousness of the contents of an object, as of a being which exists independently of our cognitive relation to it; notwithstanding all efforts to avoid or modify it, we attempt to sanction this precise concept of knowledge. But if it is such, then a primary relation of potential *possession* of the object necessarily precedes knowledge—without which cognition and knowledge are as inconceivable as is impossible the conscious achievement of a goal without the anticipation of this goal, and as is impossible any activity on an object which we do not have in our hands. We try to show that this primordial possession of the object, which is prior to any turning of the consciousness towards it, is possible only in a circumstance when the subject and object of knowledge are not rooted, as is generally thought, in some kind of consciousness or knowledge, but in *absolute being*, as a primary unity which is directly and integrally present with and within us, on the soil of which the knowing consciousness and its object are first of all possible.[10]

Frank expressed this clearly in a talk he gave at the defense of *The Object of Knowledge* in 1916, "The Crisis of Modern Philosophy": "Knowledge, which is in opposition to being, is knowledge about being, that is knowledge-judgement, knowledge as a system of concepts, or, concisely, abstract knowledge. But once we *know* being in its *distinction* from our knowledge, then we have another knowledge. This is knowledge as a living possession of being, knowledge-intuition, knowledge-life. In this knowledge we know being not as something distant from us, but in the way we know our own existence. We know being, because we ourselves exist and live, and that primary being which is evident to itself and which we call *life* exudes directly into us."[11]

In this sense, there are two worlds for Frank that correspond to two epistemological kingdoms. It is thus that he attempts to overcome the division between idealism and empiricism. The outside world is immanent to consciousness because it already belongs to the same absolute being. It nevertheless remains a transcendent world because in the world of reason it remains separated and distinct. The two worlds, however, are not abstractly separate; it was for this that Frank criticized Bergson. They are interrelated, although in keeping with Frank's preference for intuition over reason, it is the latter that depends on the former. For Frank, the formal logic of concepts and distinctions depends on the "transcendental or objective logic" of this other world of total-unity.[12]

In Frank's logical terminology, individual objects are termed A, B, C, and so on. Each object, A, is defined in opposition to what it is not, non-A. This combination, A-non-A, is itself drawn from the indefinable "metalogical" whole, x, which is the source of all definitions.[13] With the x, therefore, there is an unknown, mysterious element in all knowledge. The object, A, is connected to the cosmic total-unity and is thus part of a system where everything is interconnected: "The thread connecting the separate definitions . . . passes through the depth of their primordial unity, out of which they grow, and in which they are rooted, just as the leaves of a tree are not united by being adjacent to one another (where on the contrary they are separated from one another), but only in their common link in one trunk and root."[14]

When consciousness attempts to get to know the world through its attentive gaze, it is really attempting to get to know the total-unity. This leads to the meaning of the title of the whole work. The object of knowledge, in its profoundest sense, is total-unity. The attentive gaze is directed toward the absolute. This total-unity—because it is the condition of all abstract, logical, rational definitions—cannot itself be described in a rational way. It is the condition of reason. It is the realm where distinctions and differences, which are the essence of logic, are overcome, of Nicholas of Cusa's "coincidence of opposites" (*coincidentia oppositorum*).[15] The mind, then, is directed at an unknowable realm. The unknowable is present in all knowledge.

There is undoubtedly a strong artistic element in Frank's theory of knowledge. In his 1910 essay on Goethe's epistemology, Frank praised Goethe for his synthesis of the intellectual and the artistic. Goethe, he wrote, had combined a respect for discipline of thought with an intuitive, creative penetration of reality. His mind was directed at the whole, not at its parts. He believed many intellectual issues resulted from dividing up what God had made as unified. Instead, the true intellectual gaze should be focused on the whole, as embodied in the concrete object. For Goethe, Frank wrote, "truth is always concrete." "'Objective' or artistic thought is the direct opposite to logical or abstract thought."[16] Frank's use of the word "objective" here is significant. He uses the same word in *The Object of Knowledge* to describe transcendental thought. Clearly, Frank's living knowledge involves an artistic or creative element.

Goethe, Frank wrote, was not a romantic, in the sense that he did not idolize self at the expense of the rest. Neither was Frank, for the same reason. However, in a very broad sense, Frank's epistemology does contain a romantic element. He writes of "the ascent of consciousness to a height" at which it can for a brief moment gain a profounder intuition into the world. He writes that the intuitive penetration into the world "has the form of a sudden 'enlightenment,' a kind of unexpected gift from above."[17] What Frank has in mind can perhaps best be described in poetry. When William Wordsworth writes in "Tintern Abbey" of the eye that, touched by harmony and joy, "sees into the life of things," he is describing something very similar to Frank's "living knowledge." Nevertheless, Frank rarely uses the language of inspiration. He wanted living knowledge to be the foundation for all knowledge. It was not to be the exception but the condition.

One of the main aims of *The Object of Knowledge* was to provide protection for philosophy against the inroads of psychology. In his attacks on pragmatism, Frank had attacked the potential subjectivism of Kant. He stated his views on this very clearly in "The Crisis of Modern Philosophy." Kant, Frank wrote, declared that outside knowledge there is nothing to compare knowledge with and concluded that any understanding of being—ontology—must result from knowledge, that therefore epistemology precedes ontology and provides the bases for it. For Kant, the construction of knowledge on the basis of ontological assumptions was a dogmatic prejudice. The problem arose that it was difficult to discuss the problem of knowledge in separation from the carrier of knowledge. To assume the carrier meant to assume some form of being: that is, to have an ontological assumption. The result of this in modern epistemology was a struggle against such psychological assumptions. Modern epistemology, in its attempt to rid itself of all assumptions, had reached its ultimate limit in the work of such philosophers as Hermann Cohen, who declared that in speaking about thought, he was not speaking about human thought.

For Frank, this did not work. If epistemology was separated from ontology, it would still be stained by psychologism: "As far as epistemology is constructed in conflict with ontology, as far as it wishes to speak only about consciousness and knowledge, as something separated from being and in opposition to it, it refers not to an all-embracing primary source for everything else, but only as a certain *partial* sphere, which notwithstanding all the reforms in the concept of it, inevitably preserves a connection with the concept of psychic life and thus this conception of epistemology is fundamentally poisoned by psychologism." Epistemology cannot rid itself of ontological assumptions: "Epistemology reveals that it has always been ontology and cannot exist without it."[18] The task now, according to Frank, was to form the right kind of ontology, not the assumed dogmatic ontology Kant battled against, but another form of it, the kind that modern epistemology seemed to be unable to avoid. The concept "my consciousness," Frank wrote, assumes *my* existence. My existence assumes the existence of being outside me. Consequently, modern epistemology leads to a concept of being that lies both within and outside me, as a "unity rising above the opposition of the subject and object."[19] Only such a unity could provide common ground on which to examine the link between the subject and the object; thus epistemology was impossible without this unifying ground.

The problem for Frank was how to avoid the ontological idealism of Fichte, Hegel, and Schelling in which the world simply became the pale extension of mind. He believed that the reduction of everything to an aspect of an idea unfolding itself in the world might satisfy the rationalist mind but could not satisfy those who wanted more than a logical explanation of things. The popularity of Bergson was testimony to this. To answer this, Frank presented his philosophy of "ideal-realism." The world of ideas or ideal being is given a nonlogical foundation in *"life"* as opposed to a system of concepts or reason. Thus Frank understood the common ground between the subject and the object to be *life.*[20]

Frank gave his philosophy various titles: "absolute realism,"[21] "intuitivism," and "ideal-realism." He wrote: "That unity, which in Kant is already a higher epistemological concept is not the unity of consciousness, but absolute *unity*, uniting consciousness and being. In this sense the new (monistic) realism or intuitivism is *ideal-realism.*"[22]

Frank is often bracketed with Losskii as an intuitive philosopher. There is reason for this. He wrote to Losskii that *The Object of Knowl-*

edge was an attempt to build on Losskii's work by establishing the conditions of intuition. It was, he wrote to Losskii, an attempt to discover "the ontological conditions of the possibility of intuition as a direct apprehension of a reality independent of our cognitive acts."[23] However, it would be wrong to associate Frank too closely with Losskii. The two were never close on a personal level, and *The Object of Knowledge* makes a number of implicit criticisms of Losskii's work. Losskii's epistemology centred around the concept of "coordination." The attentive consciousness directly apprehends outside objects through a process of "coordination." Frank was critical of this approach in *The Object of Knowledge,* for he suggested that such intuitivism is inclined to underplay the independence from consciousness of the transcendent object.[24] During the Second World War, Frank wrote to Struve that he did not share in any way Losskii's "naive realism" and "dogmatic rationalism," and compared his thought to the oversimplifications of Tolstoi and Chernyshevskii.[25]

Frank's philosophy is closest to those who attempt a synthesis that goes beyond reason, those who stress life over thought. In describing his system, Frank declared that total-unity means "life": "Absolute total-unity is . . . a living eternity or living life, an eternity as the unity of rest and creation, the complete and the inexhaustible."[26] Frank appreciated Bergson for his "[elimination] of the monopoly of the prevailing rationalist epistemology and [satisfaction] of the need for a more living philosophy which would not tear away the cognitive spirit from reality itself."[27] Frank found in the German philosopher Wilhelm Dilthey a similar approach: "The basic idea with which [Dilthey] has enriched philosophy is specifically the idea that the basis of any systematic knowledge is rooted in *experience,* in the concrete whole reaction of the subject to the impression of being."[28] Although his thinking had undergone many changes since he wrote "On Critical Idealism" in 1904, the idea of the world as a system of *"integral spiritual life"*[29] clearly in some sense remained. In the same way as Bergson desired to view time as a process rather than a line of consecutive moments, so Frank thought of true knowledge not as knowledge of a multiplicity of units making up the world but as an experience of the life and wholeness of that world.

With his stress on inner experience, Frank offered an inherently antirationalist philosophy. Losskii noted this when he criticized Frank's thought for having an insufficient respect for reason.[30] Certainly, Frank laid himself open to the charge; for example, he wrote that "all abstract knowledge is in a certain sense only *symbolic.*"[31] Although he attempted to fit logic into his system, Frank's heart was with "living" as opposed to "rational" knowledge. The tendency to pantheism, present throughout his thought, was due to this. In stressing the dependence of reason on "primary intuition" and thus the dependence of the finite things of the world on a system of total-unity, Frank's theoretical framework always ran the risk of allowing the individual to become submerged in the cosmos. Berdiaev, Losskii, and Zen'kovskii all believed that Frank's system was pantheistic. Berdiaev accused Frank of having no sense of the creative element in man.[32] Losskii commented that in Frank's thought there was "too great an approximation between God and the world."[33] Zen'kovskii declared that "the problem of evil finds no place in [Frank's] system."[34] All these criticisms stemmed from the sense that Frank was trying to offer a seamless whole and that freedom and man were easily lost in it. Frank was well aware of the problem but believed that the monodualistic system he had adopted preserved individuality and multiplicity within the framework of total-unity.

The pantheistic side of Frank put him very much in the tradition of Spinoza, whom he much admired. He took seminars on Spinoza's *Ethics* at the Bestuzhev Courses, (1910–11, 1914–15).[35] In 1912 Frank published an extended article on Spinoza's theory of attributes in *Questions of Philosophy and Psychology* in which he touched on many elements which then appeared in other forms in his philosophy. For example, he wrote that in Spinoza "substance or the cosmos as a whole is one being . . . a single object of knowledge in distinction from the content of knowledge which is expressed in logical definitions; any partial definition . . . does not capture the substance itself, but only talks *about it*, expresses a particular feature of it." Here, Spinoza's idea that there are two kinds of knowledge has its obvious parallel in Frank's thought. Frank also described Spinoza's thought as "mystical."[36] This is an expression that could equally be applied to his ideas; indeed Lapshin described Frank's own system as "mystical rationalism."[37] Certainly, the mystical element in Frank's thought is present in *The Object of Knowledge* and his subsequent philosophical writing.

Frank is often thought of as a disciple of Vladimir Solov'ev's system of total-unity. Philip Swoboda, however, notes that the adjective for total-unity, "*vseedinyi,*" as Frank first started to use the word in 1909, was originally associated in his mind with Goethe and Spinoza, not with Solov'ev. In a letter written in 1941, Frank, in a very concise description of his basic philosophical intuitions, admitted the Spinozistic element in his early thought: "My basic philosophical and metaphysical intuition consists (and has always consisted) in a combination of the Platonic dualism between the next and this world, of an inner spiritual reality and an empirical, rational reality (what in *The Object of*

Knowledge comes out as a duality between intuitive and conceptual knowledge and now as a duality between the Kingdom of God and this world) with the pantheistic motif (in my youth I was even an inspired Spinozist) wherein everything of this world is in the roots of its being nothing but a revelation of the next world in its otherness."[38]

Frank's philosophical interests at this time were nevertheless strikingly similar to trends in earlier Russian philosophy. A suspicion of pure rationalism and a desire to bridge the division between subject and object were typical of Slavophiles such as Ivan Kireevskii and of course Solov'ev. In *The Object of Knowledge* Frank accepted that his views were similar to certain trends in Russian philosophy,[39] and in regard to Solov'ev specifically, stated that he was in many points very close to his position on epistemological matters, referring very positively to his *Critique of Abstract Principles*.[40] At the same time, his contemporary work made very little mention of Russian philosophy; his writing was filled with references to recent German and European philosophy. If he was influenced at this time by the Russian tradition specifically, it would have been more through the general atmosphere of inquiry than direct influence.

In his stress on life, Frank argued that thought has a life of its own, a dynamism. This suggests an Hegelian influence. The pure mind moves from one idea to another; there is a process and movement in thought. It is a dynamism that results from the fact that thought belongs to absolute being, which in Frank's system can be described as the unity of movement and rest. Frank, in an Aristotelian phrase, called this life "entelechy."[41] He used Aristotle's term "first philosophy" as a description of his own work, confirming that *The Object of Knowledge* was an attempt at an all-embracing explanation of everything that is.[42] For the moment, though, Frank's thought was basically Platonist in its sense of the otherwordly nature of total-unity. It always remained such, but the Aristotelian element reemerged during the Second World War.

Frank regarded his philosophy as an expression of the Platonist tradition of Plato, Plotinus, Augustine, and Nicholas of Cusa.[43] The influence on *The Object of Knowledge* of these figures, however, is difficult to gauge. Frank always regarded Plotinus and Nicholas of Cusa as the two philosophers with whom he had most in common. However, although he mentioned them in his introduction to *The Object of Knowledge*, he stated that he discovered them only after his own philosophical system had formed.[44] The immediate influences were probably Bergson, Spinoza, and Goethe, as well as German idealism and neo-Kantianism. In this connection, Philip Swoboda argues that Frank's philosophy is a combination of *lebensphilosophie* (a term used to describe the primacy of life, intuition, and freedom over necessity, abstract analysis, and mechanism, and associated with Nietzsche, Simmel, Bergson, and Dilthey) and neo-Kantianism.[45]

Whatever the influences on Frank, he was undoubtedly not the product of one school. In the Russian context, he was neither a Slavophile nor a Westernizer. Although he was influenced by ancient philosophers, he was locked into the philosophical issues of his day. In these senses, he was a universal thinker.

The Object of Knowledge was the foundation of Frank's philosophical system. Although his total-unity was occasionally referred to in a religious sense—as, for example, an "all-embracing divine consciousness"—there was a broad attempt to keep religion and philosophy separate. In later years, as Frank's religious interests grew, total-unity became interchangeable with God. The division between the infinite and the finite had already been foreshadowed in Frank's anti-utopian political writings. Later, this division was clearly expressed as a duality between absolute and relative moral kingdoms. In his idea of the individual as rooted in the absolute Frank saw the potential for a philosophy of community as well as the individual. Because of the underlying total-unity, Frank wrote in *The Object of Knowledge*, the psychic subject, "in the sphere of spiritual life," "can go beyond the limits of himself and spread out, in principle, to unlimitedness." In doing so, he can relate to the "other I."[46] It was from these ideas that Frank developed his social philosophy. Thus, in religious, moral, and social fields, *The Object of Knowledge* was the key to Frank's thought.

Frank defended *The Object of Knowledge* on 15 May 1916 in front of a large crowd and three official opponents, Vvedenskii, Lapshin, and Losskii, and the dean of the faculty, F. A. Braun. It was clearly a success. The committee discussed the possibility of giving him his doctorate immediately as well as his Master's, but Vvedenskii said that he might as well write another book, so he had to be content with the Master's.[47] Struve was also present at the occasion and in the public discussion expressed a hope that Frank would move away from abstract philosophy toward social sciences.[48]

Frank himself arranged for the publication of *The Object of Knowledge*, assisted by a donation from the Historico-Philological Faculty of the university. In spite of what Frank described as the "outer and inner heaviness" of the work, it sold very well, and Frank regretted that only 525 copies were put on sale.[49]

9

War and Revolution

AFTER *THE OBJECT OF KNOWLEDGE*, Frank started work on his doctoral thesis, *Man's Soul*. He was engaged in a very ambitious task, to construct an all-embracing philosophical system. *The Object of Knowledge*, concerned with the bases and limits of abstract knowledge, had been the first part of a proposed trilogy. *Man's Soul*, subtitled "An Attempt at an Introduction to Philosophical Psychology," which appeared in July 1917, was the sequel. The final part, *The Spiritual Foundations of Society*, which appeared only in 1930 in an abridged form, addressed the foundations of social life.

In *Man's Soul* Frank outlined his theory of human nature. It was a defense of the soul in the face of an empirical psychology that viewed psychic phenomena as simply manifestations of the outer objective world,—a critique, he said later, of the "sensualist materialism" of William James and Carl Lange.[1] Frank argued that psychology had been hijacked by positivists and materialists and turned into a branch of physiology. Modern psychology would not accept certain kinds of spiritual experience: "Only one thing is unquestionable: the living integral inner world of man, the human person, that which outside of all theories we call our 'soul,' our 'spiritual world'—is utterly absent in these sciences [of empirical psychology]."[2]

In Frank's view, the soul was a reality, and the objective aspect of man's nature concealed a magnificent inner world:

This objective psycho-physical aspect of man will henceforth be for us only a small peak emerging above the surface, beneath which we know the being of the immeasurable abyss that ever expands into the depths. Man in his outward aspect in the objective world has the modest appearance of a small particle of the universe and, at first glance, his essence is exhausted by this his outward nature; but in reality that which

93

is called man is—in itself and for itself—something immeasurably greater and qualitatively wholly other than a fragment of the world: it is a hidden world, outwardly imprisoned in a modest frame, of great, potentially infinite chaotic forces. And its subterranean depths resemble its outward aspect as little as the interior of a gigantic mine, hiding both riches and suffering, resembles the small opening of the shaft connecting the mine with the habitual world of the earth's surface.[3]

For the empirical psychologist, consciousness is made up of the sensations and ideas that present themselves to it. Frank argued, however, that the soul is the carrier of consciousness, the thing that makes consciousness possible. What man values in his life is this deeper soul that is unique and unrepeatable. This soul is made up of three fused but nevertheless different "I"'s. There is a lower empirical "I," the cluster of ideas, moods, feelings, and lusts that have a strong influence on the peripheral side of a person's life. Then there is an intermediary volitional "I," exhibited when a person makes a choice to overcome the lower "I" and exhibits courage or determination in the face of it. Finally, there is a pure and higher "I," seen in the experience of moral obligation or divine calling:

> [The experience of this higher "I"] is most obviously typical of the domain of so-called morality, i.e., for the ideal normalization of behaviour and relations to people. [It also occurs] whenever we are conscious of the supra-empirical, supra-individual agency of our "I," in the form of a "call," of Socrates' "daemon," of every higher "voice" in us. An artist who is drawn by a powerful call to create images . . . ; a thinker who feels the necessity to communicate a truth revealed to him . . . ; a statesman who is conscious of himself as called to lead people to a goal revealed only to himself; a saint who has heard a voice which draws him to a life of holy exploit; even someone who is in love, in whose soul love has opened like a great force, illuminating his whole life and giving it meaning—all experience the action of the higher, spiritual or ideal-rational unity of their "I." . . .
>
> This experience and the higher or deeper essence of the soul revealed in it [can be seen] in that aspect in which it is *living knowledge or revelation* in the broad sense of the word.[4]

It is thus clear how Frank's thought in *Man's Soul* complements his earlier work. The higher "I" of the soul merges with the living metalogical reality he had described in *The Object of Knowledge*. The essence of the soul is "living knowledge"; once again Frank's linkage of epistemology and ontology is clear.

There are two infinities in Frank's universe. There is the divine infinity. The soul of man, rooted in the depths of absolute being, reaches into a divine infinity. On the other hand, through consciousness, the soul also encounters the infinity of the objective world:

> If outwardly, at its periphery, the soul through objective consciousness touches and is fused with the *objective side of being* and thus becomes the bearer of a subjectively illuminated and formed "external world"—inwardly, in its very root, the soul is anchored in the absolute subject and is, as it were, a subjective channel through which psychic life becomes its subjective bearer. Thus the soul is not only the "image" of the *world* but also *the image of Spirit or God,* the pure light of reason, though refracted in the element psychic life. . . . Two infinities, issuing as it were from the unfathomable depths of being (the infinity of the pure, all-embracing light of knowledge and the infinity of the universe illuminated by the knowledge), narrowing and being refracted in an obscure and limited medium, encounter each other at a small point; and this point is the *individual consciousness.*[5]

In *The Object of Knowledge,* Frank made the point that knowledge is possible because it is already given to the individual in the ground of his being. In essence, this is a continuation of that argument. Total-unity unites both the individual and the objective world. On this basis, consciousness can penetrate beyond the outer form of things: "We 'feel' the sadness or merriment, the pleasantness or somberness of *another* person, the beauty of a landscape, the dolefulness, turbulence or playfulness of a musical melody, the sad splendor of Botticelli's subtle images and the noble rigor of Rembrandt's light and shadow."[6]

Much of Frank's writing here is concerned with the nature of the individual soul, but as in *The Object of Knowledge,* it is clear that individuals are not isolated from one another. Although Frank describes the soul and consciousness in distinction from one another, he makes it clear that they are fused together and that it is only an abstraction to separate the two. As Heraclitus (whom Frank greatly admired) said, there are no limits to the soul. This sense of the interconnectedness of things is the background for Frank's belief that nations as well as individuals have souls:

> Just as the objectivity and universal obligatoriness of objective knowledge are possible only in virtue of the rootedness of individual consciousness in the light of one reason, so all commonality of human life, . . . the presence of a mutual understanding of life, the objectivity of spiritual culture (religion, art, moral and juridical life) are possible only by virtue of this inner unity and fundamental commonality of spiritual life. . . . [We] are *obligated* to recognize the being of not only singular "souls" or consciousness but also the being of common-generic, national, common-human, universal "souls." Such entities as "a national soul" or

the "genius of mankind" are not empty abstractions, not merely "verbal" unities but genuine living, concrete unities.[7]

Thus, Frank believed in the reality of national identity and group consciousness in general. This was partly a continuation of his interest in social psychology, as outlined in his 1905 essay "The Problem of Power."

Man's Soul turns out to be a justification and defense of many key concepts in Frank's writing. The nation, the soul, culture, morality, religion, reason, empathy, insight, knowledge, consciousness—all find an explanation. For Frank, a meticulously careful thinker, it was no good simply to criticize materialism as wrong. He stated in this work that nonmaterial realities not only exist but can be explained as part of a particular kind of universe. *Man's Soul* was about the structure of souls in that universe.

Frank finished *Man's Soul* while staying in Staritsa in Tver Province in 1915. His work and life were not greatly affected by the war, and the family did not feel the hardship of those years. However, Frank related his philosophical thought to the First World War. It is unlikely that his ideas were actually stimulated by the war, but the war gave him a useful opportunity to apply them in a practical way. Certainly he felt that they were relevant. In November 1914, Théodore Ruyssen, a French philosopher, published an article in France, "Force and Right," to which Frank responded positively in *Russian Thought*. Ruyssen, according to Frank, had done well to attack the prevailing German view that force is a higher principle than law; however, he lacked a real philosophical foundation for his defense of spiritual values: "The issue of the relation between force and law seems to be insoluble when confined to the framework of empirical 'social psychology,' because . . . law is a phenomenon of *spiritual* life, and spiritual life is something more than a pure psychic fact. On a purely empirical plane, the idea of the primacy of force is irrefutable because in that sphere a legal consciousness is only one of many empirical forces and, consequently, is not in conflict with the concept of force and does not rise above it. . . . A belief in the insuperability and primacy of this higher force [of law] can be derived only from a religious-metaphysical worldview."[8] Frank's philosophy, then, can be seen as a real attempt to offer this "religious-metaphysical worldview."

How to interpret the war was a major issue for the Russian intelligentsia. Struve gathered a group from *Russian Thought* to discuss the war in his flat. One religious philosopher, D. V. Boldyrev, called it a Christian war; another thinker, D. Muretov, defended the ethics of nationalism; and the historian E. D. Grimm declared the war a zoological battle for survival. Frank talked of the need to be loyal to absolute moral principles.[9] Struve's view of the war was imperialist, although he would never sanction anti-German feeling: "The war of 1914 is called to lead the external expansion of the Russian empire to its conclusion, so establishing its imperial task and its national calling."[10]

Frank was also present at another gathering with the princes Grigorii and Evgenii Trubetskoi on the issue of Poland. Grigorii Trubetskoi had coauthored with Struve Nicholas II's appeal to the Poles to rise up against Germany, promising Russian support in their fight for freedom.[11] It is unlikely that Frank had close touch with people in the administration, but certainly these discussions suggest that he had a wide range of contacts. Struve, as ever, seems to have been his main avenue into the social and public arena.

On 6 Oct 1914 the Moscow Religious-Philosophical Society met to discuss the war, and the speakers on the subject included Bulgakov, Ern, and Evgenii Trubetskoi. The general tone was Slavophile, and for Bulgakov and Ern, extremely so. Bulgakov declared that Russia had managed to avoid the humanistic individualism that characterized modern European culture and was now ready to lead the mystical, apocalyptic revolution that had been prophesied in *Revelation* and would lead to the kingdom of Christ. "Europe is the means, Russia is the end," he wrote. "The Russian era in world history is now approaching . . . . Once again we have come to believe in Russia."[12]

Ern, in "From Kant to Krupp," offering an interpretation that became famous, stated that modern German militarism was a direct product of German intellectual history, and in particular of Kantian thought. The abandonment of metaphysics and the accompanying deification of morality in the "categorical imperative" had opened the door to the modern devotion to the state and the worship of the German nation. Germany had killed God in its philosophy, and the First World War was the consequence. Ern represented the extreme Slavophile tendency that felt not only that the German spirit was flawed but that Western culture as a whole was fatally rationalist, believing that Russia stood for the true divine "logos."[13]

Evgenii Trubetskoi's piece was more sober than Bulgakov's and Ern's, although he too was inclined to see Russia as possessed of a historical calling to be a liberator in international affairs, now specifically in Poland and Serbia. Nevertheless, he had the grace to point out that her task as a liberator also coincided with her national interest, and he warned against Russia falling into the narrow nationalism exhibited by Germany. "Would [Russia] succeed in overcoming her own inner monster, that terrible and hellish beast which hides in the soul of every people?" The possibility of victory depended on this issue, on the preservation of the right sense of national identity.[14]

Frank found himself in an interesting situation. This was a social milieu he moved in naturally. He had sympathy with some of these writers; yet his mother's family had originally come from Germany, and he belonged to the Jewish minority. The Jews had often been the victims of Russian nationalism. Whether he was at the Moscow meeting is unclear, but he responded to the speeches with an article in *Russian Thought* and not surprisingly adopted a very different tone.

In "In Search of the Meaning of the War," Frank responded to the addresses by stating that Russia was right to be fighting the war but that the war should not be interpreted as a battle between two national ideas. Specifically replying to Bulgakov and Ern, he said it would be wrong to identify absolute goodness with one side or another. The basis for this view was the same as the one that was to be articulated in *Man's Soul:* "Every national being—as also the being of an individual person—in its final roots, in its very being, must be thought of as one of the manifestations of the divine."[15] To believe that the soul of another nation is essentially evil would be simply to sanction one's subjective interests: "We must understand this war not as a war against the national spirit of our opponent, but as a war against the evil spirit which has taken over the national consciousness of Germany—as a war for the establishment of those relations and conceptions under which it is possible to freely develop an all-European culture in all its national expressions."[16]

Frank went on to describe the great spiritual history of Germany and lamented that she had abandoned it: "Separating herself from her great wise men, [Germany] has fallen to the temptation of unprincipled, irreligious national self-esteem. The war is not between East and West but between the defenders of might and the defenders of law, between the preservers of the sacredness of the all-human spirit, including the true elements of the German genius within it, and its detractors and destroyers. Only as such can one get a true justification of the great European war."[17]

Here again, the spirit of *Man's Soul* is evident. Frank's concept of nationhood came from his belief that national identity grows out of the spiritual foundations of life, and it is evident that he regarded the roots of the German nation as the same as those of Russia. Elsewhere in the same essay he wrote that without a belief in such deeper uniting values, the kind of self-sacrifices needed in such a war are impossible. Also, the absence of such a belief precludes a sense of "moral responsibility for the disasters which war brings with it."[18] Frank clearly felt that there could be no gloating over victories; even a victory in war would be accompanied by violent deeds for which the victor should feel no pride.

In a another essay, published in October 1915, Frank continued in the same vein. This time he was writing in the shadow of German military successes. The central question was the root of these successes. Frank's view was that the German nation still had a moral cohesion that made such power possible. Military victory is not possible without a moral force behind it. The problem lay in the fact that this moral force was a distortion of something originally good. In this case, perhaps influenced by Ern, Frank suggested that the courage of the German soldiers was due to the unifying concept of the "categorical imperative" and that this imperative had come to be identified with service to the state. Nevertheless, Frank defended Kant, and Bismarck, referring positively to the latter's "deep *realpolitik*" as a dramatic contrast to its "giftless caricature" exhibited by his successor.[19] He described the Germans as typified by an active, practical quality, what he called "effectiveness" (*deistvennost'*).

Germany's moral strength, Frank argued, was due to her earlier barbarian civilization, which was destroying her great spiritual tradition and manifesting itself in a new paganism. The central issue of the war was for Germany to rediscover her spiritual roots and for Russia to appeal to those roots. Also—and here Frank was clearly picking up on the theme raised earlier in the paper of Evgenii Trubetskoi—Russia was prey to the same spiritual war going on in Germany. The Christian Russia of Pushkin, Tiutchev, Dostoevskii, and Tolstoi was in combat with the darkness, evil, laziness, and irresponsibility of the Russian Xerxes. "We know," he wrote, "that the socio-political weaknesses of Russia are only manifestations of her religious moral sins and that in the final analysis responsibility for these sins lies in the whole people, in the very soul of Russia." In Frank's view, the establishment of goodness and truth at the heart of political life was the responsibility of every individual. The victory of the Russian Christ over the Russian Xerxes would be effected only through individual moral change.[20]

Frank's specific political analysis clearly depended on his belief that both individuals and nations have souls and that within those souls there is a battle between good and evil. The source of the goodness was the "all-embracing light of reason" in which both individuals and nations had their ground. The source of the evil was something he attempted to explain in different ways in later life. It is clear that he considered the political and military world dependent on this spiritual world operating at a deeper level. His understanding of nationhood is also notable. He clearly disliked the kind of Slavophilism displayed by

Ern and Bulgakov, and his writing is a clear rebuke to it. Yet he also had a clear belief in national identities, national souls, even national callings. If it is nationalism at all, it is clearly very different in kind. In writing about Germany, Frank seems to suggest that Germany could find her national identity in a European context. In another essay written during the war, an essay suggesting that Frank had a remarkable knowledge of wartime German thought, he states this very point, although he does not elaborate on what he understands by "Europe": "Believing in the future of general European culture, it is impossible not to believe also in the preservation of the living, deep forces of the German spirit."[21] Frank's conviction that identities are rooted in the spiritual world meant that national identities and international solidarity need never be in competition with each other. This was another of the opposites he attempted to reconcile on the basis of a deeper unity.

Frank was not alone in holding to these more moderate views while supporting the war effort. In fact, Struve had a slightly similar concept of the two Germanys. In his view, it was the positive Germany of Bismarck and idealist philosophy that was in conflict with the negative modern bourgeois Germany.[22] Struve, according to Frank, also shared his views on the active and Kantian elements in the German character.[23] Their views attracted some notice on the edges of the Russian administration, and they were invited in the autumn of 1915 to give a talk to a group called the Solov'ev Circle. The event took place in the flat of Prince A. D. Obolenskii, a member of the State Council and former procurator of the Holy Synod, and was also attended by A. V. Krivoshein, the former minister of agriculture, and Prince Ukhtomskii, the editor of *Peterburg News* (*Peterburgskie vedemosti*). According to Frank, they had a lively discussion on the theme of his essay about the spiritual essence of Germany.

Obolenskii, a supporter of government reform and a great admirer of Solov'ev, was also concerned about anti-German feeling. He had written to his wife in September 1914: "The idea of nationalism has been put before God and there now remains only the cult of hatred towards the Germans. . . . There only remains to us to try in every way to conquer the Germans without any hatred towards them."[24] Struve too had German blood and in spite of his imperialist ideas, denounced calls for a boycott of German goods and suspension of German instruction in schools.[25]

The implication is that there was a meeting of minds and that Frank at least intellectually belonged to a certain section of the "national liberal" grouping in which Struve was a leading figure. It is unlikely that he had the strong Russian imperialist feelings Struve revealed at the time, particularly in his hostility to Ukrainian nationalism, and he was much more religious than Struve. However, the term "national liberal" fits Frank's thought to a considerable extent. He believed in the Russian identity and the importance of the Russian state, and he believed in the need for real reform. The formal term Frank later used to describe both his and Struve's political views was "liberal conservatism."[26] At the same time, religious ideas play such a big role in Frank's thought that it is difficult to define his ideas outside a specifically Christian or spiritual context.

Frank's contact with Struve continued into the revolution. His sympathy with the "national liberal" grouping is confirmed by his close participation during 1917 in the League of Russian Culture. This was an organization set up by Struve to bring together people of different political views with the purpose of preserving and propagating Russian national values. Struve believed that it was much easier to build up the material prosperity of a society than to preserve and create its spiritual heritage. It was the league's aim to do that, to foster the values which would hold the nation together. There were two criteria for being a member of the league: "First, [members] should be united by the awareness that a society lacking in established principles guiding its social and legal culture disintegrates into incoherent mobs of bestialized men, interspersed with bodies of frenzied fanatics who acknowledge no responsibility, who have no sense for the past and no foresight. Secondly they should feel themselves Russians, loving their national culture in all its historical richness and diversity."[27]

The league was headed by a five-man Provisional Committee: Struve; Kartashev, who became chief procurator of the Holy Synod in Kerenskii's second coalition government; M. V. Rodzianko, the last chairman of the Duma and one of the leaders of the Octobrist Party; N. V. Savich, another Duma deputy and Octobrist; and V. V. Shulgin, one of the leading figures in the Nationalist Party. Frank was one of the founding members of the league, as were Berdiaev, Bulgakov, and Izgoev. Other members included Kotliarevskii, Maklakov, S. F. Oldenburg, and Andrew, Bishop of Ufa. Even Aleksandr Blok joined. Special rooms were set aside at the offices of *Russian Thought* for those wishing to join, and Frank recalled them crowded with visitors.[28]

Clearly, the league represented the kind of people Struve had been associated with, a mixture of intellectuals and politicians with a general leaning toward Russian nationalism, reform, and religion. Struve also started the journal *Russian Freedom (Russkaia svoboda)*, which had close connections with the league and in which Frank played a major editing role. *Russian Freedom* was similar to *Polar Star* and came out weekly, but Struve was very busy with other things; not least, he was head of the Economics Department of the Ministry of Foreign Affairs under Miliukov. Frank did most of the technical editorial work. Toward the end of the summer the journal began to appear less frequently. The official publishers were Struve, Maklakov, and N. N. L'vov, one of the founders of the Octobrists.

Under the influence of Struve, the general tone of the journal was very negative about the revolution. Although Frank agreed with this in principle, he was clearly doubtful about the effectiveness of Struve's attitude: "Many of us vainly tried to persuade P. B. that, in the interests of the practical influence of our ideas, the tone of accusation should be softened. I had a strong feeling that this undertaking was useless; I used to tell P.B. that we were making a hopeless attempt in the pages of *Russian Freedom* to stop up a dam which had been burst by a huge raging torrent."[29] The mentalities of the two men were very different. Frank was concerned that the excesses of the revolution might be followed by an equally excessive reaction. Struve, as the summer of 1917 wore on, grew more violent in his opposition to the revolution. Frank's loyalty to Struve was very strong and this probably kept him involved in the undertaking despite his doubts.

Frank welcomed the first days of the February revolution: "The first days of the revolution were brightly painted in a spirit of nobility. The popular soul . . . brightened, became kinder and ennobled; it became easy to breathe, people became more attentive and polite. . . . Russia came to be led by the best Russian people, whose names were dear to and valued by everybody."[30]

Precisely who Frank specifically admired in the first Provisional Government is not clear, but it included a number of prominent Kadets, including Miliukov, minister of foreign affairs, and the new minister of education, A. A. Manuilov, who had been one of his lecturers at Moscow University.

Although Frank later pointed out that it was the monarchy that had held Russia together,[31] there is no evidence that he was upset by the fall of the monarchy. Defending the February revolution against further onslaught from the radical parties at the end of April 1917, he stated, "For any educated . . . and honest socialist, it is absolutely obvious that in the conditions of free political life, with absolutely guaranteed freedom of speech, assembly, professional and political unions, with democratic suffrage, all the interests of the working class can be upheld by peaceful legal means."[32] This should not be taken as a defense of socialism, but it indicates that Frank had some common ground with the moderate, socialist parties and that he approved of the transformation of Russia into a society founded on democratic suffrage and law.

In spite of Frank's enthusiasm for the revolution, he was worried about the course it might take from the very beginning. He expressed this in the first issue of *Russian Freedom* (March–April) in an article entitled "Democracy at the Crossroads." He stated that a remarkable revolution had occured that had united groups as diverse as the Nationalists and Socialist-Revolutionaries into one movement. Now, however, Russia faced a choice between two moral roads, two totally different kinds of democracy:

> Democracy can establish the religious ideal of people-power, as the people's free construction of higher truth on earth. For this ideal, the power of the people is not self-government . . . but such a disinterested, self-sacrificing *service* of higher truth, as all power should be. . . .
> The other road is the road of the materialistic worldview. For it, democracy is simply a means for making the people master over the material goods of the country and thereby giving them over to a full life of pleasure. For the people here, power is simply a right and a force, but not an obligation and a service. In establishment, this path of deification of the people and their material interests leads, on the one hand, to a cruel Jacobin tyranny of the uncultured masses over the educated section of society; on the other hand, it leads to a licentious exhibition of egoistic passions. . . . This is the road of hatred and tyranny, the road of licentious, dark, base instincts. . . . One can predict with certainty that if the fanatics who are ideologically organizing class hatred achieve their goal, they themselves will be swept away in an elemental wave of *pugachevshchina.*[33]

These comments indicate that Frank was deeply uneasy about the course of the revolution by the beginning of April. Precisely when he wrote the article is not clear. However, Frank understood the revolution at this stage to be a battle between *two* ideas: a religious conception of man and power and a materialist one.

The nature of Frank's "two democracies" becomes clearer in the light of Frank's next article, "The Moral Watershed in the Russian Revolution," which came out in the second issue of *Russian Freedom* on 26 April. Although the article was probably written before the street demonstrations of 20–21 April in which the Bolsheviks were a major force, it is clear that Frank already regarded Lenin and his followers as the main representatives of the lawless form of democracy:

> However much they tell us about the struggle between the "bourgeoisie" and the "proletariat" . . . this division has no essential political meaning at the present moment, and is almost only verbal. Kerenskii and Plekhanov only use different words from Miliukov and Guchkov but they

are saying and doing the same thing; from another angle, the socialists Kerenskii and Plekhanov in their real aspirations have nothing in common with the socialist "Bolsheviks" and Lenin, and the struggle between these two different trends within socialism is at the current moment perhaps the most important and deeply gripping political struggle. . . .
. . . [This natural watershed in the Russian revolution] passes between the followers of law, freedom and the value of the individual . . . and the followers of violence, tyranny, the display of class egoism.[34]

On 20–21 April, following the publication of Miliukov's note to the Allies reaffirming the government's commitment to the alliance, there were major street disorders in which the Bolsheviks were prominent. On 25 April Frank completed his next article for *Russian Freedom*, "On Nobility and Baseness in Politics," in which he expressed deep concern about the "hurricane of class hatred" and "moral poison of violence" eating way at the national organism. According to Frank, it was on Labor Day, 18 April, that "man-hating speeches had rung out from numerous platforms" and had prepared the way for the "great storm" that broke three days later. Frank declared that since the arrival of Lenin, who had introduced an atmosphere of extreme sectarianism ("*khlystovskie radeniia*"), the country had been plunged into perpetual suspicion of the presence of counterrevolutionaries. As early as this, 25 April 1917, Frank wrote: "It is terrible to think it, but it seems that we are heading irrepressibly into an abyss."[35]

Frank believed that the Bolsheviks represented the same lawlessness as the Germans did in the war. Both believed in the primacy of violence. "Is it really true," he asked, "that in these last days on the streets of Petrograd we have seen this slogan ["force is stronger than law," "the clenched fist decides everything"] painted on cars, mounted by little Russian Wilhelms who remind their internal enemies of the violence of the sword?"[36]

The idea of the "soul of nations," put forward in *Man's Soul*, was very much in evidence in Frank's writing of 1917. "The Russian revolution," he wrote, "has not been prepared by anyone . . . ; people have not brought it about, but the instinct of the popular soul."[37] He believed that the battle between force and law was taking place in the Russian soul. In this, philosophical and political views were bound together.

A mystical expression of this combination appeared in a short article Frank wrote in June 1917, "The Dead are Silent," in which he argued that it was the memory of the dead of the First World War that caused the revolution. He argued that memory of the dead remained very much alive in the popular soul and was necessarily associated with the motherland they had sacrificed themselves for. If in the current situation their self-sacrifice was not respected, if the new nation that had resulted from their sacrifice simply offered a license for "democratized pillage" and a "shameless banquet in their graveyard," then, though they remained silent, they might exact a horrible revenge. Frank warned that the silent dead were unavenged and unsatisfied, so consequently "we can at any moment expect a fresh and sudden shock in our historical soil, which in its elemental blindness could destroy and wipe from the face of the earth not only the evil, but also the goodness of all our new life."[38]

There was one expression in Frank's thought of April 1917 that marked the beginning of a stage in his thinking that was to develop considerably in emigration: "[The expression] 'evil only gives birth to evil' . . . so long seemingly inapplicable to politics . . . [has now become] the self-evident and very necessary truth of a *genuine realpolitik* (*real'noi politiki*)."[39] Frank did not believe that politics need be governed by selfish interests, and this was the area of political thought in which he had the greatest interest. It seems ironic that such views were expressed at that time, more so that *Man's Soul* appeared in July 1917, the month of the first major Bolshevik insurrection.

Frank's material situation became difficult in the winter of 1916–17. During this time his relationship with Struve remained close, and Struve often tried to help him. In the autumn of 1916 he had proposed to the Economics Faculty of the Polytechnical Institute that Frank start a philosophy section in their department to broaden the intellectual range of the students. In the end, the initiative came to nothing. Then, during the winter of 1916–17, when inflation was high, the Franks began to find it difficult to operate financially. Frank's salary could not meet their expenses, and they decided to rent out one of the rooms of their apartment, a decision that in the current conditions, Frank wrote, was "distressing and heroic."[40] They told the Struves about it, and before they had time to act, Struve telephoned to announce that he was raising Frank's salary on *Russian Thought*, and they were able to continue as before.

The Franks were clearly living in difficult conditions in 1917. Nevertheless, they still had servants of some kind, and they were able to spend the summer with the Struves in a large house near Usikirko station in Finland, two hours from Petrograd, and Frank would travel to Petrograd to do his editorial work on *Russian Thought* and *Russian Freedom*. Sometime after the February Revolution, the servants, with the exception of Natalia's governess, Olga, decided they were no longer servants and left. This put Tatiana in a difficult situation because she had never cooked before. Attempting to cook chicken for the first time, she put the chicken into boiling water with the giblets still inside.[41] This story shows the extent to which the Franks naturally presumed a reasonably comfortable lifestyle. Until that point, they had apparently not considered saving money by doing without the servants, so the revolution forced them to adjust their way of living.

S. F. Oldenburg was made minister of education in July 1917, and he put V. I. Vernadskii in charge of all universities and scientific institutions. Also in the ministry was I. M. Grevs, who was responsible for the creation of faculties. All three knew Frank, and they invited him to become dean and ordinary professor of the new Historico-Philological Faculty at Saratov University. Frank, needing the security of a job, accepted and left, somewhat reluctantly, to take up the appointment in September 1917.

10

Saratov

LIFE IN SARATOV was difficult, and the city experienced tensions similar to those in Petrograd. The Bolshevik influence in the Saratov Soviet increased steadily in the summer. Conditions in the city became very bad. The local harvest was a disaster, 45 percent down from the previous year, and by October the city was sometimes without grain for a whole day. September saw an outbreak of typhoid. Strikes broke out. The Bolshevik takeover in Petrograd was soon followed by one in Saratov, and the ensuing months were tense and full of rumors that the Bolsheviks had been overthrown in Petrograd. These were accompanied by the continual threat of a military reaction—for example, from the Orenburg Cossacks, who at the end of 1917 were stationed on the Lower Volga.[1]

Saratov University had previously consisted only of a medical faculty and was just at the beginning of an expansion. Whether Frank, as dean of the Historico-Philological Faculty, had responsibility for selecting staff is not clear. The faculty that autumn included the famous Germanist scholar V. M. Zhirmunskii and the Slavist M. R. Fasmer. N. S. Arsen'ev, a specialist on European literature, taught there from 1918 to 1920. G. P. Fedotov, the religious thinker and historian, was a professor of history there in 1920–22.[2] Fasmer, Arsen'ev, and Fedotov, like Frank, all ended up in emigration. Another friend of Frank's on the university faculty was the economist L. N. Iurovskii.

Frank opened the term on 13 October and emphasized the importance of the "humanities" to a community. Alexis Babine, an American teacher of English at Saratov University, recorded the occasion in his diary: "[Frank] is a dull speaker. The lecture was fairly well attended and courteously applauded. Its purport was healthy and conservative—calling for broader culture in order to save the country from conditions similar to the present ones."[3]

Frank was based in Saratov between the autumn of 1917 and the autumn of 1921, although he spent a good part of those years on the German Volga. The official Soviet history of the university records only that he had a chair in philosophy there in 1917–18.[4] According to the surviving archives, he did six hours of teaching and lecturing per week in the years 1917–20, the subjects of which were logic, Kant's metaphysics, ancient philosophy, psychology, (including James, H. Höffding, and Vvedenskii), and social philosophy, including Simmel. He was also chairman of the university's Philosophical-Historical Society and led a student philosophical circle.[5]

The total academic staff of the university, 146 in 1917, rose to 210 in 1920. Student numbers in these years rose dramatically: from a total of 2,251 in 1917 to 16,508 in 1919. In 1917, the Historico-Philological Faculty accepted a total of 189 students, of whom 117 were not committed to any formal course. By 1919, the faculty had split into two departments, historical and philological, which in total numbered 1,172.[6] The Department of Philology did not begin to graduate specialists until 1921, so Frank's lectures were probably introductory and bearing in mind the massive increase in numbers, addressed to uneducated audiences. Life in the university was not easy. Sometime after the revolution, Babine ironically reported: "The long oppressed members of the university—janitors, messengers, laboratory hands, and the like—have raised their heads under the Bolshevik regime, [and] are demanding economic equality with the teaching body. . . . The university library closes at 2 P.M. every afternoon to enable the staff to attend the rabble's 'emancipation' meetings."[7]

This increase in numbers was accompanied by the politicization of the university and a steady increase in Party influence. In April 1918, the faculty of the university sent a delegate to the Bolshevik Department of Education in Moscow to protest against Party violations of university autonomy.[8] A student communist union was set up in the autumn of 1918, and student revolutionary committees were set up in the faculties. The university administration was forced to allow students and teachers on its governing council and to give them the deciding vote. In October 1919, a general student conference moved to fight against so-called outmoded ways of thinking and in favor of self-government. Students and teachers were sent to the front to fight against Denikin. Later the Faculty of Social Sciences, into which the Department of History merged in 1919, became the focus for Marxist thought in the university.[9]

By 1921, the situation was very difficult ideologically. In March of that year, three professors were thrown in jail for giving a series of lectures at one of the city's churches in which they said that natural phenomena could not be explained by chemical interactions alone, and that some power, which might even be called God, seemed to be present in the world. In December 1920, a secret document sent to different institutions called for Party supporters to "keep track of anti-Soviet remarks and statements of professors in their lectures and to report the same to proper authorities."[10]

Another danger was anti-Semitism. Just after the revolution, on 28 October, Babine recorded the rumor of a Jewish pogrom,[11] and the Jews were sometimes accused of hoarding food and subject to hostile searches. Frank's children encountered anti-Semitism for the first time. The brother of Vasilii El'iashevich was in Saratov, and his son was teased at school for being a "Yid." Frank's children took part in the teasing too until Tatiana heard about it, told them off, and explained that they were half Jewish.[12]

When the Franks first arrived in the city, they were given a very large flat, and the first months were comfortable.[13] However, things soon changed. Babine recorded that in April residents of the better houses were being turned out of their flats and that in the summer he had four families living in his flat.[14] This happened to the Franks in the autumn. Ten relatives of Tatiana and the family of a friend, N. I. Boldyrev, numbering three people, moved in with them. Along with servants, this made twenty-three in the flat, which became like "a cross between a coaching inn and a furniture shop."[15] Fortunately, they all got on well. Frank, who loved peace and quiet, found it difficult to work.

The major cause for concern was the lack of food. The city filled up with refugees from the surrounding area. According to some sources, prices had shot up by 900 percent since 1914.[16] Just to stay alive demanded a great deal of energy. In October 1918 Frank wrote: "We are now living in a state of devastation. . . . We receive a quarter of a pound of bread a day."[17] Babine recorded in January 1919 that there was no meat in the city except that for the Red Army, that butter was at 50 rubles a pound, a chicken 80–100 rubles, and that there was no rice or lentils.[18] In spite of this, Frank recalled that they "did not go hungry, even in the worst years."[19] Tatiana would sometimes go to the country to get food. Each morning a pile of sunflower seeds was divided among the children, a process they nicknamed "the commune."[20] In the deteriorating situation, the family decided to move out of Saratov.

They spent the summer of 1919 with a group of Russian intellectuals in a small town, Volskoe (Kukkus), in the German settlement area along the east side of the Volga to the south of Saratov. In July 1919 Denikin's army occupied the southwestern districts of Saratov Province and was at one point stationed across the Volga not far from Volskoe. The Franks considered joining the White movement and leaving. However, they decided against it.[21] Frank's life was continually under threat. At this time, he left the family and went back to Saratov. Tatiana heard a rumour that he had been arrested and rushed home to discover it was not true.[22]

Mainly because of the food situation, the Franks moved permanently to the German Volga in the autumn of 1919 to stay in another village to the south of Volskoe, Rovnoe (Seelman), with a population of about 8,000.[23] They were based there until the spring of 1921, although Frank was sometimes back in Saratov.[24] The pretext for the move was that Frank was to do some lecturing, but in reality the food situation was better there than in the city. Rovnoe was about two days' journey from Saratov, and there were no roads to reach it, so they used horses.

Initially it was pleasant, and they lived in a comfortable flat, but soon life became difficult there too. Tatiana decided to become like a peasant and acquired a pig, chickens, geese, and a cow. Since money was almost valueless by that time, she bought them in exchange for her jewelry. The cow came in exchange for a watch with a long gold chain. Frank was very impractical, one of the many Russian intellectuals whose minds were brilliant but not well adapted to coping in such situations. He suggested that since he could play the piano, he might be able to milk the cow too, but Tatiana did it. The cow had a calf, and during the winter when it was very cold the calf came to live in the flat with them. There was no heating in the flat. The boys, Viktor and Aleksei, would go out and get bags of straw and pour them onto the floor of the flat whence they put the straw into the stove. There was also a shortage of electricity in the village, and it would be turned off for some hours every afternoon. When it was winter and dark, the family would simply stay at home and do nothing. Often in the darkness the parents sang the children extracts from operas. In July 1920, Vasilii, their fourth child, was born. It was a difficult pregnancy, and Tatiana nearly died. She was taken to another German village nearby, Privalnoe (Warenburg), where there was a good doctor. She was in such a bad way that Frank took Viktor to see her and say good-bye, but she survived and paid the doctor with a dozen silver spoons.[25]

The atmosphere at this time was tense. Frank had a close friend who was killed by his peasants. Natalia said it was the first time she had seen her father cry, and they mentioned him in their evening prayers. El'iashevich's brother, who lived nearby, had been a tsarist officer in the Great War, and the children were strictly instructed not to refer to this fact. Frank returned to Saratov after Vasilii was born. Exactly when he left is not clear, but food requisitioning had become common at the time, and conditions were deteriorating badly. The communists came looking for Frank, but he had gone. However, they shot or hanged a number of the intelligentsia who were living in Rovnoe. At this point one of the bandit armies operating in the area occupied the town. It was probably that of Piatakov, whose band ransacked the local government grain stores and murdered over a hundred Party officials.[26]

Eventually the Red forces recovered control of the region, and the local commissar demanded that Tatiana vacate her flat within twenty-four hours. The nanny, Olga, and another old lady who was staying with them were also there. Tatiana had to get them and the family back to Saratov. This was in the spring of 1921 when the ice was beginning to melt on the Volga. She found some peasants who were still willing to cross over, bribed them, arranged for the cow to be tied to the sleigh, crossed the river, and returned to Saratov.[27] A snowless winter in 1920–21, followed by a drought, led to a catastrophic famine in the German Volga later in 1921.[28]

The events and atmosphere of these years must have had an effect on Frank. He was clearly lucky to survive. In 1923, in an article he wrote on his arrival in Germany, "Reflections on the Russian Revolution," Frank stated that the Russian revolution was a peasant revolution. This was not just the result of detached analysis but his experience of it. Saratov and the surrounding Volga region experienced an enormous upheaval in these years. A terrible famine, marauding bandit armies recklessly massacring people, Civil War—all this must have affected his perception of the revolution. Frank understood the revolution to be an outpouring of pent-up popular energy, and this was what he and his family experienced during the Civil War years. When he claimed in the same article that the only way to overturn the Bolsheviks was to master and control the energy unleashed in the revolution,[29] this was surely due to his experience of that energy. The terror was not confined in any way to the Bolsheviks. The White and bandit armies showed no mercy either. It is not surprising that in emigration Frank clashed with Struve's passionate desire to see a White victory in the war and believed that the defeat of Bolshevism needed a long-term change in the popular consciousness.

Back in Saratov, Frank was given a room in an institute. It was not possible to stay with Tatiana's family because their flat had forced guests in it. The food situation was as bad as ever. Babine records Frank complaining about the real weight of his academic food rations: "[Frank and three other professors] had brought back their portions stating that they had weighed them in one of the university laboratories and found them 2½ and 2¼ lbs. short of the 7 lb. due to them."[30]

As the summer of 1921 wore on, refugees began to pour into Saratov from the German Volga area to avoid the famine. NEP, introduced in March 1921 at the Tenth Party Congress, which restored a measure of free enterprise in the countryside, had not yet affected the city. It seems that Frank was no longer working at the university by this time, or at least not tied to it. Certainly the family found no reason to stay on in Saratov and decided to move to Moscow.

The population of Moscow had decreased by 40 percent during the Civil War. However, an influx of over 50,000 occurred in 1921, mainly people escaping from the Volga famine.[31] In 1920, Berdiaev was made professor of philosophy at the University of Moscow. He did not get a high salary, so he had to work elsewhere to supplement it.[32] Philosophy was assigned to a special institute attached to the university, and Frank was offered a job there, which he accepted. Frank went first to Moscow with Iurovskii to look for accommodation, a major problem. The number of apartments in the city had fallen by nearly a fifth during the Civil War as many buildings were gutted for firewood and because the government had taken up a lot of space since it moved there in March 1918. Eventually Frank found two rooms in a large communal flat on Medvezhii Pereulok. Then the family joined him.[33]

The food situation remained very bad, but the Franks were lucky. The Zhivotovskiis, Frank's sister Sofia and brother-in-law, had fled just after the revolution, first to Sweden and then to Paris. They were still wealthy and had made money even during the Great War. In the West, Sofia initially lived by selling off her jewelry, and through an American aid organization, probably the American Relief Administration, she sent large cases of food to the Franks filled with chocolates, sugar, and other things.[34]

When Frank arrived in Moscow, he discovered an enormous interest there in spiritual and philosophical subjects in a population tiring of atheist propaganda. He wrote in 1923: "Just as before, our seminaries were seedbeds of atheism, so now all the schools of communism, due to the deathly soullessness, giftlessness and monotony of the doctrines preached therein, are more than anything provoking a sense of protest and boredom in those participating, and a hunger for something new and opposite. . . . Among the democratic youth, you can see . . . a deep disillusion with the trite communist-atheist worldview and a hunger for a new, deeper faith."[35]

One of the foci for this was the Free Academy of Spiritual Culture, an organization founded by Berdiaev in the spring of 1919 for the "preservation and development of spiritual culture in Russia."[36] The Spiritual Academies (there was also one in Petrograd) were a kind of replacement for the former Religious-Philosophical Societies but were much broader and provided instruction and courses as well as simple discussion. Berdiaev gathered some of the best minds in Russia, including Belyi, Viacheslav Ivanov, F. A. Stepun, and B. P. Vysheslavtsev, to give lecture courses on a variety of spiritual, cultural, and philosophical issues. Frank joined the academy and read his own course, "Introduction to Philosophy." In addition to the courses, they organized fortnightly lectures followed by discussion on a variety of themes such as Polish messianism, Indian mysticism, Solov'ev, Russia and Europe, and Oswald Spengler's *Decline of the West.* Frank took part, along with another friend, Iu.Aikhenval'd.

The academy was officially registered with the Moscow Soviet of Workers' Deputies and since it had no buildings of its own, was permitted to hire rooms at the Women's University. The courses, seminars, public meetings, and debates they arranged attracted huge numbers, ranging from communists to churchmen. Some of the lectures became so popular that the auditorium, made for an audience of three hundred, could hardly manage, and they had to repeat some of them. "On [one] occasion," Berdiaev wrote, "I received a note during the lecture from the management of the Women's University, to the effect that there was danger of the floor giving way under the weight of such a number of people."[37]

In the spring of 1922 Frank and Berdiaev founded a Faculty of Philosophy and Humanities under the auspices of the academy, which was designed to provide a chance for systematic study for the students. Frank was the dean of the faculty, but it had to close at the end of the summer when Frank and most of these other philosophers and thinkers were arrested and exiled.[38]

The reference to discussion of Spengler is an interesting one because his work clearly aroused great interest in Frank and his colleagues. Perhaps a book with such an apocalyptic theme was bound to interest Russians at that time. Frank, along with Iurovskii and another friend, Ia. M. Bukshpan, a former pupil of Struve, had set up in 1921–22 a publishing house called Bereg.[39] One of its publications was a collection of four essays by Frank, Berdiaev, Bukshpan, and Stepun, *Oswald Spengler and the Decline of Europe,* which aroused the ire of one of the main Marxist philosophical journals, *Under the Banner of Marxism* (*Pod znamenem Marksizma*). Frank, in his essay "The Crisis of Western Culture," stated that the revolution marked the end of a dying secular civilization that had begun with the Renaissance and referred his readers to a hidden spiritual stream in European culture that had begun with St. Francis, Dante, and Nicholas of Cusa, had gone underground, and reemerged with romanticism and German idealism. In

Frank's thought, Nicholas of Cusa represented Christian humanism. In Frank's view, society needed to turn away from humanism to find a Christian foundation for man's aspirations. Frank and his colleagues were accused in *Under the Banner of Marxism* of nationalism, bourgeois attitudes, and promoting an outlook similar to Struve's: "From this collection to a new 'Great Russia' is as near as *Landmarks* was to *Great Russia* on the eve of the war."[40]

The Soviet authorities were well aware of Frank's ideological leanings. Bereg published a detailed work by Frank on sociological methodology in 1922, *An Essay in the Methodology of the Social Sciences*, which marked an important stage along the journey to his mature social philosophy. Frank rejected a variety of "isms"—materialism, rationalism, historicism—in favor of a broader approach to society that would stress the interrelatedness of disciplines and the existence of the ideal realm of aspirations and values as part of the real, concrete world. As he had outlined in *Man's Soul*, society as a whole has an inner spiritual being and can be examined as such as well as studied in its particular aspects and manifestations. Frank's book aroused more opposition, again for presenting bourgeois views, this time from a Soviet monthly critical journal with which Lunacharskii was associated, *The Press and Revolution* (*Pechat' i revoliutsiia*). Frank was attacked for a belief in God, for stating that the ideal rather than material world is the greatest influence on society, and for believing in human freedom: "In Frank [the issue of freedom] is resolved very poorly. He comes to the conclusion that there is no necessity in people's actions, he talks of 'spontaneous, inner spiritual causes.' But surely the purpose of natural science is knowledge of necessity."[41] Bearing in mind the potential for determinism in Frank's thought, this latter criticism is notable. Frank was attacked for believing that people are responsible for their actions. Also in 1922, Frank published his *Introduction to Philosophy in Short Form*, this time with the Academy Press in Petrograd, which seems to have been connected with Bereg.[42] Here he sketched his understanding of philosophy in a form that was close to the lecture courses he had read in previous years.

The easier atmosphere that prevailed in Moscow at the beginning of NEP did not last long. At the Twelfth Party Congress of 4–7 August 1922, the decision was made to deal forcibly not only with the Socialist-Revolutionaries and Mensheviks but also with the upper echelons of the "bourgeois-democratic intelligentsia."[43] In August 1922 the Franks took a dacha outside Moscow. One day the local peasants came to warn them that the Cheka was looking for Frank. They had a number of compromising documents with them, probably correspondence, so they went outside and threw everything into the nettles. Then three people arrived, arrested Frank, and took him to Moscow.[44]

Frank was one of about two hundred Russian, "bourgeois" intellectuals who were arrested at this point and subsequently exiled in the autumn. It is perhaps testimony to Berdiaev's and Frank's influence that they were accused of corrupting youth.[45] Frank's influence had been clearly felt, as shown by a declaration written to him by a group of his students at Moscow University:

> It is sad for us to think that our studies under your direction have come to an end. We have worked with you for only a year, but, all the same, you have managed in this short time to captivate us with your lectures in which we saw, beyond the limits of the problem of abstract knowledge, the living face of the divine total-unity, to a life's union with which you so inspiringly called us in your works. We wanted to thank you, dear Semyon Liudvigovich for your teaching, and to say to you, that your philosophizing, which combined rigour of thought with an inspired search for life's truth, [and] your ideal of concrete knowledge[,] will always give light to us in our deepest aspirations, to penetrate into the kingdom of truth. We believe that the time will come, when once again we can work with you, dear Semyon Liudvigovich.[46]

Frank was obviously a loved and admired figure and clearly had no qualms, even under the Soviet regime, of teaching philosophy as he understood it. However, whatever Frank's influence in 1921–22, he would have been a marked man, irrespective of these educational activities; the Bolshevik opposition to *Landmarks* would have ensured that. He would never have been considered a political danger to the Soviet regime, but he was a capable exponent of a totally opposite worldview.

On arrest, Frank found himself in the Lubianka with, among others, Prince S. E. Trubetskoi, the son of his old friend Prince Evgenii, who had died in 1920, and Metropolitan Kirill of Kazan.[47] Those arrested had to answer questions on their political views, attitudes to communism and Soviet power, the church, and other groups such as the Socialist-Revolutionaries and the *smenovekhovtsy*.[48] Then they were offered the chance to go abroad or into internal exile. Frank, like most of them, chose the former. It meant signing a document to say that if he ever returned to the Soviet Union, he was liable to be shot. Others who were sent abroad included Berdiaev, Bulgakov, I. A. Il'in, Izgoev, Karsavin, Kizevetter, Lapshin, Losskii, Stepun, and Vysheslavtsev—in effect a whole generation of Russia's foremost philosophical figures. The German government agreed to give them visas, and after a few weeks to say good-bye, the men and their families departed by boat from Petrograd to Stettin in two parties in September and November.

On their way out, the Franks stayed in Petrograd with their Saratov friends the N. I. Boldyrevs. Tatiana went to look for the furniture they had left in 1917, and on visiting the university porter's flat, she found herself sitting on their old sofa with their pictures on the walls. The porter said that it had all been given to him.[49]

When they got on the boat, everyone was searched to prevent them taking out diamonds or other jewelry. They went through Vasilii's hair.[50] The exiles were allowed to take 50 rubles worth of gold and silver and an additional 200 rubles for each member of their party. They had to cover all expenses themselves, including fees for passports. The British Foreign Office estimated that "those who have worldly goods can, thus, in the most favourable circumstances, cross the frontier with a capital of 25 pounds: most of them have next to nothing."[51] On leaving Petrograd, Tatiana came up on deck to find Frank crying and saying that he would never see Russia again. He was right. But he was lucky to get out. As he realized later, he would never have survived if he had stayed.

Frank understood the Bolshevik revolution as a kind of biblical catastrophe. He expressed this to Gershenzon in December 1917: "Our weak intelligentsia souls are simply incapable of conceiving abominations and horrors on such a *biblical* scale and can only fall into a numbed and unconscious state. And there is no way out, because there is no longer a motherland. The West does not need us, nor does Russia, because she no longer exists. You have to retreat into the loneliness of a stoic cosmopolitanism, i.e., start to live and breathe in a vacuum."[52]

In the middle of 1918, while he was in Saratov, Frank wrote one of his most important essays, which expressed this Old Testament sense of calamity very powerfully. By that time, the *Landmarks* group had dispersed to different parts of the country. Struve was in Moscow from February 1918 and wrote to a number of his friends inviting contributions to a collection of essays expressive of opposition to Bolshevism. Those who participated were Askol'dov, Berdiaev, Bulgakov, Viacheslav Ivanov, Izgoev, Kotliarevskii, V. N. Murav'ev, Novgorodtsev, I. A. Pokrovskii, Struve, and Frank. The collection, which was in effect a sequel to *Landmarks*, went to the printers in midsummer 1918, but because of the "Red Terror," was stored in a warehouse. A number of copies were distributed to the public during the Kronstadt uprising in March 1921, but the remainder were confiscated, and the book was republished only later in emigration.

The title of the collection, on the suggestion of Frank and taken from his essay, was *From the Depths* (*Iz glubiny*), drawn from a line in Psalm 130: "Out of the depths have I cried unto thee, O Lord." Taken as a whole, the essays were varied, but throughout there was a consistent religious and national theme and a sense of lamentation over the fate that had befallen Russia. It was a response to what Frank called "the suicide of a great nation."[53] Frank's own contribution to the collection, "De Profundis," was one of his most effective political essays and was expressive of his emerging political thought. The underlying message of the essay was that Russia had fallen into a spiritual abyss and needed a resurrection. His intellectual framework was the same as that in *Landmarks:* the revolution was a consequence of the secularization of European society. However, Frank believed that unlike the West, Russia did not have the deep spiritual traditions that were at the roots of Western reforms and gave them stability.

As in *Landmarks*, Frank was highly critical of socialism. Socialism, he wrote, is based on an "inner lie": the disparity between the high ideals of its adherents and the real motives that lie behind them. This was nothing new for Frank. What was interesting was Frank's answer to another question: Why did the moderate liberal and conservative parties prove ineffective in face of the Bolsheviks?

Frank was just as critical of the liberal parties as he was of the socialist:

> The basic and final cause of the failure of our liberal party is spiritual; it lies in the lack of a viable, positive *social worldview* and in its inability as a result of this, to inspire the political *pathos* which forms the magnetic strength of any strong political party. Our liberals and progressive figures are partly state-enlightened socialists . . . and partly half-socialists, people who see their ideal as *half* of the negative program of socialism, but disagree with its full establishment. In both cases, the defence of the principles of statehood, law and social culture is not sufficiently deeply grounded and is really a tactical device rather than a clear principle. . . . The weakness of Russian liberalism is the weakness of any *positivism* or *agnosticism* in the face of *materialism, or,* which is the same, the weakness of a cautious nihilism which is sensitive to human complexity in the face of a direct, completely blind and thus secular nihilism. Only great, positive ideas have an organizing power. . . . In Russian liberalism, a belief in the value of the spiritual principles of the nation, the state, law and freedom is unclear and religiously uninspired. . . . This is why in the battle with the destructive nihilism of the socialist parties, it could dream, through logical arguments and references to common sense and political experience, only of *changing the mind* of its opponent—in whom it continued to see rather a rational ally, but it could not light the fire of religious disapproval of its destructive acts, and gather and

strengthen an active social battle-line for its active irradication. What is now called the "state inexperience" of the liberal Russian intelligentsia is not an absence of the appropriate *technical* knowledge, know-how and practice . . . but an absence of living moral experience in relation to a succession of the basic, positive principles of state life.[54]

Frank's diagnosis here is noticeably similar to his earlier analysis of the lack of principle in the Kadet Party in 1905.

The conservatives, in Frank's view, suffered from a similar problem. Although they at least had some spiritual heritage to draw from, they had abandoned it with fatal consequences:

Russia had no small number of gifted conservative thinkers and activists with real moral, intellectual and spiritual depth—one needs only recall our Slavophiles. But they remained superfluous and powerless cells, because the prevailing conservatism did not wish to use them . . . as living carriers of an idea which awakens the social consciousness. Russian conservatism which officially depended . . . on a specific religious faith and national-political ideology deprived itself of strength . . . through its actual disbelief in the living force of spiritual creativity. The most remarkable and tragic fact of modern Russian political life, which points to a very deep and general feature of our national soul, is the inner similarity of the moral visage of the typical Russian conservative and revolutionary: the same incomprehension of the organic spiritual foundations of society, the same love of the mechanistic means of outer violence . . . , the same combination of hatred of living people with a romantic idealization of abstract political forms and parties.[55]

The weaknesses of Russian liberalism and conservatism were thus the same. Both were inadequately grounded in the deeper spiritual world. Frank believed that the political world is not the primary force in history; political parties, governments, and nations are not the goal of life. Rather, they are a product of a truly grounded life. For Frank, liberal and conservative could have the same spiritual foundation, although the parties expressed different opinions. With that in mind, it is not surprising that he was never a party man. It was not simply a matter of an apolitical temperament, although that may have had a lot to do with it; it was also that Frank did not regard political parties in themselves as fundamentally important. The important thing is what they are grounded in.

The lack of spiritual grounding in the thinking of the political parties was accentuated in Frank's mind by the passivity of the religious culture: "The Russian religious consciousness gradually moved away from and out of life, to study and teach the need to be patient and suffer, but not fight and create life; all the best strengths of the Russian spirit came to be spent on suffering and long-suffering, passivity and inactive dreaminess. . . . The Russian religious spirit a long time ago stopped strengthening the people in their daily working life, stopped permeating their earthly economic and legal relations with moral energy." This meant a process of despiritualization: "The people were torn away from the spiritual root of life and began to find satisfaction in unbelief, in purely negative freedom."[56] It is interesting that Frank did not refer to the church here but to the religious spirit of the nation. Not only does this fit his philosophy; it also fits his theology: the underlying religious spirit rather than the institution is the essential church.

Politics, Frank wrote, depends on two things: an inspired minority that takes charge of the leadership and the moral, intellectual, and cultural condition of the masses: "[The political arena] is defined by the *interaction* between the content and level of the social consciousness of the masses and the ideological tendencies of the ruling minority."[57] This understanding of the nature of political power was central to his essay "Reflections on the Russian Revolution," which strongly focused on the need to address the underlying spirit of the nation. Frank's reluctance to support Struve wholeheartedly in 1917 was due to his conviction that you cannot simply fight for a change of leadership in a difficult situation; you have to understand and affect the popular mood: "Only he can overcome the revolution and overthrow the power which it has set up, who can *master its inner forces and direct them on a rational path.* Only he who can—as the Bolsheviks did in their time—find a starting point for his own aspirations . . . only he will be able to victoriously establish his own political ideals."[58]

In this sense, Frank saw the Bolsheviks' strength as their great understanding of how to use and master the social consciousness of the country. The essence of revolution, he wrote, is to "overcome one idea with another,"[59] and by doing that, the Bolsheviks had been able to seize the mentality of the population and seize power. Many years later he wrote that an opposition movement would have needed a similar understanding of how to exploit popular grievances to have saved Russia from Bolshevism: "The only possibility of saving Russia in the first years of Bolshevism lay in some kind of anti-Bolshevik peasant movement under the slogan 'land and freedom,' a movement led by some brilliant political demagogue."[60]

11

Rebuilding a Life

GERMANY, AND BERLIN in particular, was the main center of the Russian emigration. By the autumn of 1920, there were well over 500,000 Russians in Germany, many in transit to other countries. At the beginning of 1922, the estimate of numbers had fallen to 250,000 but returned again to half a million in 1922–23. From 1923 onward there was a general exodus of Russians from Germany. The disastrous German inflation rate of the early 1920s benefited the Russians, many of whom had foreign currency, but when the mark stabilized, the situation became difficult, and many left. The German census of 1925 recorded over 250,000 people in Germany who had lived in the Russian Empire in 1914. Of these, nearly half were Russian Germans and Jews. By 1930, there were less than 100,000 Russians living in Germany, compared with nearly 200,000 in France.[1]

In 1922, at the Treaty of Rapallo, Germany became the first Western government to recognize the Soviet state. After that, the Trust Office for Russian Refugees was set up in Berlin to assist Russians with legal and administrative problems. One of the main problems for the arriving Russians was their legal status. In response to this, the Nansen Committee of the League of Nations drew up a special document called the Nansen Passport that was issued to all Russians claiming émigré status. The passport could be used to apply for visas and to get permission to travel abroad, and it entitled the holder to petition for permanent residence.[2] However, the Franks, like other exiles who had to leave in 1922, were not given Nansen passports. They continued to be holders of their Soviet passports in spite of the fact that the last page of Frank's passport stated that he could never return to the USSR, on pain of execution. This was to cause some difficulty when the family came to leave Germany in 1937–38.

The Russian community in Berlin was mainly composed of two not always distinct social groups: the Russian intelligentsia and the upper classes. One commentator noted: "The Russian emigration in Berlin was a pyramid whose point was the only part which remained. The lower and middle classes were missing. . . . Instead there were army officers, bureaucrats, artists, financiers, politicians and members of the old court society."[3] The Russians in Berlin lived mainly in the southwestern suburbs of Schöneberg, Friedenau, Wilmersdorf, and Charlottenburg, and there were so many Russians there that the area almost became a Russian suburb. It had been the high-income residential area of Berlin before the war and contained many attractive buildings and parks.[4]

Until the mark stabilized, Berlin was the center of a highly sophisticated Russian cultural milieu in which every variety of opinion was represented. In particular, the city became a focus for poetry and the arts. Visitors or residents included Belyi, I. G. Erenburg, Gor'kii, V. F. Khodasevich, V. V. Maiakovskii, L. O. Pasternak, and M. I. Tsvetaeva. There were a great number of publishing outlets. It is estimated that between 1918 and 1928 there were 188 Russian émigré publishing enterprises in Berlin.[5] The main Berlin daily newspaper was *The Helm* (*Rul'*), which was founded by a triumvirate of Russian Kadets: V. D. Nabokov, who had been head of the Secretariat in the First Provisional Government; I. V. Gessen, who had coedited *Speech* with Miliukov; and A. I. Kaminka, who along with Nabokov had founded the prerevolutionary legal paper *Right* (*Pravo*). The main rival to *The Helm* in the emigration was *Latest News* (*Poslednie novosti*), which Miliukov edited in Paris.

The intellectuals who were exiled in the autumn of 1922 came out of Russia in two groups. Frank was in the first group, made up mainly of those from Moscow, which arrived in late September, and included Aikhenval'd, Berdiaev, and Kizevetter. The second group, coming from Petrograd, which had spent a longer time in jail than the Moscovites, included Izgoev and Losskii and arrived in early November.[6] Berdiaev described his mood on leaving Soviet waters: "Many had a feeling of being out of danger: until then no one was certain that we would not be sent back. . . . A new life was opening before us. . . . Yet in me the sense of freedom was transfused by a sense of intense pain at parting, perhaps irrevocably, with my native land."[7]

Frank and his colleagues, who on their arrival in Berlin were treated to a series of evenings and dinners, soon discovered that the emigration was bitterly divided. The most difficult aspect of this for Frank was the tension that now appeared between him and Struve. Frank arrived in Berlin exhausted by his experiences and very concerned about those like Izgoev who were still in prison. The sharply anti-

Soviet attitude of those like Struve seemed to Frank and his friends provocative and dangerous. For example, Patriarch Tikhon had been put under house arrest in June 1922, and they were astounded to read a highly anti-Bolshevik report of this by S. S. Oldenburg in the June–July issue of *Russian Thought*. Struve seemed to Frank to have no sense of responsibility for the fate of people in the Soviet Union: "We have formed the terrible impression that politicians here consider people living in Russia today . . . to be worthless material, which is doomed to destruction for the sake of unbridled free speech in the emigration."[8] Frank was clearly frustrated. He felt that Struve and the emigration were irresponsible in their reckless criticisms of Soviet life and biased in their picture of Russia: "Although the Kremlin is occupied by the Bolsheviks, the heart of Russia is still in Moscow and not in Prague."[9]

The Franks were met in Berlin by the Zaks. Lev Zak and his wife, Nadezhda Braude, had gone to the Crimea during the Civil War and escaped out to the West via Constantinople. The Franks brought very little with them; they were badly dressed and physically exhausted.[10] They decided to stay in Berlin. Frank turned down an invitation from Struve to go to Prague. This was partly because of the difficulty of their relationship but also because of the problem of finding accommodation there. The situation in Berlin was initially good for anyone with foreign currency, which Frank had, and Germany was really a second home. Losskii, on the other hand, took up an offer of financial support from the Czech government and moved to Prague. In a letter to El'iashevich, Frank indicates that he turned down a possibility of moving to France: "Life in France is so much more expensive than in Germany, that to move there even temporarily would be completely impossible."[11]

The first thing the Franks had to do was to find accommodation. The housing situation for Russians was not easy, and many relied on the help of organizations such as the YMCA or the Russian Social Committee for Help to the Hungry. Foreigners were not popular because they were thought to be wealthy and were not allowed to rent unfurnished accommodation because of general shortages. Landlords often demanded advance payment. Nevertheless, the Franks found a four-room flat on Karl Schraderstr. in Schöneberg. The landlady lived on the premises.[12]

The Franks' financial situation in Berlin was unstable. There is a story that Karsavin was once asked by a German professor, "How do you Russians exist financially?" He replied, "Quite simply, Frank and I continually borrow money from each other."[13] Before leaving Russia, Frank had sold a number of his books and possessions and got some

English currency for them. When converted into German money, this was enough to last for a year and was their immediate source of finances. Their financial situation was always precarious in the next years, but they were still able to have a German maid in to help and a Russian lady to assist with Vasilii. Frank was clearly grateful to find the flat. He wrote to El'iashevich: "After many years I have once again a secluded corner for my work and I dream of devoting myself to academic activity."[14]

In subsequent years, the Franks lived in six different flats. It was impossible for a foreigner to buy or become the main tenant of a flat, only to be a subtenant. Only later were they able to rent a flat of their own.[15] Until then, since it was their custom to go to the country for the summer every year, they often had to move. Frank had to rebuild his life from scratch, and it was not an easy process. Three years later, in 1925, he wrote to Struve: "In former times, in my youth, I never 'made a career,' and did not know how to do it, but now, an old man and in a foreign country, it is all the more difficult."[16]

On their arrival in Berlin, Berdiaev and Frank came into contact with the YMCA, which had had some influence on Russian student life in the years before the revolution. The YMCA had both a missionary and social function, and many of the Russian refugees benefited from its provision of food and clothing. The Franks, for example, had a YMCA bath towel.[17] Its overall leader was John R. Mott, and its chief representative in Berlin was Paul Anderson. Two of his workers were to have close contact with the Franks over the next years in emigration: G. G. Kullman, who was assigned to work directly with students, and Theodore Pianov, a Russian without higher education who had been on the YMCA staff in Russia before the revolution and was assigned to seek Russian professors the YMCA might be able to work with. Berdiaev described Kullman, who later joined the League of Nations, as "a man entirely representative of the Western spirit and yet sharing our spiritual and intellectual experience."[18]

Anderson felt that the Russians might be able to help the YMCA: "One day it came to me that perhaps we were looking at them from the wrong angle—how to be of help to them—whereas we should solicit their aid to us." The YMCA was an American Protestant organization, but it subsequently identified itself, according to Anderson, with "creative Orthodox doctrine" and made its overall policy in the Russian community "the preservation and development of Russian Christian culture."[19] Soon after their arrival in Berlin, Berdiaev and Frank met with Anderson and in relating the success of the Free Academy of Spiritual Culture in Moscow, declared that they would like to set up a similar thing in Berlin. Anderson agreed to fund such a venture, and

Pianov was assigned to organize it. They were able to rent for evening use the building of the French gymnasium. The result was the Religious-Philosophical Academy.

The faculty of the Religious-Philosophical Academy was made up from the exiled group of intellectuals. Prior to this there had been a Union of Russian Philosophers in Berlin, under the leadership of Zen'kovskii. The YMCA made an attempt to merge these two groups, but Berdiaev would have nothing to do with the émigré group, which, lacking the charisma of a leader like Berdiaev and American capital, eventually came to an end. Relations between Berdiaev and Zen'kovskii remained strained for the rest of their lives.[20] Zen'kovskii became the president of the Russian Student Christian Movement, which was also funded by the YMCA and based in Prague.

The Religious-Philosophical Academy had its gala opening night on 26 November 1922 in front of a huge audience of distinguished Russian émigrés: "The public stood as a thick wall in the aisles, and many could not get in at all." Bolshevik and church representatives were there. Berdiaev, Frank, and Karsavin were the speakers. The whole project was bold and determined. The academy set its task as the awakening of spiritual interests among Russians abroad. The initial program for the academy declared that the epoch of external catastrophes should be followed by a focus on inner religious experience. Russia and Europe could not recover from their malaise through treatment of the symptoms alone. Politics was not enough. What was needed was a spiritual healing. The basis of life had been poisoned, the primary will of people and nations diseased and smashed, and only a turning to God could transform the situation.[21]

Russians expected to return to Russia when the Bolshevik regime was overthrown and were therefore anxious to bring up their children in a Russian milieu. In addition, there were students of university age, some of whom had started courses back home, who needed a good education. The fees of the academy, which were obviously a problem for the new immigrants, were 1,000 marks for unmatriculated students, and 1,500 marks for ordinary students for two hours a week for five months. The program of courses for the first term involved a wide variety of speakers and included Aikhenval'd on the philosophical motifs of Russian literature, Arsen'ev on the ancient world and early Christianity, Berdiaev on the philosophy of religion, and Stepun on the essence of the romantic movement. Frank taught courses on the foundations of philosophy and Greek philosophy.[22]

Until Berdiaev left Berlin for Paris in the summer of 1924, the academy in Berlin was a major focus of Russian intellectual life, attracting considerable numbers and a wide variety of speakers. Bulgakov came from Paris; the German philosopher Max Scheler gave a talk. However, Berdiaev was clearly the moving force behind it, just as he had been in Moscow. Although it continued after his departure, it gradually petered out in Berlin.[23] The focus moved to Paris, and although Frank gave a couple of lectures there in 1926,[24] he could not maintain a close connection. The St. Serge Theological Institute, which became a centre of Russian Orthodoxy in emigration, was founded in Paris in 1925, and likewise, while Frank had contacts there, he was not part of the regular faculty. The academy in Berlin was not a registered educational institution, and professors were paid by the lecture, not as tenured staff. Nevertheless, this was a great help to Frank. Four hours of lectures a week brought in eight dollars a month, about a third of the monthly budget.[25]

The contact of the Russian émigrés with the YMCA was the beginning of a fruitful working relationship. In the summer of 1923 Frank wrote an article called "The Religious-Historical Meaning of the Russian Revolution." It appeared a year later in a collection of essays put out by the YMCA, *Problems of Russian Revolutionary Thought (Problemy russkoi revoliutsionnoi mysli)* whose specific purpose was to affect the student mind in an inspirational way. The book was an example of Protestant-Orthodox collaboration, one in which the Protestant YMCA made an attempt to promote Orthodox thinking.[26] Eventually the YMCA press in Paris became the main outlet for Russian religious thought in the emigration.

The desire to create a community of Russian émigrés united by common religious convictions led to the formation of the Brotherhood of St. Sophia, originally founded by Bulgakov in 1919 in Russia but revived in emigration in 1923. The membership included many of the great names of the Russian religious renaissance: Arsen'ev, Bulgakov, A. V. Elchaninov, G. V. Florovskii, Frank, Kartashev, Struve, G. Trubetskoi, and Zen'kovskii. Berdiaev and Losskii were affiliated. Their unity was maintained through simultaneous prayer and communion, in private and in church, and occasionally they would meet.[27] In correspondence with Tatiana, Frank refers to two meetings of the brotherhood in Prague in September 1924.[28]

Another enterprise Frank was heavily involved with was the Russian Scientific Institute, which was also initiated in the winter of 1922–23. Its aim was to provide a formal educational institution for émigré scholars. Specifically it aimed to support independent academic research in Russian culture, to enter into dialogue with other academics, and to provide systematic courses for Russian students educated in Germany. It also aimed to complete the education of young people who had not finished high school in Russia. Its leading figures included those associated with *The Helm*, Gessen and Kaminka, and a number of the exiled group, including Berdiaev, Frank, Il'in, and Karsavin. The main financing came from private German sources, including a million marks each from Nordische Bank fur Handel und Industrie and Deutsche Nordische Bank.[29]

In December 1922 Gessen was chosen as the original chairman of the project to create the institute. In January an organizing committee was set up that included Aikhenval'd, Berdiaev, A. Chuprov, Frank, Karsavin, and Losskii. The first term opened at the old Architectural Academy in Berlin on 17 February 1923. There were 446 enrollments, which included 260 students in the Philosophical Department where Frank was based. Berdiaev, Frank, Kizevetter, and Struve all gave courses at that time, and the success was considerable. In the autumn of 1923, the academic program was changed so as to make an open attempt to offer education of university standard. Frank, made dean of the new Historico-Philological Faculty, taught an obligatory course on the history of ancient philosophy and a seminar on philosophy. At the opening of the academic year he gave a talk on the importance of preserving and developing a Russian national culture. Il'in was dean of the Law Faculty, Prokopovich of the Commercial Faculty, and V. I. Iasinskii rector of the institute. In his opening speech, Iasinskii expressed the hope that those who started courses at the institute might finish their courses in their own country. Students completing the three-year courses received diplomas similar to those given by prerevolutionary higher educational institutions.[30]

In Berlin, the institute was sometimes referred to as the Russian University in Berlin. In spite of its success, however, it was in a precarious situation. Many of the leading Berlin intellectuals soon left for Paris and Prague. Already by the autumn of 1923, the institute itself had partly moved to Prague, which became a major center of Russian academic life in Europe. It also suffered from political infighting, polemics between anti-Bolshevik émigrés and those who had more sympathy with the Soviet regime. Funds were given by the YMCA and the League of Nations, and it continued to operate until 1933. Frank remained a central figure in the institute, becoming its director in 1932. He gave many courses and lectures—for example, on psychology, modern philosophy, Leont'ev, and the Christian worldview.[31]

Another academic group in which Frank played a part was the Russian Academic Union, which was mainly concerned with providing assistance to Russian students abroad. *The Helm* reports Frank as a representative of the union at the Russian Academic Congress in Prague in September 1924, as being elected a member of its school commission in December 1924, and as secretary for 1925.[32]

All this suggests that Frank was continually occupied with administrative as well as academic reponsibilities in these early years in Berlin. It is unlikely that he enjoyed this. He did not have a gift for admin-istration and in later years would say that he would prefer not to teach if only he could devote himself entirely to academic work.[33] In August 1923 he wrote to Tatiana: "I have almost completely decided to give up the running of the Institute . . . and to earn these 10 dollars by writing."[34] Nevertheless, administrative work was one of his few sources of income, and he was forced to do it.

Frank thought that it was in academic work that he could make the greatest contribution to Russian cultural life. And, just as after 1905, he did not wish to get involved in intelligentsia politics for this reason. He had a philosophical calling:

> The main task of my life I see as before in academic work, at the current moment in writing "social philosophy"; first of all I feel this organically—and for me, as an "amoralist," that is the decisive thing. But I also think that it is perhaps the maximum that I can give to Russia. Because to leave Russia the fruit of spiritual creativity in the form of new intellec-tual ideas also means to do something for history. Along with that, of course, I am attracted by educational activity. In the last year in Mos-cow, when I could not think about anything else, my activity at the uni-versity and the Academy of Spiritual Culture gave me the deepest satis-faction; I was conscious of inspiring my listeners and I created a whole group of disciples.[35]

Frank struggled with disillusionment. Nowhere does he specifically state this, but his writings of these early years in Berlin were attempts to discover a meaning to life in a world where there seemed little hope. The combination of the triumph of Bolshevism in Russia and the struggle for existence in a Germany in a chaotic state gave him lit-tle cause for optimism. Apart from the official lecture courses he gave, there were discussion groups in the Franks' flat.[36] Younger people would come and ask Frank for his advice, and there was real interest in religious and philosophical issues. One of the groups Frank got se-riously involved with was the Russian Student Christian Movement, which was founded in 1923 at Přebov, Czechoslovakia. The aim of the movement was to offer students a bridge between their spiritual and their practical interests, which was in sharp contrast to the division between church and secular life in imperial Russia. The movement called for the renewal (*otserkvlenie* and *ozhivlenie*) of the church. Frank, in his own words, was one of its "ideological leaders."[37] It was for these young people who had lost their country that he felt most deeply.

Consequently, Frank's writings at this time more than any other were missionary in their purpose. *The Collapse of the Idols* (1924), *The*

Meaning of Life (1926), and *The Foundations of Marxism* (1926), were written for younger people. At the same time, as Frank pointed out, it is impossible to give something to others if you do not have it yourself, and these writings, particularly *The Collapse of the Idols* and *The Meaning of Life*, contained a striking element of personal search and struggle.

The Collapse of the Idols was written in the summer of 1923 while the Franks were on holiday with a group of Russian intellectuals at the beach resort of Zingst in northern Germany. It was based on a speech he gave at the Congress of Russian Students in Germany in May 1923, which had been organized by the YMCA. It was not meant to be a philosophical work or some kind of spiritual sermon. He called it a "sort of confession of a typical, spiritual journey of a modern Russian soul."[38] It was an attempt to diagnose the causes of Russia's tragic experience and mark pointers for a new path. Frank denied in the introduction that it was a specifically personal confession, but in a letter dedicating the work to Tatiana, he wrote that he had put "almost [my] whole soul" into it.[39] *The Meaning of Life* was completed in Berlin in August 1925. Once again, Frank described it as an "expression of the personal beliefs of the author."[40] This time it grew out of conversations with members of the Russian Student Christian Movement, and the book was an attempt to express his spiritual beliefs in accessible form. Although it was written in a theoretical style, it was more a book for spiritual meditation than a work of philosophy.

Much of these two books was a reiteration of the basic themes of *Landmarks* and Frank's religious philosophy. He declared that the emphasis on external as opposed to internal transformation and the primacy of political over spiritual change led to the idolization of worldly ends and ended in tyranny. The gods of the modern world were revolution, politics, society, and culture. These would have to be replaced by the one real God. The social and political arena should never be seen as an end. The only true end is God:

> This hierarchy of values—this primacy of aim over means, of the fundamental over the secondary, must be firmly asserted in the soul once and for all. . . .
> . . . No earthly human matter . . . can give life meaning, and when it has been given a meaning from another source—through its ultimate depth, then it is given meaning all through. . . . You cannot look for light in the darkness, and the darkness is opposite to the light; but the light gives light to the darkness. It would be completely false, and opposed to the Christian consciousness . . . to separate God from the world, to get absorbed in God, and fence oneself in from the world in suspicion of it. . . . All human life, enlightened by its link with God and

affirmed through it, is justified. . . . The one condition of this is the demand that man does not serve the world, "does not love the world and what is in it" as final goods, but that he sees the world as the means and instrument of the Divine, that he uses [the goods] for the *service* of absolute good and genuine life.[41]

All worldly aims, then, are idols. That by definition means any political structure or any social project. It does not invalidate the project. The project will find its meaning in the service of good—as a means. But as soon as the means becomes an end in itself, tyrannies become possible.

One thing Frank had formerly regarded as an aim now turned out to be, in *The Collapse of the Idols*, a means and was condemned as such: culture. Formerly Frank had had a deep faith in the accumulated spiritual culture of mankind: "In the pre-war period, in that recent time which is yet so long ago and which seems like a lost golden age, we all believed in 'culture' and in the cultural development of mankind." Frank believed that the First World War and the Russian revolution had put paid to the progressive view of history to which this belief belonged. Now Frank no longer made culture a priority; for him, it had become a rather "foggy idea." It was simply a by-product of man's search for truth: "If we find the truly good, a true task and the meaning of life, and we learn how to realize it, we will also participate in the creation of true culture. But we can in no way formulate our ideal, our faith, by referring to that which is accepted as culture."[42] Thus Frank had come to see culture as part of the external organization of society, and to make anything external a priority was idolatry.

This disillusionment with culture was accompanied by the most hostile comments on European culture and politics that Frank ever made. Frank expressed the view that the Versailles settlement had confirmed that "merciless exploitation of the weak is the normal, natural condition of European international life." He declared that the democratic ideals of Western Europe were a charade. He railed at the leaders of Western societies for putting their material interests before principle and for praising the barbaric Asian socialism of the Soviet Union. Western society was not what it had been made out to be. It was totally materialistic. Man had been turned into a "slave of things, machines and telephones." "And democratic ideals?" he asked. "Maybe it is possible and even necessary to accept them in an abstract sense . . . , but it is impossible to believe in them or bow down before them."[43] Coming to the West, Frank found a society that was also concerned with the outer man, and for him, any concentration on the outer was idolatry. Spengler's suggestion that the West was in deep decline had met with a positive response from the Russian exiles. Frank, although he disputed Spengler's historical relativism, described him as "one of the subtlest . . . historical minds of our time,"[44] and his own diagnosis belonged with Spengler's general tone of postwar disillusionment.

Frank's strongest invective, however, was a continuation of his former attacks on idealistic or utilitarian morality. This had been the theme of his articles in *Problems of Idealism* and *Landmarks*, and it was of great importance to him. In *The Collapse of the Idols*, his thinking on this issue was at its clearest. Frank distinguished between two ethical codes: Kantianism and Christianity. The former, he declared, leads to tyranny, the latter to personal wholeness. The problem with Kant's categorical imperative was that it elevated morals to abstract moral principles standing outside the human being and demanded his obedience. The Christian moral code, which in Frank's view was no less demanding, suited the makeup of human nature. Frank, holding to the view of the neoPlatonist Tertullian that "the soul is by nature Christian,"[45] effectively offered an argument from natural law. The divine nature is at the foundation of the human, and by living according to the Christian moral code, man becomes more himself. The difference between the two moral codes is that the Kantian is external to human nature whereas the Christian is internal.

In practice, Frank illustrated the two moral codes regarding sex. He commented that the exceptional inner frustrations that any young person feels in relation to this subject need very sensitive treatment. People go through agonies over the subject: "We ourselves do not know . . . where in our souls the cult of the blessed Madonna ends and Sodom begins."[46] The answer is to see morality not in terms of condemnation but salvation. Christ stated that he came not to judge the world but to save it. Cold, critical judgment is of no help to people at their moments of crisis; what is needed is the understanding, sympathetic and saving morality of the pastoral approach. Instead of becoming a victim of the tyranny of the categorical imperative, man can battle against the enslaving side of his nature and remain in contact with his true spiritual home, which is God.

The idea of a divine foundation to human nature was Frank's answer to the various idols he had diagnosed. In his famous poem "The Second Coming," the Irish poet W. B. Yeats observed that the world was no longer held together by a set of unifying values: "The centre does not hold." Frank, writing for a generation of younger people with no center, no foundation, and no beliefs to fall back on, wanted to draw attention to the inner center, the aspect of man on which a life and a calling could be constructed. For an exiled community that had lost touch with its country, this could not have been more relevant. There was no need to search for some support to lean on. The support, man's inner contact with God, was already there. This Christian foundation had its own strict laws, and it demanded constant vigilance. Frank used Pascal's phrase "order of the heart" (*ordre du coeur* or *logique du coeur*) to describe the nature of this Christian foundation to human nature: "This 'order of the heart' cannot be breached without punishment, for it is the condition of meaning, the stability of our life, the condition of our spiritual equilibrium and therefore of our being."[47]

This already fitted in with Frank's overall philosophy and his concept of the soul as outlined in *Man's Soul.* Typically, *The Meaning of Life* contained statements such as "The human person is as it were outwardly closed and separate from other beings; but inwardly, in the depths, it communicates with everyone, and merges with them in a primary unity." The philosophy of total-unity stood, as ever, at the foundation of Frank's social analysis. This relates to one subject that came up continually in *The Meaning of Life*—self-revealing truth. Frank declared:

> Surely in the act of cognition it is not we who do anything . . . : we only recognize truth, the light of knowledge illuminates us.

> If I turn now to my own *search* for truth, then I clearly see that it . . . *is the very manifestation in me of that reality which I am searching for.* The search for God is already the action of God in the human soul. . . . [God] *is specifically with and in us,* He acts in us.

> [Absolute being] is for knowledge of the heart a self-evident truth.

> The metaphysical almightiness of the Good is made certain in its empirical weakness, the impossible for people is not only possible, but self-evidently *is* with and through God.[48]

This is a key element of Frank's religious worldview. God is acting, illuminating himself to people. This was of importance for Frank's students in their search for stability. God is the actor, and if man looks within, he will discover God as he continually reveals himself. Frank quoted Augustine: "Go not outward, but into yourself, and when within yourself you find yourself limited, transcend yourself." He called for a slowing down of life so that people could search for this inner light: "Non-activity is actually more important than the greatest and most blessed action."[49]

Later in the 1920s Frank made an eloquent critique of the external-ization of modern life:

> For the modern Western world—i.e., for the tendency of "Americanism"
> . . . there is a common desire to turn the human individual wholly into
> the so-called "active man," that is into a *cynic*, who has lost feeling and
> taste for the inner life and finds his full satisfaction in technical activity. . . .
> Such a person, it is true, is an "individualist"—he has an individual life,
> he even looks at his life from the point of view of his interests and suc-
> cess, but the individuality in the sense of inner reality is destroyed in
> him. Genuine love which satisfies the inner demand of the spirit is re-
> placed by outer, transient ties based on feeling, and the whole aim of life
> comes to consist in outward success—in the acquisition of wealth, glory,
> power, in a word, in seizing the best place in the world, in subjecting the
> world in some sphere to oneself—this expressing itself in the terms of
> "sport"—in the "breaking" of some kind of "record."[50]

With all that, Frank defended himself in advance from possible charge of quietism.[51] He denied that to declare the primacy of spiritual over political life meant to withdraw from the world. In this, of course, he was absolutely right. Nevertheless, Frank may have had the temperament, if not the doctrine, of the quietist. The melancholy Frank always exhibited runs throughout *The Meaning of Life*. The message of the book is not depressing, the very opposite in fact, but the general mood is wistful. The sense that the whole world without exception is corrupt, evil, and compromised is present throughout.

It is not possible to know whether this melancholy was a consequence of Frank's general character or the atmosphere of the emigration; probably it was a mixture of both. Frank undoubtedly had a tendency to melancholy. Lev Zak, in his memoir on Frank, stated that Frank's Christianity was deeply intertwined with a strain of Greek humanism and that the aspects of Christianity that were in conflict with that humanism were deeply alien to him. He also wrote that Frank was very sensitive to the presence of evil in the world.[52] During September 1923 Frank and a number of other Russian intellectuals were invited to give lectures in Rome by Professor Lo Gatto of the Institute for Eastern Europe.[53] Frank went sightseeing in Rome and wrote to his wife: "These two days from morning to evening I have been studying antiquity—there is a beauty alongside which one would want to die, before which one's whole life seems meaningless." Frank reported that in front of one particular Venus "I almost cried."[54] This is typical of Frank's melancholy; it was a sadness at the vision of a beauty that is inaccessible in this life.

For Frank, the early years in Berlin represented an attempt to find meaning in a world that offered little hope. The revolution had happened because Russia had lost contact with her inner spiritual life. As Frank said, Russia was "a living, real creature," an old mother who was "spiritually ill."[55] Perhaps what Russia had lacked in 1917 could be born in emigration.

12

The Dispute with Struve

ON HIS ARRIVAL in the West, Frank discovered that he had so diverged from Struve in how to respond to the revolution that a close relationship with him was no longer possible. The Struves instinctively felt that those who had lived in Russia under Bolshevism had compromised with evil. In his letters to the Struves, in which he analyzed their ideological rift, Frank referred to the old editorial board of *Russian Thought* as a distinct and united group of people, having in mind in addition to himself men like Berdiaev and Izgoev, and referred to "those of us who have lived these years in Russia."[1] In reply, Struve, who after the revolution had joined the Whites and become foreign minister in General Wrangel's government, wrote of the strength of "our" position, identifying himself with the White emigration.[2] The two men had thus entered different camps of opinion. Frank went to see Struve in Heidelberg in November 1922, and they had a conversation that lasted two or three days, but they could not overcome their differences.[3]

Frank was unimpressed with the spirit of the Russian emigration. It suffered, he thought, from being distanced from the realities of Soviet life and from becoming an inner, closed society obsessed with its own experience. In a letter to El'iashevich he wrote: "The majority of emigrants do not understand the revolution at all—whether it be as counter-revolutionaries or as *smenovekhovtsy*. I, along with those who formerly shared his outlook, have had a fundamental break with Struve."[4] Struve, he felt, failed to see that "the emigration, through the immanent sociological laws of its being, is destined to political fruitlessness and is the classic place for political divisions and factionalism."[5] Nina Struve wrote a letter "full of passionate accusations," suggesting that Frank lacked a sense of responsibility for Russia. Frank wrote back that unlike twenty years before, when he worked

134

with them on *Liberation*, he now had sufficient strength to stand on his own feet. In his turn he suggested that the Struves were so egocentric as to believe that Prague and their activities were the center of the world. In consequence, he wrote, "your love acquires an inevitable tinge of despotism." But he added: "I am not a moralist, and do not wish to remake anybody, least of all my own friends, so I love you all the more for your accusations."[6] A few months later he wrote a postcard to Nina: "I hurriedly tell you that I remember and love you all as before."[7]

The anguish these men felt at losing their country is evident from a meeting convened in Berdiaev's flat at the end of 1922. Struve accused the new exiles of not understanding the White movement, and Frank, supported by Izgoev, declared that the White movement should never be seen as an end in itself. Berdiaev flew into a rage, began to shout, and accused Struve of "godlessness" and "materialism." The landlady threatened to call the police.[8]

This was a matter of particular anguish for Frank because he still regarded the Struves as his closest friends. Of those who were exiled, he had become quite close to Berdiaev and Izgoev, but they did not offer intimate companionship. He wrote to Nina: "Apart from you both I have no friends in the genuine sense. Tania, during these years, found herself a close friend in Eliz. Vas. Boldyreva, but I have no one apart from you. . . . I came here with the dream of living and working with you, and if I thought that in some way I could do that in Prague, I would move there without any hesitation."[9]

The problem of how to respond to the revolution was the central question of the emigration. What had happened to Russia in 1917, and what should be done about it? The essence of the argument between Frank and Struve lay in whether to plan for the overthrow of the Bolshevik regime. Frank's mentality and philosophy led him to see the revolution as the product of a deep internal illness of the Russian popular soul. It was no good trying to orchestrate the overthrow of the communist regime because the political system in Russia depended on its inner spiritual condition. The only long-term solution was to work for an inner moral and spiritual transformation that would then affect the political reality:

> Those of us who have lived these years in Russia, and who have deeply felt the organic nature of what has happened, have at the same time a living relationship with the concrete face [*lik*] of the motherland, in her condition of illness. Firstly, we have all understood that Bolshevik power is just the scum and foam of the revolution, and not its essence, only the symptom of an illness (which of course, in its turn, complicates

the illness and slows its treatment), but not its actual cause. I think you agree with this. . . . From this comes our non-belief in some kind of mechanistic form of treatment and belief only in healing through an inner reeducation in the process of the revolution itself, that is a spiritual reaction to the prolonged experience of revolution. The narrow-minded dream about the return of a lost paradise on the very day which follows a coup, seems to us simplistic and false.[10]

Frank believed that the road of inner transformation was the path of the political realpolitik he had learned from Struve himself:

The spirit of "realpolitik" for which I am personally most indebted to you, which flows not out of outer tactical considerations, but from the religious-moral conviction of the organicity of all political processes—this spirit must find its actual trial right now. In Russia, of course, there are many people who have simply become embittered, or on the contrary have been corrupted and have drowned in the bog. But people of your spirit, living in Russia, have had to endure a *necessary* mixture of unconditional spiritual steadfastness and hatred for evil with an attentive, patient, careful relation to actuality, as an expression of the organic processes of the popular soul. I have to say about myself that dropping behind and perhaps even weakening in these years of deprivation—in the area of abstract academic creativity—I have for the first time in these years acquired a real spiritual maturity in the area of a whole, concrete attitude to life. And in this regard, I have felt myself to be a true expresser of *your spirit*, in which I now, if I am not mistaken, stand in opposition to you.[11]

Frank, then, declared that in this "concrete attitude to life" he and his colleagues such as Berdiaev were following in the footsteps of Struve and were thus the true apostles of the *Landmarks* tradition.

With this in mind, Frank was highly critical of the White movement's very attempt to overthrow the Bolsheviks by force. Their approach was the same as that of the revolutionaries they hated; they believed in the primacy of political over spiritual life, of the outer over the inner. Anti-Bolshevism might turn out to be as violent and cruel as the ideology it criticized. In addition, it represented a narrow constituency: "The practical political conclusion to which I came . . . was that the White movement, recruited to a significant degree from former representatives of the ruling classes, was from the start destined to failure." Frank believed that Struve's passionate opposition to the revolution was typical of the narrow intelligentsia mentality. Dominated by his hatred of the revolution, Struve had become a "revolutionary counter-revolutionary,"[12] and he warned him that "black bolshevism" would prove no better than its red variant.[13]

Frank regarded Bolshevism as a symptom and not a cause—an ideology reflecting something deeper, an "elemental Russian piggishness." Bolshevism was not so much alien to Russia as a disease that inevitably accompanied a spiritual crisis. To Struve he wrote: "[The process of the revolution is]—such is my deep conviction, which might seem to you the greatest heresy—an illness of the *growth and development* of the Russian people, something analagous to the phenomenon of spiritual collapse, perversion and crisis, which accompanies the movement from childhood to maturity in the individual organism."[14] In August 1923 he even suggested that Bolshevism had passed away: "[The Russia we return to] will not be a Bolshevik Russia, but in essence that no longer exists anyway: but it will be that new Russia, which in essence is already now, in many ways painful for us, but ontologically and nationally real."[15]

Struve, who had worked tirelessly for the White movement and had made every effort to form a united stance on the revolution in the Russian emigration, was not impressed by Frank's analysis. It seemed like "political indifferentism."[16] This talk of the spiritual reeducation of the nation seemed to him simply a recipe for inaction. Surely Bolshevism was damaging the Russian nation and was not just a symptom. Frank's attitude was an acceptance of the revolution, and in his view "fact-acceptance" (*faktopriatie*) was "historically the greatest evil in the world." A merciless battle should be fought against all evil, against "fact-acceptance" and "psychologism."[17] (Struve presumably meant the passivity brought on by blaming historical events on the psychology of a nation.) What was needed was a heroic struggle to overthrow "the socialist syphilis" that had got into the soul of the Russian nation: "It is now necessary to instil into the Russian soul an *heroic* consciousness, because in the end even the very best Russians are guilty of a weakness and flabbiness of soul. And insofar as 'realpolitik' suggests paths which are convenient for such weakness and flabbiness, then it is evil and an untruth."[18]

A central issue of the argument between the two men, then, lay in the area of political realism. Frank strongly believed that his position was the "realist" one. Evidently he believed it was not passive or cowardly; it was characterized by the ability to look at things as they really are, by the Goethean "objectivism" he owed to Struve himself. He vigorously defended the "fact-acceptance" to which Struve felt so hostile: "'Fact-acceptance' is principled *realism* . . . [which] flows out of a religious, i.e., concretely-moral relation to historical reality."[19]

A concrete example of Frank's "realism" came up in his attitude to the divisions within the Orthodox Church that appeared after 1917. Patriarch Tikhon had initially been hostile to the Soviet government but after the autumn of 1918 had changed his position to political neutrality. Frank approved of such an attempt to come to terms with the new political authorities. The very survival of the Orthodox Church depended on some kind of mutual agreement. He regarded Tikhon's "fact-acceptance" as a heroic deed analagous to the deed of Aleksandr Nevskii when to save Russia, he chose to bow down before the Horde. Tikhon was successfully saving Orthodoxy among the people and in his religious realism had turned out to be perhaps the only politician who had won back certain essential positions from the Bolsheviks.[20] Later he commented that Tikhon was right to steer the church away from a political position.[21] Struve saw the issue very differently. Without denying that Tikhon might have made the right tactical decision, he did not accept his actions as necessarily moral: "I am completely alien to rationalism and abstract idealism, but I am simply convinced of the objective power of truth and the 'heroic' principle which stands beyond it."[22]

Struve's idea of heroism was different from Frank's. It involved actively opposing evil. The Struves felt that the new arrivals were weak willed. Frank defended them vigorously. Berdiaev, he wrote, under the threat of being shot, had given lectures on the difference between religion and socialism in Moscow. Such people could not be accused of cowardice, but their heroism, based on a belief in spiritual renaissance, was not of the same revolutionary type.[23] Struve's reference to abstract idealism is important. In essence, Frank was accusing Struve of objectivizing good and evil, approaching it in such a way that different people, organizations, or movements could be identified as the representatives of good and evil in the world. The two men had differing understandings of evil. Frank did not believe that evil could ever be eliminated by force because it could never be identified with a specific social order. Struve believed that the world was in a deep crisis that Frank underestimated. The crisis was so immediate that it should be opposed with all the means available, even the use of "black bolshevism."[24]

The result of this was the maintenance of very different attitudes toward those whom they disagreed with. Frank differed strongly with Struve in his attitude to Eurasianism, an émigré intellectual trend that saw the revolution as part of the organic development of Russian history. It took the position that Russia, with its geography and its Asian and Byzantine heritage, had a distinct non-Western historical road. Writing in 1925 to one of the Eurasians, P. P. Suvchinskii, Frank said that while he could not suscribe to Eurasianism, he agreed with its political analysis. Indeed he regarded Eurasianism as the only original current of thought in the emigration.[25] He also published his *The Foundations of Marxism* and *Religion and Science* (1925) with the Eurasian Press in Berlin, although he was anxious not to be labeled a Eurasian. Frank's link with the Eurasians appalled Struve, who in a letter of 1927 accused him of "an absence of moral taste." Frank replied that he was not a Eurasian and never would be and that as a movement, it was ideologically and morally lightweight. Yet, he declared typically, you do not have to agree with someone to appreciate his work. Just as, not being a Kantian, he had published work in Kantian journals, so he had adopted a similar attitude to the Eurasians.[26]

Similarly, their concepts of history were different. Struve believed that the human will was primary. Struve published Frank's "Reflections on the Russian Revolution" in *Russian Thought* at the end of 1923 but wrote a criticism of it in which he said that their basic difference was in their "volitional relation to reality."[27] He wrote that "historical life is made up of the projects and designs of people, of the . . . results of their actions."[28] In this sense, Struve was suspicious of Frank's historical diagnosis because it took the individual out of the history-making process and resorted to vague concepts of "class" and "people." Frank also believed in the influence of the individual but did not wish to make this into a universal category. General historical forces also played a part.

Frank's "personless" view of history is quite curious. It undoubtedly fits his philosophy, but it is strangely abstract. It seems to be a concept typical of a philosopher for whom people are subject to invisible social or spiritual forces, and it carries a determinist coloring. Yet Frank was not a determinist and believed that individuals have a role in history. This tension between determinism and freedom in his thought was in fact the inevitable result of his philosophy of total-unity. As ever, the individual could easily get submerged in the absolute.[29]

The differences between the two men were in a way as much of temperament as of substance. Frank observed that Struve had an active moral nature while he liked to be an observer—"according to the Spinozistic principle 'not to cry, laugh, hate, but to understand'—first of all to objectively orientate oneself in what has happened, to understand the general sociological nature . . . and historical meaning of the revolution."[30] This amounted to the difference between a political and a spiritual outlook.[31]

Frank tried hard to smooth over the differences with Struve. He felt that their objectives were the same, although their approaches to them were different, and he concluded that the division was a result of different experiences. He wrote to Struve to say that through meeting the White youth in Berlin, he had come "intuitively" to understand his experience. He stated that their political disagreement was not a difference of conviction but of evaluation. With time and a return to their own country, their differences would pass away.[32] In reply to that, Struve pertinently objected: "Each of us himself *chose* and created his own experience."[33]

Frank's efforts at a reconciliation were not initially successful. The differences surfaced again over the newspaper *Renaissance* (*Vozrozhdenie*), which was founded in 1925 by the Russian businessman A. O. Gusakov and backed by Grand Duke Nikolai Nikolaevich, the imperial representative abroad, and A. P. Kutepov, General Wrangel's former right-hand man. Struve was the editor from 1925 until he was dismissed in August 1927. Frank refused to participate in the paper because he felt it represented the emigration rather than a movement in Russia itself, and he described it as "pure spiritual barbarianism," full of the "false fanaticism of revolutionism." He felt that Struve was a much greater figure than his assistants, whom as a group he described as "block-heads and bourbons." His affection for Struve remained unaffected: "In my personal relations to him love for his personality overcomes my disgust for what he is doing."[34]

Frank remained generally concerned for Struve's health and well-being. For example, in a letter to El'iashevich in 1928, he suggested that money should be raised to help him as he was then living in very poor conditions in Belgrade.[35]

With time, the dispute began to dim. Frank believed that hindsight had proved his views right.[36] Nevertheless Struve's comments about his views were also very perceptive. By the end of the decade, they were in frequent correspondence. Frank contributed a number of articles to Struve's new paper, *Russia and Slavdom* (*Rossiia i slav'ianstvo*). In the spring of 1930 Struve arranged for Frank to stay with him in Belgrade and to read a two-month course of lectures at the Belgrade Russian Scientific Institute. At that time Frank wrote "Beyond Right and Left," an essay in which he argued that with the similarities between fascism and communism, the old terms "Right" and "Left" were now dated. Struve said that he agreed but commented that it was still a typical "intelligentsia" approach in that it was "an opinion divorced from real political life." In the spring of 1931 and the summer of 1932 Struve stayed with the Franks in Berlin. By this time, their friendship was almost as it had been before the revolution. On the first occasion, Struve even introduced Frank to an old pupil of his, V. F. Hoeffding, with the idea that Frank might counterbalance the extreme right-wing influences that were preying on him. Implicitly, Struve accepted if not the correctness of Frank's political judgments at least his moral evaluation of some of the extreme figures of the right-wing emigration.[37]

As he had written to Nina Struve, Frank initially regarded his work on social philosophy as his main task in emigration. The foundations for his maturing social philosophy were built in 1925 when he published two essays, "I and We" and "The Religious Foundations of Community." In 1927 Frank wrote to Struve: "I am living in complete loneliness, and am engrossed in writing a large academic work on social philosophy, in German. It is the one serious thing which remains for me here."[38] In spite of the reference to German, this work, *The Spiritual Foundations of Society*, was published in Russian by YMCA Press in 1930.

The reasons for Frank's interest in this subject were various. In part, he wanted to continue and complete the philosophical system he had begun to develop in *The Object of Knowledge*. However, he also felt that the assumptions of modern social and political thought needed revision. The interwar world was characterized in his view by a crisis of belief. Some, it was true, continued to believe in Christianity, or science, or man, but very few people retained a faith that touched on all aspects of a person's life and offered a clear distinction between good and evil. The faith of the modern era had been socialism, but after the events of the Russian revolution, that was no longer credible. If there was any other typical worldview, it was historical relativism, and if that was taken to its logical conclusion, it led in its denial of absolute principles to nihilism. The modern world had no beliefs of its own, only a belief in the relativity of all other beliefs.[39]

The answer, as one would expect from Frank, was to rethink the foundations. He criticized modern philosophy for its lack of the classical idea that the world is a living cosmos, operating as a united order.[40] His interest was to understand and explain that order. It was an order that he found in the Bible in the idea that the word of God is not something to be searched for in the heavens but is already implanted in the heart of man and in thinkers like Heraclitus, who declared that "all human laws are fed by one divine law."[41] In *The Spiritual Foundations of Society*, Frank quoted a statement from Thomas Carlyle that even if the majority are in favor of it, a ship will not get around Cape Horn if a storm prevents it. The democratic majority is powerless in the face of the natural forces of the world: "To prosper in this world . . . there is but one thing requisite—that [a] man or nation can discern what the true regulations of the universe are in regard to him and his pursuit, and can faithfully and steadfastly follow these."[42]

Frank's thought is intricately tied to such a worldview. For example, in his social philosophy he does not offer his reader a choice between Christian and secular approaches to social life. He says that the origins of social life are necessarily religious. It is in man's nature to serve God. He cannot avoid doing it, and moral ideals of any form are a by-product of that service and reflect its depth. And in the political sphere acceptance of state power and adherence to the law are in some way imitations of the supreme service that should be offered to God."[43]

In this very broad sense Frank believed that all societies are necessarily theocratic.[44] And history itself is the story of man's relationship with God: "The history of society, as the history of spiritual life, is the dramatic fate of God in the heart of man,"[45] or as he came to express it after the Second World War, "[It] is the Godmanhood process."[46] History reflects the struggle that goes on in every human heart between God and the world, between the inner spiritual home and the outer, material life. Each individual chooses. As Frank says, "The dividing line between the divine and the human, between the church and the world passes only through the depths of the human heart."[47]

Frank's social philosophy comes out in his understanding of the true nature of democracy. In his writing in general Frank used three concepts of democracy. The first was one he associated with Western liberalism. He welcomed the "young democracy" introduced by the 1905 revolution,[48] and associated it at the time with a range of liberal principles. Early in emigration he wrote of the "democratic Europe" built on "universal franchise . . . parliaments and governments."[49]

The second appeared in the form of an elemental mass movement; this was the "materialist" democracy that Frank warned of in 1917. Thus he read the Bolshevik revolution as a combination of "atheistic revolutionary radicalism" and "democratization,"[50] using the latter word to mean the releasing of a popular movement—in the Russian case, a popular peasant revolution. "Democracy in this sense," he wrote, "should not be understood as some *form of government* or *state organization.* . . . The Russian revolution is a democratic movement of the popular masses, led by a vague, essentially politically unformulated, more psychological ideal of arbitrary rule and independence."[51]

The third type of democracy, which Frank also began to formulate in 1917, was well expressed in *From the Depths* and is best termed "spiritual" or "Christian democracy." It was the kind of democracy Frank believed would be the real answer to Bolshevism; it would be part of what he later called the task of "[saving] the very *idea* of democracy."[52] In *From the Depths*, he had called for "a spiritually wise and enlightened *fortitude* [*muzhestvo*]." This would be "a creative fortitude, founded on a humble consciousness of one's dependence on higher powers, and rootedness in them." It involved a form of spiritual chivalry. Frank lamented the lack in Russian culture of "the spirit of religiously-enlightened activity, the spirit of true knighthood [*rytsar-stvo*]." He associated this democratic culture with the Slavophile dream of the organic development of culture out of national traditions, the same idea that Dostoevskii had defined in the concept of *pochvennost'*.[53] When the popular will grows out of its spiritual foundations, it results in "the establishment of the genuine ideal of *democracy*": "[This ideal democracy sees] the political activity both of individuals and the whole nation not as some arbitrary gamble guided by the transient needs of the moment . . . , but as humble service defined by faith in the intransient meaning of national culture and the duty of each to generally guard the legacy of one's ancestors, to enrich it and then transfer it to those who follow."[54]

Frank's concept of service goes back to his theoretical philosophy and his understanding of the link between man's soul and God. In *Man's Soul,* he argued that there are sides to human need that express sacred obligations, and he outlined this in terms that suggest a profound personal experience of the subject:

> In the life of every man there are moments when all the serviceable and derivative goals, values and strivings of his life are apprehended precisely in all their relativity . . . and are blocked by the consciousness of the fundamental essence or striving of his "I," which he is then conscious of as precisely something absolute. The most common example is the profound erotic passion which grasps the very essence of a man: then he is immediately conscious that, without unification with the loved one or, in general, without some consummation or other of the passion— his life loses its meaning; he is conscious, in other words, that in this passion he is dealing with not some subjective need or other but with the very essence of his "I." And this "I" itself is for us not a particular, relative reality but a being of an absolute order, whose demands are sacred, and which we as purely empirical beings must serve. All the tragedies in the world that have ever been experienced or described are genuine tragedies only insofar as they are reducible to the struggle, perils, hopes, and failures of this absolute essence of our "I."[55]

Frank's concept of democracy is tightly tied to his idea of service. In "I and We" and *The Spiritual Foundations of Society*, he outlined the foundation for his social philosophy. The primary categories of social life, he wrote, are the "I" and "We," both of which are inconceivable without the other but in turn are dependent on a higher uniting principle. This higher principle is God. The individual and the community are rooted in God and find their rightful identity in his service: "Since the principle 'We' is not more primordial than the principle 'I' but is correlative to the latter, this conflict [between the two principles] cannot find higher resolution within the conflicting principles themselves. *Stable harmony and reconciliation can be found only through the groundedness of both principles in a higher principle: the service of God, absolute truth.* Thus, the ultimate source of social unity lies in the principle of service, in the groundedness of the social unity in holiness."[56] Not only is God thus the uniting factor in society, but he is the condition of self-realization: "The genuine 'I,' like the genuine 'We,' and at the same time their genuine dual-unity, is only realizable where *'I' give myself* and *'We' give ourselves* to the higher principle—God."[57]

Frank's view of society as rooted in God was also hierarchical. He believed that all are morally equal before God but that all have different gifts. This means that everyone has a different role to play and that there are some people who are born to be leaders. Democracy, as founded on the principle of equality, has as its genuine foundation the common aristocratic character of all people as sons and free co-workers with God. This aristocratic principle of democracy demands as a counterbalance the aristocratic principle of inequality and hierarchy, the natural distribution of people into a higher and a lower order according to the level of their intellectual, moral, and spiritual perfection.[58] Frank's idea is very close to that of St. Paul: all people are part of the body of Christ, although everyone has a different role to play.[59]

These concepts of democracy must be understood in terms of what Frank called "the genuine ideal of democracy." Since as he saw it everyone is a child of God having a divine and distinct calling, true democracy will exist only when the universal free service of God becomes a reality. At one point he called this a free theocracy: "The rebirth of life can only happen through a theocracy, the leadership of God, not in the normal sense of the enforced rule of the priests, but in the sense of a free theocracy, of the free and peaceful cooperation of all the potential of the human spirit in the construction of a God-filled life."[60] He believed that such a perfect democracy or theocracy was unrealizable in this world, so there were no utopian implications in his vision. However, the value of his ideas was in explaining more clearly the link he always made between the inner and the outer layers of social life. In *The Spiritual Foundations of Society*, Frank offered two forms of communality: *sobornost'*, the inner spiritual unity of a society or social group, and *obshchestvennost'*, its outer social manifestation.[61] *Obshchestvennost'* depends on the quality of *sobornost'*, which in turn depends on the quality of free service offered to God. Paraphrasing this, it means that the outer social life of a country depends on the spiritual life of its individual members and the community as a whole, or that the social sphere is dependent on the spiritual democracy of the nation.

Since Frank believed that the idea of service is fundamental to human nature, he used it to explain freedom. Since man is not living in a pluralist universe, the idea of freedom cannot be defined in a purely liberal context. This means that human rights must be defined not as the right to express one's own opinion but as the right to serve truth. Freedom is thus made dependent on the right to serve:

> The individualistic idea that the individual has a right to a definite, strictly fixed, inviolable area of freedom . . . an idea that is based on the false notion of the "innate" rights of man, must be rejected as incompatible with the supreme principle of *service*, which can alone justify the idea of individual freedom. In practice, not even the most liberal and democratic society in the world knows and actually allows such unshakeably fixed individual rights. In periods of social emergency, these rights are inevitably curtailed. . . . The very interests of general freedom, of free social construction, often require restrictions on individual human "rights," which are always relative and derivative, for they are only a secondary manifestation and means for the realization of the *principle of service* and the associated principles of solidarity and freedom.[62]

In Frank's view, there are two elements in society that must be balanced: the "We" and the "I," the community and the individual, tradition and freedom, the past and the future. The best political systems are those that incorporate both elements, of which he regarded the constitutional monarchies as perhaps the best. However, he also felt that a republic could provide the same sense of continuity and that "universal suffrage gives greater assurance than election by parliament or national assembly" of that tradition. This was due to the fact that historical principles are "more firmly rooted in the masses of the people than in the consciousness and will of party leaders."[63] Although he believed in the hierarchical structure of the world, he also felt that all state institutions should be open to the public and that people should freely find their places in society.

In addition, Frank believed that access to and the right to property is "the condition of realization of the principle of freedom" without which social life is inconceivable. Denunciations of the right to property do not take into account that man is a corporeal being: "In its immanent, inner essence, private property is the necessary *extension* of the human *body*, as the organ of spiritual activity." Man can only be free if he has an "intimate connection with a specific part of the material world."[64] Frank's committment to private property was thus very strong.

As ever, Frank wished to avoid universal prescriptions for political illnesses. Every situation must be judged on its merits, using the necessary realism. Politics is like medical treatment: "Even as a doctor determines necessary therapeutic measures not only on the basis of general laws of physiology and pathology, but also in relation to the state of the organism of the given patient, . . . so the politician is guided [to apply] the principles of social life to the given state and needs of society."[65]

Frank offered his reader the "organization of freedom."[66] It involved a balance between respect for the interests of the state and awareness of its spiritual foundations coupled with a belief in the sanctity of the individual. Frank offered a conservative view of the world but often suggested a liberal political system. The context was conservative, the content liberal. According to Frank, his thinking mirrored Struve's "liberal conservatism" or "conservative liberalism."[67] It was a combination of principles he also saw in Pushkin and described in a famous essay, "Pushkin as a Political Thinker," which he wrote in 1937: "The political worldview of Pushkin is *conservatism* . . . injected with liberal principles."[68] Frank's purpose was to redefine freedom in a conservative context. "In practice, liberalism . . . contains a considerable amount of truth. But this truth usually receives an incorrect philosophical explanation."[69]

It must be said, however, that Frank was emotionally against traditional "liberal" language. The conservative element in his thought often outweighed the liberal, at least in the theory. Perhaps the best description of his political ideas is "spiritually free conservatism": "True, ontologically grounded politics is essentially always the politics of *spiritually free conservatism*, not stifled by prejudices and dead habits . . . is always the politics of innovation which draws its creative forces from reverent respect for the living content of the spiritual life of the past."[70]

Frank's conservative instincts continued into the Second World War. In his meditation *God with Us*, written in 1941, Frank declared that "great statesmen, genuine masters of life, people like Cromwell, Napoleon, Bismarck, were always also religiously wise people."[71] Frank did not explain what aspects of the religious life of these men he most valued, but his choice of leaders reflects his admiration for great and heroic individuals in history. He had a similar enthusiasm for Churchill. Taken as a group, these men were autocratic; their genius was for leadership from above. When the issue of Indian independence came up in the late 1940s, Frank felt that it was too soon for independence and said that as soon as the British left, the Indians would start to kill one another.[72] It was the same instinct at work.

Frank's desire to put human freedoms in a religious framework also had an historical aspect. In his essay "The Religious-Historical Meaning of the Russian Revolution," Frank expanded on an argument he had used in *From the Depths* to lament not only the decline of spiritual values in Russia but the secularization of European culture that had proceeded from the Renaissance. The Middle Ages, he argued, had preached love without freedom, and the Renaissance, in reaction, had emphasized freedom and individuality, but without the original religious context. The European idea of freedom was thus "identified with rebellion." The liberalism and democracy that stood at the end of this process had basically lost touch with the spiritual foundations of European life and were based on an "empty humanistic belief in man in general."[73] Russia was tied to this historical process and had suffered by embracing the secular aspects of European society without appreciating their religious roots. Frank, then, was continuing to write in the tradition of *Landmarks*, calling for a religious, Christian humanism.

13

Lonely Years

FRANK WAS ALWAYS a private person and was never surrounded by friends. His son Vasilii heard him use the "ty" form of address only to three people: Struve, El'iashevich, and O. E. Buzhanskii, an old student friend who in the emigration lived for a time in Berlin and then left for Paris.[1] Life in Berlin involved an increasing sense of loneliness and isolation. The dispute with Struve deprived Frank of his closest friend, and even when their relationship returned to normal, they lived in different parts of Europe.

Frank and Berdiaev remained in close contact even after the latter's move to Paris. In February 1926 Frank visited Paris and wrote back to Tatiana that he had had a wonderful visit with him, that "Berdiaev had poured out his whole soul to me."[2] Berdiaev tried to help Frank financially through his contacts in Paris and took a keen interest in all he was doing. In turn, Frank was a regular contributor to Berdiaev's religious journal *The Way* (*Put'*), which was a major outlet for religious philosophy in the emigration. In spite of this, the two men were never really close. In 1922 Frank wrote to Nina Struve: "Over the last year, I have become ideologically close to Berdiaev, but in relations with him there is an inevitable personal coldness, although he is very sweet, sympathetic and warm-hearted."[3]

Frank was never close to Berdiaev or Bulgakov, who established himself as a controversial and influential theologian in Paris. In 1945 Frank wrote: "[With Berdiaev and Bulgakov] I have been friends almost half a century, admitting their talent . . . but I have always considered their thoughts rather as certain "absurd ideas," than as truth; these thoughts . . . did not help me. So, for example, I never could understand the meaning of Bulgakov's sophiology; and the ideas of Berdiaev which made him famous throughout Europe, for example on social and political issues, and generally his 'rebellion,' seem to me in their naivity and vagueness almost the thoughts of a schoolboy; I do

Semyon Frank as a baby, with his mother, Rozaliia Moiseevna Frank.

Frank and his sister Sofia: later Sofia Zhivotovskaia.

Frank's father, Liudvig Semyonovich Frank.

Frank's maternal grandfather, Moisei Mironovich Rossiianskii.

*Frank as a pupil at the
Lazarevskii Institute
of Oriental languages.*

*Frank, 1898, while a student at
Moscow University.*

The Frank/Zak family, around 1898, from left to right: Semyon Frank, Sofia Zhivotovskaia, Abram Zhivotoskii, Lev Zak, Vasilii Zak, Sara Rossiianskaia, Mikhail Frank, Rozaliia Frank.

*The young Tatiana
Sergeevna Bartseva.*

Tatiana as a young woman.

Semyon and Tatiana Frank on their honeymoon, Grefenburg, Austria,
summer 1908.

Tatiana, Aleksei, Semyon, Viktor, 1911.

The Frank family in Berlin: Natalia, Aleksei, Tatiana, Vasilii, Semyon, Viktor.

The children in Berlin: Aleksei, Vasilii, Natalia, Viktor.

Semyon and Tatiana Frank.

P. B. Struve.

Lev Karsavin.

The Russian Scientific Institute in Berlin, 1923–24, from left to right; starting with Frank (front, fourth from left): Frank, Iasinskii, Berdiaev, Aikhenval'd, Prokopovich, Karsavin.

St. Serge Theological Institute, Paris. Frank front, fourth from left.

*Frank and Struve, during
their last meeting at
Bussy-en-Othe, 1938.*

*Semyon and Tatiana Frank,
during the Second World War.*

Frank, as painted by Lev Zak.

A drawing of Frank, done a few weeks before his death in 1950, by Lev Zak.

Frank, Grenoble, 1945.

not feel any maturity or responsibility in them—which does not prevent me from accepting that he has a very talented and lively mind."[4]

Izgoev, the other colleague from *Landmarks*, with whom Frank had worked closely on *Russian Thought* and probably had more in common, left Berlin to take up a teaching post in the Baltic. Another colleague at the academy was Karsavin, one of the leading thinkers of Eurasianism, whom Frank admired very much. "Karsavin," Frank wrote, "in spite of his cynicism and love of boasting, is essentially a very remarkable person."[5] However, in their relationship there was also a difference of temperament. Karsavin was a man of provocative opinions. On one occasion in late 1924 there was a meeting of the Religious-Philosophical Academy in Berlin at which Karsavin made a number of insinuations about the newly opened Religious Academy in Paris.[6] This was not Frank's style. Karsavin moved to Lithuania in 1928, where he became a professor at the University of Kaunas, and eventually perished in the Gulag.

Aikhenval'd was one of Frank's closest friends in Berlin. Also of Jewish background, he was not overtly religious, saying that "God did not give [me] the gift of belief."[7] Frank admired him greatly and called him "a knight of the Holy Spirit."[8] Frank fainted with shock when he heard that he had been run over and killed by a tram in December 1928, and in a letter to Berdiaev he wrote of the great loneliness he felt in Berlin after his death.[9]

The atmosphere in Berlin accentuated the loneliness. Frank commented to Berdiaev that there were only two groups left in Berlin: the extreme Right, Black-Hundreds, and the left-wing Jewish Masonic circles. He did not meet the former and did not like the latter. Nor, it seems, did the latter like him. In the two obituaries he wrote on Aikhenval'd, he referred to his religious nature, and this caused them great annoyance: "They have started to persecute me, accusing me of calling Aikhenval'd a man with a Christian soul and even accusing me of wilfully burying him in an Orthodox cemetery (!) and forcing Jews to go to an Orthodox requiem. It's rather amusing, but you cannot say that it is fun to live in this kind of atmosphere."[10]

The atmosphere of bitter division that characterized the emigration was wholly alien to Frank. By nature, he had a considerable gift to get on with people he disagreed with. On one occasion years before he had written to Gershenzon that although disagreeing with all his ideas, he sensed the goodness of his motivations and appreciated him for it.[11] It was typical of Frank that he was able to distinguish a person's ideas from the person. This was not a characteristic typical of the Russian intelligentsia. Struve had bitter disputes with people and was eventually to have such a strong rift with Berdiaev that in later years in Paris he would cross the street to avoid meeting him.[12] Berdiaev had a similar fiery nature, so that one commentator stated that "throughout his life, he seemed almost to feel that losing an argument was putting himself in bondage to his opponent."[13]

The factional atmosphere cut straight across Frank's life at the Russian Scientific Institute. He wrote to Berdiaev in 1925: "I am suffering in a vise—between the stupidity of the frenzied right-wing elements and the stupidity of Iasinskii. I live only on the dream of possibly finding some kind of German work, which would deliver [me] from participating in age-old Russian affairs."[14] He said he felt himself sandwiched between the right-wing groups that were "morally extremely unclean" and the left-wing elements he found "spiritually very alien."[15]

The atmosphere did not contribute to the hoped-for religious renaissance in the emigration. In 1923 Frank noted that in Berlin "no one has any belief." At the end of 1924 Frank wrote that "the moral corruption of the emigration has gone forward at great pace and has captured those circles which were until recently foreign to it." Obviously Frank had hoped the academy would offer an antidote to such a moral collapse: "[In regard to the academy,] we are doing everything possible, but with the absence of Russian people in Berlin, the poverty, the abundance of intrigues, it is impossible to gather together a lot of money."[16]

The youth work suffered, and the circles Frank and Berdiaev had been responsible for came under the influence of the increasingly right-wing atmosphere. The likelihood is that on a purely intellectual level the Berlin students were not very good. Berdiaev commented that at the academy "the standard of intellectual interest and culture among the young people was on the whole rather low. The majority were mainly preoccupied either with ways and means of overthrowing Bolshevism and with the White movement or with stuffy, ritualistic piety."[17] While on a visit to Prague with the Russian Academic Union in September 1924, Frank wrote back to Tatiana: "I have bumped into some such wonderful young Orthodox people here who are completely different from those in Berlin. . . . I felt with emotion that Russia is alive and will live."[18] He wrote to Berdiaev in 1925: "Even religious thought develops in Russia in a healthier and more fruitful way than with us in emigration. . . . In Moscow we had immeasurably greater influence than here. In the youth, there are spiritually-healthy elements, but they are terribly primitive."[19] In 1925, after Berdiaev had moved to Paris, Frank wrote to him, "Our influence on the young people, judging by real results, is nil, but of course don't tell that to Kullman and the Americans."[20] The influence of the Russian Student Christian Movement also declined, especially in its activities in Berlin and Germany. By the end of the 1920s, according to Frank, the young people had lost interest in spiritual things, and the organization began to focus on scouting, sports, camping, and singing.[21]

The disillusionment was increased by the growing sense of permanence exhibited by the Soviet regime. "The everlasting belief in return"[22] began to fade. Frank, like many of his friends, had believed that emigration was temporary. He wrote to Struve in January 1924 that he thought they would return to Russia in two years.[23] He addressed the Russian Academic Union in September 1926 in the context of "when we return to Russia."[24] By the end of the 1920s, the illusions had given way to a more realistic assessment. The heroic days had passed.[25]

One of Frank's colleagues at the institute was I. A. Il'in, who had also been exiled in 1922 but in the discussions with Struve had been very supportive of the White movement, contributed to *Renaissance*, and generally associated with right-wing groups in emigration. In 1926 Il'in published *On Resistance to Evil with Force*, in which he argued that although violence was never an attractive political option, there were extreme occasions when it might prove necessary. The book caused considerable controversy in émigré circles. Struve was highly supportive of the thesis; Berdiaev opposed it. Others took different sides: Losskii came down in favor of Il'in; Aikhenval'd, Stepun, and Zen'kovskii against him. Although Frank did not actively participate in the debate, he sided with the latter group.[26] Frank had a low opinion of Il'in. He thought that he was morally corrupt and at the end of the 1920s suggested that he had compromised himself with German right-wing circles.[27]

Il'in's supporters in this dispute included Metropolitan Khrapovitskii, who was head of the Russian Orthodox Church Abroad, and Bishop Tikhon of Berlin. After the revolution, two sources of authority appeared in the Russian Orthodox Church: the Moscow Patriarchate, increasingly under Soviet control, and the Bishops' Synod at Sremski Karlovci in Serbia, which had a right-wing imperial leaning. The Bishops' Synod appointed the former archbishop of Volhynia, Evlogii, to head the Russian church in Western Europe, with headquarters in Berlin. However, the Moscow Patriarchate then appointed Evlogii to be its metropolitan of the Russian church in Western Europe. This was initially accepted by the Bishops' Synod, but then the synod took an openly monarchist position, and the Moscow Patriarchate ordered its followers to renounce political utterances in the name of the church. Metropolitan Evlogii accepted the order and consequently came into conflict with the Bishops' Synod. The result was a split in the Russian Orthodox Church.

Frank found himself at the center of these disputes in Berlin, where the Bishops' Synod appointed Bishop Tikhon to be its representative. Frank had a very low opinion of Bishop Tikhon and felt that the Bishops' Synod mixed up its political and religious aspirations.[28] Tikhon refused to be subject to Metropolitan Evlogii and was banned from taking services. Of the twelve members of the local parish council in Berlin, eight came out in favor of Evlogii, including Frank, as did the majority of parishioners. There was a fractious debate on the issue at the Russian Academic Union in September 1926. Frank spoke and declared that Evlogii, appointed from Moscow, had the canonical right of leadership.[29]

However, the atmosphere was very unpleasant, and division was caused in both families and the community. The church was the center of Russian social life in emigration. In a letter to his old friend Prince G. N. Trubetskoi, Frank lamented that of the followers of the position of Metropolitan Evlogii only two or three were motivated by belief in his cause; the rest were simply Tikhon's personal enemies: "The division therefore carries the character of a disgusting émigré squabble." The principled supporters, he wrote, "are very alone." Although, unlike Tatiana, Frank was probably never a strict churchgoer, he had become seriously involved in church matters. However, through this dispute he became disillusioned with church politics and within a few years discontinued his involvement. In 1929 he wrote: "I have already long ago stopped taking an active part in church matters relating to the division, basically because I came to believe in their complete hopelessness and in the impossibility, in the given psychological circumstances, to contribute to a rational and worthy resolution of them."[30]

Frank believed that Metropolitan Evlogii was canonically in the right. A compromise in practical affairs between the factions was, he believed, not out of the question. However, in spiritual affairs "there is a church *truth*," which could not be altered. Evlogii's position was something that could not be changed.[31] Frank thought that the Moscow Patriarchate was the canonical church and should not be abandoned in its hour of greatest need. This came out most obviously in his attitude to the successor to Patriarch Tikhon, Metropolitan Sergius Stragorodskii. In 1927 the Soviet government abolished the post of the Moscow patriarch. Metropolitan Sergius, who became the acting head of the church, abandoned the apolitical stance of Tikhon in favor of a position of loyalty to the Soviet government in political affairs. Initially, Evlogii managed to come to some compromise with this position, but in 1931 he felt compelled to transfer his loyalties to the jurisdiction of the Patriarch of Constantinople. A small group fo clergy and believers refused to accept this and decided to remain loyal to Moscow.

Frank, along with Berdiaev, belonged to this group. In a lecture he gave at the beginning of the 1930s, Frank, pointing out that Metropolitan Sergius was not a free man, expressed sympathy with his attempts at agreement with the Soviet authorities. No one, he wrote, should attempt to judge him on a personal moral level because only God could make such judgments. Frank pointed out the complexity of the situation facing Sergius and commented that he and his fellow bishops, while bringing upon themselves the "martyrdom of shame" at the apparent moral weakness of their actions, had nevertheless kept the church open for thousands of believers and had indeed presided over a deepening of church life in the face of the persecutions of the Soviet government. The church, Frank wrote, would never sit easily under the Soviet system. The decisions it had made should not be condemned out of hand. "One must oneself stand," he wrote, "in a responsible position within the hell of the Soviet state, take responsibility for the fate of the church, thousands of its servants and millions of its believers, in order to be in the position to pass judgement on it."[32]

Yet another area where divisions appeared in the emigration related to the YMCA. The idea of fostering a religious renaissance among young people soon proved illusory. Not only was the harvest of souls not very great, but it turned out that different people had different aims. One of Paul Anderson's representatives in Berlin was a Methodist, E. MacNaughton. MacNaughton did not approve of the Russian Orthodox focus of the Russian Student Christian Movement (RSKhD) and wanted it to become more interdenominational and part of a broader YMCA strategy.[33] According to Frank, he wanted to turn it into a typical American youth organization. This caused considerable tension. Although he was not directly concerned by these things, Frank was involved in both YMCA and RSKhD operations in Berlin and found the situation extremely difficult. On behalf of Pianov, Frank wrote to Berdiaev: "Somehow have a word with Anderson and MacNaughton. . . . The YMCA can only operate among Russians if it relies and trusts the 'Movement,' and it will inevitably collapse if it tries to act independently and with American methods."[34]

From the beginning, the growing tensions in German society made life difficult for the Franks. This manifested itself in the children's education. In the autumn of 1923, Natalia entered a German school and befriended two foreign girls. They quarreled with some German girls, who complained to the headmaster. He then came into the class, called the three girls in front of the class, and said that they were living in

Germany at the expense of the native population, whom they had also offended. The German girls shouted their agreement, and Natalia burst into tears and went home. On the advice of a friend in the Ministry of Culture, she was transferred to a Roman Catholic School.[35]

Viktor, who of all the children most took after his father, also went to a German gymnasium. He was hit in the face by a teacher. It was a common thing in Germany, but for Russian children, it was a terrible insult. Viktor left the school. On visiting the headmaster, Frank suggested that it would be very bad for a pupil's character to accept a slap on the face in a submissive way.[36]

In spite of such incidents, Frank became angry with the children if they insulted Germany. Natalia, in her German book, replaced *"über"* with *"unter"* in the German national anthem, and he was very annoyed with her. He said that whatever country you live in, you have to respect it and its national anthem.[37]

The main difficulties in bringing up the children, however, related to Aleksei. He refused to go to a German school and at Frank's insistence was thrown out of his Russian one. He went to ballet school. When he started dancing, the family had to go and meet him when he received his pay packet to prevent him inviting all his friends to a restaurant to get drunk. On one occasion he and a friend were arrested after they broke the glass of a shop on the Korfürstendam to steal the photograph of a ballerina with whom they were in love. It was all over the newspapers. Aleksei would get into serious depressions and twice tried to commit suicide, on one occasion with Frank's sleeping pills. Once he tried to escape to America and got as far as Hamburg before he was found by the police. Even Frank, who was very rarely cross, became annoyed with Aleksei, and would raise his voice to tell him that he had no sense of responsibility. Frank, very much the philosopher and intellectual, had difficulty relating to Aleksei, whose mentality was so different. Naturally, he and Tatiana were upset by the suicide attempts and realized that they would have to treat him in a different way. At the end of the 1920s he joined a ballet company and eventually left Germany.[38]

Apart from Viktor, who eventually became a well-known writer and journalist in his own right, none of the children had great promise academically. Tatiana was fond of paraphrasing Sofia Tolstoi, saying that nature tried so hard over Semyon Liudvigovich that it was having a rest with the children. Nevertheless, with the other children, Frank enjoyed bringing philosophy down to a childish level. He would go off to the park to philosophize with Natalia and come into her bedroom and read her poetry. They would sometimes go to museums, where he loved to look at antique sculpture. When Vasilii was about 6, they had philosophical talks with each other. Frank would say, "What am I; why am I 'I' and not someone else?" They had a game with two spoons, which they would lick, exchange, lick again, and then become each other.[39]

When he was in his teens, Vasilii would go off drinking with his friends. Although Frank was not very enthusiastic about it, he did not try to prevent it. He suggested that he keep a diary and in his personal advice to him said that he should be faithful to himself and not do things that were against his nature.[40] As moral advice, it clearly fitted his own experience.

Frank was a private person, and the milieu he lived in was his family. Until the Second World War, even a radio was regarded as an invasion of privacy. Tatiana was Frank's greatest inspiration and support. She took on all the organization and material worry of the household, so that there was a joke that she was the only Jew in the whole family.[41] She was also possessive and moody and had the habit of ignoring her children when there were differences of opinion. Frank adored and idolized her. The letters he wrote her whenever he was away on lecture tours were full of tenderness and gratitude. He wrote, "You are my only friend"[42] and would frequently comment that their marriage had been ordained by Providence. Writing for their twentieth wedding anniversary, he declared: "Not only do I love you much more deeply that 20 years ago, I simply religiously bow down before you. And if marriage has a mystical meaning, and we will answer there in heaven together, then I believe that your love and active goodness will expiate my hard-heartedness and all my sins."[43] The hard-heartedness he referred to relates to a sense of inadequacy he always felt in regard to doing things actively for other people. In later years he regretted that he had not done more concretely to help others. Tatiana was the one who would raise money for other Russian families in difficulty and do charitable works.

Frank had a deeply religious view of marriage. His words "I simply religiously bow down before you" were no accident. True love, he believed, involved seeing the divine element in the other person. In his confessional work written in 1941, *God with Us*, he wrote that erotic love ends in disappointment and even hatred unless its focus becomes not the appearance of the beloved but "the absolute value of the beloved's personality as such": "True marriage is a path to such religious transfiguration of erotic love, and it may be said that the sacrament of marriage consists precisely in this mysterious 'divinely-human' process of transfiguration."[44]

With the help of Tatiana, Frank was able to establish a certain routine, a schedule he kept throughout his life. He would work from

9 A.M. to 2 P.M. and then have lunch. He always slept in the afternoon, sometimes for two hours. This was partly because he suffered badly from insomnia. When he did sleep, he had to have complete darkness in the room, so that whenever they moved into a new flat, Tatiana would install heavy curtains. Sometimes he would put a mask over his eyes. Tea was a traditional time of day when the family would gather around the table and often eat something sweet. After tea, Frank would sit down and play the piano. His favourite composers included Beethoven, Schubert, Mozart, and Tchaikovsky. They crossed themselves before meals. Although he smoked heavily, Frank almost never drank and said that once, when he was a student, he had tried some champagne and had pains in his shoulders.

Frank's absorption in his thoughts sometimes made him oblivious to the world around him. He could do practical things, but he did not wish to overburden his mind, so he would say to Tatiana, "Go and get angry with the children."[45] He was very short-sighted and wore spectacles, and he always wore a suit, waistcoat, and a tie.

Both had problems with their health. Tatiana seems to have been prey to bouts of extreme anxiety, about which he once wrote her: "I know your dispositions to psychic imbalance, and I do not wish to preach at you that you need to fight against them, but I only wish to say that it is a cross that it is necessary to carry, like any other, not falling into despair."[46] During the summers Frank would rest in the country and read lighter books; for example, he liked the novels of D. H. Lawrence and Charles Morgan. During the summer of 1929, he suffered from a kind of nervous depression and talked to himself, almost to the point of hallucinating. Tatiana arranged for him to go to a sanatorium in Badenweitcr to recover, and he was very much helped by a psychiatrist who, in Frank's words, "almost rocked [me] to sleep like a good nanny."[47] His lack of strength culminated in some heart problems in early 1936 that laid him up for a number of weeks. The local Russian doctor treated him without charge.

Frank was unquestionably homesick. News from Russia was bleak. He was very upset at the arrest and death of his old friend from Saratov L. N. Iurovskii. Iurovskii had decided to stay in Russia in 1922 and became a prominent economist in the Ministry of Finance. He was allowed to travel abroad and stayed with the Franks on one occasion. He was arrested in the early 1930s, accused of liaising with counter-revolutionaries in the West, and eventually perished. During the Ukrainian famine, Tatiana declined to buy exported food like cheap goose from the Soviet Union because of the terrible situation there.[48] Frank was frustrated that the world did not seem to understand what was happening. About Einstein, for example, who was hostile to Western anti-Sovietism and had pacifist inclinations, with whom he corresponded at the end of the 1920s, Frank supposedly said, "He might be a genius in his field, but he is a complete idiot in regard to politics."[49]

When M. Fasmer became head of the Russian Department at Berlin University, he arranged for Frank to give lectures there in 1931–33. The lectures were consistently popular with students. One of his pupils recalled how they contrasted with the drama of life in Berlin in 1931–32. Hitler's popularity was growing, and frequently there was fighting in the streets. In Frank's classroom all was quiet. His lecture style was less professorial than meditative. He would not analyze the texts but used books as starting points for reflection. He had notes but did not refer much to them. He spoke very slowly and had a magnetic face and eyes. It was the same at home: Frank would be surrounded by lots of noise but remain completely calm and unruffled.[50]

Frank made every effort to get involved in German life, although the children lived exclusively in Russian circles. In November 1925 he wrote to Struve that the Russians and Germans were very much alike, that he had just given a talk at the Society of East European Studies, and that he was slowly getting into German academic life.[51] In the following years he gave a number of public lectures at the Kant Society, published articles in *Kant Studies* (*Kantstudien*), *The Grail* (*Der Gral*), and extracts from *The Object of Knowledge* in the German edition of *Logos*. He also got involved in a high-church movement, Hochkirchliche Vereinigungen, led from 1929 by the well-known Marburg theologian Friedrich Heiler. Heiler, whom Frank knew and admired, had a similar interest in mysticism and universalist Christianity, and in 1934 Frank wrote a couple of articles for his journal, *A Holy Church* (*Eine heilige Kirche*). Also in these years Frank wrote articles for *Highland* (*Hochland*), a Catholic journal with a social orientation founded by the publicist Carl Muth.[52]

But opportunities were sparse, and for financial reasons Frank was forced to move beyond an academic audience. He did a range of speaking engagements for a religious aid organization called Russische Bruderhilfe based in Lemgo near Berlin and wrote some popular articles for its journal, *Love One Another* (*Liebet Einander*). This was not work he much enjoyed. His audience was not well educated, and he had difficulty relating to it. In a letter to Tatiana in 1931 he lamented: "Bit by bit I am learning how to talk to peasants, I have put aside the talk I had thought out. . . . Of course, this is a terrible degradation—none of my ideas are needed by anyone . . . it's like teaching the alphabet to children; but mainly I find it immeasureably more difficult than lecturing to students."[53]

In spite of all his efforts, Frank's attempts to get into German life were not very successful. The one philosopher he had been in active communication with was Max Scheler. He died in 1934, and Frank wrote in that year that Berlin had become like a desert and that he lived like a hermit.[54] Eventually, Frank felt cut off from everybody. In early 1937, responding to an invitation from El'iashevich to go to Paris, he wrote: "Over the last few years I have got out of the habit of believing that I could be of any use to anyone . . . ; I have almost no more Russian links left here, and there are only a few pleasant and comforting contacts with Germans, but—with all my Europeanism— the difference of nationality is nevertheless a barrier to a real personal relationship in all its fulness."[55]

Frank noticed early that not all was well in Germany. In 1922 he contrasted the radical mood in Germany with that in Russia by noting the absence of any beliefs, even false ones, in Germany and suggested that the moral and economic disintegration of Germany would lead to state collapse and her enslavement by France.[56]

Frank associated fascism with the vulgarization of modern culture, with what he called the "new barbarianism." In 1926, in a lecture he gave at the Union of Russian Jews, he commented that romantic love, as praised in the literature of all countries from the troubadours to Turgenev, had disappeared from modern thought. This, he believed, was linked with such things as the legalization of nudity, the feminization of male fashion, jazz music and dance, and cinema. He saw all these things as somehow a return to the primitive and believed that a similar primitivization was visible in certain phenomena of political life. This was true with fascism, representing the renaissance of the primitive state system where attempts were made by one leader to dominate a country through physical force.[57]

In 1933, when Hitler came to power, Frank did not foresee what was going to happen. He was shocked at the degrading of German culture and amazed by the German support for Hitler, but at the time he felt that the Jews who were leaving the country were exaggerating the danger.[58] Nevertheless, he wrote to Berdiaev in April 1933 asking him whether he could find work for him in Paris with the YMCA and saying, "I wish the Germans every success in their national renaissance, but being a foreigner and moreover of another creed, I cannot be active on the ideological front and I wish to help the Germans with one thing—by not burdening them with my presence any longer."[59]

In early 1934 Frank gave a lecture entitled "The Legend of the Grand Inquisitor" in which he attacked attempts forcibly to improve life on earth and to take away man's responsibility for his actions and put it into the hands of an elite. Freedom, he declared, is the foundation of spiritual growth, and that is fruitful only in combination with love. After the talk, a member of the Gestapo said to Viktor: "Tell your father to be more careful. We well understand what he has in mind in his lecture."[60]

Frank's financial situation was always extremely bad in Berlin. As early as 1924 he wrote to Struve: "We have a real lack of money and life has become very difficult."[61] He made repeated efforts to find work in other cities, including Paris, Warsaw, and Belgrade, but they were all unsuccessful. He also went on lecture tours abroad to earn money, including to the Baltic countries, Bulgaria, Czechoslovakia, Holland, Italy, Serbia, and Switzerland. In 1930 he wrote to El'iashevich to accept a previous offer of money so that he could have a proper holiday in the country.[62] The worry about finances forced the family to get rid of their hired piano. In their final flat in Nestorstr. in 1933–37, they had neither a fridge nor hot water.[63] In the early 1930s Tatiana took a refresher course in massage and would go out in the early mornings to earn money. The job that Frank took at Berlin University was a considerable help. But when Hitler came to power, he was deprived of the opportunity to lecture at the university almost immediately because he was a Jew.[64]

In November 1934, while on a visit to Amsterdam, Frank met the Swiss psychologist Ludwig Binswanger, who became one of the pioneers of existential psychoanalysis. The two began to correspond regularly and developed a friendship that in subsequent years became extremely close. The contact also proved vital for financial reasons. By the middle of 1935, even Tatiana had difficulty getting work. A close friend of the Franks, Maria Gurevich, wrote secretly to Binswanger that the Franks were without income or the possibility of finding it and completely isolated: "Professor Frank himself, in his mystical submissiveness, with all his reconciliatory nature and mentality, is preparing for a death from starvation. And . . . I fear that such a thing could indeed happen."[65]

Binswanger, naturally, wished to come to the rescue and sent Frank one hundred marks. Frank reluctantly accepted the money, although he stated that Maria Gurevich's secret letter to Binswanger was like a violation of his chastity.[66] He did not like receiving money as a gift and wished to depend on no one. In the next couple of years he visited Binswanger twice at his home in Kreutzlingen, Switzerland, but always made every effort to give paid lectures to pay for his visits.

For some years Frank had been working on a major new philosophical work in German, *Das Unergründliche*, which he hoped would offer him an opening into the German market and give him a European as well as a Russian audience. He also hoped that royalties might bring in some money. However, all his attempts to find a publisher ended in failure. The problem was partly that he was a Jew. In 1938, by which time he was in France, a Swiss publisher, Fritz Karger, became interested in it but realizing that Frank was a non-Aryan, decided that it was not financially viable to publish it. There would simply be no market for it in Germany or Austria.[67] The book eventually appeared in Russian in 1939 under the title *Nepostizhimoe* (*The Unknowable* or *The Unfathomable*).

In May 1936, with Viktor and Natalia back home after being abroad, Maria Gurevich, against what she called the "stubborn will of the professor," reported to Binswanger again. She said that the five Franks were living on 200 marks, which Viktor and Natalia earned monthly. After the flat and school fees were dealt with, this left 94 marks for everything else. She and her family were preparing to leave Berlin and intended to leave the Franks 25 marks a month and 20 marks from some friends in Paris. "If," she wrote, "we could succeed in getting together the sum of at least 100 marks monthly, we would present it to the family as coming from a support fund for Russian scholars in New York."[68] The catastrophic situation was real enough, although the Franks never actually went hungry and Maria Gurevich may have exaggerated the situation. On occasions, Vasilii would collect gifts of food for the family from friends. Binswanger agreed to Mme Gurevich's proposal and sent 60 marks monthly. Frank was not told about the real situation and continued to receive the money as if from a foundation in New York at least into the first part of 1937 and probably until he left Berlin at the end of 1937.[69] Frank never referred to this source of money in his letters to Binswanger, and it is not clear whether he ever discovered where the money had come from.

In the mid-1930s Viktor and Natalia, who were members of the International Student Club, received a questionnaire about their ancestry. There was growing ideological interference at Vasilii's school, the Grunewald Gymnasium. Frank and Tatiana witnessed anti-Jewish demonstrations in which Jewish shops were attacked. In the summer of 1937 the Franks rented a house outside Berlin and advertised in the Jewish press for holiday residents. This was one of Tatiana's ways of raising money. The landlady, however, accused them of irregularities in payment and took them to court. She explained to the judge that Jews had invaded her village. The case lasted two to three months, and Frank won. (Such events as winning this court case made Frank liable to think that the Nazi regime was more liberal than its communist counterpart. No Bolshevik judge would have had such independence.)[70]

In 1937 Frank was summoned by the Gestapo more than once, probably twice. The family became very worried and decided it was time for him to leave.[71] Frank wrote to Binswanger, who invited him to Switzerland.

The difficulty of leaving Germany was that they still had Soviet passports, which they had had to renew yearly. Viktor would go and get his father's renewed just in case the Soviet embassy decided they wanted to detain him. To get out of Germany was very difficult. France would give visas only if they could prove that they could return to the country from which they came, and Germany would give exit visas only on the condition that they never return. Kullman, formerly with the YMCA, now worked for the League of Nations, and he used his influence to get the visas.

So at the end of 1937 Frank hurriedly left Germany exhausted by the tensions of those years. Frank once said to Natalia that "the main thing in life is to remember that it is a journey."[72] Certainly that was his experience. His sense of gloom had been heightened by the unexpected death in June 1937 of his sister, Sofia, whom he had not seen since he was last in Paris ten years before and whose funeral he was not able to attend. He stoically reflected to Binswanger that it was wrong to hope for happy relationships on this earth: "One behaves like a small child, in whose child's world a power from another, higher world intervenes."[73]

14

The Unknowable

FRANK'S LAST YEARS in Berlin were occupied with writing *The Unknowable*, which in a letter to El'iashevich in 1937 Frank described as the "the best and deepest thing which I have so far written."[1] He imagined it as something like the *Prolegomena* to Kant's *Critique of Pure Reason*.[2] It was the culmination of his intellectual and spiritual development in Berlin, indeed probably the boldest and most imaginative of all his writings, containing a synthesis of epistemology, social philosophy, and personal spiritual experience. Initially he wrote it in German, beginning work on it in the early 1930s. He finished it at the end of 1935 but on failing to find a publisher, rewrote it. After his move to France in 1938, he translated it into Russian, and it was published in Paris in early 1939.

Frank's Berlin period was in part a continuation of his polemic with philosophies that have no place for the soul of man. The world crisis seemed almost more acute than during the First World War. At the root of the problem, in Frank's view, was a crisis of humanism. In an essay of 1932, "Dostoevskii and the Crisis of Humanism," Frank declared that the optimism of the rationalist, romantic, and naturalist views of man had collapsed. Man had become an orphan in the world. Dostoevskii had seen this collapse most clearly and offered a humanism that recognized both the fundamental evil instincts of man and the divine foundation to his personality.

Frank welcomed any signs of a turning away from a "soulless" view of man—for example, what he saw as a convergence of religious and scientific thought. This, he believed, was manifest in the acceptance by science of the role of prayer and faith in the treatment of physical maladies.[3] On the other hand, he disagreed with much of modern psychoanalysis. Freud's psychology was "biological materialism"; in his view, it turned man into a slave of sex.[4] (According to Frank, Freud, like Marx, was completely blind to things of the spirit, an attitude he described as "typical of a religiously-uprooted Jew.")[5]

Frank's anthropological work was part of a broader interest in personalist philosophies. The most obvious example is the similarity of his "I-We" philosophy with the "I-Thou" thinking of Martin Buber, whose *I and Thou* had first appeared in 1923. For Buber, a person becomes an individual only through his relationship with others. Through that relationship he comes to know God. The relationship with the "Thou" becomes a relation to the "Eternal Thou."[6] Frank never met Buber, but he was in close communication with Max Scheler, another thinker with personalist interests. Frank welcomed Scheler's book *The Position of Man in the Cosmos*, which appeared in 1928. Although Frank did not agree with Scheler's hostility to traditional Christian views of God, he was much in favor of his openness to the spiritual as opposed to the purely rational or material sides of man.[7] Another thinker whom he admired was Ferdinand Ebner, whose *The Word and Spiritual Realities* addressed similar interests. Buber, Scheler, and Ebner, all mentioned in *The Unknowable*, reveal that Frank belonged to a broader body of thinkers who were interested in personalist or spiritual approaches to philosophy.[8]

Frank, then, was not alone in his interest in personalism. Nor was his mysticism an isolated phenomenon. For example, the first chapter of *The Unknowable* opens with a quotation from the Islamic mystic al Hussayn ibn-Mansur al-Hallaj, whom Frank later described as "the greatest religious figure after Christ"[9]: "To know is not merely to see things but also to see how they are submerged in the Absolute." Louis Massignon's famous biography of al-Hallaj had appeared in Paris in 1922. In *The Unknowable*, Frank referred to this and to Christopher Dawson's essay "Islamic Mysticism," which had appeared in his *Enquiries into Religion and Culture* of 1933.[10]

In 1934 Frank went to the World Congress of Philosophy in Prague, and in his speech made a very strong defense of the relevance of the themes he was working on in *The Unknowable*—in particular, his theories of the coincidence of opposites. He believed that his apparently abstruse theories were of great importance for a world in crisis:

> The *docta ignorantia*, absolute realism . . . is the philosophy of fulness and many-sidedness, of equilibrium in diversity. It is—in contrast to the currently-preached "either-or," to the philosophy of one-sidedness and fanaticism—the philosophy of "both-and." It is the philosophy of tolerance, not in the sense of a formal toleration of error, but in the sense of a factual appreciation of the many-sidedness of truth, and consequently the relative entitlement of different principles. . . . It is a phi-

losophy of respect and love, in contrast to the current tendency to contempt and hate, to the destruction of the enemy. There is also no need to worry that in the "both-and" all contrasts, all definite certainties are neutralized and extinguished. The absoltue is not a night in which all cats are grey . . . but a bright rich unity of diversity.[11]

Whether the assumed pertinence of *The Unknowable* was the reason Frank was confident in the success of the book in not clear, but he did express optimism about the future of the book to Binswanger.[12]

The Unknowable, a work of religious philosophy, is subtitled "An Ontological Introduction to the Philosophy of Religion." For Frank to write a work of philosophy that was unashamedly religious was not unexpected. Frank believed that philosophy as a discipline was necessarily religious. As far back as 1922, in his lecture at the opening of the Religious-Philosophical Academy, Frank declared that God is *"the only object of philosophy."* This was an extension of his belief that total-unity, which is at the foundation of all being and consciousness, is the one object of knowledge. By "God," Frank meant the foundation of all being, the source and life of all things.

A philosopher who is not concerned with this is no philosopher at all; he is, Frank believed, simply an expresser of arbitrary opinions:

> If one does not sense [this first-foundation of being], breathing as it were this invisible atmosphere, it is not generally possible to philosophize, but only possible to pronounce idle "philosophical" words or to come up with empty, unrealizable, inwardly incomprehensible and unnecessary, apparently philosophical but in essence purely-linguistic ideas. Not turning towards the absolute, not raising one's whole existence to it, it is altogether not possible to be a philosopher, *to have* philosophy; [in such a case] one can only imitate a philosopher, be occupied with philosophy, i.e., fill one's head with verbal concepts from philosophical books. In order to see the object of philosophy, it is therefore necessary, as Plato said, "to turn the eyes of the soul." It is necessary to effect some kind of fundamental spiritual revolution by which a primary illumination of one's whole spirit is attained, and the obscuring shroud will fall from one's spiritual gaze. Thus, philosophical creativity assumes a religious frame of mind, a religious direction of spirit; a *religious intuition* lies at the foundation of all philosophical knowledge.[13]

The reference to Plato is important. Frank believed that there was nothing illegitimate about a philosopher concerning himself with God. In this essay Frank referred specifically to Heraclitus, Plato, Augustine, Malebranche, and Boehme as philosophers whose thinking was religious, but generally he regarded anyone with an intuition of a fundamental foundation for all reality as a religious thinker. Plotinus, Nicholas of Cusa, Hegel, and Spinoza were among the many others he regarded in such a way.

Frank's way of talking about philosophy is interesting. There is almost a form of holiness about having a philosophical calling. In this lecture of 1922 he wrote that philosophy in its highest sense is "the humble service of truth itself—a service in which the will of God Himself is fulfilled."[14] Frank dedicated *The Unknowable* to Binswanger, suggesting that the two of them were "initiates" in the school of philosophy.[15] In 1939 Frank declared that *The Unknowable* was a symphony of Plotinus, Nicholas of Cusa, and Binswanger. The issue, he wrote, was not to be an expert but to have a sense of that primary reality. Writing to Binswanger at the end of 1935, Frank, on the basis of his own experience, suggested that even the philosopher can be completely taken over by a religious spirit: "I am firmly convinced (because I know it from experience) and am not ashamed to confess it, that any profound deep-digging philosophy comes close to the precipice of madness. Plato certainly knew that because he spoke of Holy Mania. In any case that is how it seems when one is writing a book about the 'unfathomable.'"[16]

This sense of the holiness of philosophy was accompanied by a belief that as Aristotle believed, all knowledge is a product of amazement at the world. In this, both religion and philosophy, feeling and objective knowledge, are united by a metaphysical consciousness based on a sense of the infinite breadth of the universe.[17] Frank much admired Isaac Newton for his statement that in spite of all his discoveries, he was just like a child who had found some shells on a beach.[18] Societies that lose that sense of awe fall into decline.[19] *The Unknowable*, as the philosophy of the unfathomable and mysterious, is an expression of that mentality of perpetual amazement.

Frank, then, was confident about the religiousness of his philosophy from the moment he arrived in emigration, and that is the context in which *The Unknowable* must be approached. It is interesting that his diagnosis of the crisis of modern philosophy had become so distinctly religious. In his speech of 1916 "The Crisis of Modern Philosophy," Frank had called for bringing together idealism and realism in what he described as "concrete idealism or ideal-realism."[20] In 1932, in an essay on Hegel in which he addressed the same problems, Frank made the same diagnosis but called this time for "concrete ideal-realism or religious ontologism."[21] Frank was talking about the same thing but in clearly religious language. "Religious ontologism," in fact, is a good description of *The Unknowable*. To Binswanger Frank wrote that *The Object of Knowledge* was an ontology of knowledge and although it provided the basis for all his later work, did not touch on ethical, religious, and personalist issues.[22] *The Unknowable*, on the other hand, had gone "much further in the direction of a transrational, personalist ontology."[23]

In one sense, *The Unknowable* is an exercise in transcendental thought; that is, it is thought about thought and the presuppositions of all rational discourse. That at least is its starting point, for Frank travels a long way from there. All rational knowledge, he states, is based on the principles of noncontradiction. It is essentially founded on the principle of negation. An object or definition is itself because it is not something else. However, that negation reveals at another level a relation between the objects or definitions, a relationship of "both-and." Thus the principle of negation is itself negated and gives way to a higher unity. The problem here is obvious. This "something else" is simply a negation of rational thought and therefore no different from it. So Frank affirms not a unity based on rational thought but a unity that somehow transcends logic. It is thus transrational thought, and the unity in which opposites are reconciled is a metalogical unity. The transrational and the metalogical thus become Frank's primary interest. Frank is trying to tell his readers about something that cannot, strictly speaking, be described in language.

The title page of the book contains a quotation from Nicholas of Cusa: *"Attingitur in attingibile inattingibiliter"* (the unattainable is attained through its unattainment.)[24] This puts Frank's work firmly in an apophatic tradition. Through revealing the limitations of language and what words cannot express, Frank hopes to say something about the inexpressible. This is the doctrine of "wise ignorance," or *"docta ignorantia,"* which was first affirmed by Socrates and declares that the beginning of wisdom is knowledge of one's ignorance.

Nicholas of Cusa is Frank's principal mentor in these matters. In his introduction Frank wrote:

> My entire thought is founded on that *philosophia perennis* which I perceive to be the essence of Platonism, especially in the form (i.e., neo-Platonism and Christian Platonism) in which it traverses the whole history of European philosophy, from Plotinus, Dionysius the Areopagite, and Augustine to Baader and Vladimir Solov'ev. In principle, philosophy coincides here with speculative mysticism. Among many great minds of this orientation, I wish to single out one thinker who, combining in a grandiose form the spiritual achievements of antiquity and the Middle Ages with the fundamental problems of the modern period, attained a synthesis that has never again been attained by the European mind. I mean Nicholas of Cusa. In a certain sense, he is my only teacher of phi-

losophy. And in essence, my book is intended to be nothing more than a systematic development—on new paths, in new forms of thought . . . —of the basic principles of his world-view, his speculative expression of the universal Christian truth.[25]

Frank quotes Nicholas of Cusa: "It is a great thing to be firmly rooted in the unity of opposites." In a sense, this unity is nothing new for Frank. He calls his whole approach "antinomian monodualism," clearly an idea with its roots in his earlier reading of Goethe. However, Frank is now more confident of his thought. In fact, he is bold enough to declare that "God is *the simple transrational unity of opposite and conflicting determinations, both of which are conserved in Him in all their force.*"[26] An examination of the limitations of reason leads Frank to assert the presence of a primary foundation for all things, which he calls God. This God is unfathomable, for to understand him would be to say something about him, and that would be to limit him to the finite. He is thus transfinite. Even to say that he exists would be illegitimate because as the source of existence, he cannot be limited to existence.

In *The Meaning of Life* Frank argued that knowledge that the world is somehow meaningless is already an indication of a higher realm of truth that makes that knowledge possible. There is a kind of "inner truth" that illuminates and evaluates the outer world. This idea of an inner truth is essential in Frank's thought in *The Unknowable.* Using the same transcendental arguments, Frank suggests that the self-evident truths of certain rational discourse must acquire their self-evidence from somewhere. For rational, objective knowledge to be valid, it must look to something outside itself for authority. Truth that is limited to reason necessarily implies a higher truth that is not limited. Through this kind of argumentation Frank posits a primary truth that stands at the foundation of all thinking and all things and gives them meaning. This truth stands as a kind of transrational intuitive source of rational thought.

Frank's view of truth is the same as his view of God. He much admired Augustine's idea that man would not be able to search for God if he did not already possess him in some way. "In the domain of the spiritual and absolute reality," he wrote, "we *also have all that we lack,* for if we did not have it we could not be conscious of its absence."[27] In searching for truth and God, man must already possess them. They are the a priori givens of the search.

Transcendental thought, then, leads Frank to posit a primary foundation for the principles of logic and the search for truth. He describes this unfathomable primary reality as a metalogical unity or living truth. In turn, they are both called God. If these are God, then this is surely the God of the philosophers—abstract and incomprehensible, an idea without a trace of personality to it? However, Frank's unfathomable God turns out to be highly personal, and this is perhaps where *The Unknowable* is most interesting.

In Frank's social philosophy, personal identity, in the form of "I," is possible only because of the relationship of "I-Thou." That in turn results from the primary "We." These categories of social being—"I," "Thou," "We"—are in contrast to objective descriptions of people— "He" and "They." Thus Frank argues that there is a personalist foundation for social life.

These ideas are integrated into *The Unknowable* with the added factor that God himself is also a "Thou." The whole thrust of Frank's argument is that the primary reality, total-unity, or living truth—he has many names for it—is not objectifiable. It cannot be defined in the third person, as an "It" or a "He." For as soon as this is done, the unknowability has been destroyed: "God is the unconditionally unknowable, absolute primordial ground, experienced and revealed in experience as 'Thou.' And His 'Thouness' is experienced as somehow belonging to His essence and mode of being. To speak of God in the third person, to call Him 'Him,' is blasphemy from the religious point of view, for this assumes that God is absent, does not hear me, is not directed at me, but is something objectively existent. . . . The religious consciousness of God is expressed not in speeches *about* God but in words directed *to* God (in prayer) and in God's words *to me*." God reveals himself only through *my* being and thus reveals himself in the form of a "Thou." The unfathomable total-unity of God is present in the concrete depths of *my* being. The two form a united intimacy that cannot be described in rational language. This argument, which leads Frank to see God as a "Thou," is in part at least an argument based on Frank's earlier concept of living knowledge. God, Frank declares, reveals himself to people "only through religious experience."[28]

The fact that God can be understood only through personal experience means that he cannot be experienced outside a relationship:

> The "idea" of Divinity cannot be separated from the living, concrete experience of Divinity, from *my* experience of Divinity. . . . In its essence Divinity is always "God-with-us" (Emmanuel) and, in the final analysis, "God-with-me." For what is revealed to me is not only God "as such" but precisely "God with me," the concrete fulness of the inseparable and unmerged dual-unity of "God and I." . . .
> . . . That great Nameless or All-Named which we conditionally designated as Holiness or Divinity becomes God—*my God*. God is Divinity

as it is revealed to me and experienced by me in complete otherness, in
relation to me, and in inseparable unity with me. . . . Divinity becomes
"Thou" for me, reveals itself as "Thou"; and only as "Thou" is it God.

Not only is Frank's God personalized; the relationship with God is described as that of love. God is love. His very essence is a creative over-
flowing of his bounds, a giving of himself. His immediate presence is a
flow of life that rushes into people, gives birth to them. The "Thouness" of God is creative love itself. According to Frank, it is "only in
love [that] we gain living knowledge of the unknowable reality."[29]
    This, then, is the essence of Frank's philosophy. It turns out to be a
philosophical defense of a personal God. But Frank denies that he is
writing as an apologist for Christianity. His writing is "only an attempt
to see in an unprejudiced way and to describe the truth in all its fulness."[30] How, then, is the reader to evaluate it? Frank presents conclusions that although normally associated with mystical theology, he
vigorously defends as philosophical. Yet it is difficult to know how to
describe this philosophical thinking. For to try to analyze it means to
try to evaluate it rationally, and it is Frank's purpose to describe something that is only transrationally understandable.
    In essence, *The Unknowable* is an attempt to put into language
Frank's experience of what he had earlier called "living knowledge." It
is an attempt to provide a philosophical framework where living religious experience can be accepted. It therefore involves a certain kind
of empiricism. In a work published in 1926, *The Russian Worldview*,
Frank distinguished between two brands of empiricism: English empiricism, based on sensual evidence, and Russian empiricism, based
on inner experience. For the Russian, he argued, experience is "not the
outer contact of things, as it seems to sensual perception, but the acquisition of the complete reality of objects through the human spirit in
its living wholeness." The distinctive feature of Russian philosophical
thought was this idea of life-experience, *lebenserfahrung*.[31] This life-
experience is really an awareness of total-unity. Other philosophies in
which Frank identified this broader approach included William James's
"radical empiricism" and Husserl's phenomenology. To describe it
simply, Frank was attempting to describe man's inner intuition of God
in philosophical terms. To do this, he was trying to go beyond rational
philosophy. As he wrote, "The only true philosophy that deserves the
name is the *philosophical overcoming of all rational philosophy*."[32]
    Frank's philosophy is clear in his treatment of the subject of evil.
For Frank, the almightiness and all-benevolence of God conflicted
with a fallen and sinful world. The challenge was how to overcome

this dualism. Frank attempted to overcome it by referring to experience rather than logical explanation:

> *The only way we can know evil is by overcoming it and extinguishing it* *through the consciousness of guilt.* Rational, abstract theodicy is impossible, but living theodicy, attainable not through thought but in living experience, is possible in all its unknowableness and transrationality. When the gentle, consoling, and reconciling light of God shines through the terrible pain of the awareness of sin, that which is experienced as incomprehensible separation, isolation, perversion, is also experienced as undamaged and inviolable being with and in God. That which is in irreconcilable conflict is perceived as being in primordial harmony. In this form the fundamental principle of antinomian monodualism reveals its action in relation to the problem of evil and in the living victory over evil.[33]

What is logically an unsolvable problem is thus overcome through personal experience. This is the essence of Frank's empiricism. It is clear that he is going beyond the ordinary bounds of philosophy. He is saying that understanding demands participation. Certain problems cannot be understood by the objective observer; a solution is left to the one who is involved.

It is notable that Frank draws so extensively on German mystical thought. At the end of *The Russian Worldview*, Frank lists a series of great German mystics, including Meister Eckhart, Nicholas of Cusa, Boehme,[34] Angelus Silesius, Baader, Schelling, Hegel, and Goethe— all also quoted or referred to in *The Unknowable*.[35] Frank regarded German mystical thought as the great source of thought about life-experience. In an unpublished lecture, "The Russian Mentality in its Relation to the German," Frank explained that in spite of the apparent difference between the Russian and German characters, there was a deep likeness between the two nations. In neither country did the individualism associated with Roman culture fit easily. In the Roman world, the individual feels separated from being. (Frank presumably had in mind the Cartesian division between being and consciousness.) But in the Russian and German minds, the individual feels rooted in being, inwardly connected to rather than outwardly attached to being. This means that it is "not the *striving for God* but the *being in God*" that is their prevalent religious mood. Frank saw the roots of this in both cases as the Platonic element in their intellectual outlook, which had manifested itself in mystical, speculative philosophy rather than the concrete, logical thought associated with the Roman world.[36]

The obvious dilemma for any philosophy concerned with "being in God" as opposed to "striving for God" is the problem of pantheism. If one is inwardly connected to God, where is the division between God and man? The division between the two becomes blurred. In Frank's case, as his comments on German thought reveal, his thought opens the way to a vague distinction between being and God: the individual's root in being becomes a root in God as the source of being. Frank was well aware of this difficulty and attempted to answer it using his traditional method of the coincidence of opposites. Drawing on the ideas of Nicholas of Cusa, he declared that the world is neither God himself nor something logically other than God and alien to him. The world is the vestment or flesh of God, the "other of God" in which God is disclosed or expressed. Creator and creation together form a unity that does not exclude their difference and opposition. Man's thought thus enters into the "heaven of the coincidence of opposites." Frank stated that anyone who suspects this view to be pantheism is simply ignorant.[37]

Frank was keen to resist the charge of pantheism. In a critique of Hegel, he criticized Hegel for the very things he himself is sometimes accused of: "The powerful conception of Hegel's philosophy is poisoned by the one-sidedness of pantheism; it breaks on the bitter fact of the fall of man."[38] Frank appeals not to a logical refutation of the tendency toward pantheism present in any philosophy of total-unity but to a refutation based on the coincidence of opposites. It is implied by reason but not proved by it. In a sense, it is once again an argument from experience.

The link between God and man is at the heart of *The Unknowable*, perhaps the central issue of the work. In *The Object of Knowledge*, Frank's fundamental intuition was the relation between the whole and the part: the whole is more than the sum of its parts; the parts belong to the whole but maintain their distinctness. At the time, this was a mystical philosophical intuition akin to Bergson's concept that time is a dynamic process rather than a distinct set of moments. With the growing religiousness of Frank's thought, that fundamental intuition had now become an insight into the relationship between God and man. The idea that God and man are intimately interconnected and in one sense united was now the religious expression of that original intuition. Frank's philosophy had, then, become a philosophy of Godmanhood, the philosophy of "God-with-me" or "I-with-God." Perhaps it could be described as a phenomenology of Godmanhood, an attempt at an unbiased description of the relationships between God and man.

In 1935 Frank wrote to Binswanger that their relationship was like an "I-Thou" friendship. In spite of their great differences in nationality and profession, he sensed a deep inner likeness.[39] His philosophical description of human relations seems, therefore, to have mirrored his experience of them. To some extent, Frank's "I-Thou-We" philosophy is a philosophy of friendship. There is a confessional element to his thinking. Later, in fact, Frank declared to Binswanger that all philosophy is a form of confession.[40] This seems to hold true for *The Unknowable*. Throughout the latter part of the work, there is a sense that Frank's experience is of great importance. That is implied in the empirical nature of the philosophy itself, but the writing seems to convey his spirit in a very personal way. He makes statements like "My life with God is a kind of *inner, deep, hidden* life that is inaccessible to observation or perception from outside." Such comments fit in the flow of Frank's explanations, but they also hint at his inner life. In discussing beauty, Frank argues that the harmony of the world coincides with the aspiration for beauty in the individual. This confirms his intuition of there being an underlying unity to the individual and the world.[41] It is interesting here that Frank's whole mind is always attracted by harmony; his philosophy is thus connected to what is emotionally and mentally closest to him. His philosophy of beauty is also an expression of his personal love of beauty.

This confessional quality emerges particularly strongly in his writing about suffering. In *The Unknowable*, Frank wrote the following about the nature of suffering:

> The pure essence of suffering is disclosed to us in the spiritual acceptance of suffering, in our ability to endure and withstand it. Suffering is then experienced by us not as a meaningless evil, not as something that absolutely should not be, not even as an externally imposed punishment, but as *healing* from evil and calamity, a God-sanctioned and divine path of return to the homeland, to the perfection of reality. One of the most evident laws of the spiritual life is that without suffering there is no perfection, no complete unshakeably stable bliss. "Blessed are those who cry, for they will be comforted"; . . . As Meister Eckhart puts it: "The fastest horse to perfection is suffering." Suffering is like a hot probe that cleans and expands our respiratory paths, thereby for the first time opening for us free access to the blissful depths of genuine reality. There is no need to emphasize that suffering reveals its deepest essence only when endured in *my* deep inner experience and only in its aspect as *my* suffering. And only as *my* suffering does it find meaning and justification.[42]

This is Frank's philosophical description of suffering. It turns out, however, that it comes directly from his personal experience.

During the Second World War, Frank's son-in-law, Paul Scorer, worked for air force intelligence and was killed while on maneuvers in 1943. In 1945 Frank wrote the following lines to Natalia about this loss:

A living soul cannot live on despair and hopelessness; it is unnatural as a prolonged condition. Suffering must enlighten, deepen, widen the soul and so give it life. . . . But any strong, deep and living feeling, particularly grief, must be creative, lead somewhere, open up new horizons. That is the way I approach it. Suffering is like a hot probe plunged into our lungs. Until it has reached the end, a person experiences a tortuous burning and suffocates; but at the end, he starts to breathe in a new way, deeply and freely, in a way he did not breathe before. This is not an intellectual construction; this is my experience. People who have gone through deep suffering are chosen people; they have a depth, inaccessible to others, and a quiet light shines in that depth, which illuminates and gives meaning to life. "To suffer is cruel, but having been through suffering, you have the grace of God." (Meister Eckhart) The Arab mystic, al-Hallaj, the greatest religious figure after Christ, says: "Whoever has really suffered has been visited by God; God has made his own abode in him." This is strange and terrible, but it is also a great accomplishment of the spirit; it is a real transformation of the soul. Grief turns into tenderness; a quiet, heavenly light burns in the soul; the flow of tears cleans the soul and gives it a kind of transparent, shining festive dressing. Surely we can no longer be materialists for whom everything ends with the visible world. . . . Love is stronger than death. Death, if it cannot destroy love, can neither destroy the joyfulness of love. Grief can only be the grief of parting. Of course, so-called "men of the world" will tell you that "these are all sweet words which cannot stand up in front of the rough and bitter truth of life." But, all the same, . . . love is stronger than death, stronger than any earthly forces, so that it will conquer them, and not they it. This, and only this is the true Christian faith. Evil cannot destroy goodness and blessedness. No one and nothing can take away the truth of love's happiness, and that means that evil cannot destroy them. Any experts or clever people who tell you the opposite are simply blind. The passion of Christ ended with resurrection. All the sufferings of the human soul must also finish with a resurrection to a new deepened and transformed life.[43]

These passages are worth quoting in full because they show Frank the mystic in all his grandeur. The passages are also identical in their purpose and at times in their language—in the image of the hot probe, for example. This means that Frank used his philosophical thinking in a directly advisory, spiritual sense. There was no division between his thinking and what he tried to practice in life. The key sentence in the last passage is "This is not an intellectual construction; this is my experience." If Frank's writing on suffering in 1945 is the result of his experience and mirrors almost exactly the writing of 1938, it can be assumed that in this aspect of *The Unknowable* at least Frank was writing in a confessional as well as a philosophical sense. It is not perhaps too much to go further and conclude that Frank's philosophy of Godmanhood is also the philosophy of his own religious experience.

The passages on suffering are of particular interest, bearing in mind the events Frank had lived through in the past decades and how difficult life had been. They offer the reader an insight into how Frank dealt with the lonely years he had been through. Frank's sense of the tragic is due to both his personality and his experience, and it was undoubtedly a critical factor in his mental makeup. In a letter to Binswanger in July 1937, Frank, taking the expression "bright sorrow" (*svetlaia pechal'*) from Pushkin, declared that "[bright sorrow] corresponds to the deepest ontological nature of reality" and is deeper and nearer to God than all jubilation.[44]

Frank's sense of sadness and difficulty was increased by his ill health, and this may have contributed to his acute awareness of mystical issues and his sense of the immediate presence of the spiritual world. *The Unknowable* is the work of a man who is more interested in the next world than in this. The writing had been a struggle. After the first draft of *The Unknowable*, in the first two months of 1936, Frank had serious heart problems that according to his doctor had resulted from the fatigue of working on the book.[45] In a letter to El'iashevich of January 1937, Frank wrote about his decision to rework *The Unknowable:* "I live now with a premonition of the end of my life."[46]

Problems in writing *The Unknowable* were probably accentuated by the sheer difficulty of undertaking a work that although intended to be concrete, is highly complex and extremely abstract. He always found it hard work to express his ideas in literary form.[47] In presenting a copy of the book to his daughter, Frank marked the chapters that were accessible to the ordinary reader and that she thus might understand.[48] One critic said that the book was so difficult that it was a "mockery of the reader." (Frank was encouraged when, after publication, Struve expressed great enthusiasm for it, writing: "This book will last.")[49] As he had said in reference to Plato, philosophy at times touches on the mad, and in one passage in *The Unknowable* he commented that to inquire into the meaning of the word "is" brings us to "the edge of insanity."[50] "My work is a blessed agony," he wrote in November 1935.[51] At that time he said that in writing such a book, it was almost as if he had been out of the world altogether.

In a long article he wrote for Berdiaev's religious journal *The Way* (*Put'*) on Rainer Maria Rilke, a poet he much admired and quoted in *The Unknowable,* Frank expressed great admiration for Rilke's search

for immediate religious experience and stated that Rilke, like all genuine mystics, combined a feeling of the breadth and depth of the
divine being with a sense of a personal relationship with God.[52] What
Frank said about Rilke is equally applicable to himself. With *The Unknowable*, Frank had become a mystic as well as a philosopher. His
universe had become personalized. To some extent he was always a
mystic, but life in Berlin seems to have accentuated this tendency. The
isolation drove Frank inward to his soul. Perhaps the instability of the
outer world led him to seek the permanence of a mystical reality.
However, that is speculation. What is clear is that much of *The Unknowable* is an attempt at a philosophical description of Frank's inner
religious experiences.

15

1938–1945

D URING A DANCING TOUR to Australia, Aleksei met and married an English girl, Betty Scorer. On their return, they settled in a small village between Toulon and Cannes popular with Russian émigrés, La Favière. Aleksei invited his parents to come and stay with them. Frank spent the first few weeks out of Germany with Binswanger in Switzerland and then some weeks in Paris before reaching La Favière in the early spring. After a few months, Tatiana and Natalia received their visas and joined him. Vasilii had left to live and study in England in 1937. Viktor remained in Berlin until the summer of 1939 when he left for England after being offered a grant in Oxford. He eventually got a job with the BBC monitoring service.

During his stay in Paris, Frank attempted to raise some money and arrange for his new life. He still had a Soviet passport but was in reality stateless. In his efforts to get a residence permit for France and a stipend to support him and the family, he met about twenty French philosophers.[1] Berdiaev, using his numerous contacts, tried to help him by asking people to write recommendations for him.[2] Frank eventually received his residence permit for France in May and got a grant for 1938–39 from the Caisse Nationale de la Recherche Scientifique amounting to 10,000 French francs. In addition, Binswanger loaned Frank 1,000 French francs,[3] and he was much helped by a generous gift of money from a Dutch friend.[4] However, the financial situation continued to be critical.

La Favière was attractive. Aleksei's house was ten minutes from the beach, and Frank described the place as "a doll-like little house of four rooms with a second of two rooms." Although the house was served with electricity, there was no running water. For Frank it offered conditions for a kind of Tolstoian existence, and he enjoyed the beauty of the landscape and the sea.[5] When Tatiana arrived, she got the idea of turning the place into a guest house for English holidaymakers who might wish to benefit from the favorable exchange rate. They had about five rooms to let; Tatiana turned herself into a cook, and Natalia became a waitress.

The setup worked well for the summer of 1938, but it was not easy. The Franks were worried about imposing on the hospitality of Aleksei and Betty, and Aleksei continued to live with no sense of responsibility. He would go to the next village, get drunk, and disappear for a time. Their relationship with Betty Scorer was easier, but there was always a tension in the household.

Frank's primary interest was to get *The Unknowable* published, and his failure to publish it in German was a personal tragedy. To Binswanger, he tried to put his misfortune in a broader perspective: "What is a tragedy for me personally, namely that my book cannot appear in the language in which it is thought out and written, is a small thing in comparison with the global, historical tragedy whereby for the foreseeable future, philosophical thought in the German language—the language of poets and thinkers—must be abandoned." Frank spent the summer of 1938 doing a Russian translation, and the final product, he felt, was an improvement on the earlier version.[6] This, however, was not a great comfort to him. He could not see his Russian audience, and his chance of a dialogue with a broader German audience had slipped by.

Frank's disappointment was the setting for a heart attack, brought on by a steady accumulation of fatigue, too much hill walking, and swimming. He declared to Binswanger that he had been "close to the border of the other world."[7] He was confined to bed, where he read Ferdinand Ebner's *The Word and Love*, which he described as a great consolation. Frank did not fully recover his strength until 1939.

In September 1938 the Franks left La Favière and went to stay with the El'iasheviches on their estate in Bussy-en-Othe near Paris. Living there was also difficult because the Franks felt they were imposing and living on charity. Frank, still weak from his heart attack, tried to relax by reading French novels but remained in a mood of despair. "The whole world is so miserable," he wrote. Looking back on his life, he discarded any pretension to worldly importance: "[Being a professor] is just a 'role' I once played in a sunken world, in my preexistence. Now I am nothing but a personality, and at best only a professor in a literal sense, as a confessor of my beliefs."[8] Struve came to see him and spent three days. It was to be their last meeting. Struve said, "You are now again at a crossroads," to which Frank sharply replied, "Not a crossroads, but no road at all."[9]

In December, in this atmosphere of gloom and despair and while reading Cardinal Newman, Frank conceived the idea for a book about darkness and light. "The only important thing, " he wrote to Binswanger, "is not to doubt and to believe in the light, in spite of the thick darkness which surrounds it."[10] He finished a draft of the book in August 1940,[11] but rewrote it after the war, and it eventually appeared in 1949 as *Light in the Darkness*.

The family situation underwent an important change in the summer of 1938 when Betty Scorer's brother Paul arrived to spend the summer with them and fell in love with Natalia. They were married in Paris in February 1939.

Frank was given a three-year grant of £250 a year from the Christian Council for Refugees of the World Council of Churches in the spring of 1939. This supported them in Paris, where they had moved at the end of 1938 and taken a small flat in the suburb Fontenay-aux-Roses. They considered moving to Britain, but Paul Scorer said that the £250 stipend was not enough to live on, so they decided to stay. The grant was renewed in 1942 but suspended in 1943 because of the impossibility of transferring money to France.

The Franks enjoyed Paris. Though short-lived, it was perhaps one of the happiest periods of their lives. Paris was the home of the Russian emigration, and since Frank was a famous figure in Russian thought, many people came to visit. Their closest friends there were the Zaks and the family of Struve's son Aleksei. At the same time, Frank found a kind of informal spiritual community he felt part of. This included G. Fedotov, who had been with him in Saratov; the famous Mother Maria Skobtsova, founder of "Orthodox Action" and believer in what she called "monasticism in the world"; and the Russian religious thinker I. I. Fondaminskii. Back in 1935 Fondaminskii had founded the "Circle," a discussion group devoted to religion, philosophy, and literature. Frank took part in the discussions and gave a talk on Pushkin.[12]

However, Frank never wished to belong exclusively to a Russian milieu, and Paris gave him the chance to get to know the French intellectual scene. In May 1937 *The Object of Knowledge* appeared in a French translation under the title *Connaissance et L'Être* in a series produced by two prominent French philosophers, L. Lavelle and R. Le Senne, and it won a positive response. A reviewer for the *Thomist Review* (*Revue Thomiste*) welcomed Frank's "immense logical apparatus" and his "metaphysics of total presence" but cautioned against the pantheistic Parmenidian elements.[13] Frank admired both Lavelle and Le Senne, characterizing the latter's philosophy as an attempt to synthesize Bergson and rationalism.[14] Through Berdiaev Frank probably met most of the major French religious philosophers of the time.

He had great admiration for Gabriel Marcel, specifically recommending him to Binswanger as a thinker who had much in common with them.[15]

In spite of the stimulation and variety of life in Paris, Frank was very depressed by the world crisis. Hitler's invasion of Czechoslovakia made him ill. On the eve of the war he wrote: "Inwardly, I am completely calm, but the current world situation is a real burden on my nervous system." At the end of August, following the general advice of the French government, the Franks moved out of Paris to Nassandres, a small village in Normandy. Natalia, in London, was expecting a baby in January, and Frank commented that what normally would be a cause for joy was now a cause for anguish. From Normandy the Franks moved back to La Favière. Frank stated that they were "apocalyptic times."[16] He began work on *Light in the Darkness*. They then moved to Le Lavandou for the winter, a town near La Favière with better accommodation.

The Franks were able to correspond with Britain until France was divided in two. Nevertheless, they were increasingly isolated from the outside world, and the following years became a struggle to survive.

In their isolation, Ludwig Binswanger became a lifeline to the world. It was through him that the Franks had most news of the family, and it was to him that Frank poured out his thoughts and emotions. Frank wrote to him in 1942 that his friendship was "the greatest consolation of these last years of my life," and at the end of the war he singled him out, with Struve, as his most precious friend.[17]

The friendship, although founded on common intellectual interests, was not built on a unanimity of viewpoint. Their philosophical tastes were different. Binswanger, for example, was an admirer of Freud, whom Frank disliked, and was not guided by a religious faith as Frank was. Their letters are characterized by a deep seriousness of outlook. They suggest a common quest for truth, a respect for the world, and a belief in the importance of what they are doing. They are interesting for their lack of any cynicism. In spite of the war and its atrocities, neither writer displays any note of bitterness or desire to prove anything about himself.

Although they differed in their approach to religion, Frank felt spiritually very close to Binswanger: "Although I ideologically stand closer to Christian belief than you, you have both ideologically and existentially taught me what *love* is. And love and God are known to be the same, so you have become my teacher of theology."[18]

Binswanger's help was financial as well as spiritual. Frank called him his banker.[19] In May 1941 Frank estimated that he needed 2,500

French francs a month to live. Until the middle of 1942 he continued to receive money from the stipend given him by the World Council of Churches. Apart from that, Binswanger was the main source of money. Frank's letters to him refer to payments of about 1,000 French francs. Frank assured him that after the war it would be possible to pay him back, but Binswanger probably realized that this was a slim possibility. The total amount owed at the end of the war was 1,553 Swiss francs.[20] Binswanger was generous in the extreme, dispatching food parcels, books, newspapers, medical advice when Frank was ill, and news of the family from England.

Frank, who in Berlin had stubbornly refused to ask for money, lost all his inhibitions. He finally had to accept being entirely dependent on the generosity of somebody else. Whenever he was in need, he turned to Binswanger.

Life was filled with uncertainty. Not only was there a shortage of money, but it was impossible to know what would happen next. At one point the Franks were arrested and kept in a temporary camp in Toulon for a couple of days, then released. The Vichy French rounded up many of the Russians in the south of France when the Molotov-Ribbentrop pact was broken. In 1942 the Franks tried to get out of France to England through Portugal. Everything was arranged, including the visa for Britain and the plane ticket from Lisbon, but the Portugese transit visa came too late. It was a great disappointment to them, and Frank, his plans upset, had to turn to Binswanger to ask for "as much money as you could lend me without difficulty for yourself."[21]

One of the greatest difficulties was fear about the children. News was sporadic. Viktor had a tuberculosis operation in the autumn of 1939 and married a Canadian girl in the autumn of 1940. In 1942 Vasilii came down with spinal meningitis, and when he recovered, went with the Allies to North Africa. Natalia had two children and remained at home in London. However, Paul Scorer volunteered, worked on intelligence missions, and was lost in action in the Bay of Biscay in the autumn of 1943.

At home, Aleksei continued to give his parents cause for worry. He spent part of the time with his parents, but Betty had a flat in Grenoble, and he spent time there. His drinking was still a problem, and Frank even consulted Binswanger about it. But more generally, Aleksei was just unable to be responsible for himself and his family. In 1940 Frank expressed his anguish to Tatiana over Aleksei's failure to understand any moral or intellectual principles. According to Tatiana, he was "grieved by his lack of understanding of religion and God" and was puzzled that "[Aleksei could] grow up in our family and not understand . . . us." By 1943, he seems to have resigned himself to Aleksei's wayward character. The problem, he felt, was that Aleksei from birth had no willpower.[22] Betty and their daughter, Marusya, left for England in the middle of 1942. Aleksei remained, was arrested twice for being a suspected non-Aryan, joined the resistance, left it after quarreling with some communist members, and found himself on the run from them and the Germans.

The radio was the link with the outside world, and Frank's English improved considerably as a result of listening to the BBC. He would also listen to music. He wrote to Binswanger in December 1940: "Now and again, I hear some good music on the radio, which is also a great comfort, and I have—strangely—perhaps for the first time, felt with complete clarity that music really opens an entrance to the beyond, to the so-called 'thing-in itself' or even more the 'unfathomable'—as Schopenhauer taught."[23] Music was always an inspiration to him. He once said that Mozart was the best proof of the kingdom of God.[24]

The war was intellectually a productive time for Frank. He finished work on *Light in the Darkness* and at the end of 1941 wrote a spiritual testament, *God with Us*. It was written on individual sheets of paper and sent by letter to Viktor in England, who edited it. Not one of the sheets was lost, and it first appeared in English in 1946. Frank yearned for a philosophy that dealt with real life, a philosophy without abstraction, something perhaps akin to the dynamism of Bergson's thought. The theme of "creativeness" [*tvorchestvo*] became particularly important to him in these years. In creativeness he saw "perhaps the deepest secret of life," which made the categories of cause and substance seem superficial. Many of his ideas on this theme were expressed after the war in his last major philosophical work, *Reality and Man*. Frank's wartime thought, as a whole, was typified by a thirst for life as opposed to theory: "Before all the horrors of the current life, and feeling my own death to be near, I am engaged in a work of spiritual life and all abstract theories (my own included) seem to me something rather childish."[25]

Frank worked hard, but access to books was a special problem. Binswanger sent some; others came from Aleksei Struve in Paris. Frank found a local library in Le Lavandou and a cemetery with cyprus trees where he could meditate. At one point he also had access to a philosophy library in Montpellier. He read widely, including Dante for the first time, and the French writer Charles Péguy, whom he greatly admired. The books were important, for they provided Frank with stimulation.

Perhaps the greatest problem of the war was the temptation to despair. The loneliness was one reason for this. Another was Frank's health, which was never good. He had chest pains and prostate and bowel problems, and was usually in a state of exhaustion of some kind. As ever, he was prone to morbid reflections: "I would prefer to die in the old Europe, perhaps along with the old Europe." At times he fell to despising himself, writing to Binswanger: "There is nothing to admire in me."[26]

Frank's inner battle with despair was well illustrated by his changing attitudes to Providence and fate. Throughout the war, Frank had a sense of being protected by Providence. In August 1940 he thanked Binswanger for sending 1,000 francs, saying: "As always in these situations (such is my experience of harsh years) the money arrives just in time, when one has no other way out." At the end of the year he commented: "As far as my financial position is concerned, I have the experience which is already familiar to me from last year, that Providence does not abandon me—and not only through the agency of real friends such as you." Sometimes, however, his faith in Providence seems to have given way to a form of stoicism, though of a benevolent kind. On one occasion he stated: "I believe that this hell on earth will last for years. . . . I look at this prospect in a stoical way—in spite of everything, I have had a happy life, both on a personal and a spiritual level, and when it comes to an end, one has to be grateful for the good." Frank reflected that all needs are relative and wrote that "one must first of all yield to fate." Failing to get the Portuguese visa in time, he declared: "It remains for us to await our destiny patiently and calmly."[27]

It is clear, then, that although Frank sincerely believed in Providence, he did not always make a clear distinction between Providence and fate, and this underlines the presence of Greek elements in his Christianity. Frank's grandest expression of resignation came in his notebook of 1942:

> The commandment not to worry about tomorrow—there is trouble enough today—is, in general, not a demand, but an exhortation, expressing an ideal of perfection. In the general conditions of human life, this ideal is not fully realizable; it contradicts the very mechanism of the volitional life of man. Our thought, our concern, our interest is always directed to the future, tomorrow, next month, next year etc. The earthly life of man would have no meaning without it: and the gospel commandment simply reminds us that we should not ascribe to this circumstance unconditional significance, as it were get completely absorbed in it, but that it is incumbent in all our worries to preserve a lightness without worry, trust in God. But there are situations when all the human worries actually become purposeless, when one has to submit oneself to fate and the will of God. Then one has actually and seriously to change one's mentality and in the literal strict sense of the word to think only

about two things: about the needs of today and eternity. The very difficult and ordinarily impossible becomes in practice the one thing necessary and reasonable[.] Children live for today and wise men for eternity:
everything else is vanity. . . . Between the tranquillity of carelessness
and the destruction of the soul caused by despair there is no mid-point.
If such a circumstance exceeds human strength, then it is necessary to
call on the higher power of grace for help. What is impossible for man is
possible for God.[28]

In spite of this interior struggle between hope and despair, Frank
was determined to be optimistic. Although tempted to nihilism, he also
hated it. In a long letter to Binswanger, he made a strong critique of
Martin Heidegger, whose philosophy he understood to be a declaration of isolated individualism. Such thinking, he felt, was a recipe for
despair: "Heidegger is spiritually a dead end. . . . His "ground" is not
a true ground which one can stand on. It is like a rock onto the edge of
which you can cling while in full view of the abyss. I always ask: Why
the fear—and not the trust? Why should anxiety be an ontologically-
grounded state, and trust just accursed theology? . . . A true foundation is only that which is more than my own existence; a true foundation can only be 'home,' floor, we-being."[29]

This statement is remarkable. Frank's view of Heidegger changed
dramatically in the months before his death. Here, his comments are
an affirmation of his own beliefs, and they carry a striking force. Written in the middle of 1942 when life was exceptionally difficult, they
amount to a chosen creed. In *The Meaning of Life*, Frank declared
that although the world gives no grounds for hope, one can nevertheless be certain that everything has a true meaning. There is a ground
to stand on. Frank had every reason to bow to Heidegger's *angst*.
Through the war he kept a capsule of poison with him in case the
Germans came for him. He said after the war that suicide was of
course a sinful option; however, he felt he would not be strong enough
to bear it if they treated him as they did other Jews.[30] With the perpetual possibility of such an event, Frank's declaration of trust rather
than fear reveals a remarkable determination.

The Franks stayed in Le Lavandou until August 1943, by which
time life had become too expensive, and the lack of food meant a continual threat of starvation. In addition, with the Allied invasion of
North Africa, the Italians had diverted to the south, leaving the French
riviera to the Germans at the end of 1942. This left Frank, as a Jew, in
great danger. From Paris, the Zaks had gone into hiding near Grenoble. The Franks followed. An Orthodox priest, Father Bakst, invited

them to go and participate in a small religious community in Isère. There was a promise of food, some kind of philosophical work for Frank, and housekeeping duties for Tatiana. Frank described the move as a "new epoch in my wandering life."[31]

Unfortunately the Franks were again disappointed. There was food in abundance, but it was a desperate situation. The house they were given near the small village of St. Pierre d'Allevard had no water, heating, or cooking facilities. It was an uncomfortable place, inadequate for a cold winter. Frank described it as a kind of pavilion, a "dry, unheated shed, without a kitchen or stove, fitted with something resembling rooms."[32] They had to cook on a bonfire in the open air, and when it rained, Frank held an umbrella above Tatiana. Frank consoled himself by saying that "nevertheless we are thankful that destiny made us leave Le Lavandou and installed us here."[33] The gloom was deepened by news of the death of Paul Scorer in September.

Happily, they moved in October 1943 to accommodation in St. Pierre d'Allevard, but in an even more remote place. Frank's health was poor. He commented: "Unfortunately spirit and body are not working together as harmoniously as Plato thought."[34] However, the conditions were much better and quieter. It was a separate house with a kitchen, a main room, and a primitive outside loo.

There was no atmosphere of poverty, and the local farmers had plentiful food. Nevertheless, it was much more expensive, and the local villagers were not always friendly to the foreigners. In April 1944, for example, Frank wrote to Aleksei Struve that they had been without bread for a week and that the local peasants, fearing a breakdown of the transport system, were storing and not selling their produce. Aleksei responded by sending herring and tea.[35]

Near Grenoble there was a perpetual fear of the Germans, who came around looking for Jews to arrest. Tatiana wrote later: "We were like hunted animals, hungry and lonely." At one point they contemplated going across the mountains to Switzerland but decided against it. A number of Jews had tried this, but the Swiss were inclined to refuse them entry, and various people had failed to get through and been taken prisoner. Every time there was a raid, the Franks, like all the other Russian Jews, would head off into the forests to hide. Frank's life was in effect in the hands of Tatiana: "It was a terrible time, the Germans behaved like beasts, tried to catch Jews; often my landlady told me that the Germans had flown in to a nearby place, and I, with shame and pain in my soul, would take Semyonushka into the hills to hide him there, often coming back down to get him food or tea. I can never forget the burning shame [I felt] for people, whenever I saw that man, when I looked into his face."[36] The Zaks, who lived about ten miles away, had the same experience and in June 1944 escaped a search by the Germans only by hiding in the attic of their church.[37]

It is remarkable, considering Frank's fragile health, that he came through these experiences. He slid easily into depression and had nightmares: "One night, Semyonushka woke me up with his cries, he woke up from a nightmare [.] Although he did not see, for such things cannot be seen, he felt the reality and strength of evil[.] He was in the hands of evil, he felt that he was suffocating and dying . . . he begged me not to leave him. [He said that] 'love overcomes evil.'"[38]

The fact that Frank was never touched increased their belief in the help of Providence. Tatiana later said: "Semyonushka's life was in danger. . . . He could have been arrested at any moment and sent to a camp, never to return. For myself, I decided I would go with him wherever. Even to camp. . . . Why was he not arrested? I still cannot understand, do not know. Alesha was arrested twice and sent to a camp for undesirable foreigners. Semyonushka wasn't touched."[39]

Frank was as devoted as ever. "If you die first," he said in August 1941, "I will die on your grave like a loyal dog." Later he said: "Looking at you, I understood all the great power of sacrificial love."[40] When Frank in his nightmares during the war claimed that love conquers evil, he had this relationship in mind. His philosophy of love was surely partly built from it.

The financial situation, always bad, worsened with the move to this new accommodation. Frank estimated that he would need about 6,000 francs a month to live. It seems that 3,000 of that was covered by various academic funds, and that left another 3,000 to find. Aleksei Struve sent 1,000 francs.[41] Struve, knowing of Frank's financial difficulties, approached El'iashevich to ask him to help. This eventually led to Frank receiving at least 10,000 francs from El'iashevich in the winter of 1943–44.[42]

They built up some large debts. Frank estimated in September 1944 that they amounted to 30,000 francs.[43] This had to be paid before they could contemplate moving to Britain. They were suddenly helped by the unexpected appearance of Vasilii, a visit that caused his parents such joy that Frank wrote: "I now understand that one could die of happiness."[44] While in North Africa Vasilii started to collect things for his parents, which he managed somehow to keep with him. When he reached France with the Allied advance, he persuaded his commanding officer to give him a 1,500 cwt. lorry, which he filled with boots, shoe polish, cigarettes, tins of corned-beef, alcohol, and other things. He arrived early one morning without any warning at the end of September 1944. The Franks were overwhelmed. They put all the things out on the floor, and the neighbors came and chose items in exchange for their debts. Then Vasilii went with the Allies to Greece.

In May 1943 Nina Struve died. In early March 1944 Frank got news of the death of Struve. It was a great shock. In a letter to El'iashevich he described himself as "orphaned," declaring that Struve was a "genius," a man of extraordinary qualities. The duty of all his friends was to preserve the memory of his personality.[45] In a similar vein, in a letter to Aleksei Struve, he wrote that apart from his family, Struve had been "the closest and dearest person in the world" to him.[46] He declared that it was as a person rather than a thinker that Struve should be remembered. To Binswanger he wrote that Struve had been at the forefront of the struggle against materialism and positivism in prerevolutionary Russia and compared him to Péguy and Herzen.[47] Frank immediately set out to write his reminiscences of Struve, which eventually appeared posthumously as *A Biography of P. B. Struve.*

In the letter to El'iashevich Frank was prompted by Struve's death to pour out reflections about his own life journey:

> Everyone of us, of course, has had his own life and path, and everyone his own sins. As someone rightly said, every old man is a King Lear, but every old man, and especially those who have felt themselves called to something, is aware that he is a sinner, and is tortured by the feeble torments of repentance. I know from P.B. that he, who worked unceasingly all his life, zealously fulfiled his duty, and burned with a sacred fire, had a bitter sense that his genuine creative intention remained unrealized. Not long before his death, he wrote to me that his tragedy lay in the fact that he had only now matured intellectually and spiritually when his strength had diminished. And I answered him that I felt exactly the same. Every old man, as far as he consciously looks back on his life believes himself a "cunning and lazy slave." . . . I feel about myself that not only have I vainly wasted a mass of energy and many years on unnecessary things, betraying myself and my calling, but that even in my most academic and creative work, have not been sufficiently honest, responsible, and strict with myself, not sufficiently true . . . in my thought. I am now ashamed of the banal courses which I gave, and often think how intelligently and responsibly I could give those lectures now—now, when I am without energy and no one needs me. And all my academic works seem to me rather childish, and I feel that I have sacrificed strict, unbiased truth to please either the favoured, preconceived "ideas," or the logical harmony of constructions—in a word I feel them to be of the "second rank"—when I could and ought to have, if I had been sufficiently strict with myself, offered the "first rank." Only now, at once taken with ideas in two directions—the philosophy of creativeness, in which I think I have caught the "deepest secret" of being, and a con-

scientious evaluation of my own religious convictions and doubts, do I feel that I have now become at last "myself."[48]

The Franks were liberated on 22 August 1944 and moved into Grenoble. The subsequent months were very difficult. With the general lawlessness in France, there were hangings in the streets, and some women who had associated with Germans were painted with tar and shaved. When the Americans arrived, Aleksei offered his services. He was taken straight to the front, where in October 1944 he was badly wounded. He was on a jeep that exploded on a mine and lost an eye and part of his hand. It was a terrible shock to the Franks, and any thought of an immediate move to England had to be put aside. Tatiana in particular had great difficulty accepting what had happened.[49] He was transported to England by the American military in the spring of 1945.

In the summer of 1945 the Franks went to spend some days in Aix-Les-Bains to help Tatiana's rheumatism. Back in Grenoble at the beginning of August, they had news from Viktor that the English visa had finally come through, and they left for Paris. Frank's nervous system seems to have been very bad. At least Tatiana thought it was. She laid him out on the compartment sofa and went out into the corridor, declaring to anyone who wanted to enter that an extremely ill and infectious man was in there. "Thus," she wrote, "I gave him the chance to have some sleep and rest."[50]

In Paris they stayed with Aleksei Struve and Tatiana Lampert, a close friend of Tatiana from before the revolution. Eventually all the documents for the move to England were processed, and they took the boat train through Dieppe to Newhaven, arriving in London on 15 September. Earlier in the year Frank had reflected to Binswanger: "I have had quite enough of world history for my life."[51]

16

Religious Experience

F RANK'S WARTIME THOUGHT was a continuation of his previous work. In *The Unknowable*, he emphasized the importance of personal, mystical experience. The idea of a philosophy of religious experience had become central to his work, and he had grown more confident in expressing it. In a letter to Struve in May 1943, he admitted this. Describing the development of his ideas, he declared: "I now recognize the moment of 'empiricism' to be basic in knowledge, and I have broken with the vain desire to 'prove' and 'deduce' everything. Here, as in everything, the highest wisdom is in humility." Frank also stated that this new empiricism involved in his most recent work a "concretization" of his ideas, a result, he said, of his acquiring "an intuitive recognition of the moral foundations of being," and attaining to "a full clarity and inner freedom and breadth in religious beliefs."[1]

During the war, Frank's writing was primarily religious rather than philosophical, and this was because his interests were increasingly religious. He did not consider an understanding of the world as important as an experience of God. And God, he increasingly believed, cannot be experienced philosophically. At the end of 1942 Frank wrote in his notebook: "The link to God, life through love of God and trust in Him—this is like being in love, a possession of the soul whereby *you stop thinking* and you perceive higher truth with your heart and not your mind."[2] Frank's original conversion to Orthodoxy was not a dogmatic conversion and because of his experience of Marxist dogma, he was always suspicious of set systems of thought. Although he created his own system of thought, it is no accident that his chief work, *The Unknowable*, was devoted to what cannot be known or understood.

Frank wrote *God with Us* in the autumn of 1941 and expressed there his personal religious beliefs. A very private person, he never found it easy to reveal his inmost thoughts. At the end of his life he wrote to El'iashevich that he was not a "'biographical' person," that he wanted to keep his personal life to himself and answer for it to God alone.[3] Nevertheless, *God with Us* is a personal work; it lies somewhere between an argument for the validity of religious belief and a personal confession of what Frank had experienced. Its essence is antidogmatic and hostile to conceptual theology.

The central issue in religion, Frank wrote, is that God reveals himself to the souls of people. They do not need rational proofs of God because knowledge of God is not primarily rational. Any theology constructed primarily around dogmas is inadequate. What the world calls blind faith, a faith without rational explanation, can also be a certainty of the truths of faith. This is because certainty in religious experience is a product of the inner self-revelation of God, who is the voice of conscience in the human heart: "But one thing is important: we experience in the intimate depth of our heart the living presence and action of a certain force . . . , which we immediately *know* as the force of a higher order and as a *certain message from afar* which has reached our soul from a region of being which is different from all the ordinary everyday world."[4] The whisper of God in the human heart is thus the argument and foundation for religious belief. As Frank wrote to Binswanger, "The true method of cognition in the field of the spirit is a form of higher empiricism."[5]

Cardinal Newman once described dogma as the "fundamental principle" of his religion and associated the antidogmatic position with liberalism.[6] Frank admired Newman but by his definition, was definitely a liberal. In Frank, dogma is secondary to experience. The measure of the truths of dogma is their persuasiveness, their correspondence with the data of inner experience. God cannot be defined in concepts, which is what dogmas are, and any attempt to fix God into specific definitions leads to a narrowing of consciousness.

The extent to which Frank believed that dogma is a product of experience is well illustrated by his attitude to the resurrection as he expressed it a few months before his death: "Faith is never founded . . . on historical fact," he said to Viktor. "If you go to the Gospel as a researcher, then it could kill your faith, faith is born out of inner experience."[7] During a conversation with Viktor about Catholicism and the meaning of faith, Frank declared that there was no such thing as objective faith outside experience: "If you go to the Gospel text from the point of view of the judicious observer, then the account of the resurrection does not stand criticism, there are only contradictions in it. But if you live and think into the personality of Christ, then it becomes clear that he could not die, that in him the spirit overcame the flesh."[8]

Frank was actually less hostile to dogma than he made out. He did not regard it as unimportant. Just as a seafarer steers by the stars on the horizon, so, he believed, man should be guided by the dogmas that are on the spiritual skyline.[9] Dogmas are landmarks. They are of great importance but should not be regarded as the destinations. They are symbols of that inexpressible higher reality.

At the heart of this is Frank's ontology. Frank followed Kant's critique of "dogmatic metaphysics." God, for Frank, is the source of being and not being itself. God is not an object, not a "thing" that remaining invisible nevertheless occupies a place in the universe. So dogmatic descriptions about God are limited from the start because they fail to take into account that he does not belong to being.

For Frank, God is both transcendent to and immanent in every human being. His immanence is the source of the idea of Godmanhood. As he expressed it in *The Spiritual Foundations of Society*, a man becomes more himself the more he serves God because at a deep level of being man is part of God.

Writing to Binswanger, Frank declared that Binswanger, lacking a deep religious belief, had nevertheless become his teacher of theology. It is here that Frank's religious beliefs start to work out in action. Intellectual assent to faith is not enough: "The Christian world must stand united in the face of the growing menace from the enemies of faith—not from those who deny it intellectually, but [from those] who in practice reject its moral teaching." Love and the search for truth, rather than correct opinion, are the signs of God's presence in the human heart. Disbelief, since it results from a refusal to accept the evil of the world, may be faith in disguise: "Whoever searches and longs for truth, searches and longs for Christ, for Christ is truth."[10]

In January 1945, Frank wrote to the Russian philosopher M. I. Lot-Borodina, whom he had known in Paris before the war, "I am becoming more acutely aware that truth and untruth, in the deepest religious sense, do not at all coincide with the ordinary division of people into religious believers and non-believers. One must show, for example, the person who believes in justice and love of people—let us say a nonbeliever . . . but a well-intentioned socialist—that without knowing it, he believes in God and Christ; and one must show some other church person that he himself does not believe in God, but in the devil and mammon."[11]

This emphasis on the word "truth" reveals the extent to which Frank's philosophical and religious views are interlinked. In his philosophy, the idea of truth is the transcendental foundation for all thought. In his religion, the voice of truth is the voice of Christ in the human heart.

This truth is the foundation for what amounts to a kind of Christian universalism. The voice of truth can be found in all the religious traditions. Christ is at the heart of all:

> All the great religions of humanity contain an element of truth, which we not only can but must apprehend. Moses, the Jewish prophets, Buddha, the creator of the Upanishads, Lao Tse, the ancient religious sages, Mohammed—they must all be our teachers, wherever they adequately express genuine truth, the voice of God. *Precisely because* the Christian sees the absolute expression of God and His truth in Christ and his revelation, he knows that this truth is universal and that its echoes have always and everywhere been audible to the human soul and have found their partial expression. To accept one religion as true does not mean to reject all the others as false; it only means to see in it the fulness of truth, and a measure for the relative truth of other religions.[12]

Although Frank was suspicious of all theology, it is true that some of his own work is theological, and he was aware of that. In a letter to Binswanger, he ironically commented that *Light in the Darkness*, an attempt to describe his experience of the moral dualism of the world, had ended by becoming very much an expression of Christian theology: "The more firmly I grasp the problem, the closer I come to some of the foundations of traditional Christian theology. So, indeed, at the end of my life, I have come to set the stock of my life-experience in the ground of Christian belief."[13] However, if this acceptance of Christian theology involved some appreciation of dogma, he did not regard it as the primary aspect of religion. In a letter of August 1944 Frank expressed himself most fully:

> After careful reflection, I have come to the clear realization that in Christian religious thought and theology there are *two* completely *different* concepts of God, which are . . . *completely irreconcilable.* I will call them "philosophical" and "religious" views of God. The first was ideally, logically developed by Thomas Aquinas,—the second is what Pascal called "the God of Jesus Christ." For Thomas—God is absolute— the absolute first- principle, the foundation, the all-embracing, all-defining power *of everything in general.* . . . Such a God is necessary for pure philosophical thought, but to pray to and worship him, to be comforted by him . . . is impossible. "The God of Jesus Christ," the God of the human heart . . . is quite another being [*sushchestvo*]. . . . Both "Gods" undoubtedly *exist*—one is discovered by the mind, the other by the heart. But to bring these two—in effect the God of Aristotle and the God of Jesus Christ—together into one God is . . . absolutely impossible, at least *rationally.*[14]

Frank sides with Pascal over Aquinas. As he expresses it in *God with Us*, a religious Christianity is not faith in the teachings of Christ but faith in Christ himself as the incarnation of God.[15]

Frank's religion, then, is firmly rooted in the individual's relationship with God. In *God with Us*, Frank declared that faith does not appear by chance in the human heart: "Faith demands from man a certain strength of will, defined by a *moral decision* to seek what has the highest value." This will to believe is a "will to attend," a "will to *see.*" It means to *"direct the gaze* at the object of religious experience." "It is the will to open the soul to meet truth, to listen to the quiet, not always distinguishable 'voice of God,' in the way that we sometimes, amidst deafening noise, listen to a quiet sweet melody, which reaches us from far away."[16]

On the other hand, man cannot *take* faith, for it appears as a gift. Yet it is a gift that cannot be only passively received: "What is difficult here," Frank wrote, "what demands moral exertion, committed moral will, is simply our readiness to receive this gift, to go to meet the giver." This was a point he evidently believed to be very important. In his notebook of 1943, writing specifically on this point—that faith must be sought—he declared his enthusiasm for the verse in the Gospel of St. Matthew that states: "The kingdom of God is taken by violence." This idea was "my final testament and principle."[17] By this he meant that the responsibility for faith to a great measure rests on a choice to seek God. Faith is not an accident.

Frank's evident hostility toward systematic descriptions of the world had significant implications on a purely philosophical plane. It led him to declare in the summer of 1944 that all philosophers who attempt to explain the world are "liars" and "fools." Philosophy as a catechism about the world is impossible as a subject. He declared: "I search not for philosophy, but for *wisdom.*" The fact that Frank expressed this difference between philosophy and wisdom indicates an awareness that his thinking was to some extent antiphilosophical. If philosophy is about logical explanations, Frank was not a philosopher. Frank, of course, did not stop calling himself a philosopher. He was simply asserting his belief that any philosophy, to be adequate, must express a whole and not simply a rational view of the world. His work, based on the *docta ignorantia*, was an attempt, as he put it, to *"philosophically prove the impossibility of philosophy."*[18]

Frank's general approach to dogma is most clearly borne out in his attitude to Catholicism. Viktor's Canadian wife was Catholic, and at the end of the war he converted to Catholicism. This prompted a lengthy correspondence with his father.

In Frank's view, there are two aspects to the life of the church. On the one hand there is free individual experience where the essential mark of the spirit is complete liberty and independence from all rules and controls. Christ was a form of heretic, and the essence of Christianity, as a religion of freedom, cannot be put into any orthodox set of ideas. In this respect, everyone has his own road to God: "Strictly speaking, every person has his own God, his own individual religion." But along with this there is the organization of moral and spiritual life on earth. Since man is imperfect and grace alone is insufficient, he also needs an organized and disciplined spiritual life. This is the order necessary to prevent anarchy in the world and is provided by the organization of the church. Catholicism, he believed, had very strongly developed the latter element, partly at the expense of the former. It distorted the essence of the Christian spirit by overemphasizing church authority over free experience.[19]

By this, Frank did not declare that Orthodoxy was the supreme alternative. Indeed, he made a number of statements that were positive about Catholicism. In *God with Us*, he declared that Catholicism had done more for the Christian education of humanity than any other denomination and in the dark hour of the Second World War offered the greatest earthly hope.[20] After the war he described Catholicism as the "natural leader of Christendom."[21] To Berdiaev he wrote: "I envy the Catholics, clearly differentiating between personal values and objective church discipline."[22] Catholicism, he believed, had managed to retain a universal quality, whereas Orthodoxy and Protestantism had got into the hands of terrestrial rulers. During the war Aleksei Struve's wife converted to Orthodoxy, which Frank welcomed for the religious unity it gave to the family. However, he added: "I am not so absolutely convinced of the supremacy of our faith over Catholicism to see in [this conversion] the acquisition of truth."[23]

In his letters to Viktor he expressed fears that Viktor was not converting out of deep conviction but because of some kind of alienation from the atmosphere of the Russian emigration and worried that by separating himself from the faith of his background, he would become an internally divided person. Thus, he said, his concern for Viktor was not due to any dislike of Catholicism but to a concern for Viktor: "You know that I am without any fanaticism. . . . If I tried to dissuade you from converting to Catholicism, then I would probably have tried to dissuade a Catholic in your position from accepting Orthodoxy."[24]

Frank, then, affirmed his own Christian universalism. He was primarily a Christian rather than an Orthodox:

In my conversion to Orthodoxy, I was much helped by the fact that from childhood, in spite of my Jewish upbringing, I got accustomed to the ringing of bells, the appearance of churches, Russian holidays and so on, but nevertheless, this conversion, I can now say, was not really successful. My attitude to Orthodoxy is different from your mother's, for example. After a stormy enthusiasm for the Orthodox church, I now . . . find our spiritual soil in the consciousness that I am a "Christian," a member of the universal church of Christ, but not . . . a member of any specific denomination; there is something very valuable in Orthodoxy, incomprehensible to Europeans, which is very close and dear to me, but in principle I can only say that I am Orthodox, Catholic and Protestant, but none of them in separation and isolation.[25]

These comments are especially interesting because they indicate some change in Frank's religious views. Previously, he says, he was Orthodox in a committed sense, but this was no longer the case. This change may have been connected with the experience of exile. Frank remarked that being an emigrant made one realize that one never has a true home in this world. It was brought on by the church schisms of the 1920s. Frank wrote to Berdiaev in 1935 that he "had become detached from [*otstal*] the patriarchal church,"[26] which, since he always remained loyal to Moscow, means either that he had a weaker sense of commitment to the Orthodox church in Berlin by that time or that he felt less commited to the church as a whole. In any case, Frank's Christian universalism in its most confident expression belongs in the 1940s.

Nevertheless, in spite of Frank's breadth and universality, he was not convinced by aspects of Catholicism and the Roman tradition. He believed that the New Testament taught personal freedom and that Catholicism was in opposition to that. In letters to Viktor he wrote:

Christianity itself, in distinction from for example Old Testament or Mohammedan religiosity, consists in the awakening of such a "masculine" principle of individual, religious responsibility, of such a realization that the final issue for me is what God says *to me myself*, and *only to me myself*. (Here Catholicism . . . is inclined to deny this "masculine" principle.) But practically what is currently most important for me is that I somehow cannot believe that specifically you could find real inner satisfaction in such a "feminine" or "childish" type of religiosity.

I see your decision as the capitulation of a person who fears inner spiritual freedom in the face of the imposing power of a great and historically-influential collective.

Viktor wanted the security of a group to support him when, Frank declared, "only through the yearning of loneliness is true happiness acquired."[27]

Frank hastened to add that with all this, Viktor should not doubt his parents' continuing love for him. Tatiana, he wrote, had taken the conversion much more painfully than he, but they accepted what he had done: "We both, of course, have fully accepted the right for our children to choose their life's path completely independently and we only wish they find happiness and satisfaction on their chosen path. There is no question of any kind of 'condemnation.' Even if, by deep inner conviction and aspiration you became not a Catholic, but let us say . . . a communist, we would not condemn you, but would continue to wish you happiness on your new road and would give you our "parental blessing." . . . Our love for you and wish for your happiness cannot be hindered or diminished by any ideological differences."[28]

There was, however, an inevitable tension over the issue. In September 1946 Viktor published two articles in the English Catholic newspaper *The Tablet* in which he questioned the wisdom of those who after the schism in the 1920s had remained loyal to Moscow, questioned the judgment of Metropolitan Evlogii, and suggested that the postwar Orthodox Church in Western Europe was in some difficulty. The articles caused considerable controversy in the Russian community in Britain, prompting Father Lev Gillet, one of its most influential representatives, to warn that there would be a considerable scandal if Viktor continued to write such articles.

Frank was upset by what had happened and felt that Viktor was both unwise to write such articles and historically incorrect in aspects of his analysis. He stated that Viktor was making a moral mistake in writing critically of the Orthodox Church in Western publications. It was the "Russian patriotic duty" to attack the Soviet system but not to expose the Russian community to foreigners: "You must be a follower of Vladimir Solov'ev, and not of the arrogant Latin, Western people who despise Russia." Viktor's comments were implicitly critical of his father's position, and Frank defended himself vigorously: "The majority of the followers of the Moscow Patriarch act out of a feeling of religious duty, and themselves experience their position as a tragic one."[29]

After the war Frank had a brief exchange of letters with Viacheslav Ivanov, who after leaving the Soviet Union settled in Rome and converted to Catholicism. He was a firm believer in the visible church and did not respond to Frank's universalist approach. Ivanov questioned the value of having believing Christians outside the church, to which

Frank replied that the lack of a humanist element in historical Christianity had led to a deep cleavage between believing Christians and those who fought for reforms and democracy. The churches had seemed in some way against man. The chance to build a Christianity with a humanist face, which had been offered by great figures such as Nicholas of Cusa and Erasmus, had been missed. The result was that today those outside the church had a kind of mission to the secular world:

> Your question: in what do I see the use of the existence of free Christian souls beyond the bounds of the church? I answer: in that they are the one remaining bridge between the church and the atheists and are in this sense essentially missionaries with a calling in their relations with the latter. The church—the Catholic church—is in principle catholic, that is universal; but Christian revelation, which has invisibly overflowed in souls, is in one sense still more universal than the face of the church as historically formed. For this reason I come to a practical conclusion in regard to papal infallibility. I accept its practical usefulness: in the *ecclesia militans*, as in any army, there must be a supreme commander; but if an ordinary soldier, while fulfiling his order, retains the right to his personal opinion, then—even more so—this right is inalienable for the Christian. After the fashion of the orthodox Catholic Pascal I thus preserve my own right "from the court of the Pope to appeal to the court of Christ."[30]

Frank, not surprisingly, approved of the ecumenical movement and saw great potential in it. The key to its success, he argued, was not a solution to all the doctrinal differences between the churches but a new relationship and understanding. His approach here was in effect built around the ideas of his social philosophy: outward social life, or *obshchestvennost'*, depends for its quality on the inner unity of its members, or *sobornost'*. So the doctrinal unity of churches could result only from a deeper relationship of love. In the prewar period, the ecumenical movement had had two wings: the meetings in Stockholm, entitled "Life and Work," and those in Lausanne under the title "Faith and Order." While expressing admiration for both groups, Frank gave preference to the former for its emphasis on the spirit of reconciliation and working together as opposed to the latter's concern with dogma. The spirit comes before the letter. Dogmatic unity, while important, could result only from the right kind of relationships.[31]

In *God with Us*, Frank declared that there was a real basis for a growing unity of the churches. The dogmatic essentials in common were belief in Jesus Christ; his nature as both divine and human; salvation facilitated by his redemptive act; and most important, God as love and love as a divine force. Some of the doctrinal divisions between the churches were not as essential as they seemed. One of these, Frank argued, was the dispute over the *filioque* clause of the creed. The Catholics take the Holy Spirit as proceeding from both the Father and the Son; the Orthodox creed declares that the Son is "eternally begotten" of the Father and that the Holy Spirit "proceeds" from the Father but that they are both in an equal position before him. Frank argued that although with some doctrines such as those relating to grace and nature it was important for practical life to get the thinking right and precise, in regard to the *filioque* it was of no practical significance how one interpreted it. The doctrine was a mystery anyway. "I think," he wrote, "that not one serious, honest theologian could say in what consists the essential religious meaning of the Catholic formula of the *filioque*, and the Orthodox teaching about the procession of the Holy Spirit from the Father."[32] Consequently, Frank believed, there was room for some real progress in the dialogue on this issue.

Another area of difference was in attitudes to the transcendence of God. The Eastern churches stressed that man and God were linked, whereas the West, influenced by Augustine's belief in the transcendence of God, saw a great gulf dividing them. This difference, Frank argued, was not really essential. It was not a case of choosing between them but appreciating that they were both valid expressions of a divine spirit that reveals itself in many ways. As he said in 1946, "The differences between the two forms of Christianity as regards rites and theology must be viewed as a diversity of gifts and vocations which is perfectly consistent with the oneness of the Holy Spirit. . . . What we need now is a truly 'Catholic' latitude of mind which would acknowledge that Christ had revealed his truth to a world in its manifold human diversity."[33] While clinging to the fundamentals, then, certain doctrinal differences could be constructively addressed.

Frank actually regarded the Orthodox expression of the relations between the Trinity as more accurate than the Catholic. Using a formulation of the *filioque* clause frequently found in Orthodox tradition, he declared in his notebook in January 1943, "The Orthodox formula is more precise: the Holy Spirit proceeds from the Father, but through the agency of the Son; i.e., proceeds from the Son, secondarily passing through Him." At the same time he commented that "in their essential, real, true meaning, they coincide."[34]

With this in mind, Frank attempted to address constructively the issue of the *filioque* and church unity in an article in *The Tablet* in 1946:

I do not think that a formal, irrevocable schism ever took place at all, since on neither side did any authoritative body sanction a schism by excommunicating the other side. What we are now faced with is rather a protracted and deeply-rooted estrangement. Personally, therefore, I hold myself entitled to consider myself a member of the One and Indivisible Universal Church and as such, as being in communion with the Western church.

. . . The Catholic Church has deemed it possible not to insist on the *filioque* formula by the Catholics of the Eastern rite. I do not think that there would be any insuperable religious scruples which would prevent the Eastern church from acknowledging in one form or another the *sovereignty* of the Pope as the Supreme Bishop of the Universal church (as she did indeed before the separation). Such an agreement would in my opinion satisfy the urgent needs of Christendom in the present state of spiritual anarchy.[35]

The Tablet reviewer pointed out in reply that although the Catholic Church permits omission of the creed, it insists on acceptance of the doctrine.[36]

It is striking that Frank concluded his comments here by appealing to the state of the world. Current spiritual anarchy required a united voice from the churches, and it was time that certain doctrinal disputes were put to one side. Frank's thinking was therefore very much related to what he saw as the spiritual needs of modern society. It is in this sense that his universalism, although his personal belief, was a recipe for the world's ills. Frank wanted to see a gathering of the forces of good to tackle the forces of evil. In fact, not only did he want the Christian churches to work together, but he wanted a gathering of all believers, "including members of other, non-Christian denominations and even people, who are theoretically non-believers—in so far as the power of love *in practice* lives in their hearts."[37]

In the general process of Christian renewal, Frank saw a great role for the layman. Once again, his view of spiritual life involved a kind of duality. There was the conservative force at work in religious life, which preserved the great traditions of the past, handed them on to the new generation, and acted as the guardian of vital truths that should not be lost. Frank associated this with the church. At times of spiritual darkness, such work was of exceptional importance. However, the task of prophetic spiritual renewal was different. It found its source in the layman, working to introduce spiritual truths into everyday life. Frank saw confirmation of this division between the roles of the church and the layman in the history of monasticism where monks were always regarded by those in the church hierarchy as lay people.

The lay activities of societies such as "Action Catholique" should be encouraged:

> There should appear [Christian organizations of laymen] with the task of the active renewal in the spirit of Christian truth of all of life in the multiplicity of its aspects—there should appear Christian unions of different classes and professions, Christian societies to satisfy human need, Christian organizations for the reconciliation of all kinds of human conflicts. . . . And if here it is natural to have organizations united by having their confession in common, then, along with that, societies with members of various Christian denominations on the soil of a general Christian activity could have an absolutely distinct and providential mission.[38]

This thinking, perhaps comparable with that of Frank's friend Mother Maria Skobtsova, expresses in more detail what he had in mind by Christian humanism: the church at the service of the world.

In a review of *God with Us* in the *The Tablet,* one writer pinpointed the doctrinal dilemma Frank poses. His universality is very attractive, but it is arguable whether experience on its own is enough for a complete Christian theology. The writer suggests that Frank's thought is inadequate on two counts. First, he is not able to distinguish adequately between truths revealed to inner experience and those revealed to man by God and accepted on authority. Second, the distinction between natural humanity and humanity elevated by grace is ignored, and in consequence the potential sanctification of human nature, which is the gift of grace, is treated as inherent in that nature, as though the Incarnation itself were but the fulfilment and perfection, though freely bestowed by God, of a natural human possibility.[39]

These comments are extremely pertinent. Frank's philosophy of Godmanhood and its potential for pantheism means that it is always the immanent rather than the transcendent nature of God that predominates. In regard to revelation, Frank had argued in *The Unknowable* that "both philosophy and theology are based on general, eternal revelation." There was an interconnection between them: the former focuses on general truths, the latter specifics, but the two are certainly not absolutely distinct.[40] The immanence of God is also the reason for Frank's approach to natural humanity. Frank believed that Augustine, Aquinas, and the medieval mind had been wrong to stress God's transcendence and had therefore overemphasized man's sinfulness.[41] God's creation contains his spirit and is holy. With that, of course, the idea of Christ restoring a completely broken relationship of man to God is lost. Berdiaev put it simply and in another way in a review of *The Unknowable:* in Frank, "'ought' and 'value' coincide with reality."[42]

Even then, Frank is elusive in these matters. Frank valued revealed dogma and in his list of the essentials of Christianity included the dual nature of Christ, a doctrine that has caused immense dogmatic controversy in the church. In a way, Frank relied on the dogmatic tenets of the church. In regard to pantheism, he was always anxious to overcome the charge. For these reasons, Frank's position is not easy to define. He was, of course, an expert in finding grounds for agreement amid irreconcilable opposites.

Nevertheless, Frank was not a theologian. His thinking was mystical rather than theoretical. *God with Us*, for example, is an appeal to the heart as much as the mind, and it often achieves a poetic quality. "The human heart," Frank writes, "is so constituted that its centre of gravity and its resting place is in another world, beyond the range of the sensuous, bodily reality. It can preserve its balance only if the invisible cup of its scales, hidden in the depths of 'another' dimension of being, is full; if it is empty, the other, visible cup, in virtue of which man belongs to 'this world', helplessly sinks to the ground, unable to support itself."[43]

Even on dogmatic issues, Frank's mind could easily fly off in imaginative meditations. In January 1943 his thoughts moved to the Trinity. The Father is "the abyss, the transcendent, absolute first principle and source of all, the Creative Foundation, the Unknowable, the Inexpressed, the All-Nothing, God Concealed." The Son is "the expression and incarnation of the Father, God revealed . . . , the Concentration and Sun of Being, God in coincidence with the final depth of humanness, the human spirit, Godman and Godworld, Immanent God." Finally the Holy Spirit is "emanation, divine atmosphere, God as light distributed everywhere and penetrating everything; the life-giving principle." Again, the Trinity is like music. It involves "the creative conception of the composer, musical matter, consisting of distinct, exact, mathematically exact sounds, [and] the musical atmosphere, stemming from there and given by it." While these reflections are clearly thought out, they are not just philosophical descriptions. This is the writing of a man intoxicated by faith. It is Frank the poet, and with such a man, it is not surprising that he did not regard the doctrinal dispute over the *filioque* as important. Such writing suggests that Frank was not only a philosophical mystic but a religious one.

17

Christian Politics

A NUMBER OF Frank's family and friends died in the Holocaust. His sister Sofia's husband, Abram Zhivotovskii, and his son Leonid both perished in the concentration camps. Michel and Raissa Gorlin, Russian Jewish poet friends, died. Mother Maria Skobtsova died at Ravensbruck, exchanging her life for another. I. Fondaminskii, arrested like Mother Maria for helping Jews, died in a camp. Earlier in the war his old friend O. Buzhanskii had committed suicide in Paris: his family had objected to his decision to obey the Nazi order that Jews wear a yellow star. Frank took the suicide badly. When the Franks came through Paris in 1945, they met their old friend from Berlin Pianov, who had just come out of Buchenwald and was in a terrible condition. Frank went to see him in hospital and was shaken.

This was the bleak world which Frank, from what had amounted to internal exile in France, returned from in the latter part of 1945. He was not a disillusioned man, and his spirit had not been destroyed. Yet he had little hope for the world. He regarded the use of the atom bomb as a terrible sin and thought that humanity might easily destroy itself. And God, he thought, in his disillusionment at mankind's ways, might even permit such a destruction.[1]

The West seemed politically naive. Frank considered Roosevelt's judgment at Yalta disastrous, and it was not until Churchill's speech at Fulton in 1946 that some of his faith in the West was restored. Not only Roosevelt seemed confused. During his stay in Paris Frank had a meeting with Berdiaev, who at that time enjoyed a brief flirtation with the Soviet regime and advised Russian emigrants to return to their homeland. He believed that the Soviet regime's achievements in the war suggested that it was returning to the family of nations. It was a view Frank found incomprehensible, and they had a heated argument in which Frank became quite indignant.

Frank believed that the world was faced with an ideological war. In an unpublished article, "Soviet Imperialism," that he wrote after the war, he took up the issue of the long-term nature of the Soviet system. Hopes, he wrote, that communism might evolve into something different were illusory. Soviet power, in its very essence, was merciless and despotic. Its full character had not been displayed in 1917 but in 1929–30 during the collectivization of the peasantry. Lenin had started the process, but it had grown to fruition under Stalin, who having destroyed those of his colleagues with a more romantic vision than his, set out to create a totalitarian society based on an idea of slavery. "The Soviet system," Frank wrote, "is a totalitarian state in its maximum, most absolute form, because it is based on a *principled* denial, not only of political, but also of civic freedom."[2] With oppression its only mode of survival, the Soviet system returned to the idea of Asian despotism with the addition of technology to put the idea into practice. Fascism, for Frank, was the pupil of Bolshevism.

Since the end of the war, Frank declared, the Soviet Union had become open to corruption from without. Fearing Western democracy, which it perceived as absolutely alien to the Soviet idea, Stalin had built Eastern Europe as a buffer to prevent this outside influence. The aim was "the creation of an *eastern bloc*, covering a wide strip of the Asian world, the eastern Mediterranean and Europe from the Baltic to the Aegean."[3] This empire was dangerous to the West not so much as an expansionist power like its tsarist predecessor but as an ideological opponent. The only answer, Frank argued, was some kind of spiritual renewal in Russia, which he hoped might be possible after the war. The key thing was for the West to hold out long enough.

The ideological war demanded a broad-minded response. In *God with Us*, Frank had argued that the forces of good in the world were actually more numerous than Christians realized. Often, nonbelievers were allies of the universal church. This was a theme he considered in another essay, "The Real Meaning of the War." Frank commented on the fact that there were many people in the world burning with communist convictions. At the same time, he said, democracy had ceased to be an idea that could really inspire people in Europe, and the quality of it in the West had also deteriorated so that what people called democracy was in fact materialism, the same materialism that lay at the root of Soviet communism. So beneath the outer forms of the ideological struggle in the world Frank perceived another conflict, the conflict between the materialist and religious views of man. This conflict was not so much between believers and nonbelievers as between those who believed that there was good and evil and those who did not. This assessment, Frank argued, might be unacceptable from a strictly ecclesiastical viewpoint, but it was vital in the context of the terrible world situation.

As a hypothetical example, Frank took two figures from the French Left: Léon Blum, leader of the French Socialists, and Maurice Thorez, secretary-general of the French Communist Party. If the two were asked whether one should suspend one's moral principles for the sake of achieving a politically useful end, Blum would say never, and Thorez would say that one was obliged to suspend them. Thus, while both men were politically on the left, one, Blum, stood firmly for moral principle and therefore the sacred idea in man; the other, Thorez, belonged in the materialist camp.

This was Frank's message to the Christian democratic parties of the new Europe. The Christian view of the world needed to be broadened to include nonbelievers. Frank feared that the new Christian Democratic parties might ally with the wrong people, failing on occasion to realize that they had many friends in the traditionally left-wing camp or at other times allying with people on the Left who were its moral enemies. Only a deeper moral criterion, which went beyond Right and Left, would be adequate.

Politically, Frank declared, a Christian renaissance drawing on the traditions of the past yet creatively relating to the needs and aspirations of millions of contemporary nonbelievers was of vital importance. Without it, "neither the wealth of America, nor the wisdom of politicians and diplomats and even more no atomic bombs will save the world from inevitable ruin."[4] Thus, Frank asserted, the political health of the world depended on the rediscovery of spiritual life. This was the *Landmarks* analysis for the postwar world.

However, beyond the immediate practical, political issues, events such as the Holocaust raised deeper problems. What had happened? How did the Nazis come to do what they did, and what kind of world was it where such terrible things could occur? What kind of politics would be sufficient to deal with such challenges? These were the issues Frank particularly reflected on during and after the war, and his reactions to them marked the culmination of his political and social philosophy.

In November 1942 Frank wrote in his notebook: "In this terrifying war, in the inhuman chaos which reigns in the world, he who first starts to forgive will in the end be victorious."[5] This belief in the necessity of forgiveness was at the center of Frank's thinking. The cycle of revenge had to be stopped. For this reason Frank was strongly against the Nuremburg trials, in which he felt the defendants were presumed guilty from the start and was shocked at the death sentence meted out to the former prime minister of Vichy France, Pierre Laval. (Frank was always against the death penalty.)

The essence of Frank's postwar political thought was an attempt to justify ideas like forgiveness in the political arena. He was concerned to combat the idea that "realpolitik" is always cynical, always presumes that the most realistic political option will prove the bloodiest or most dishonest. For a hopeless and hate-filled world, forgiveness had to be the choice of the realist. Mankind, Frank believed, would have recovered easily from the destruction of the war of 1914–18 if the spirit of hate and revenge had not poisoned the economic and political life of the following decades.[6] This mode of thinking was the thrust of an unpublished postwar essay, "The Christian Conscience and Politics":

> In spite of all its cruelty, war, in as far as it is resistance to a politically organized criminal will, may be directly prompted *by love*—and, moreover, by love not only for the victims of the criminal attack, but also of the enemy himself. . . . But because there are tragic situations in which we are morally compelled to cause suffering and even to deprive other human beings of life, it does not in the least follow that there are situations in which we must renounce the commandment of love and be guided by hate. . . .
>
> . . . No bombs, not even atomic bombs, none of the cruelties of war cause so much destruction of normal conditions of life or are the cause of so much ruin and evil as the *spirit of hatred.* Comparatively soon, ruined houses will be rebuilt: the slain will be buried. . . . But hatred which has entered the world has the capacity of prolonging itself indefinitely. Leaping like a spark from one soul to another, the spirit of revenge gives birth to ever new fits of hatred. . . . Are there not many otherwise quite kind and intelligent people who preach fervently that the German people . . . should be utterly destroyed for the good of humanity? This is the way in which the diabolical Nazi doctrine of racial hate, vanquished in open battle, marks a triumphant recovery in the hearts of men. . . .
>
> This shows clearly that the Christian commandment of love—of love to all men, including one's enemies, of sacrificial love capable of renouncing egotistic gain for the sake of another's good is not only far from being a "Utopia" incompatible with "real politics," but is, on the contrary, the only possible "realistic" politics. The fundamental tasks of "real politics" in our terrible time may be summed up in a few words: in this war of hitherto unheard-of extent and cruelty, *the true victor will be he who first begins to forgive.* . . .
>
> . . . The call to repentance and non-judgement has not been made for moral edification alone. Like every other religious doctrine it is

imbued with a deep understanding of the spiritual order of man's being.
. . . It is bound up with the *awareness of the collective interdependence
of human destinies*, and, hence, for the joint responsibility for the evil
reigning in the world. It is based on a deeper insight into the *causes* of
evil, and is, therefore, of primary political importance. . . .

. . . The responsibility for evil [lies] not only with those who actually
commit it, but also with all their contemporaries, with all those who help
to create and share in the common conditions of life—to wit, with *all of
us*. . . .

. . . Hitlerism and German militarism . . . arose not from the Germans' will to evil, or at least not from it alone; they would have been impossible without the general political and economic prostration, i.e.
without the decay and moral and political paralysis of the whole of Europe during the two decades which preceded the wars.[7]

Frank's comment that everyone is responsible for evil in the world
echoes the position of Dostoevskii's Father Zossima, who declared
that mankind would be saved only when everyone took responsibility
for everyone else.

Frank wanted to provide a theoretical foundation for the politics of
love. He attempted to do this in *Light in the Darkness*, which he re-
worked in the months after arriving in London. It was a challenging
task, and Frank enjoyed it: "A book written on this theme in 1939–1940
sounds in 1945 as if it was written in the 18th century—infinitely too
feeble and friendly. One must now for the same ideas find other words
and I am just working on that now. This is a lot of fun for me, and as
always, I find the meaning of life only in precise creative action, in
words squeezed out of thought."[8] Unfortunately, when it was finished,
Natalie Duddington, who translated *God with Us* into English, refused
to translate *Light in the Darkness* because of its antipacifist senti-
ments. It was eventually published by YMCA Press in 1949. Considering what had happened in 1939–45 both in the world and in Frank's
life, a book on Christian politics was a remarkable idea.

In Frank's philosophy there is a dualism essential to everything he
wrote, a division between the exterior "material" and the interior
"spiritual" worlds. This dualism appeared in his religious thought in
the form of a morally divided universe. This was the basis for *Light in
the Darkness*. In regard to this, Frank rightly argued that *Light in the
Darkness* was not a theological work,[9] because its origins were in his
philosophical system.

Light in the Darkness starts with a quotation from St. John's Gospel: "The light shineth in darkness, but the darkness comprehendeth it
not." The world, separated from God, is in darkness but is lit by the
light of God. The location of this spiritual meeting between light and

darkness is in the depth of every human heart. Thus, two worlds meet in the human heart. The two aspects of human nature lead to two tasks in life: personal self-perfection or being with God and the moral improvement of the world in the context that it is not perfectible. In the political arena, the politician must combine absolute and relative moral demands. The ideal democracy, which is the goal of the absolute demands of the inner world, must be balanced against an appreciation of the sinfulness of society and the need to fight for goodness on the basis of the way things actually are. The result is the same form of realism which Frank wrote of in his letters to Struve of 1922–23: "The necessity to take into account in the make-up of the moral life of the individual—within the limits of his being in the world—this duality, this combination of holiness, of the obligatory nature of the moral foundations of real human life with their imperfection defines what one can call *Christian realism.*"[10]

Christian realism is thus a form of arbitration between different moral demands. It involves an intuition of the link between the "outer" and the "inner": "Social reforms are fruitful and lead to the good only insofar as they take into account *the given moral level* of the people for whom they are intended. . . . The best intentions of social and political reforms not only are fruitless, but can even lead to fatal results if they do not have support in definite, suitable human material."[11]

Frank's Christian realism is in fact a kind of anti-utopianism. The world's fallen state must be accepted. Frank's description of "natural law," for example, is built around this. In the conditions of the fallen world, God has instituted certain principles to protect man against evil but that reflect the fallen state of the world. They are marriage, private property, and the state. Utopian attempts to be rid of these things "are unnatural attempts to tear man's being from the soil of the world in which it is rooted." In heaven, these principles will not apply, but it is highly destructive to try to abolish them in a worldly environment. "Genuine Christian wisdom necessarily includes *the consciousness of the inevitability in the world of a certain minimum of imperfection and evil.*"[12]

In *Light in the Darkness*, Frank argues for Christian realism with pacifism in mind. In his view, pacifism, motivated by a desire to preserve one's personal perfection in the face of the onslaught of evil, is a totally irresponsible option. An individual is responsible for himself and his salvation, but also for the fates of other people. And if that means using violence, for example to oppose violence, that will in some cases be legitimate. If this sounds like an argument for arbitrary moral relativism, Frank is at pains to stress that to use evil means to defend oneself against evil does not make those actions good. They remain evil. He warns that "any sin, even the *morally-necessary* burdens the soul, and with an inadequate attention of conscience, if it becomes a habit, can corrupt it." And elsewhere: "It is a question not of rational, utilitarian calculation of means for the attainment of a certain end, but of a certain *integral solution of moral tact*, which is guided by the striving to find, in the given concrete conditions, a way out, that is *least burdened* by sin."[13]

Back in 1905, Frank and Struve in their articles on culture had discussed the problem whether violence could ever be justified and did not rule it out, although they were extremely adverse to violence. Only "moral tact" could decide those few occasions when it would be justifiable. Frank's Christian realism is a culmination of that idea of "moral tact." Christian realism must deal with the situation at hand. It cannot implement policies that do not fit the moral state of the population. There is no ideal system. The goal is service of a higher truth, but every society is at a different stage in its fulfillment of that service, and thus every situation demands a different response. Frank's Christian realism is a form of pragmatism with an ideal spiritual goal as its aim. It is an eloquent justification for an ennobled pragmatism.

It is pragmatism with a vision. Although the world is not perfectible, man is compelled to fight for goodness: "Not being able to overcome and destroy evil completely, and conscious that he himself is responsible for evil, he must do *everything possible* to effectively counteract evil." This has two aspects to it: "Perfection can be an essentially-moral introduction of good into human souls, that is, moral education and spiritual correction and the enrichment of life; or it can be directed at the *order* of life, at the norms which act within it, relations and forms of life, and in this case it is social-political perfection. . . . Both make up the task of Christian politics in the wider sense."[14]

In regard to legislation, Frank distinguishes between two types of policy: the policy that will protect society from evil but in itself cannot actually improve conditions and the attempt to influence society through a process of moral reeducation. This reeducation, if applied, should not mean a kind of outside compulsion. Changes effected through this approach will be effective when they influence the wills of people rather than trying to force them to be virtuous. In this sense, the policymaker will still operate according to the vital maxim that the inner world is the key to the outer.

The basic heresy of modern times, in Frank's view, was the idea that human nature in itself does not need improvement. Personal improvement leads to social improvement. It was precisely through this path "from inside outwards" that all the great achievements of the Christian culture of Europe had been built. In regard to slavery, for example, "[Slavery] had been gradually dying out before it was legally abolished."[15]

Frank offers an explanation of the way the individual, through his spiritual life, influences society. Between the erotic life of man and the laws of society that govern sexual relations there is an intermediate sphere of moral habits, concepts, and values through which the moral life of individuals eventually influences the laws. In the sphere of the material needs of people there is an intermediate realm of customs of courtesy, kindness, and compassion or, alternatively, coldness, reserve, and indifference through which the individuals of a nation come to influence its laws. "Through this intermediate sphere," Frank writes, "the general legal order normalizing the general structure of collective human life is, in the final analysis, an expression and product of the personal spiritual life of the members of society, the degree of their moral perfection or imperfection." The Christian politician will understand the way the individual influences society. Acting on the basis of that, he can try to Christianize society, *"creatively Christianize the general conditions of life, to reform these conditions in the direction of their maximal agreement with Christian truth."*[16] This process is Christian politics.

In earthly conditions, Frank suggests that "it is possible to have a Christian state, a Christian economic and social order, a Christian attitude toward property, and especially a Christian family."[17] These, however, will never be perfectly achieved because the world is not perfectible.

The greatest problem with Frank's political realism is in the area of application. "Moral tact" is a fine idea in principle, but what are the criteria by which the active politician should make decisions? Who is to tell him when the moral level of the population has descended to such a low level that the universal franchise should be suspended? How should he decide whether to use violence at a given moment? There is also a theoretical problem. Frank seems to offer a dualistic world; there is the inner challenge of self-perfection and the outer task of moral improvement that necessarily involves some kind of compromise. Frank attempts to overcome this dualism and any cynical attempt to misuse his idea of "moral tact" with his idea of the "politics of love."

Typically, Frank is interested in uniting contradictions in a higher unity, in a "center." He argues that man's inner life with God should radiate outward in his activity in the world. There need never be circumstances when the principle of love need be suspended: "[In the face of man's responsibility for his neighbour,] irresponsible sentimental love, unarmed for battle against evil . . . and politics guided by goals other than love for people, are both inconsistent. Truly responsible active love inspires us to 'politics,' the system of intelligent actions that takes into account the concrete conditions of human life. . . . In a world that suffers from the politics of hate and from dreamy, irresponsible love, we must affirm the courageous Christian idea of the politics of love."[18]

Frank's vision for Christian politics is a noble one. *Light in the Darkness* closes with an eloquent vision of "inspired" statesmanship similar to that in *From the Depths:*"Christian realism not only does not lead to passivity, but requires *maximum intensity of moral activity.* . . . [Genuine moral activity combines] the inexhaustible power of faith with a reasonable account of reality—the activity . . . of a servant of the God of love, who has no need to become a Don Quixote in order to be a fearless and tireless knight of the Holy Spirit in the world. In its essence, Christian activity is *heroic* activity."[19]

Here, Frank places great emphasis on the role of the individual. The individual can be a knight, a hero, a visionary. Frank's Christian political thought considers intuitions and motivations. He does not really offer concrete political advice. There is no blueprint. He tells how to be a politician. Obviously, then, he puts as great a stress on the policymaker as the policy. For it is the policymaker who will bring the necessary intuitions and motivations to further the realization of the right policies. Here, then, we see his deep belief in the importance of the individual. In Machiavelli's thought, the effective prince utilizes his *virtù*, his intuitive understanding of the needs of the moment and the changes of fortune, to consolidate his power and the power of the state. Frank offers something like a Christian *virtù*.

Frank's Christian politics, typical of his writing, is concerned with finding a synthesis of contradictory demands. It is a manifestation of the broader intuition present in his thought at the time of *Landmarks* that there must be a reconciliation in European thought between the Christian and atheist currents. This reconciliation would lead to a new Christian humanism. This was the feature of Solov'ev's thought that Frank most admired: "In his teaching about Godmanhood, Solov'ev was the first in history to give a principled, religious-dogmatic foundation to what one could call Christian humanism."[20]

Thus, *God with Us* and *Light in the Darkness* must be read as part of the completion of this train of thought. It is a theme Frank continually insisted on, and it indicates the extent to which he regarded the Second World War as part of a historical process. Just as after 1917, Frank argued that the Bolshevik revolution was a product of sociological factors and a process of secularization of European thought, so he now does similarly for the Second World War. In a sense the Second

World War is a product of an age-old fault in European intellectual history.

For all his love of Augustine (and throughout Frank's work, Augustine is quoted with admiration), Frank traces this fault back to the Augustinian rejection of the goodness of man. From that point on, man was regarded as bad and God as good. There was an element of truth, Frank argued, in the Pelagian heresy Augustine fought against: namely, that man could freely choose the grace of God.[21] The result was that the Renaissance and the Reformation declared the power of man in opposition to the idea of God. European intellectual history split in two. The need now was for a philosophy that would be both totally Christian and totally humanistic. Christian morality could not be separated from the Christian religion. As Frank explained to Binswanger, morals without metaphysics are not adequate. A secular Christian morality, Frank believed, was a product of the "barren . . . superficial humanitarianism of the 19th century," a creed that could not appreciate the nature of evil.[22]

Frank lamented that Christian socialist and Christian democratic movements had lacked "the ardent faith that can move mountains." Such a faith depended on a new understanding of Christian revelation: "This spiritual flame can flare up only when its deepest religious and dogmatic source is recognized—when the Christian revelation is seen to be a new revelation not only about God but also about *man*. This 'Christian humanism' was indicated by thinkers like Nicholas of Cusa, Erasmus and St. Francis de Sales. Faith in man might have developed in the bosom of the Christian church itself, and then the whole social and spiritual history of Europe might have followed a different and more harmonious path."[23] Others Frank labeled as Christian humanists were Thomas More and the famous Russian bishop Tikhon Zadonskii, who had been the model for Dostoevskii's Father Zossima.[24]

Frank's view of history, expressed in *The Spiritual Foundations of Society*, was that it reflects the story of man's relationship with God. Frank's writings during and after the Second World War suggest a strong sense of history. Writing to Binswanger after the war, he declared: "Old European culture is approaching its fatal end. . . . All cultural and historical eras must have an end."[25] In 1950 he quoted Lord Acton in his notebook: "Religion is the key to history."[26] Frank's work of the time was a response to this diagnosis and reveals an acute historical consciousness; to some extent, it also reveals an acute historical relativism. Christian realism is a complete focus on actual social and political conditions. However, that relativism is combined with clarity about where history should ideally go—toward the ideal free democracy he outlined before the war.

Although Frank outlines where history should go, he does not hold definite hopes that it will do so. History, for him, is not by necessity moving in that direction. Progress is not inevitable. The Second World War could not be called part of a progressive development. Rather, it was the culmination of a false road in European culture. The divergence of the Christian and humanist currents in history had reached a climactic conclusion. To some, this view deprived history of any overall direction or meaning. The Russian theologian Georgii Florovskii described *Light in the Darkness* as a "thoroughly pessimistic book" because, he believed, it lacked any sense of growth in history. Florovskii suggested that "Frank had no hope for history. It was for him a tragedy without any immanent catharsis."[27] Frank would partly have agreed with such an evaluation. On one occasion Binswanger suggested to Frank that he was an optimist, but Frank replied that to the extent that he did not believe in the inevitable victory of good over evil and since he believed that God is like any human artist and cannot always be assured of success, he was a pessimist.[28] However, Frank did not argue that there is no meaning to history. His philosophy was geared to finding meaning not in progress toward a goal but in the foundation of life itself. The linear progression of time was for him less real than the ultimate reality that lay beneath.

Related to this, Frank did not believe that Christ's mission could be measured by its success in the world. The sign of the almightiness and success of Christ's task was simply *"the irrepressible craving for Him of the human heart."*[29]

Frank's aspiration for synthesis was also evident in his thinking on nationhood. In 1949 Frank published an essay entitled "Pushkin on the Relations between Russia and Europe." Although it was concerned with Pushkin's thought, it was also a reflection of Frank's views. Its thrust was that neither the Slavophile nor the Westernizing traditions in Russia were adequate. Pushkin had had the wisdom to reject the extremism of both these trends, searching for a genuine synthesis between the two. According to Frank, distinctiveness in national identity does not preclude universality: "The deeper and more distinctive [an individual is] . . . the more universally human he is; a nation is the same."[30] Frank's political views in this area were not far from his religious opinions. He did not like exclusive creeds. This was why, although he loved Russia and much appreciated certain aspects of the Slavophile tradition, he never accepted Slavophilism. In his search for a universal approach he felt cut off from much of the Russian emigration. He regretted, as he expressed it in a letter to Fedotov, the lack of Solov'ev's broad-mindedness in the Russian tradition: "[Russian nationalism] is permeated with a false religious exaltation. . . . Slavophilism is . . . an organic and evidently incurable disease of the Russian spirit (which is especially strong in emigration). It is characteristic that Vl. Solov'ev, in his battle with this national self-admiration, has had no follower. Everyone whom he influenced in other ways—Bulgakov, Berdiaev, Blok—turned onto the comfortable path of national self-admiration."[31]

Frank's enthusiasm for Solov'ev is not surprising. What is surprising is that Solov'ev's influence on Frank seems to have been indirect. In the introduction to *Reality and Man*, which Frank wrote between 1945 and 1947, he denied that Solov'ev had been the inspiration for his thought. Although the thesis of *Reality and Man* was similar to the philosophy of Solov'ev, Frank declared, "the similarity became clear to me only when my own theory had finally taken shape." Solov'ev's influence had been "unconscious."[32] This seems confirmed by the fact that Frank's main work on Solov'ev took place after 1945 when he edited an anthology of Solov'ev's work and gave a series of talks on him for the BBC that were published in *The Listener*. In an article on Solov'ev he wrote in 1950, Frank stated that since Dostoevskii's famous Pushkin speech in 1880, every Russian had considered himself a universal person. "Too often," he wrote, "this has been an unjustified, empty pretension."[33] Nevertheless, Solov'ev, he declared, had really been a universal figure.

In his introduction to the anthology of Solov'ev's work, which he edited after the war, Frank's description of Solov'ev's Christian thought could be equally applied to his own:

[Solov'ev] combines a bitter awareness of the power of the evil, unconquerable till the end of history, . . . with a keen sense of the Christian's responsibility for the world's evils and insistence upon active struggle for Christ's truth in every domain of human life. Solov'ev preaches an *heroic* Christianity which has no need of optimistic illusions for carrying on its arduous moral activity. . . . There grew up in his heart and mind a kind of grand synthesis between the spiritual attitude of the first Christians, the medieval faith in the Church as the spiritual guide of mankind and the humanitarian faith of modern times. True, he did not definitely formulate this synthesis; he called it his religion of the Holy Spirit. It points the way which Christian thought must follow—the way which Péguy sought after him and to which the most sensitive minds of our day are unconsciously drawn.[34]

As he implied, Frank was not a disciple of Solov'ev in a formal sense. Nevertheless, their outlooks on both metaphysical and social questions were strikingly similar, and the phrase "religion of the Holy Spirit," if used to refer to Frank's belief in the universality of truth, is an apt description of his Christian thought.

18

London

FAMILY LIFE IN London was acutely difficult, mainly because of the condition of Aleksei. His marriage with Betty Scorer came to an end. In subsequent years he lived with Natalia and his parents in London, but he had continual drinking problems accompanied by epileptic fits resulting from his injuries. He had not been registered as an American soldier when he was injured and was thus unable to get a war pension. Tatiana was worried about him, almost to the point of obsession. Frank's health was bad, and he and Tatiana worried that they were imposing on Natalia. The result of all this was continual tension in the household.

The grandchildren Misha and Peter Scorer were in the house, although they had to circumvent a regime established by Tatiana and rigorously enforced; the house had to be absolutely silent not to disturb Frank's work. For this reason and because Frank did not grapple with the practical details of his life in any way, the impression created was that Frank lived in a world created entirely for him by his wife, isolated from reality. He looked at the family, at least, through her eyes.[1] Nevertheless, he enjoyed the grandchildren and would sing songs and tell them stories.

Viktor worked in London through and after the war for the BBC, then went to work for Radio Liberty in Munich. Vasilii found a job at the Allied Control Commission in Vienna as an interpreter.

The Franks had very little money. In spite of Frank's promises to Binswanger to pay his debts after the war, he was never able to do so. Before his death he asked Viktor and Vasilii to pay Binswanger, but Binswanger refused to accept anything. The family relied greatly on outside grants. Although there was no money available from the Christian Council of Refugees, as before the war, through his contacts in the World Council of Churches, Frank received £243 from the Gene-

214

va Secretariat of the Ecumenical Refugee Commission in 1946 and £100 from the organization Christian Reconstruction in Europe in 1948.[2] In 1947 he had written to the World Council of Churches offering his services: "The experience of these years has taught me much, and I would be happy to take part in the hard work of the spiritual regeneration of the world, according to my powers."[3] When Vasilii reached Austria, he sent about £25 a week. After Frank's death, Tatiana managed to get a pension from the German government as the widow of a Jew who had to leave Germany.

Contact with British life was limited. Frank wrote some articles for *The Tablet* and gave his talks on Solov'ev for the BBC. He admired the English philosophical tradition, Bradley in particular, but he had little contact with British academic life. On one occasion he had a brief meeting with Isaiah Berlin but was disappointed to be told that Oxford philosophy lacked Hegelians and was dominated by empiricists.[4] Frank's social milieu was the Russian community. Nikolai Zernov, cofounder of the ecumenical Fellowship of St. Alban and St. Sergius, was a frequent visitor. Lev Gillet was a close friend. There were visitors from abroad, including Berdiaev and Zen'kovskii. On one occasion the young theologian Aleksandr Schmemann came and so impressed Frank that he compared him with Struve.

While in London, Frank took on the editing of an anthology on Russian philosophical and religious thought. This eventually appeared posthumously and included extracts from the works of Berdiaev, Bulgakov, Fedorov, Florenskii, Viacheslav Ivanov, Merezhkovskii, Rozanov, Shestov, Solov'ev, Tolstoi, E. Trubetskoi, and Frank. He wanted to include Struve, but his publisher did not permit it. Frank also edited an anthology of the writings of Solov'ev. It was commissioned by Mania Harari, a Catholic of Russian background from Collins publishers, but after a controversy over Solov'ev's attitude to Catholicism, it was eventually published by the Student Christian Movement Press in 1950. *God with Us* was published in 1946 by Jonathon Cape. However, until the end of 1947, Frank's energies were primarily devoted to *Reality and Man*, a work that marked the culmination of all his thought. The origins of the book went back to 1942.

During the war, when Frank started to think about a philosophy of creativeness, he believed he was doing something of immense importance, that he was approaching the inner secret of being. He was attempting to grasp the moment of Bergsonian dynamism in the world. In Berdiaev's original critique of *The Object of Knowledge*, he had identified two approaches to "being" in Frank's work—those of Parmenides and Heraclitus—and stated that Frank erred on the side of Parmenides. In some ways, Frank's interest in creativeness was an attempt to redress that balance.

On 5 April 1943 Frank wrote to Struve: "Being all my life a Platonist (and in one sense still remaining one) I have only recently (better late than never) recognized the huge positive value of Aristotelianism—of a living motif, which incarnates itself in concrete reality, and the idea which forms it (entelechy)—and the falseness of the cult of abstract idealism. My basic ontological intuition is that the essence of being and life is creativeness, formation, incarnation, the introduction of the creating ideal principle into inert 'matter.'"[5] The idea of creativeness and the discovery of Aristotle were evidently related here; Frank was trying to find a clearer place for the concept of entelechy in his overall philosophical system.

In the same letter to Struve, Frank declared that he wanted to create "a universal philosophical system" built from natural science and the humanities, resulting in a logical and religious-philosophical synthesis.[6] He had kept up with the latest developments in mathematics and physics and believed that certain discoveries had their parallels in the spiritual world. In April 1943 in his wartime notebook, Frank referred among other things to Werner Heisenberg's uncertainty principle and Sir Arthur Eddington's observation that the behavior of electrons cannot be fully defined. If true, Frank believed, the work of these men destroyed the mechanistic view of the world and introduced the possibility of uncertainty and thus a form of freedom.[7] Perhaps, as Leibniz suggested, the customs of nature change; perhaps there is a creative spirit in the natural world, as there is in the human. Frank thus wanted to build a philosophy of creativeness that would bridge these two worlds.

Such, then, was Frank's broad purpose. He felt he could glimpse the beginnings of a new Kantian synthesis: "I can only see the basic 'personalist' organic foundations of being—the principle of 'creativeness' (as a primary, as yet unrecognized category) and the corresponding principle of 'inertness'—which I spy everywhere, beginning with physics and ending with the area of language in spiritual-social life."[8]

Although he clearly believed he had arrived at something new and important, Frank's understanding of creativeness belonged to his philosophy of total-unity and Godmanhood. In his anthropology, Frank presents man as tied to God. Man becomes more human the more he transcends himself. Frank's concept of the creative force in the world involves the idea that God is revealing himself in his creatures and in the objective material world. Some of the phraseology in Frank's notebooks suggests the Hegelian idea of the Creator positing himself as the objective world and creating an "other": "The first principle, incarnating itself, differentiates itself into Creator and creation; as it were from its own womb it gives birth to material." The world, Frank declares, is not yet perfect; it bears the marks of God's continuing creative agony.[9]

In regard to man personally, as opposed to inorganic nature, creation is for Frank a form of cooperative work with God. It is obedience to the will of God. Creativeness is the expression not of the personal existence of the creator but a wider superpersonal reality. Man as creator is a conductor or herald: "The great creator creates not his but God's will. Creation begins at the moment of readiness to resign one's will, when we say 'Let it be *Your* will'—the higher creating will." Such is the case in artistic, scientific, political, or any other creative work. "For creation is not there where we think and do, but where something *is born* in us apart from and against our will, like a baby in the womb of a woman." Frank differentiates his concept of creativeness from that of love. Creativeness involves the striving to create something new, whereas love is concerned to preserve what already exists. However, both have their source in the higher divine power. Maternal love, sacrificing itself for children, occurs in both the human and the animal world and suggests a divine foundation in both these worlds.[10]

At the end of 1945 Frank commented to Binswanger, "Whether I will be in a position to realize my planned systematic philosophical work (on 'creativeness' as the basic principle of being), I doubt; perhaps, however, I will manage to bring to maturity at least part of the problem." In November 1946 he wrote that his philosophy of creativeness, although much worked upon, was not succeeding.[11] Frank struggled with the ideas for the work on creativeness and in the end did not manage to write it as he had foreseen. However, the ideas in his notebooks of 1943 reappear in his last significant philosophical work, *Reality and Man*, which he completed at the end of 1947 and was published in 1956 only after his death; the ideas reappear as an important feature of the work and thus of Frank's final testament on the metaphysics of human nature and the world.

Thus, in *Reality and Man*, Frank affirms that the creative principle stands both at the foundation of personal human actions as they cooperate with God and at the root of organic and inorganic processes in the nonhuman world:

In the experience of creative inspiration, in which the superhuman creative principle directly passes into human creative effort and is merged with it, man is conscious of himself as creator; that means that he is aware of his kinship with the creative primary source of life and of his participation in the mysterious metaphysical process of creation. It is as a creator that man is most conscious of himself as the "image and likeness" of God. In the domain of reality, experience is the ultimate criterion of truth, since experience is self-revelation of the reality present in it; there can therefore be no question of illusion or error here, as in the case of our knowledge of the world of fact. Hence we are entitled to express it in ontological terms and say that man is co-partner in God's creativeness. . . .

. . . Such is the general correlation between God and His creatures manifested in the mysterious presence of creative processes in cosmic nature itself. It was recognized by Aristotle in the doctrine of purposive form or entelechy, but during the last three centuries the world has been regarded as a lifeless machine. In our own time, beginning, approximately, with Bergson's doctrine of "creative evolution," the presence of creativeness has once more received recognition, at any rate in regard to organic nature; and the development of modern physics inclines scientists to admit that something similar may be found in the so-called inorganic nature as well.[12]

In 1943 Frank wrote that his denial in *The Unknowable* of the value of exploring the origins of sin had been correct from a moral and ethical standpoint but could not be justified from a religious metaphysical angle.[13] In *Reality and Man*, Frank used the concept of creativeness to try to address the problem. The creation of the world was not an event that took place in time. It is continually going on. God is not a cosmic superman who stands at the beginning of the process. Rather, he created the world out of himself as his other, which is seen as pure potentiality and dynamism (as opposed to the unity of potentiality and actuality that constitutes God's being). This explains why, from man's perspective in time, the world is not yet perfect: God is continually, and creatively, working on its perfection. The world, as a reality apart from God, is a formless dynamism or potentiality.

Creation of the world, which from the point of view of man is a temporal process and from the point of view of God timeless, involves God's arrangement and distribution of this dynamism and potentiality by instilling into it his own perfection and actuality: "We may say with Bergson that the very character of temporality inherent in cosmic being, i.e., time itself as the dynamism of transition and duration, is an expression of creativeness, of creative striving, lying at the root of existence. From that point of view, the world is not so much the result or the fruit of Divine creativeness as its immanent manifestation. . . . The history of the world and of man with all its disasters is the expression of the struggle of God's creative power and the chaotic disorder and elemental obduracy of his material, i.e., of the sheer dynamic potentiality of being."[14] These comments suggest that Frank's view of history was not deeply pessimistic. History involves God's continual perfection of the world. It has a deeply divine meaning.

Whether Frank was fully happy with this explanation of the imperfection of the world, however, is open to question. Certainly Lev Zak doubted it.[15] According to Zak, Frank was always tormented by the question asked by Ivan Karamazov: Is God's harmonious world acceptable at the price of the sufferings of a small child? It is doubtful that Ivan Karamazov's reservations would have been assuaged by Frank's solution.

As his social philosophy makes clear, Frank was hostile to any kind of individualism. This was the reason he never liked Berdiaev's thought. As he said to Berdiaev in 1946, "I differ from you where your philosophy carries the character of groundless rebellion and individualism. . . . I accept the lawfulness and truthfulness of rebellion but only as a subordinate moment."[16] The thrust of *Reality and Man* is that man is not an isolated unit separated from the world. In this sense, the philosophy of creativeness, which is at the heart of it, is of great importance. Frank understood the work as in part an attack on existentialism. In November 1946 Frank declared to Binswanger that his philosophy of creativeness was not working but that he was attempting a "philosophy of philosophy" that would justify the worth of philosophy against obscurantist thinkers like the existentialists and that if he succeeded, he would be completing an important mission. In April 1947, while writing *Reality and Man*, he said that it would be "in part in polemic with existentialism."[17]

Frank understood existentialism to be a manifestation of modern individualism. "Modern 'existentialism'," he wrote in 1948 to M. I. Lot-Borodina, "is the bitter hangover of our era after the long period of the deification of man."[18] On completing *Reality and Man* in December 1947, Frank reported to Binswanger that the fundamental tendency of the book was "to attempt to bring the problems of human 'existence' (the theme of existential philosophy) into a synthesis with real metaphysics, with the perennial philosophy (which for me means Christian Platonism)."[19]

In *Reality and Man*, Frank describes individualism as an idea that "primary reality coincides with the closed-in and finite sphere of 'one's own' inner life or *Existenz*."[20] He states that Heidegger's existentialism is a modern example of it. During the war and after, Frank was hostile to what he perceived to be Heidegger's individualism and described him in 1948 as "a very sharp thinker, but malicious and hateful to me."[21] In 1950, however, he changed his mind with the publication of Heidegger's latest work, *Woodpaths*, which he described as a "real event in the history of the European spirit":

You know what repelled me from Heidegger: the idea of the unity of the soul, "existence" as it were in a vacuum—the opposite to my metaphysical life-picture. Now, the whole meaning of the new book is that Heidegger has broken out of this prison, and has found the way into the open air, into true being. This position remained closed to the whole of the German philosophy of the last 100 years. Therefore this work is an event. . . .

It could not be more meaningful and joyful for me than that at the summit of my life, I discover that the greatest German thinker comes on his own ground to the conclusion which as a fundamental intuition, as it were as a revelation, has guided all my creative work for 40 years. You understand, that this satisfaction has nothing to do with my personal vanity, from which I feel free. I am also glad that Heidegger in his way has described this intuition much more vividly and meaningfully than I managed to do.

Should European culture be on the road to destruction, then Heidegger's last book will be its best postscript.[22]

In conversation with Viktor on 31 August 1950 Frank expressed great admiration for Heidegger's new work. In that context, he recalled his revelation of 1913—"*cogito, ergo est esse absolutum*"—and suggested that Bergson was the only other thinker who had a similar intuition.[23]

Frank's late enthusiasm for Heidegger puts into perspective the purposes of *Reality and Man*. He had seen in Heidegger and modern existentialism generally the lack of the very creative spirit he believed was so important, a lack of the Godmanhood of man. As soon as Heidegger abandoned the idea of "existence in a vacuum," Frank welcomed him. In this context, *Reality and Man* can be read as an attempt to see man as rooted in a higher reality, to understand his "ground." Thus, the importance of "creativeness" in Frank's thought becomes clear: in creativeness, he sees man's kinship with reality as a whole and with God.

Frank admitted the great value of Christian existential thinkers like Augustine, Pascal, and Kierkegaard but believed that they had a one-sidedly tragic conception of man's place in the world. Their work needed to be "completed and balanced by the opposite elements of trust in the final, metaphysical foundations of being, of the consciousness of the closeness between man and God."[24] *Reality and Man* was an attempt to complete the work of the Christian existentialists. It admitted both the imperfection of the world and man's secure foothold in the divine reality. The very possiblity of tragedy, Frank argued, presupposes spiritual depths in which man is secure.

In this, *Reality and Man* is a declaration of hope, a dramatic assertion that the world has a definite meaning. Just as with *Light in the*

Darkness and its Christian humanism, Frank attempts to offer another foundation for a destroyed European culture:

> Man's life is tragic because his spirit is solitary in the natural world . . . ; he is compelled to waste his powers on the arduous and never wholly realizable task of preserving and perfecting his life, and to take part in the work of outer and inner creativeness, imparting form and light to the world around him. But however great his sorrows and disappointments . . . , in the ultimate depths of his spirit he is securely rooted in God, and through this is in inner harmony and joyfully-loving unity with all that is. The pain of discord and the peace of harmony dwell in his heart side by side; indeed the discord and tragedy of his existence have their source in his privileged, aristocratic position as a being superior to the world, a child of God . . . and bears witness to his inviolable security in the bosom of Divine holiness and omnipotence.[25]

The emphasis on "man" in the title *Reality and Man* is important. The fact that Frank takes man as his starting point suggests that a change had taken place in the focus of his philosophy. Prior to *The Unknowable*, Frank had suggested that the proper study of philosophy was God. However, he states in *Reality and Man* that religion takes God as its starting point, whereas philosophy must start with the "immanently-given nature of man."[26] There is no doubt that Frank's mind had gone through a process of reassessment. In a revealing letter to Binswanger in 1946 Frank suggested that his work had suffered from an insufficient distinction between philosophy and religion yet that he would still love to find a synthesis between the two:

> I have fundamentally understood Pascal's saying . . . that between pure thought and the field of the religious . . . there is just as deep a gulf as between thought and material being. Many of my writings suffer from a haziness towards this gulf, even though my fundamental intuition, of which I recently wrote you . . . contains at least in embryo the possibility of really overcoming it. It is very good that I at least understand that now. It is only to the greats—Plato, Plotinus, Nicholas of Cusa, and in recent times perhaps also Kant—that it was given to achieve here a real synthesis. In Thomas Aquinas, his grandiose metaphysical system crushes the purely religious element (on this he movingly testified, when he rejected his *Summa* completely and said: "Everything that I have written up until now is nothing but straw!"). My creative work and thought is now chiefly moving in two quite sharply differentiated directions: the philosophical-systematic . . . and the existential religious, although I see this [division] as a spiritual scandal and have in mind a work of complete synthesis, which I do not really have time or energy to do.[27]

Frank's assessment of his own work is interesting. His comments reveal an awareness that his thought could be accused of making an insufficient distinction between philosophy and religion. However, his statement that acceptance of such a division was a form of "spiritual scandal" for him reveals the extent of his deep desire to reconcile and bring together these currents. His hopes and dreams in the world of philosophy related to creating such a synthesis.

In September 1947, three months before he completed *Reality and Man*, Frank wrote that he was searching for a middle position between an "objective ontology," or Kant's "dogmatic metaphysics," and subjectivism or existentialism. This meant a bridge between the objectivist and subjectivist views of the world. Man was to be the middle position—a point in the outer objective world to whose inner life a higher reality reveals itself. Accomplishing this task, Frank wrote, would bring his life's work to a completion. This confirms that *Reality and Man* represents an attempt by Frank at such a synthesis. It was obviously a work of great importance for him. He said that he worked on it in a "a kind of ecstasy and spiritual drunkenness," and in 1949 he described it as "the maturest product of my mind."[28]

In spite of all that, it did not perhaps represent the all-embracing synthesis Frank had hoped for. In his vision for a synthesis of natural and humanitarian sciences, as he expressed it to Struve in May 1943, Frank kept a place for a theory of language. This was not featured in *Reality and Man*. Frank wrote to Binswanger in 1948 that he had long conceived of a plan to write a philosophy of language that would accompany a philosophy of creativeness. He doubted he could achieve it but said that he had done a great deal of reading in linguistics over the previous seven years. His theory, as he briefly outlined it to Binswanger, was an extension of his theory of creativeness. Speech is a creative expression of spirit in sensual material. Speech, like art, expresses a music that arrives from a higher source. In October 1948 Frank had in mind another work, this time on intuitive epistemology, and also considered writing a philosophical testament.[29] None of these projects came to anything, and they indicate that Frank's mind was not satisfied with the completion of *Reality and Man*.

In spite of the declaration of hope that *Reality and Man* represents, Frank's life in London was not easy. One continuing cause of unhappiness was the lack of a Russian audience for his books. The émigrés were dying out and with the Soviet regime in power, there was no sign that his books might be read in his native land. In a notebook of quotations he wrote out for Vasilii in 1948 he included a line from Edmund Burke: "Never despair, but if you do, work on in despair."[30] Frank may not have despaired, but he had a sense that life was passing by. In London he heard the news that his brother Mikhail had died after a long illness in 1942; that left Lev Zak as the only surviving member of his original family.

Bulgakov had followed Struve to the grave in 1944. In spite of his disagreements with Berdiaev in 1945, Frank had maintained warm relations with him. Berdiaev died in 1948. Frank wrote to his sister-in-law E. Iu. Rapp that the "last comrade of the old guard has left." In spite of their differences, Frank said, they had always maintained a close relationship and had "a deep, spiritual solidarity . . . in the most essential area—in the free search for truth." He declared himself "spiritually orphaned" by Berdiaev's death.[31] In May 1949 he published an article on Pushkin, "Bright Sorrow," in which he characterized Pushkin's tragic consciousness as one of "mournful resignation—sadness softened by acceptance."[32] It could have been about himself.

Frank, as ever, was unwell. Precisely how unwell is difficult to ascertain. In Paris he had been diagnosed with angina pectoris, but one of his English doctors could find no trace of it. It may be that Tatiana exaggerated the extent of his health problems; nevertheless, when walking a distance, he would get a pain in the chest and have to stop. For such circumstances he always carried pills with him. He continually used sleeping tablets.

Frank fell seriously ill in August 1950 with cancer of the lungs. He was confined to his room and remained there almost continually until his death in December. Although the nature of his illness was concealed from him, he realized he was dying. El'iashevich came from Paris to say good-bye. Lev Zak came and remained with him until he died. The illness was exceptionally painful, particularly in its last weeks, and Frank relied heavily on the comfort of Tatiana. She rarely left his side and kept a notebook for the things he said. It was the time of the Korean War, and he felt a sense of guilt that he was dying surrounded by family while others were dying on the battlefield. Returning to the memory of his mother, he attributed the comfortable surroundings in which he was dying to the fact that his mother had forgiven him for his lack of love.[33]

These last months were spiritually the most important of his life. His mind was intoxicated by religious ideas. He had certain experiences of a mystical nature that led him to believe that everything he had written was wholly inadequate to the truth he then experienced. He said that it was like reaching the summit of a mountain and discovering the view to be very different from what you expected. "Philosophy has already gone old for me," he wrote.[34]

Zak, a close confidant at that time, provided the best description of the most important of his experiences, which took place in the first part of November:

> One morning, a few days before the end of S.L., I found him agitated by something and joyfully surprised. Then I heard the following from his own mouth: "Listen," he said to me, "during the night I experienced something very remarkable, something very surprising. I lay in torment, and suddenly felt that my torments and the sufferings of Christ were one and the same suffering. In my sufferings I communicated in some kind of liturgy, and participated in it, and at the highest point communicated not only in the sufferings of Christ, but, dare one say, in the essence of Christ. The earthly forms of bread and wine—are nothing in comparison with what I had: and I fell into a state of blessedness. How strange it was: it was surely something outside of everything I have thought about for my whole life. How did this suddenly happen to me?" I think that this mystical experience, given to Semyon Liudvigovich, was the highest point of all his former searchings and the crowning moment of them.

Zak added: "His spiritual journey was also a repentance (He said: 'I am a resounding gong or a clashing symbol, I did not know love'), a humble renunciation of his will and acceptance of God's will (He always used to say: 'Nevertheless let it be Your will and not mine') and love for God ('I got to know blessedness through love; the highest thing is love of the sinner for the holy'). . . . He said to me, 'I live from a living source. Everything expressed is already not it.'"[35] Zak, who had known Frank longer than anyone else, believed that Frank changed very deeply during this first liturgical mystic experience. He felt that Frank's mind was deeply permeatcd with the pessimism of classical Greek thought and that only in these last experiences did he find a new quality: "Undoubtedly, during his illness, something quite new revealed itself to him, something wholly foreign to him throughout his whole life."[36]

Frank's spiritual experiences were closely tied to the agonies of his illness. He continually stressed that suffering is the road to God. He also stated that the idea of the deep religious value of suffering is what distinguishes Christianity from other religions and what distinguishes the New Testament from the Old. Suffering as a positive idea belongs with the figure of Christ: "Suffering is the road to Christ."[37]

Frank had a deep belief in the next world. He loved, for example, C. S. Lewis's religious classic about heaven and hell, *The Great Divorce.* At one point during these months, Natalia had an extremely vivid dream of her dead husband, Paul, who mysteriously said to her, "Everything is ready." When she related it to her father, he said, "That is reality."[38] To the end, then, the invisible world was his reality.

He always refused morphine, but on the last day, 10 December, he accepted an injection of it and did not wake up. The Orthodox priest Father Anthony Bloom gave him last rites while he was unconscious. Frank once said that he would be quite glad to be cremated rather than buried because there was no theological difference. However, Tatiana favoured burial, and he was laid to rest in Hendon, north London. Some lines that he loved from the Book of Wisdom was written on his grave: "I loved and sought wisdom from my youth. Perceiving that I would not possess her unless God her to me, I appealed to the Lord."[39]

Conclusion

BERGSON ONCE REMARKED that every philosopher has one basic point to make and that everything he writes is a variation on it. This is true of Frank. Frank's primary intuition was that everything finite is rooted in an all-embracing whole or unity. In his philosophy, he always tried to offer a synthesis between the absolute and the relative, the monistic and the pluralistic. His gaze was directed at the presence of synthesis or relation. In this sense, his philosophy is summed up in the words of al-Hallaj quoted at the beginning of *The Unknowable:* "To know is not merely to see things but also to see how they are submerged in the Absolute."[1]

At the same time, the word "absolute" does not fully embrace the spirit of Frank's work. In *The Unknowable* in particular, Frank is attempting to personalize the absolute. "Total-unity" develops into the expression in philosophy of the idea of a personal God. That is why the "I"-"Thou"-"We" relationship is so important to Frank. The absolute or God cannot be understood purely through analysis; they are best approached through a relationship. In this respect, Frank could be compared to Dante, whose cosmic vision ends with a picture of God as "the love which moves the sun and the other stars."[2] Frank's philosophy is about love and creativeness as well as unity.

That Frank can be compared at all with men like al-Hallaj and Dante is a strong indication of the nature of his philosophy. To the positivists, his work, which was a system of speculative metaphysics, will be seen as just an attempt to ask questions that cannot be addressed by reason. To them, the "unknowable" simply cannot be known. Frank's reply would be that the presuppositions of reason and knowledge must be explored first. Nevertheless, it is not a vision of philosophy that sits easily in the twentieth century. Charles Péguy, the French thinker whom Frank much admired and compared to Struve, once

226

described philosophy in terms Frank would undoubtedly have approved of: "A great philosophy is not one [that] goes unchallenged. . . . A great philosopher knows that he and others travel alongside [one another] and that each faces a reality which daily grows greater and more mysterious."[3] For Frank, then, philosophy is a kind of personal journey and sacred calling.

The weaknesses in Frank's ideas are obvious. In spite of his protests to the contrary, his philosophical system contains pantheistic elements, and the result is that his treatment of the problem of evil is never very satisfying. Consequently, his religious thought does not deal adequately with the problem of Original Sin. His religious ideas are so closely connected to his philosophy that doctrine and revelation are not addressed in a way that would be fully satisfying to a theologian. The reason for this is the extent to which his philosophical and religious ideas are one and the same thing. In the end, the two are not really separate. He was aware of this. As he wrote to Binswanger in 1946, he believed that his work suffered from a hazy distinction between the two disciplines. At the same time, his fundamental intuition was based on a belief in the interconnection of things; he wanted to overcome this distinction and create a synthesis. He never claimed to be a theologian but was a philosopher with a religious perspective, belonging to a long line of thinkers in Russian and European thought whose philosophy was of that kind.

The issues Frank raises are certainly close to the concerns of traditional Russian philosophy. Typically Russian concepts like "living knowledge," "*sobornost*," and "total-unity" find expression in Frank's work. Yet while it is true that Frank admired aspects of Slavophile thought and in particular the work of Solov'ev, his work fits more easily into a European tradition. Indeed, it is difficult really to know how much the Slavophiles and Solov'ev influenced Frank's philosophical development because his early works contain so few references to them.

Frank's work should be seen as part of the current in European thought and philosophy that has been open to metaphysics. He drew heavily on the neo-Platonism of Plotinus and Dionysius the Areopagite, as well as from the "coincidence of opposites" of his "chief mentor," Nicholas of Cusa. Spinoza and Goethe were important in the development of his philosophical system. Although he had on the surface of it broken with the idealism of Fichte and Hegel, his universalism retains much of the approach of the German idealists. In the twentieth century, he chose Bergson and the late Heidegger as those closest to him, but his interest in the philosophy of relationship also puts him in the company of writers like Martin Buber and Gabriel Marcel. Frank cannot be understood outside this European tradition; in this sense, he is not just a representative of Russian philosophy.

At the same time, Frank's work clearly grew out of the needs and experiences of his inner life. His son Viktor wrote that his father's true biography was in his philosophical work,[4] and this is surely true. His fascination with total-unity, for example, was partly a philosophical response to a love of beauty. His neo-Platonism was connected to his inner sense of sadness, to the melancholic Hellenism that was present throughout his life and that according to Lev Zak, he overcame only on his deathbed. Indeed, Frank said something very similar in a letter to Binswanger shortly before his death: "The longer one lives, the more the immanent tragedy of life comes to consciousness, and the necessity . . . of finding a secure hold on the spirit, on the transcendent. Such an inner, isolated spiritual tranquillity was born into me, [and] my whole philosophy is generally nothing else but its expression."[5]

Frank was an extremely private man. The intimate side of life was very important for him, even sacred. He once wrote to Binswanger: "It is strange that one can be much more open in letters than in conversation. For lovers and friends, distance is a great blessing because only then can they really express themselves. And it demands much tact at the next meeting to be silent about what was openly discussed in the letters."[6] A sense of sacredness in life is surely connected to the expression of the sacred in philosophy. Frank evidently had a sense of the sacramental about his marriage and profoundly valued his friendships with Struve and Binswanger. His philosophical exploration of God and of personal relationships surely fits with this. He was attempting to grasp in philosophical terms the sacred nature of life and true human communication.

It is this link between Frank's experience and his philosophy that gives his life its great unity. His philosophical and religious views were in part declarations that in spite of everything, the world has a meaning. Even during the Second World War, which was probably the most difficult time of his life, his life and letters confirm that this was his personal belief. In his darkest moments he forcefully argued against a nihilistic picture of the world. Where there was sadness and doubt, it also found an outlet in his work, as in his 1949 essay on Pushkin, "Bright Sorrow." Binswanger wrote to him during the war: "Of all those whom I have encountered in life, you are the only man whose teaching, nature and life form a complete unity."[7] Frank's ideas flowed from his experience; he was not a secretly divided person.

Frank's search to express his inner intuitions was also a kind of struggle. His quiet, even passive personality may obscure the fact that his work was an attempt to give a new direction to European civilization. He did not like the materialisms of either Russia or the West and the accompanying relativization of truth. In this sense, he was engaged in a task: to save philosophy from psychologism by rooting "thought" in "being" and to save man from an isolated individualism by presenting him as a creature rooted in God and community. In his memoir of 1935 Frank wrote that weakness of character had been the "basic hindrance" of his whole life,[8] and he probably had in mind his feeling that he did not do enough actively to help people. In spite of this, Frank set himself the enormous task of creating an all-embracing "first philosophy," and at the end of his life he was talking about creating the first major philosophical synthesis since Kant. Although at the end of his life he was not fully satisifed with his achievement, he cannot be accused of settling for limited objectives.

In political philosophy Frank was trying to develop a theory that would be an adequate response to the horrors of Bolshevism and Nazism. The term "liberal conservative" accurately reflects the nature of his political ideas. He clearly had a profound conservative belief in the organic nature of society and opposed both rampant individualism and revolutionary change. At the same time, he was very much a liberal, believing in economic freedoms, private property, the rule of law, and elected governments. Frank could also be called a "national liberal" to the extent that he identified with certain national liberal ideas in prerevolutionary Russia and because he defended the idea of the nation in his work. At the same time, he was never a nationalist, never moved as far to the right as Struve, and was not at home in right-wing political circles.

Nevertheless, a term like "Christian liberal" or "Christian democrat" is probably closer to the spirit of Frank's later political thought. *Light in the Darkness* is really an attempt to provide a Christian basis for postwar European political life. It is his new stress on motifs like love, forgiveness and repentance that gives his later work a more directly religious quality. In this area, his Christian realism has something in common with the thinking of Aleksandr Solzhenitsyn, whose 1973 essay in *From Under the Rubble,* "Repentance and Self-Limitation in the Life of Nations," addresses similar problems. Frank was looking for a new, overtly spiritual dimension to modern political life.[9]

In spite of this, Frank warned the Christian democratic parties not to be narrowly Christian. Kindred spirits, he declared, would not be found by listening to speeches but by looking at actions. That sums up an essential feature of his political and social philosophy. In *Landmarks,* when Frank declared that Marxism and populism were at heart very similar doctrines, he meant that the methods revolutionaries use determine the outcome of their struggle as much as the policies they advocate. If violence is chosen as a method, it affects the policy. For Frank, the means help to determine the end.

Frank's anti-utopianism, so powerfully expressed in *Landmarks* and *Light in the Darkness*, foreshadowed the critiques of maximalist political doctrines that can be found in many later writers. There is a community of thinkers whose social and political ideas were formed in reaction to their experience of communist dogmatism. Many of the Russian and Eastern European dissidents belong in this community, some having chosen secular and others religious alternatives to communism. In a way, Frank and the rest of the *Landmarks* group are also part of it. Frank's thought specifically fits into a kind of postcommunist Christian democratic position. It puts him in the company of writers like Czeslaw Milosz, Leszek Kolakowski, and indeed Solzhenitsyn who are hostile to any form of totalitarianism but are concerned to combat the moral bankruptcy that can accompany pure individualism.

Frank's political thought is based on universalist Christian anthropology. His openness to all religious traditions comes out in the fact that he believed that Indian Brahmanism contained the first expression of the ontological proof;[10] referred positively in *God with Us* to Buddha, *The Upanishads*, and Lao Tse; and drew from al-Hallaj. In one of his copies of the New Testament that survived his death, it is notable that the Gospel and Epistles of John were the heavily underlined works.[11] This was no accident. Frank's intuition of the world was closest to that of St. John's Gospel, to the belief that Christ gives light to every man who comes into the world. It is not a question of Christian or non-Christian but of loyalty to that inner light. In fact, Frank believed that human nature as a whole is cosmically defined.[12] In his view, secular ideologies fail to account for this. The soul of man, as Tertullian put it, is by nature Christian, even if also fallen. Thus, the laws of God are natural laws and are disobeyed at man's peril.

For Frank, society as well as the soul withers without Christian values. In his view, the causes of the Bolshevik revolution lay in a profound collapse of moral and spiritual values in the nation. He believed that the moral struggle that occurs in each soul also takes place in communities and countries, and his social philosophy was constructed around that belief. In his notebook of 1950 Frank quoted Arthur Koestler's view that "ethics is not a function of social utility, and charity not a petty-bourgeois sentiment but the gravitational force that keeps civilization in its orbit."[13] This was Frank's conviction: the fundamental answer to Russia and Europe's maladies was a return to a sacred view of man and society. Here, Frank's metaphysics, politics, and religion come together. They are part of the same vision.

Frank regarded himself primarily as a philosopher. His social and political ideas thus belong to his metaphysical system rather than vice versa. Consequently, his politics and social philosophy, like his religion, are really extensions of his overall philosophical system. The result of this is that his political and social ideas sometimes read like abstract moral counsel rather than concrete analysis. Topics of study like social cleavages and even institutions do not receive much, if any, treatment. Nevertheless, these were not Frank's focus. He was interested in the moral actions and understanding of the policymaker and the spiritual rather than the economic or political foundations of society. When in 1918, Frank declared that the Russian liberals had, in their understanding of the state and law, lacked not technical ability but "living moral experience," he was approaching the problem in this way. They failed to understand that a state has a moral life, and that politics must therefore be informed by a moral and spiritual vision. In this, while retaining a profound belief in the institutions of state, Frank nevertheless believed in the preeminence of spiritual life over the political. Politics was not an autonomous discipline, and therefore his political ideas belong more in the world of moral philosophy than political and social science.

Once Frank is understood for what he is, he should be read and appreciated in his own terms. He persuasively interpreted the Russian revolution within the framework of a broader religious understanding of man, society, and the world. He produced a genuinely complete philosophical system, that offers a theoretical basis for a sacred vision of the universe. He managed to link enormous abstract problems with the personal needs and intimacies of the soul. His work was dedicated to showing the interconnections of things. In the context of his turbulent life, it is a remarkable achievement.

Notes

ABBREVIATIONS

BA:	Columbia University, Bakhmeteff Archive
GARF:	Gosudarstvennyi Arkhiv Rossiiskoi Federatsii
HI:	Hoover Institution, Boris Nikolaevskii Collection
NN:	Possession of Natalia Norman
NS:	Possession of Nikita Struve
OR-RGB:	Otdel rukopisei, Rossiiskaia Gosudarstvennaia Biblioteka
PD-IMLI:	Pushkinskii Dom, Institut Mirovoi Literatury i Isskustva
RGALI:	Rossiiskii Gosudarstvennyi Arkhiv Literatury i Isskustva
RGIA-St.P.:	Rossiiskii Gosudarstvennyi Istoricheskii Arkhiv—"Sankt-Petersburg"
SA:	Archive of Aleksandr Solzhenitsyn

INTRODUCTION

1. V. V. Zen'kovskii, *History of Russian Philosophy*, vol. 2, pp. 853, 872.
2. See N. M. Zernov, *Russian Religious Renaissance*, pp. 131–64.
3. S. L. Frank to Ludwig Binswanger, 12 July 1942, NN.
4. Viktor Frank, "Semen Liudvigovich Frank," p. 2.

CHAPTER 1: EARLY YEARS

1. Frank, "Predsmertnoe," p. 108.
2. Story passed down in the family (interview, Vasilii Frank).
3. "Predsmertnoe," p. 107; Moskovskii Gorodskii Arkhiv, f. 418, o. 308, delo 1020, l. 21.
4. "Predsmertnoe," p. 107.
5. J. Darlington, "Education in Russia," p. 125. In his dissertation, Swoboda

suggests that M. M. Rossiianskii was one of the First Guild Jewish Merchants who were granted legal permission to settle in Moscow in 1859—part of Alexander II's policy of granting privileges to well-educated Jews. See Swoboda, "Philosophical Thought of S. L. Frank," p. 121, referring to S. M. Dubnow, *History of the Jews in Russia and Poland*, Philadelphia, 1918, vol. 2, pp. 161–62; and L. Greenberg, *Jews in Russia*, vol. 1, p. 75.

6. L. Zak, Semyon Frank Papers, BA, box 16, p. 2.
7. Ibid., p. 1; interview, Natalia Norman.
8. "Predsmertnoe," p. 109.
9. Zak, Frank Papers, p. 2.
10. S. Vertel', "Statisticheskie dannye," pp. 34–37.
11. "Moskva," *Evreiskaia entsiklopediia*, 11, pp. 331–40.
12. Swoboda, "Thought," p. 123; Dubnow, vol. 2, p. 350; Greenberg, vol. 2, pp. 34–35; Darlington, p. 147.
13. *Istoriia Moskvy*, pp. 263, 268; Bradley, "Moscow," p. 17.
14. A. Krymskii, "Lazarevskii Institut," pp. 247–48.
15. G. I. Kananova, *Semidesiatipiatiletie Lazarevskogo Instituta*, table 2.
16. M. F. Vladimirskii, *Ocherki rabochego*, pp. 6–7. After the deportations of Jews from Moscow in 1891, only wealthy merchants and graduates were allowed to remain in Moscow (Swoboda, "Thought," p. 124; Greenberg, p. 44).
17. M. A. Krotov, *Iakutskaia*, pp. 5, 437–38; see Vilenskii-Sibiriakov, *Deiateli revoliutsionnogo*, vyp 3, p. 1131; Nogin, *Na poliuse kholoda*, p. 131.
18. Zak, Frank Papers, p. 3.
19. "Predsmertnoe," p. 110.
20. N. O. Losskii, *Vospominaniia*, pp. 40, 75.
21. S. Bulgakov, *Avtobiograficheskie zametki*, p. 30.
22. Losskii, *Vospominaniia*, p. 41.
23. Bar. Liudmila Vrangel', *Vospominaniia*, p. 27.
24. S. Ia. Elpat'evskii, *Vospominaniia*, pp. 209, 211.
25. S. Galai, *Liberation Movement*, pp. 60–61.
26. Record of conversation between Frank and B. Nicolaevskii, HI, box 525, folder 1. At the end of 1896, when he was back in Nizhnii Novgorod, Frank was at a dinner where he made a speech honoring Korolenko on behalf of the students ("Predsmertnoe," p. 119).
27. R. G. Robbins, *Famine in Russia*, p. 136.
28. N. M. Naimark, *Terrorists*, p. 232.
29. S. I. Mitskevich, *Na grani dvukh epokh*, p. 89.
30. Ibid., pp. 90–91.
31. M. A. Silvin, *Lenin v periode*, p. 18.
32. Moskovskii Gorodskii Arkhiv, f. 418, o. 308, delo 1020, l. 14; Bar. Vrangel', p. 27.
33. See Darlington, p. 141.
34. Interview, Natalia Norman.
35. "Predsmertnoe," p. 110.
36. See I. M. Frank, "Mikhail Liudvigovich Frank," p. 268.
37. Silvin, p. 19.
38. Mitskevich, *Na grani*, p. 91.

39. M. G. Grigor'ev, "Marksisty v Nizhnom," p. 112. An important figure in the Silvin circle was A. A. Kuznetsov, who was later described by the police as the leader of a Nizhnii Novgorod workers' group, with whom Frank was associated and in whose flat they used to read Marx's works; GARF, f. 102, oo., ed.khr. 451, l. 2; f. 63, o. 1898, ed.khr. 111 (4), l. 243; Grigoriev, p. 112.

40. Grigor'ev, p. 89.

41. Ibid., p. 102.

42. "Predsmertnoe," pp. 110–11.

43. Viktor Frank, "Semen Frank," pp. 1–20.

44. Zak, Frank Papers, pp. 3–4.

CHAPTER 2: MARXISM

1. V. I. Maslennikov, "Stranichki proshlogo," p. 121; see also J. Keep, *Rise of Social Democracy*, pp. 49–50.

2. "Predsmertnoe," p. 111.

3. L. P. Menshchikov, *Okhrana i revoliutsiia*, vol. 1, p. 420.

4. See N. Harding, ed., "Appeal to the Workers," *Marxism*, p. 146.

5. Vladimirskii, "Iz istorii Moskovskoi," p. 98.

6. Zak, Frank Papers, p. 5.

7. Interview, Natalia Norman.

8. Viktor Frank, "Semen Frank," pp. 5, 6.

9. A. Kremer and Iu. Martov, "Agitation," p. 200.

10. "Predsmertnoe," p. 112.

11. Frank, "Na iuridicheskom fakul'tete," p. 4.

12. Ibid.

13. Frank, *Biografiia P. B. Struve*, pp. 14, 17. On "Legal Marxism," see M. A. Kolerov, "'Legal'nyi Marksizm'."

14. For explanation, see R. Pipes, *Struve: Liberal Left*, p. 185.

15. P. B. Struve, "Svoboda," pp. 136–37; this translation by Pipes, *Liberal Left*, pp. 187–88.

16. *Biografiia*, pp. 17–18.

17. "Predsmertnoe," p. 119.

18. Ibid., p. 123.

19. Menshchikov, vol. 2, p. 158.

20. *Biografiia*, pp. 20–21.

21. Ibid., pp. 21, 20.

22. Interview, Natalia Norman.

23. See A. A. Kizevetter, *Na rubezhe*, pp. 218–19.

24. See Bibliography, Frank: Reviews.

25. Until 1900, the reviews in *Mir bozhii* are unsigned, so it is not possible to know which ones they are.

26. Interview, Natalia Norman.

27. GARF, f. 102, oo., 1898, ed.khr. 2, ch. 1, t. 2, l. 44, 50.

28. GARF, f. 102, oo., ed.khr. 163, 1898, l. 2; the founder of this group was probably S. S. Karaseva, a student in one of the collective courses for women (Ibid., l. 7).

29. GARF, f. 102, oo, 1898, ed.khr. 451, l. 4; address: Malyi Bronnyi, Dom Girsha, no. 87.

30. This Women's Union is probably the same as the society Emancipation of Women referred to by Elpat'evskii.

31. GARF, f. 102, oo. 1898, 3 ch. 10, l. 42.

32. GARF, f. 102, d7, 1899, ed.khr. 145, l. 22.

33. GARF, f. 102, o. d3, 1899, d. 415, l. 8–9; see also V. I. Orlov, *Studencheskoe*, p. 356.

34. S. D. Kassow, *Students, Professors*, p.

35. Interview, Natalia Norman. Mikhail spent longer in jail and subsequently had major problems completing his degree.

36. GARF, f. 63, 1896, ed.khr. 1510, no. 2, l. 108.

37. GARF, f. 102, d7, 1899, ed.khr. 145, l. 23, 30.

38. Frank, *Krushenie kumirov*, pp. 64–65.

39. See Struve, "Osnovnaia antinomiia," pp. 297–306; see also R. Kindersley, *Russian Revisionists*, pp. 161–62; see also *Biografiia*, p. 23.

40. Frank, "Psikhologicheskoe napravlenie," pp. 100, 110.

41. Frank, *Teoriia tsennosti*, p. 370.

42. Ibid., pp. 263–64, 3, 289–302; for a summary, see Kindersley, pp. 166–72.

43. Struve, *Mir bozhii*, 10, Aug. 1901, no. 8, pt. 2, p. 15. See also G. Plekhanov, review, pp. 348–57; see also Kindersley, p. 171.

44. "Psikhologicheskoe," p. 84.

45. *Teoriia tsennosti*, p. i.

46. Ibid., p. 357; see Swoboda, "Thought," p. 146.

47. *Biografiia*, p. 27.

48. Notes from interview between B. Nikolaevskii and Frank, HI, box 525.

49. RGIA-St.P., f. 14, o. 1, ed.khr. 10625, l. 13.

CHAPTER 3: IDEALISM

1. "Predsmertnoe," p. 120.

2. Frank, "Na iuridicheskom fakul'tete," p. 4.

3. Some details taken from Swoboda, "Thought," pp. 77–78.

4. See A. Vuccinich, *Social Thought*, pp. 112–13. My comments on Simmel are taken directly from Swoboda, "Thought," pp. 273–82.

5. See A. P. Mendel, *Dilemmas*, pp. 196–202.

6. Struve in 1900, Introduction to Berdiaev, pp. lxiii, lxviii, as translated by Pipes in *Liberal Left*, p. 299. S. Bulgakov, "Ivan Karamazov," pp. 83–112; see also "Predsmertnoe," p. 122.

7. "Predsmertnoe," pp. 119–22. In the Crimea, they stayed on the "Oleiz" estate, which was owned by the Tokmakov family. M. I. Vodovozova, who was born a Tokmakov, was also there at the time.

8. *Biografiia*, p. 23.

9. Interview, Natalia Norman.

10. Frank to Binswanger, 28 April 1942.

11. Tatiana Frank, private memoir, p. 6, NN, SA.

12. "Predsmertnoe," p. 121.

13. Zak, Frank Papers, p. 9.

14. Frank, "O kriticheskom idealizme," p. 247.

15. "Predsmertnoe," p. 121. On 11 May 1902 Frank attended a meeting of the Moscow Psychological Society attended by the contributors to *Problems of Idealism* at which it was agreed to publish the collection and to ask the society to include the work among its list of publications; see M. A. Kudrinskii, "Arkhivnaia," p. 162.

16. Frank, "Fr. Nitsshe," pp. 187, 188.

17. Ibid., p. 141.

18. Taken from Swoboda, "Thought," on Simmel and Frank. Swoboda suggests that Frank lacks a transcendental grounding for his belief in these "phantoms" and consequently offers a psychological but not objective defense of them (see pp. 280ff.).

19. Frank, "Fr. Nitsshe," pp. 183, 173.

20. Ibid., p. 188.

21. Frank to Struve, 7 Feb. 1902, *Put'* (Moscow), p. 273; see also "Fr. Nitsshe," p. 192.

22. Swoboda, "Thought," pp. 218–19.

23. Frank, "Fr. Nitsshe," p. 187.

24. "Predsmertnoe," p. 121.

25. Frank to Struve, 24 Dec. 1901, *Put'*, p. 271.

26. *Biografiia*, p. 34.

27. Frank to Struve, 7 Feb. 1902, *Put'*, p. 273.

28. "O kriticheskom idealizme," pp. 238, 242. 264.

29. Ibid., pp. 251–58.

30. Ibid.

31. Ibid., pp. 260–61, 264.

32. Frank, review of Medicus, *I.G.Fichte*, as quoted in Swoboda, "Thought," p. 377.

33. "O kriticheskom idealizme," p. 245.

34. This is suggested by Swoboda, "Thought," p. 327.

35. Frank, "O kriticheskom idealizme," p. 245; Swoboda, "Thought," p. 44.

36. Ibid., p. 262n, 264.

37. Bogucharskii visited Frank in Yalta and told him about the journal (*Biografiia*, p. 31). That same year, Frank's stepfather sold his chemist shop in Nizhnii Novgorod and moved with his mother to the southern town of Berdnaiansk on the Azov coast. Frank spent the summer there, apparently pretending to concoct conspiracies. Lev Zak recalled: "Senia and Misha manufactured some invisible ink and wrote [things] with it. . . . They sent white letters on which there was nothing written at all." Zak suggests that the contents of their letters were quite innocent (Zak, Frank Papers, p. 8).

38. J. Billington, *The Icon and the Axe*, 1970, p. 462.

39. "Predsmertnoe," p. 113; Viktor Frank, "Semen Frank," p. 7.

40. A. Tyrkova-Williams, *Na putiakh*, p. 171.

41. *Biografiia*, p. 33.

42. Ibid., p. 35.

43. Frank to Nina Struve, 12 Nov. 1922, *Voprosy filosofii*, p. 128.

44. *Biografiia*, p. 34.
45. Ibid., p. 40.
46. "Predsmertnoe," p. 114.
47. Ibid., p. 34.
48. Frank to Struve, 11 June 1903, *Put'*, p. 278; Frank to Nina Struve, 12 Aug. 1903, ibid., p. 281; Frank to Struve, 19 Oct. 1905, ibid., p. 296.
49. Frank to Struve, 7 Apr. 1903, *Put'*, p. 274; see also Frank to Struve, 11 June 1903, ibid., pp. 277–78.

CHAPTER 4: POLITICS

1. *Biografiia*, p. 34.
2. Ibid., p. 38. This is the division of representatives described by Galai, p. 177.
3. See editorial, *Osvobozhdenie*, 18 June 1902, no. 1, pp. 1–7.
4. *Biografiia*, pp. 38–39.
5. Vodovozov, "Osvobozhdeniia Soiuz," p. 154.
6. Frank to Struve, 11 June 1903, *Put'*, pp. 278–79.
7. Frank, "Russkoe samoderzhavie," p. 430. This was an opinion he later expressed again in regard to the Russo-Japanese War; see "Inostrannaia pechat' o voine," p. 306.
8. Frank, "Po serbski ili po nemetski?" p. 56.
9. *Biografiia*, p. 37.
10. Frank, "Tsarit bessmyslennaia lozh'."
11. Pipes, *Liberal Left*, p. 341.
12. Frank to Struve, 21 Nov. 1904, *Put'*, p. 284.
13. *Biografiia*, p. 42.
14. For details on *New Way*, see G. F. Putnam, *Russian Alternatives*, pp. 54–55.
15. Frank to Struve, 5 May 1905, *Put'*, p. 285.
16. Ibid., p. 286.
17. Frank to Nina Struve, 30 July 1905, ibid., p. 290.
18. Tyrkova-Williamses: Ariadna Tyrkova and her British husband H. Williams. *Biografiia*, p. 44; Tyrkova, p. 206.
19. Ballot papers at Kadet Congress, Oct. 1905, GARF, f. 523, o. 1, ed.khr. 41.
20. Zak, Frank Papers, p. 8.
21. Frank to Struve, 19 Oct. 1905, *Put'*, pp. 294–95.
22. Ibid., p. 295; A. M. Koliubakin, left-wing Kadet.
23. Frank to Nina Struve, 8 Nov. 1905, ibid., p. 300.
24. Ibid.
25. Ibid., p. 301.
26. *Biografiia*, p. 49.
27. Frank to Nina Struve, 1 Nov. 1905, *Put'*, pp. 297–98.
28. Frank to Nina Struve, 8 Nov. 1905, ibid., pp. 300–301.
29. Frank to Nina Struve, 1 Nov. 1905, ibid., pp. 298–99.

30. *Biografiia*, p. 49.
31. A. A. Kaufman, "Poznai samogo sebia," pp. 136–45.
32. Frank, "Odnostoronnee samopoznanie," p. 132.
33. *Biografiia*, p. 49.
34. Frank to Struve, 22 Oct. 1905, *Put'*, p. 297.
35. P. B. Struve, "Ot redaktsii," pp. 2–3.
36. Frank and Struve, "Ocherki filosofii kul'tury," p. 184.
37. Frank, "Problema vlasti," p. 80.
38. Ibid., p. 121.
39. Ibid., p. 122.
40. Ibid., p. 124.
41. See *Novyi put'*, Nov. 1904, pp. 308–17.
42. See *Konstitutsionnoe gosudarstvo*, (1905).
43. Frank, "Proekt deklaratsii prav," p. 250.
44. Riha, *Paul Miliukov*, p. 97.
45. See Frank, "Politika i idei," pp. 23–24.
46. *Biografiia*, p. 45.
47. "Predsmertnoe," p. 115.
48. Frank and Struve, "Ocherki filosofii kul'tury," pp. 113–14.
49. Ibid., p. 110.
50. Ibid., p. 117.
51. Ibid., p. 184.
52. Frank, "Ocherki," p. 182; for similar arguments, see "Politika i idei," pp. 25ff.
53. By G. Shtilman; see Pipes, *Struve: Liberal Right*, p. 21.
54. Frank, "Molodaia demokratiia," p. 67.
55. Ibid., pp. 70–71. The article reflects views similar to those of Struve at this time; see Putnam, "P. B. Struve's View," p. 466.
56. Putnam, p. 469.
57. Frank, "Duma i obshchestvo," pp. 374–75; see also "Pred istoricheskimi dniami," p. 2.
58. M. N. Mogilianskaia and M. B. Pirozhkov, "Pis'mo v redaktsiiu," p. 2.
59. Struve, "Pis'ma v redaktsiiu," p. 2.
60. Frank and Struve, "Pis'mo v redaktsiiu," p. 3.
61. "Predsmertnoe," p. 115.
62. Frank to Nina Struve, 8 Nov. 1905, *Put'*, p. 299.
63. Zak, Frank Papers, pp. 8–9.

CHAPTER 5: INDEPENDENCE

1. Tatiana Frank, private memoir, p. 2, NN.
2. *Biografiia*, p. 54.
3. Frank, from an unpublished section of the original manuscript of *Biografiia*, quoted by Pipes in *Struve: Liberal Right*, p. 74, n.15.
4. *Biografiia*, pp. 67, 69–70, 106. For Frank's notes on the literary section of *Russkaia mysl'*, see PD-IMLI, f. 264, ed.khr. 26.

5. *Biografiia*, p. 70. On "national liberal" standpoint, see Pipes, *Liberal Right*, p. 169. For Frank's memoir of G. Trubetskoi, see *Pamiati Kn.G. N. Trubetskogo*, pp. 34–36.

6. Frank may have filled a hole in the program vacated by Vasilii El'iashevich; this might have meant that he was teaching general theory of law for half a year, see RGIA-St.P., f. 148, delo 256, sv. 11, l. 29; or it may have been a course in social psychology (see Course Outlines, BA, box 13). The pedagogical council of Mme Stoiunina's gymnasium included Nina Struve's father and brother and Losskii and his wife, see RGIA-St.P., f. 148, delo 256, sv. 11, l. 6.

7. RGIA-St.P., f. 148, delo 256, sv. 11, l. 66, 28, 21.

8. *Biografiia*, p. 73–74.

9. Ibid., p. 60.

10. Interview, Natalia Norman.

11. See A. I. Savinov, *Pis'ma*, p. 163.

12. Tatiana Frank, memoir, p. 1, NN.

13. Interview with Eugene Lampert, from the reminiscences of his mother, Tatiana Lampert (Gliazberg), with whom Tatiana shared accommodation at this time.

14. Tatiana Frank, memoir, p. 3.

15. Ibid., p. 9.

16. Zak, Frank Papers, p. 12.

17. Tatiana Frank, memoir, p. 10.

18. Frank to Tatiana Frank, 21 Aug. 1923, SA, folder: letters of Frank to his wife.

19. Tatiana Frank, memoir, p. 8.

20. Zak, Frank Papers, p. 11.

21. Tatiana Frank, memoir, pp. 9–11.

22. Ibid., p. 2.

23. Zak, Papers, p. 3.

24. Frank to Gershenzon, 20 Aug. 1909, OR-RGB, f. 746, k. 42, ed.khr. 60l. l. 27.

25. RGIA-St.P., f. 14, o. 1, ed.khr. 10625, l. 21; *Ves' Peterburg*, 1907–17.

26. B. Bolotnaia 4 (1909); Lakhtinskaia 14 (1910); Ropshinskaia 23 (1911–12); Krestov ostr. Esperov 7 (1913–14); S'ezzhinskaia 12 (1915–17); see *Ves' Peterburg*, 1909–17.

27. Interview, Natalia Norman.

28. See Losskii, *Vospominaniia*, pp. 163–64.

29. B. Losskii, "Nasha sem'ia," p. 148.

30. Zak, Papers, p. 7.

31. *Biografiia*, pp. 78–79.

32. Ibid., pp. 78, 93.

33. Review, *Schiller als Philosoph*, p. 270.

34. Frank, "Gnoseologiia Gete," p. 39.

35. Ibid., p. 29.

36. Frank, "K kharakteristike Gete," p. 365.

37. "Gnoseologiia Gete," p. 59.

38. Frank, "Lichnost' i veshch'," p. 217.

39. "Gnoseologiia Gete," p. 66.
40. "Lichnost' i veshch'," p. 167; see A. Vuccinich, *Darwin in Russia*, pp. 254–55.
41. "Lichnost' i veshch'," p. 215.
42. Ibid., p. 217.
43. "Predsmertnoe," p. 121.
44. Frank, "Pragmatizm kak filosofskoe uchenie," pp. 97, 99, 111.
45. Ibid., p. 113.
46. Frank, "Predislovie," to Husserl, *Logicheskie issledovaniia*, pp. viii–xi.
47. Also in 1908, Frank was removed from the list of people under police investigation; RGIA-St.P., f. 253, o. 10, delo 266, l. 152.

CHAPTER 6: *LANDMARKS*

1. *Biografiia*, pp. 75, 59.
2. Ibid., pp. 93–94, 75.
3. Ibid., pp. 73–74.
4. Ibid., p. 73; translation partly drawn from A. Walicki, *Legal Theories*, p. 382.
5. Frank to Gershenzon, 19 Oct. 1908, OR-RGB, f. 746, k. 42, ed.khr. 60, l. 6–7; published in "K istorii sozdaniia 'Vekh,'" pp. 252–53.
6. See Frank's review of Ivanov-Razumnik, *O smysle zhizni;* Ivanov-Razumnik argued that man must supply his own meaning to an essentially meaningless world, an idea Frank regarded as nonsense.
7. Frank to Gershenzon, 19 Oct. 1908, OR-RGB, l. 6–7; 11 Mar. 1909, l. 6–7; "K istorii," pp. 252, 256–57.
8. See M. O. Gershenzon, "Preface," pp. 1–2.
9. See *Biografiia*, pp. 81–82. On these differences, see Walicki, *Legal Theories*, pp. 374–76; C. Read, *Religion, Revolution*, p. 119.
10. Frank to Gershenzon, 16 Nov. 1908, OR-RGB, f. 746, k. 42, ed.khr. 60, l. 8–9; "K istorii," p. 253.
11. Frank was one of the editors and translators of a complete collection of Nietzsche's works that started to appear in Russian in 1909. See *Sochineniia*, pp. 562–63; other translations by Frank in these years were O. Külpe's *Introduction to Philosophy* and the second volume of Kuno Fischer's *History of Modern Philosophy*.
12. Frank, "K voprosu o sushchnosti morali," pp. 131–32.
13. *Biografiia*, p. 79.
14. "Spor o pragmatizme," pp. 146, 154.
15. Frank, "Ethic of Nihilism," p. 184.
16. Frank, "Filosofskie predposylki despotizma," p. 162. Swoboda notes that this essay is Frank's first serious attack on the capabilities of "reason." For his discussion, see Swoboda, "Thought," pp. 449–50.
17. See Berdiaev, "Socialism as Religion," pp. 113–38.
18. "Ethic," p. 157.
19. Ibid., p. 163.

20. Ibid., pp. 164–65.

21. Ibid., p. 166. See on this Frank "Kapitalizm i kul'tura," p. 37. Frank argues that "individual, inner, spiritual culture" and "social, exterior, material culture" develop "hand in hand"—an idea he associates with Marxism.

22. "Ethnic," p. 169.

23. Ibid., pp. 169–70.

24. Ibid., p. 177.

25. Ibid., pp. 179–80.

26. Ibid., p. 184.

27. Frank, "Sotsializm i kantiantstvo," p. 352; see also "Krushenie sotsializma kak religii," pp. 183–85.

28. "Ethic," pp. 183–84, 209.

29. Frank, "Filosofskaia raspria v Marksizme," p. 142.

30. Frank, "Priroda i kul'tura," pp. 50–114.

31. *Biografiia*, p. 83.

32. *Great Soviet Encyclopedia*, vol. 4, p. 408.

33. P. Miliukov, "Intelligentsiia," p. 105.

34. Miliukov, *Vospominaniia*, p. 256.

35. Conversation with Iu. Rostovtsev, Jan. 1988.

36. "Filosofskie predposylki," p. 160.

37. Frank, "Pis'ma A. I. Ertelia," p. 328.

38. See, for example, I. I. Petrunkevich, "Intelligentsiia," pp. iii–xv.

39. S. V. Lur'e, "O sbornike 'Vekhi,'" pp. 137–46.

40. Frank, "Kapitalizm i kul'tura," pp. 40, 42.

41. Frank, "Novaia kniga Berdiaeva," pp. 138, 141. On these issues, see A. A. Kelly, "Attitudes," p. 310.

42. Frank, "Merezhkovskii o 'Vekhakh,'" p. 2.

43. I. V. Gessen, *V dvukh vekakh*, p. 266.

44. Losskii, *Vospominaniia*, p. 148.

45. *Biografiia*, pp. 85–86.

46. A. Solzhenitsyn, "The Smatterers," pp. 229–30.

CHAPTER 7: CONVERSION TO ORTHODOXY

1. A. V. Kartashev, "Ideologicheskii," p. 69. Kartashev recalled an occasion after the shootings of Bloody Sunday when it was suggested to have a funeral for the victims to spite the very conservative Synod. Frank cried out: "That is impermissible. Demonstrate however you like, but to pray to God in order to spite whoever it may be, that I do not understand" (ibid., p. 70).

2. See Frank, "O svobodnoi sovesti," p. 417.

3. Frank to Gershenzon, 16 Nov. 1908, OR-RGB, l. 9; "K istorii," p. 254.

4. Frank, "Religiia i kul'tura," pp. 53–54.

5. RGIA-St.P., f. 148, delo 256, sv.11, l. 21.

6. Scherrer, "Die Petersburger," p. 435.

7. Kartashev in *Zapiski S-Peterburgskago religiozno-filosofskogo obshchestva*, vyp 1, 1908, p. 1.

8. Ibid., pp. 22, 24.
9. Frank, "Filosofiia religii V.Dzhemsa," p. 17.
10. *Biografiia*, p. 60.
11. Ibid., p. 90.
12. Interview, Natalia Norman.
13. Frank, "Pamiati L'va Tolstogo," p. 149.
14. *Biografiia*, pp. 91–92.
15. See his *Istoricheskii grekh*, St.P., 1907; see also Scherrer, p. 350, n. 20.
16. RGIA-St.P., f. 19, o. 127, ed.khr. 2674, l. 101.
17. Tatiana Frank, memoir, p. 16.
18. RGIA-St.P., f. 14, o. 1, ed.khr. 10625, l. 2.
19. This may have been the St. Petersburg Religious-Philosophical Society, where Cohen was a visitor in 1914, (Scherrer, p. 438).
20. Story as recounted to Isaiah Berlin (interview).
21. Frank, "Religioznaia filosofiia Kogena," p. 31.
22. "On Jewish Conversion to Christianity," BA, box 12.
23. Frank, "Die religiöse Tragödie des Judentums," p. 130.
24. "Predsmertnoe," pp. 109–10.
25. Frank, "Die religiöse Tragödie des Judentums," p. 129.
26. Frank, "Nravstvennoe uchenie L. N. Tolstogo," pp. 299–300.
27. Zak, "Semen Frank," p. 18.
28. Frank, "O natsionalizme v filosofii," pp. 162–71.
29. Tatiana Frank, "Pamiat' serdtsa," pp. 1–2, NN; also in SA.
30. Frank, "Mirosozertsanie Konstantina Leont'eva," p. 386.
31. Frank, Introduction to *Rechi o religii*, by F. Schleiermacher, p. xxx.
32. Ibid., p. xxv.
33. Frank, *Vvedenie v filosofiiu*, p. 20.
34. Frank, "Kosmicheskoe chuvstvo v poezii Tiutcheva," pp. 219, 202.
35. Ibid., p. 227.
36. Frank, "Kul'tura i religiia," p. 160.
37. Tsentral'nyi Gosudarstvennyi Istoricheskii Arkhiv Rossiiskoi Federatsii, f. 733, o. 155, delo 388, l. 128.
38. Interview, Vasilii Frank.
39. *Biografiia*, pp. 99–101.
40. Ibid., p. 101.
41. Tatiana Frank, memoir, p. 15.

CHAPTER 8: *THE OBJECT OF KNOWLEDGE*

1. Frank, "O filosofskoi intuitsii," p. 33.
2. Frank to Gershenzon, 27 Apr. 1912, OR-RGB, f. 746, k. 42, ed.khr. 61, pp. 2–3.
3. Losskii, *Vospominaniia*, p. 102.
4. Viktor Frank, "Semen Frank," p. 8.
5. Conversation with Viktor Frank, 31 Aug 1950; "Predsmertnye vospominaniia i mysli," BA, box 12; also in SA, folder: "Pis'ma rodnykh." Swoboda does

not refer to Frank's philosophical revelation in his work, partly because it is difficult to be certain that Frank remembered its date accurately. This is understandable; after all, Frank discovered "being" in 1908, not in 1913. Nevertheless, the content of the dream remains an excellent introduction to *The Object of Knowledge.*

6. Frank, *Predmet znaniia,* p. 91.

7. Ibid., p. 157.

8. Ibid., p. 391.

9. Ibid., p. 121.

10. Ibid., pp. iii–iv.

11. Frank, "Krizis sovremennoi filosofii," p. 39.

12. *Predmet znaniia,* p. 23.

13. For more on the relationship between A and x, see ibid., p. 16.

14. Ibid., p. 204.

15. Ibid., p. 220.

16. Frank, "Gnoseologiia Gete," pp. 42, 48.

17. *Predmet znaniia,* p. 307.

18. "Krizis," p. 35; also *Predmet znaniia,* p. v.

19. "Krizis," p. 36. For the connection to the concept of "intentionality," see Swoboda, "Thought," p. 619, and *Predmet znaniia,* p. 150.

20. *Predmet znaniia,* p. 38.

21. Ibid., p. 173.

22. Frank, *Vvedenie v filosofiiu,* pp. 61–62; see also Frank, "Die russische Philosophie der letzten fünfzehn Jahre," p. 91. Swoboda states: "Frank's system, in many respects, *is* Kant's system, with consciousness, as it were turned inside out, and its function in knowledge reassigned to the concept of absolute Being. . . . In Frank's thought, the necessity which, for Kant, served as the defining feature of knowledge becomes a necessity inherent in Being itself" (Swoboda, "Thought," pp. 625–26).

23. Losskii, *History of Russian Philosophy,* p. 267.

24. *Predmet znaniia,* p. 82.

25. Frank to Struve, 5 Apr. 1943, BA, box 3.

26. *Predmet znaniia,* pp. 371–72.

27. Frank, "O filosofskoi intuitsii," p. 35.

28. Frank, review, W. Dilthey, *Schriften,* p. 38.

29. "O kriticheskom idealizme," p. 264.

30. Losskii, *History,* p. 281.

31. *Predmet znaniia,* 294.

32. Berdiaev, "Dva tipa," pp. 641–43.

33. Losskii, *History,* p. 283.

34. Zen'kovskii, *History,* p. 867.

35. *Spravochnaia knizhka dlia slushatel'nits S-Peterburgskikh vysshikh zhenskikh kursov,* 1908–9ff.; also 1914–15 at the university, RGIA-St.P., f. 14, o. 3, t. 4, delo 16181, l. 16.

36. Frank, "Uchenie Spinozy ob attributakh," pp. 545–46.

37. I. I. Lapshin, "Misticheskii," p. 140–53.

38. Frank to Binswanger, 16 May 1941.

39. *Predmet znaniia*, p. 6.
40. Ibid., pp. 8, 35.
41. Ibid., p. 408.
42. Ibid., p. v.
43. "Krizis," p. 40.
44. *Predmet znaniia*, p. vi. Gläser was informed by Tatiana that Frank undertook a study of Nicholas of Cusa only in 1914; Swoboda, "Thought," p. 32; R. Gläser, *Frage nach Gott*, p. 11, n.46.
45. Swoboda, "Thought," pp. 13, 525–27, 624.
46. *Predmet znaniia*, pp. 173, 428, 434.
47. Tatiana Frank, memoir, p. 16; *Biografiia*, p. 109.
48. *Biografiia*, p. 110.
49. Frank to Gershenzon, 26 July 1916, OR-RGB, l. 28–29.

CHAPTER 9: WAR AND REVOLUTION

1. Frank to Binswanger, 29 Apr. 1935. James-Lange theory: subjective feelings are generated by bodily changes. Frank evidently had an ambiguous attitude to James, disputing his pragmatism and subjectivism but admiring his empiricism. Philip Swoboda, in his introduction to *Man's Soul*, suggests that Frank's approach to psychic life owed much to Willam James's description of the "stream" of consciousness. For other philosophical influences on *Man's Soul*, see Swoboda, foreword, pp. xvii–xviii.
2. Frank, *Dusha cheloveka*, 1964, p. 16; *Man's Soul*, 1993, trans. Jakim, p. 4.
3. Ibid., pp. 81; 60–61.
4. Ibid., p. 206–7; 167–68.
5. Ibid., p. 248–49; 202–3.
6. Ibid., p. 263; 216.
7. Ibid., p. 280–81; 230.
8. Frank, "Sila i pravo," p. 17; Th.Ruyssen, "La Force et le Droit," *Revue de Métaphysique et de Morale*, Nov. 1914.
9. *Biografiia*, p. 105.
10. Struve, "Velikaia Rossiia," p. 177.
11. *Biografiia*, pp. 103, 105–6.
12. Bulgakov, "Russkye dumy," pp. 114–15.
13. Ern, "Ot Kanta," pp. 116–24.
14. Kn. E. Trubetskoi, "Voina i mirovaia," p. 92.
15. Frank, "O poiskakh smysla voiny," p. 129.
16. Ibid., pp. 130–31.
17. Ibid., p. 132.
18. Ibid., p. 127.
19. Frank, "O dukhovnoi sushchnosti Germanii," p. 15.
20. Ibid., p. 18.
21. Frank, "Mobilizatsiia mysli v Germanii," p. 27.
22. Struve, "Krushenie dela Bismarka," pp. 5–7.
23. *Biografiia*, p. 107.

24. Lieven, *Russia's Rulers*, p. 275.
25. Pipes, *Liberal Right*, p. 205.
26. *Biografiia*, p. 123.
27. Struve, "Liga Russkoi kul'tury," pp. 3–5.
28. *Biografiia*, p. 116.
29. Ibid., p. 115.
30. Frank, "O blagorodstve i nizosti v politike."
31. Frank, "Iz razmyshlenii o Russkoi revoliutsii," p. 248.
32. "O blagorodstve," p. 29.
33. Frank, "Demokratiia v rasput'e," pp. 15–16. *Pugachevshchina:* barbarism named after the Russian bandit Pugachev.
34. Frank, *Nravstvennyi vodorazdel v Russkoi revoliutsii*, pp. 9–11.
35. "O blagorodstve," pp. 26, 27, 30.
36. Ibid., p. 27; see also *Nravstvennyi*, p. 11.
37. *Nravstvennyi*, p. 3.
38. Frank, "Mertvye molchat," p. 17.
39. "O blagorodstve," p. 28.
40. *Biografiia*, p. 110.
41. Interview, Natalia Norman.

CHAPTER 10: SARATOV

1. D. J. Raleigh, *Revolution*, p. 263; Keep, p. 184.
2. P. A. Bugaenko et al., *Saratovskii Universitet*, p. 19.
3. Raleigh, ed., *Russian Civil War Diary*, p. 22.
4. Bugaenko, p. 289.
5. Gosudarstvennyi Arkhiv Saratovskoi Oblasti, f. 332, o. 1, ed.khr. 3; *Izvestiia Saratovskogo Universiteta.*
6. Bugaenko, p. 271.
7. Raleigh, *Revolution*, pp. 19, 297; from Babine Papers, Manuscript Division, Library of Congress, sec. 1, 1917–19, p. 25.
8. Raleigh, *Civil War Diary*, p. 77.
9. Bugaenko, p. 16–19.
10. Raleigh, *Civil War Diary*, pp. 178–79, 170.
11. Ibid., p 23.
12. Interview, Natalia Norman.
13. Tatiana Frank, interviewed by Peter Scorer, Munich 1976.
14. Raleigh, *Civil War diary*, p. 76.
15. Frank to Gershenzon, 5 Oct. 1918, OR-RGB, l. 32.
16. Raleigh, *Civil War Diary*, p. 132.
17. Frank to Gershenzon, 5 Oct. 1918, OR-RGB, l. 32.
18. Raleigh, *Civil War Diary*, p. 133.
19. Frank to V. B. El'iashevich, 25 Oct. 1922, NN; also in SA.
20. Interview, Natalia Norman.
21. Natalia Norman says it was Kolchak's army they thought of joining, but only Denikin's fits the time and location; O. Figes, *Peasant Russia*, p. 21.

22. Interview, Natalia Norman.

23. F. C. Koch, *Volga Germans*, p. 310.

24. Frank to El'iashevich, 25 Oct. 1922, NN.

25. Interview, Natalia Norman.

26. Figes, p. 344; interview, Natalia Norman.

27. Interview, Natalia Norman.

28. J.-F.Bourret, *Allemands de la Volga*, pp. 281–82.

29. Frank, "Razmyshleniia o russkoi revoliutsii," p. 256.

30. Raleigh, *Civil War Diary*, p. 178.

31. R. Sakwa, *Soviet Communists*, p. 9.

32. Berdiaev, *Dream and Reality*, p. 232.

33. Interview, Natalia Norman.

34. Ibid.

35. "Iz razmyshlenii o russkoi revoliutsii," pp. 267, 268–69.

36. Berdiaev, *Sofiia*, p. 135.

37. Berdiaev, *Dream and Reality*, p. 236.

38. Berdiaev, *Sofiia*, pp. 135–36; Losev records that discussions took place in Berdiaev's flat at this time that were in the style of the the former Religious-Philosophical Societies to which Frank invited him (interview by Rostovtsev, pp. 8–9).

39. This may be linked to another project. In early 1919 Frank and Iurovskii conceived a series, "Classics of Political Thought," that aimed to introduce the public to such writers as Chateaubriand, de Maistre, Robert Owen, Renan, and Samarin; Frank to Gershenzon, 21 Mar. 1919, OR-RGB, l. 34. There also seems to have been a possibility of republishing *Predmet znaniia* at that time; ibid., 7 May 1919, l. 36.

40. V. Vaganian, "Nashi Russkie," p. 32. *Velikaia Rossia*, 2 vols., Moscow, 1911–12, a collection of essays appealing to Russian military and imperial aspirations; Struve contributed (see Pipes, *Liberal Right*, p. 185). Lenin regarded *Oswald Spengler and the Decline of the West* as a "White Guard" publication. See A. Vadimov, *Zhizn' Berdiaeva*, p. 225.

41. B. Ddoratskii, p. 239.

42. See *Bibliografiia*, p. 20; "Predsmertnoe," p. 117.

43. See M. Geller, "'Pervoe predosterzhenie,'" p. 221.

44. Interview, Natalia Norman.

45. Ibid.

46. Viktor Frank, "Semen Frank," pp. 13–14; also in BA, box 9.

47. Kn. S. E. Trubetskoi, *Minuvshee*, pp. 279–80.

48. V. A. Miakotin, in *Rul'*, 1 Oct. 1922, no. 560, p. 5. *Smena Vekh* (Change of Landmarks): An ideological group that advised emigrants to accept the revolution as an accomplished fact and welcomed the triumph of Bolshevism on the ground that it had restored state power to Russia.

49. Interview, Natalia Norman.

50. Ibid.

51. British Foreign Office: Russia Correspondence 1781–1945, F.O. 371, 1922, vol. 8205, despatch 681, p. 71; see also Geller, p. 223.

52. Frank to Gershenzon, 12 Dec. 1917, OR-RGB, l. 30.

53. Frank, "De profundis," p. 311.

54. Ibid., pp. 320–21.
55. Ibid., pp. 322–23.
56. Ibid., pp. 327–28.
57. Ibid., p. 314.
58. "Iz razmyshlenii o russkoi revoliutsii," pp. 256.
59. Ibid., p. 258.
60. *Biografiia,* p. 126.

CHAPTER 11: REBUILDING A LIFE

1. R. C. Williams, *Culture in Exile,* pp. 111–13; M. Raeff, *Russia Abroad,* p. 202.
2. Raeff, p. 36.
3. Wipert von Blücher, *Deutschlands Weg nach Rapallo,* quoted in Williams, p. 112.
4. Williams, pp. 113–14.
5. Raeff, p. 77.
6. See *Rul',* no. 562, 22 Sept. 1922, p. 3; no. 603, 8 Nov. 1922, p. 8.
7. Berdiaev, *Dream and Reality,* p. 244.
8. Frank to Struve, 10 Oct. 1922, p. 121; see S. S. Oldenburg, "Pokhod na tserkov'," pp. 343–46.
9. Frank to Struve, 4 Nov. 1922, *Voprosy filosofii,* p. 127.
10. Interview, Natalia Norman.
11. Frank to El'iashevich, 11 Nov. 1922, NN.
12. Interview, Natalia Norman.
13. Ibid.
14. Frank to El'iashevich, 11 Nov. 1922.
15. Possibly through Frank being accredited as a foreign journalist with Berdiaev's Paris-based journal *The Way;* Frank to Berdiaev, 27 Mar. 1928, Berdiaev Papers, BA. Berlin addresses: Karl Schraderstr. 1, quite a large flat; Joachim Friedrichstr. 48, 3–4 rooms with a balcony; Passauerstr.; Neue Kantstr. 27, a big flat with two balconies on the fourth floor; Hectorstr. 20, lived on the ground floor; Nestorstr. 11, a big kitchen, a small room where Natalia lived, the parents' bedroom, a study, a large dining room–sitting room, and a room where Viktor and Vasilii slept, on the first floor of a summer house (interview with Vasilii).
16. Frank to Struve, 6 Nov. 1925, GARF, f. 5912, o. 2, delo 127, l. 14.
17. Interview, Natalia Norman.
18. Berdiaev, *Dream and Reality,* p. 247.
19. P. B. Anderson, *No East or West,* pp. 32, 40.
20. D. A. Lowrie, *Rebellious Prophet,* p. 165.
21. *Rul',* no. 608, 28 Nov. 1922, p. 6; no. 599, 3 Nov. 1922, p. 8; Berdiaev, *Sofiia,* pp. 136–38.
22. *Rul',* no. 600, 4 Nov. 1922, p. 5; Lowrie, p. 166.
23. For example, its courses for 1924–25 consisted of Frank on Christian social philosophy, Karsavin on patristics, and Il'in on the philosophy of religion; *Rul',* no. 1169, 7 Oct. 1924, p. 4.

24. M. Beyssac, *La Vie Culturelle*, pp. 96, 116.

25. Frank to El'iashevich, 11 Nov. 1922.

26. See Anderson, pp. 39–40.

27. Raeff, p. 91; Brotherhood of Holy Sophia, BA, Frank Papers, box 16.

28. Frank to Tatiana Frank, 15 Sept. 1924, SA. See also Zen'kovskii, "Zarozhdenie," p. 21.

29. *Rul'*, no. 658, 28 Jan. 1923, p. 5; no. 766, 9 June 1923, p. 5; Williams, p. 130.

30. *Rul'*, no. 617, 25 Dec. 1922, p. 6; no. 658, 28 Jan. 1923, p. 5; no. 770, 14 June 1923, p. 5; no. 898, 10 Nov. 1923, p. 5; no. 1150, 14 Sept. 1924, p. 4.

31. *Rul'*, no. 890, 1 Nov. 1923, p. 5; no. 1815, 20 Nov. 1926, p. 4; no. 1828, 5 Dec. 1926, p. 9; Williams, p. 133.

32. *Rul'*, no. 1142, 5 Sept. 1924, p. 5; no. 1236, 25 Dec. 1924, p. 9; no. 1295, 7 Mar. 1925, p. 4.

33. Interview, Natalia Norman.

34. Frank to Tatiana Frank, 21 Aug. 1923, SA.

35. Frank to Nina Struve, 12 Nov. 1922, *Voprosy filosofii*, p. 128.

36. Interview, Natalia Norman; see also Berdiaev, *Dream and Reality*, p. 249.

37. Raeff, p. 135; *Biografiia*, p. 135.

38. Frank, *Krushenie kumirov*, p. 7.

39. Frank to Tatiana Frank, 1923, n.d., T.'s handwriting, SA.

40. Frank, *Smysl zhizni*, p. 5.

41. Ibid., pp. 149–51.

42. *Krushenie kumirov*, pp. 35, 50–51.

43. Ibid., pp. 38, 44, 43. Frank was appalled that the British government under Lloyd George chose to recognize the Soviet regime and shocked by Lloyd George's statement that you can trade even with Hottentots (Interview, Natalia Norman).

44. *Smysl zhizni*, p. 71.

45. *Krushenie kumirov*, p. 97.

46. Ibid., p. 62.

47. Ibid., p. 97.

48. *Smysl zhizni*, pp. 136, 85, 96, 111, 120.

49. Ibid., pp. 97, 38.

50. Frank, *Lichnaia zhizn' i sotsial'noe stroitel'stvo*, p. 13.

51. *Smysl zhizni*, p. 134.

52. Zak, Papers, pp. 6, 9.

53. Lowrie, p. 168.

54. Frank to Tatiana Frank, 28 Aug. 1923, SA.

55. *Krushenie kumirov*, p. 80.

CHAPTER 12: THE DISPUTE WITH STRUVE

1. Frank to Struve, 18 Oct. 1922, *Voprosy filosofii*, p. 123.

2. Struve to Frank, 19 Oct. 1922, ibid., p. 124.

3. *Biografiia*, pp. 128–30.

4. Frank to El'iashevich, 25 Oct. 1922, NN.
5. *Biografiia*, pp. 137–38.
6. Frank to Nina Struve, 12 Nov. 1922, *Voprosy filosofii*, p. 128.
7. Frank to Nina Struve, 20 June 1923, GARF, f. 5912, o. 2, delo 110, l. 8.
8. Berdiaev, *Dream and Reality*, p. 245.
9. Frank to Nina Struve, *Voprosy filosofii*, p. 128.
10. Frank to Struve, 18 Oct. 1922, ibid., p. 123.
11. Ibid.
12. *Biografiia*, pp. 126–27.
13. Frank to Struve, 18 Oct. 1922, *Voprosy filosofii*, p. 123.
14. Ibid.
15. Frank to Struve, 28 Aug. 1923, *Voprosy filosofii*, p. 130.
16. *Biografiia*, p. 135.
17. Struve to Frank, 3 Sept. 1923, *Voprosy filosofii*, pp. 131–32.
18. Struve to Frank, 19 Oct. 1922, ibid., p. 124.
19. Frank to Struve, 7 Sept. 1923, ibid., p. 132.
20. Ibid.
21. "Die Orthodoxie Kirche in Russland," BA, Frank Papers, box 12, p. 14.
22. Struve to Frank, *Voprosy filosofii*, p. 133.
23. Frank to Struve, 4 Nov. 1922, ibid., p. 127.
24. Struve to Frank, 19 Oct. 1922, ibid., p. 124; see also *Biografiia*, pp. 135–36.
25. Frank to P. P. Suvchinskii, 4 Sept. 1925, P. P. Suvchinskii Archive; *Biografiia*, p. 146.
26. *Biografiia*, p. 146; Frank to Struve, 16 Nov. 1927, BA, box 3.
27. Struve, "Poznanie revoliutsii," p. 303.
28. Ibid., p. 305.
29. See Zen'kovskii, "Uchenie S. L. Franka," p. 79.
30. *Biografiia*, p. 125.
31. Ibid., p. 134.
32. Frank to Struve, 28 Aug. 1923, *Voprosy filosofii*, p. 130.
33. Struve to Frank, 3 Sept. 1923, ibid., p. 131.
34. Frank to Berdiaev, 2 Nov. 1925, RGALI, f. 1496, o. 1, delo 788, l. 3. Struve's assistants on *Renaissance* included A. Borman, son of A. Tyrkova by her first marriage, and S. S. Oldenburg.
35. Frank to El'iashevich, 1 Feb. 1928, NN.
36. *Biografiia*, p. 125.
37. Ibid., pp. 158–60.
38. Frank to Struve, 16 Nov. 1927, BA, box 3.
39. Frank, "Religioznye osnovy obshchestvennosti," pp. 9–11.
40. Frank, "Ia i my," p. 440.
41. "Religioznye osnovy," p. 12.
42. Carlyle in Frank, *Spiritual Foundations of Society*, p. 28.
43. *Spiritual Foundations*, p. 82.
44. "Religioznye osnovy," p. 20.
45. *Spiritual Foundations*, p. 82.
46. Frank, *Svet vo t'me*, p. 359; *Light Shineth in Darkness*, p. 209.
47. *Spiritual Foundations*, p. 114.
48. Frank, "Molodaia demokratiia."

49. *Krushenie kumirov*, pp. 43–44.
50. "Iz razmyshlenii o russkoi revoliutsii," pp. 250–51.
51. Ibid., p. 251.
52. Frank, "Religioznyi smysl ili nravstvennaia osnova demokratii," BA, box 12, p. 5.
53. "De Profundis," p. 328. *Pochvennost'* roughly translates as "grounded-ness." *Pochvennichestvo:* The Native Soil Movement of the 1850s and 1860s.
54. Ibid., p. 329.
55. *Dusha cheloveka*, pp. 252–53; *Man's Soul,* pp. 207–8.
56. *Spiritual Foundations*, p. 111.
57. "Ia i my", p. 447.
58. See *Svet vo t'me*, p. 307; *Light Shineth*, 176.
59. For Frank on the relation of his concept of being to St. Paul's thought, see "Nepostizhimoe," p. 380; *The Unknowable*, p. 150.
60. Frank, "Deutschen zwischen West und Ost," BA, box 11, p. 2.
61. *Spiritual Foundations*, pp. 54–67. Although *"sobornost'"* is a term often associated with the Slavophile thinker Aleksei Khomiakov, Frank did not attempt specifically to link his social and political ideas to the Slavophile tradition. There is one reference to Khomiakov in *Spiritual Foundations of Society* that relates to his teaching on church unity; see *Spiritual Foundations*, p. 64.
62. Ibid., p. 139.
63. Ibid., pp. 157–58.
64. Ibid., pp. 174–75.
65. Ibid., p. 123.
66. Ibid., p. 171.
67. *Biografiia*, p. 123. Struve considered his liberal conservative political philosophy to be best exemplified in the thought and career of Boris Chicherin (see Pipes, *Liberal Right*, p. 375). Certainly, many of Chicherin's political ideas are comparable to the thought of both Struve and Frank. See, for example, his collection of essays of 1862, *Some Modern Questions*.
68. Frank, "Pushkin kak politicheskii myslitel'," p. 31.
69. *Spiritual Foundations*, p. 170.
70. Ibid., pp. 271, 153.
71. Frank, *S nami Bog*, p. 123; *God with Us*, p. 100.
72. Interview, Natalia Norman.
73. "Religiozno-istoricheskii smysl russkoi revoliutsii," pp. 37, 26.

CHAPTER 13: LONELY YEARS

1. Interview, Vasilii Frank.
2. Frank to Tatiana Frank, 11 Feb. 1926, SA.
3. Frank to Nina Struve, 12 Nov. 1922, *Voprosy filosofii*, p. 128.
4. Frank to M. I. Lot-Borodina, 24 Jan. 1945, BA, box 2.
5. Frank to Struve, 16 Dec. 1927, HI, 6, 1.
6. Frank to Berdiaev, 12 Dec. 1924, BA, Berdiaev Papers.
7. Frank, "Pamiati Iu. I. Aikhenval'da," p. 126.

8. *Rul'*, 19 Dec. 1928, no. 2453, p. 2.

9. Frank to Berdiaev, n.d., RGALI, f. 1496, o. 1, ed.khr. 788, l. 5.

10. Ibid.

11. Frank to Gershenzon, 30 Mar. 1910, OR-RGB, l. 34.

12. Pipes, *Liberal Right*, p. 366.

13. Lowrie, p. 207.

14. Frank to Berdiaev, n.d., RGALI, f. 1496, o. 1, ed.khr. 788, l. 2. Iasinskii, who was then director, had left-wing inclinations.

15. Frank to Berdiaev, 12 Dec. 1924, BA, Berdiaev Papers.

16. Ibid.

17. Berdiaev, *Dream and Reality*, p. 248.

18. Frank to Tatiana Frank, 15 Sept. 1924, SA.

19. Frank to Berdiaev, 2 Nov. 1925, RGALI, f. 1496, o. 1, delo 788, l. 3.

20. Ibid.

21. *Biografiia*, p. 152.

22. Raeff, p. 43.

23. Frank to Nina Struve, 12 Jan. 1924, GARF, f. 5912, o. 2, delo 127, l. 12.

24. Frank, Speech at Russian Academic Union, Berlin, 1926, BA, box 12, p. 2.

25. *Biografiia*, p. 149.

26. N. P. Poltoratskii, *Ivan Aleksandrovich Il'in*, p. 130.

27. Frank to Berdiaev, 6 July 1929, RGALI, f. 1496, o. 1, ed.khr. 788, l. 4.

28. Frank, "Die Orthodoxe Kirche in Russland," BA, box 12, p. 16.

29. Speech at Russian Academic Union, Berlin, pp. 1–4.

30. Frank to G. N. Trubetskoi, 21 Apr. 1926, *Vestnik RSKhD*, p. 244; 6 Sept. 1926, p. 246; 5 June 1929, p. 248.

31. Ibid., 5 June 1929, p. 249.

32. Frank, "Orthodoxe Kirche in Russland," p. 24.

33. Anderson, p. 46.

34. Frank to Berdiaev, 17 May 1927, BA, Berdiaev Papers.

35. Interview, Natalia Norman. The two schools were Staatliche Augusta Schule and Franziskus Oberlyzeum.

36. Interview, Natalia Norman.

37. Ibid.

38. Interviews, Vasilii Frank, Natalia Norman, Irina Zak.

39. Interviews, Vasilii Frank, Natalia Norman.

40. Interview, Vasilii Frank.

41. Ibid.

42. Frank to Tatiana Frank, 15 Mar. 1928, SA.

43. Ibid., 4 July 1928.

44. Frank, *S nami Bog*, p. 210; God with Us, p. 166.

45. Interview, Natalia Norman.

46. Frank to Tatiana Frank, n.d., 1923, handwriting of Tatiana, SA.

47. Tatiana Frank, SA, private memoir, p. 20.

48. Interview, Vasilii Frank.

49. Interview, Natalia Norman. For Einstein's nine brief letters to Frank, BA, box 1.

50. Interview, E. Behr-Sigel.

51. Frank to Struve, 6 Nov. 1925, *Voprosy filosofii*, p. 135.

52. For contact with Heiler, see Frank to Binswanger, 5 Nov. 1936. Among other things, Heiler was interested in Buddhism and Hinduism, and in 1925 he published his *Mysticism of the Upanishads*. Also at Marburg was the famous theologian Rudolf Otto, whom Frank admired and whose work he referred to a number of times in *The Unknowable*.

53. Frank to Tatiana Frank, 5 Sept. 1931, SA.

54. Frank to Binswanger, 30 Nov. 1934.

55. Frank to El'iashevich, 18 Jan. 1937, NN.

56. Frank to Struve, 7 Sept. 1923, *Voprosy filosofii*, pp. 132–33.

57. Frank, "Novoe varvarstvo," *Rul'*, 28 Dec. 1926.

58. Interview, Natalia Norman.

59. Frank to Berdiaev, 14 Apr. 1933, BA, Berdiaev Papers.

60. Viktor, *Vestnik*, 1977, p. 102.

61. Frank to Nina Struve, 12 Jan. 1924, GARF, f. 5912, o. 2, delo 127, l. 12.

62. Frank to El'iashevich, 5 Aug. 1930, NN.

63. Vasilii Frank, draft memoirs, Possession of V. Frank, p. 106.

64. "Predsmertnoe," p. 117.

65. M. Gurevich to Binswanger, 27 Dec. 1935.

66. Frank to Binswanger, 7 Jan. 1936.

67. See Fr. Karger to Binswanger, 12 Aug. 1938.

68. Gurevich to Binswanger, 12 May 1936.

69. See also Gurevich to Binswanger, 29 Mar. 1937.

70. Vasilii Frank, draft memoirs, p. 91.

71. Interviews, Vasilii Frank, Natalia Norman.

72. Interview, Natalia Norman.

73. Frank to Binswanger, 20 June 1937.

CHAPTER 14: *THE UNKNOWABLE*

1. Frank to El'iashevich, 22 Mar. 1937, NN.

2. Frank to Binswanger, 13 Oct. 1936.

3. Frank, "Religiia i nauka v sovremennom soznanii," p. 154.

4. Frank, "Psikhoanaliz kak mirosozertsanie," pp. 30, 44.

5. Frank to Binswanger, 12 June 1936.

6. See Buber, *I and Thou*, pp. 28, 75.

7. "Novaia nemetskaia literatura po filosofskoi antropologii," p. 133. In the 1940s Binswanger stated (28 July 1947 and 2 Oct. 1947) that Buber knew about Frank, who referred briefly to Buber in two letters to Binswanger, n.d., end of 1947; 8 Jan. 1948.

8. See *Sochineniia*, p. 598.

9. Frank to Natalia, 9 Jan. 1945, NN.

10. *Sochineniia*, p. 199; *The Unknowable*, 1983, pp. 1, 20.

11. "Die gegenwartige, geistige Lage und die Idee der negativen Theologie," p. 5.

12. Frank to Binswanger, 13 Apr. 1936.

13. Frank, "Filosofiia i religiia," Berdiaev, *Sofiia*, p. 9.

14. Ibid., p. 20.

15. Frank to Binswanger, 1 June 1936.

16. Ibid., 15 Nov. 1935, 16 Mar. 1939.

17. Frank *Religiia i nauka*, p. 23.

18. *Sochineniia*, p. 213; *The Unknowable*, p. 13.

19. *Religiia i nauka*, p. 23.

20. "Krizis sovremennoi filosofii," p. 38.

21. "Filosofiia Gegelia," p. 51.

22. Frank to Binswanger, 26 May 1937.

23. Ibid., 30 Sept. 1937.

24. *Sochineniia*, p. 181; *The Unknowable*, p. 5.

25. Ibid., pp. 183–84; x–xi.

26. Ibid., pp. 313, 315, 488; 95, 97, 242.

27. Ibid., pp. 393, 446; 161, 207.

28. Ibid., pp. 468–69, 467; 226, 224.

29. Ibid., pp. 467–68, 497, 308; 225–26, 250, 92.

30. Ibid., p. 419; 185.

31. Frank, *Die russische Weltanschauung*, pp. 8, 10.

32. *Sochineniia*, pp. 206, 314; *The Unknowable*, pp. 7, 96.

33. Ibid., p. 548; 293.

34. *The Unknowable*'s original title, *Das Unergründliche*, suggests the *Ungrund* of Jacob Boehme and Friedrich Schelling, the groundless abyss out of which God and the world are formed. Frank nevertheless differentiated his explanation of groundlessness from that of Boehme and Schelling: "My interpretation differs from Boehme's and Schelling's in that I do not include the principle of *Ungrund* in the nature of God, but find it only in the severance from God. The infinite depths of God's being are something entirely different from the groundlessness of pure formless potentiality"; see Frank, *Real'nost' i chelovek*, p. 323; *Reality and Man*, p. 175.

35. *Die russische Weltanschauung*, p. 41.

36. "Die russische Geistesart in ihrer Beziehung zur deutschen," BA, box 12, pp. 11, 18.

37. *Sochineniia*, pp. 525, 510; *The Unknowable*, pp. 274, 260.

38. "Filosofiia Gegelia," p. 47.

39. Frank to Binswanger, 24 July 1935.

40. Ibid., 12 July 1942.

41. *Sochineniia*, pp. 501, 424–33; *The Unknowable*, pp. 253, 189–96.

42. Ibid., p. 551; 296.

43. Frank to Natalia, 9 Jan. 1945, NN.

44. Frank to Binswanger, 2 July 1937.

45. Ibid., 17 Jan. 1936, 23 Mar. 1936.

46. Frank to El'iashevich, 18 Jan. 1937, NN.

47. Frank to Binswanger, 2 Dec. 1939.

48. Interview, Natalia Norman.

49. *Biografiia*, p. 169–70.

50. *Sochineniia,* p. 279; *The Unknowable,* p. 67.
51. Frank to Binswanger, 15 Nov. 1935.
52. Frank, "Mistika Reinera Marii Ril'ke," p. 68.

CHAPTER 15: 1938–1945

1. Frank to Binswanger, 27 Mar. 1938.
2. Frank to El'iashevich, 31 Mar. 1938, NN.
3. Frank to Binswanger, 14, 26 May 1938, 25 Aug. 1938.
4. Frank to El'iashevich, 31 May, 1938, NN.
5. Frank to Binswanger, 4 Apr. 1938.
6. Frank to Binswanger, 25, 31 May 1938.
7. Ibid., 25 Aug. 1938.
8. Ibid., 22, 31 Oct. 1938.
9. *Biografiia,* pp. 166–67.
10. Frank to Binswanger, 22 Dec. 1938.
11. Frank to Natalia Norman, 23 Aug. 1940, BA, box 4.
12. Yanovsky, *Elysian Fields,* pp. 164, 149.
13. Borne, pp. 501–3.
14. See, "Eine franzosische Existentialphilosophie," BA, box 11.
15. Frank to Binswanger, 4 Apr. 1938.
16. Ibid., 16 Mar. 1939, 23 Aug. 1939, 29 Aug. 1939, 27 Sept. 1939.
17. Ibid., 28 Nov. 1942, 5 Sept. 1945.
18. Ibid., 1 Dec. 1941.
19. Ibid., 7 Aug. 1941.
20. Binswanger to Frank, 29 Mar. 1945.
21. Frank to Binswanger, 11 Nov. 1942.
22. Frank, 13 Sept. 1940, 27 Sept. 1943, Tatiana Frank's war notes, SA, pp. 14–15.
23. Frank to Binswanger, 8 Dec. 1940; see also *S nami Bog,* p. 55; *God with Us,* p. 45.
24. Tatiana Frank, war notes, Aug. 1941, SA, p. 13.
25. Frank to Binswanger, 18 Feb. 1944, 15 Apr. 1944. Here and in chapter 18, I have translated the Russian concept of *tvorchestvo* as "creativeness"—following Natalie Duddington in her translation of *Reality and Man.* In some sentences, "creation" or "creativity" might be more appropriate, but for consistency I have kept with "creativeness" in most cases.
26. Ibid., 20 Oct. 1940, 25 Feb. 1943.
27. Ibid., 8 Aug. 1940, 14 Dec. 1940, 13 Feb. 1942, 25 Mar. 1942, 26 Oct. 1942, 12 Nov. 1942.
28. Frank, "Mysli v strashnye dni," 19 Nov. 1942, BA, box 15, p. 1; Viktor Frank, "Semen Frank," pp. 15–16.
29. Frank to Binswanger, 12 July 1942.
30. Interview, Nikita Struve.
31. Frank to Binswanger, 4 Aug. 1943.
32. Frank to Aleksei Struve, 26 Sept. 1943, NS.

33. Frank to Binswanger, 27 Aug. 1943.
34. Ibid., 6 Dec. 1943.
35. Frank to Aleksei Struve, 19 Apr. 1944, 17 May 1944, NS.
36. Tatiana Frank, memoir, SA, pp. 18–19.
37. Interview, Irina Zak.
38. Tatiana Frank, memoir, p. 19.
39. Ibid., p. 18.
40. War notes, 2 Jan. 1943, SA, p. 13.
41. Frank to Aleksei Struve, 5, 9 Oct. 1943, NS.
42. See Frank to El'iashevich, 15 July 1943, 7 Nov. 1943, 10 Nov. 1943, 8 Jan. 1944, 16 Mar. 1944, 14 Oct. 1944.
43. Frank to Binswanger, 13 Sept. 1944; Frank to Aleksei Struve, 13 Sept. 1944, NS.
44. Frank to Binswanger, 1 Oct. 1944.
45. Frank to El'iashevich, 4 Mar. 1944.
46. Frank to Aleksei Struve, 6 Mar. 1944, NS.
47. Frank to Binswanger, 15 Apr. 1944.
48. Frank to El'iashevich, 4 Mar. 1944.
49. Frank to Binswanger, 4 Mar. 1945.
50. Tatiana Frank, memoir, p. 21.
51. Frank to Binswanger, 21 Mar. 1945.

CHAPTER 16: RELIGIOUS EXPERIENCE

1. Frank to Struve, 6 May 1943, BA, box 3. For a discussion of Frank's use of the word "concrete," and Hegel's influence in this connection, see Kline, "Hegelian Roots," pp. 200–204.
2. Frank, "Mysli v strashnye dni," 19 Nov. 1942, BA, box 15, p. 2.
3. Frank to El'iashevich, 19 May 1947, NN.
4. *S nami Bog*, pp. 74–75; *God with Us*, p. 60.
5. Frank to Binswanger, 22 July 1945.
6. Newman, *Apologia pro Vita Sua*, p. 67.
7. Notes, 1946–50, SA, p. 3.
8. Frank, 31 Aug. 1950, "Predsmertnye vospominaniia i mysli," BA, box 12; also SA.
9. *S nami Bog*, p. 115; *God with Us*, p. 94.
10. Ibid., pp. 363–64, 137; 285, 172–73.
11. Frank to Lot-Borodina, 24 Jan. 1945, BA, box 2.
12. *S nami Bog*, p. 30; *God with Us*, pp. 24–25. While Frank knew and admired aspects of the Eastern religions, he did not accept all their teachings. On the differences between Christian, Hindu and Buddhist views of the soul, see "Uchenie o pereselenii dush," pp. 9–19.
13. Frank to Binswanger, 24 Apr. 1941.
14. Frank, letter, 13 Aug. 1944, "O nevozmozhnosti filosofii," *Vestnik RSKhD*, pp. 166–67.
15. *S nami Bog*, p. 145; *God with Us*, p. 118.

16. Ibid., pp. 80–81; 65.
17. "Mysli v strashnye dni," 27 Mar. 1943, BA, box 15, p. 9.
18. Letter, "O nevozmozhnosti filosofii," pp. 162–63, 164.
19. Frank to Viktor, 17 Apr. 1945, 5 June 1941, 13 Feb. 1945, BA, box 4.
20. *S nami Bog*, p. 328; *God with Us*, pp. 257–58.
21. Frank, Letter, *The Tablet*, 27 Apr. 1946, p. 212.
22. Frank to Berdiaev, London, n.d. 1946, BA. box 1.
23. Frank to Aleksei Struve, 19 Apr. 1944, NS.
24. Frank to Viktor, 26 May 1945, BA, box 4.
25. Ibid., 13 Feb. 1945.
26. Frank to Berdiaev, n.d. 1935, BA, box 1.
27. Frank to Viktor, 17 Apr. 1945, 26 May 1945, 17 Apr. 1945, BA, box 4.
28. Ibid., 11 Sept. 1946.
29. Ibid., 18, 15 Sept. 1946.
30. Frank to Ivanov, 17 June 1947, in *Mosty*, 1963, no. 10, p. 368.
31. See *S nami Bog*, pp. 367–68; *God with Us*, pp. 287–88.
32. Ibid., pp. 366, 372; 287, 291.
33. Letter, *The Tablet*, 27 Apr. 1946, p. 212.
34. "Mysli v strashnye dni," 11 Jan. 1943, p. 4.
35. *The Tablet*, 27 Apr. 1946, p. 212.
36. Ibid.
37. *S nami Bog*, p. 367; *God with Us*, p. 287.
38. Ibid., p. 377; 295.
39. *The Tablet*, 9 Mar. 1946, p. 125–26.
40. *Sochineniia*, pp. 479–82; *The Unknowable*, pp. 232–35.
41. "Mysli v strashnye dni," 13 June 1943, BA, box 15, p. 31.
42. Berdiaev, "O knige S. L. Franka 'Nepostizhimoe,'" p. 653.
43. "Mysli v strashnye dni," 2 Jan. 1943, BA, box 15, p. 3.

CHAPTER 17: CHRISTIAN POLITICS

1. See Frank to Binswanger, 23 Sept. 1946.
2. Frank, "Sovetskii imperializm," BA, box 12, p. 7.
3. Ibid., p. 13.
4. Frank "Real'nyi smysl voiny," BA, box 12, p. 7.
5. Frank, "Mysli v strashnye dni," 19 Nov. 1942, BA, box 15, p. 2.
6. See *Svet vo t'me*, p. 244; *Light Shineth*, p. 139.
7. Frank, "The Christian Conscience and Politics," BA, box 11, pp. 5–11.
8. Frank to Binswanger, 20 Oct. 1945.
9. *Svet vo t'me*, p. 13; *Light Shineth*, p. xxi.
10. Ibid., p. 311; 179.
11. Ibid., pp. 380, 222; 381, 223.
12. Ibid., p. 312; 179.
13. Ibid., pp. 232, 229; 132, 130.
14. Ibid., pp. 218, 332; 124, 193.
15. Ibid., pp. 373, 380; 218, 222.

16. Ibid., p. 376–79; 220–21.
17. Ibid., p. 387; 226.
18. Ibid., pp. 261, 264; 149, 151.
19. Ibid., pp. 402–03; 236.
20. "Dukhovnoe nasledie Vladimira Solov'eva," p. 176.
21. Frank to V. Fedorovskii, *Vestnik RSKhD*, p. 171.
22. Frank to Binswanger, 20 Mar. 1946.
23. Frank, *Solovyov Anthology*, p. 30.
24. See "Spiritual and Social Prophet," *The Listener*, 28 Apr. 1949, p. 710; "Einer russischer christlicher Humanist," BA, box 13.
25. Frank to Binswanger, 14 June 1948.
26. Frank, notebook, 1950, possession of Vasilii Frank.
27. Florovskii, Foreword to Frank, *Reality and Man*, p. xii.
28. Frank to Binswanger, 20 Mar. 1946.
29. Frank, typed extract from letter, probably to Viktor, n.d., NN.
30. Frank, "Pushkin ob otnosheniiakh," pp. 107, 101.
31. Frank to G. P. Fedotov, *Novyi zhurnal*, p. 289; original, 27 June 1949, BA, G. P. Fedotov Papers.
32. Frank, *Real'nost' i chelovek*, p. 8; *Reality and Man*, pp. xiii–xiv.
33. Frank, "Dukhovnoe nasledie," p. 180.
34. *Solovyov Anthology*, p. 29.

CHAPTER 18: LONDON

1. Interview, Peter Scorer.
2. Oliver Tompkins to Frank, 28 Mar. 1946, 14 May 1948, BA, box 3.
3. Frank to Bishop of Chichester, 4 Oct. 1947, BA, boxes 4, 5.
4. Interview, Isaiah Berlin.
5. Frank to Struve, 5 Apr. 1943, BA, box 3.
6. Ibid.
7. "Mysli v strashnye dni," 16 Apr. 1943, BA, box 15, pp. 13–14.
8. Frank to Struve, 6 May 1943, BA, box 3.
9. "Mysli," 4 Feb. 1943, p. 5.
10. "Mysli," 20 June 1943, pp. 47, 48–49.
11. Frank to Binswanger, 29 Nov. 1945, 18 Nov. 1946.
12. *Real'nost' i chelovek*, pp. 289–91; *Reality and Man*, pp. 156–57.
13. "Mysli," 14 Apr. 1943, p. 8.
14. *Real'nost' i chelovek*, pp. 394, 399; *Reality and Man*, pp. 216, 219.
15. Zak, "Semen Frank," p. 23.
16. Frank to Berdiaev, 1946, BA, box 1. Frank also believed that Berdiaev's thought contained gnostic heresies (see "Ein russischer christlicher Sozialist," BA, box 12, p. 6).
17. Frank to Binswanger, 18 Nov. 1946, 30 Apr. 1947.
18. Frank to Lot-Borodina, 23 Jan. 1948, BA, box 2.
19. Frank to Binswanger, 30 Dec. 1947.
20. *Real'nost' i chelovek*, p. 72; *Reality and Man*, p. 33.

21. Frank to Lot-Borodina, 23 Jan. 1948.

22. Frank to Binswanger, 30 Aug. 1950; letter published in *Logos*, 1992, no. 3, pp. 267–68.

23. Frank, "Predsmertnye vospominaniia i mysli," BA, box 12; also in SA.

24. Frank to Lot-Borodina, 23 Jan. 1948.

25. *Real'nost' i chelovek*, pp. 407–8; *Reality and Man*, pp. 223–24.

26. Ibid., p. 202; 105.

27. Frank to Binswanger, 28 Mar. 1946.

28. Ibid., 30 Sept. 1947, 30 Dec. 1947, 27 Sept. 1949.

29. Ibid., 29 Jan. 1948, 4 Oct. 1948.

30. Vasilii Frank, personal notebook, 1 May 1948, possession of V. Frank.

31. Frank to E. Iu. Rapp, 31 Mar. 1948, RGALI, f. 1496, o. 1, ed.khr. 990.

32. Frank, "Svetlaia pechal'," p. 123.

33. Interview, Natalia Norman.

34. Notes, 1946–50, SA, pp. 4–5.

35. Zak, "Semen Frank," pp. 22–23; Notes, 1946–50, SA, p. 9.

36. Zak, Papers BA, box 16, p. 6.

37. Notes, 1946–50, p. 12.

38. Interview, Natalia Norman.

39. The Book of Wisdom, ch. 8, vv. 2 & 21.

CONCLUSION

1. *Sochineniia*, p. 199; *The Unknowable*, p. 1.

2. *Paradiso*, 33, l.145.

3. See M. Villiers, *Charles Péguy*, p. 351.

4. Viktor Frank, "Semen Frank," p. 1.

5. Frank to Binswanger, 10 June 1950.

6. Frank to Binswanger, 1936, from *Sbornik*, p. 29.

7. Binswanger to Frank, 23 Apr. 1942.

8. "Predsmertnoe," p. 112.

9. On Solzhenitsyn's anti-Machiavellian position, see Stephen Carter, *Politics of Solzhenitysn*, p. 92.

10. *Predmet znaniia*, p. 443.

11. New Testament, possession of Peter Scorer.

12. In an essay of 1949, "The Heresy of Utopianism," Frank noted that although men and women should have access to equal rights, there is a "cosmically-defined difference in the intellectual and spiritual mentality and life's 'calling' of the two sexes"; Frank, "Eres' utopizma," *Po tu storonu pravogo i levogo*, p. 103.

13. Frank's notebook for 1950, quoting from *The God That Failed*, 1950, pp. 75–76.

Bibliography

ARCHIVAL SOURCES

Interviews by Philip Boobbyer

Elizabeth Behr-Sigel, Paris, Nov. 1989.
Isaiah Berlin, Oxford, May 1989.
Vasilii Frank, Munich, Nov. 1989.
Eugene Lampert, London, Dec. 1989.
Natalia Norman, London, May–June 1989.
Peter Scorer, Exeter, Aug. 1990.
Nikita Struve, Paris, Nov. 1989–Jan. 1991.
Irina Zak, Paris, Jan. 1991.

Interview by Peter Scorer

Tatiana Frank, Munich, 1976.

Interview by Iu. Rostovtsev

Manuscript of interview between Iu. Rostovtsev and A. F. Losev.

Gosudarstvennyi Arkhiv Saratovskoi Oblasti

f. 332, o. 1, ed.khr. 3: Account of Historico-Philological Faculty at Saratov University, 1917–19.

Otdel Rukopisei, Rossiiskaia Gosudarstvennaia Biblioteka (OR-RGB)

f. 109, k. 35, ed.khr. 79: six letters, Frank to V. I. Ivanov, 1911–15.
f. 348, k. 3, ed.khr. 94: two letters, Frank to V. F. Ern, 1916–17.
f. 746, k. 42, ed.khr. 60: twenty-nine letters and postcards, Frank to M. O. Gershenzon, 1907–11 (see also Published Letters).

f. 746, k. 42, ed.khr. 61; twenty-five letters and postcards, Frank to Gershenzon, 1912–19.

Pushkinskii Dom, Institut Mirovoi Literatury i Isskustva (PD-IMLI)

f. 264, delo 26: Otzyvy o rukopisiakh, postupivshikh v redaktsiiu *Russkoi mysli.*
f. 264, delo 288/289: ten letters from Frank to A. P. Mamarinova, 1913–18.

Rossiiskii Gosudarstvennyi Arkhiv Literatury i Isskustva (RGALI)

f. 1496, o. 1, ed.khr. 788/857: nine letters, Frank to Berdiaev, 1924–34.
f. 1496, o. 1, ed.khr. 990: letter, Frank to E. Iu. Rapp, 1948.
f. 2176, o. 1, no. 10: St. Petersburg Religious-Philosophical Society, discussion of *Landmarks.*
f. 2176, o. 1, ed.khr. 61: letter, Frank to A. V. Kartashev, Jan. 1914.

Moskovskii Gorodskii Arkhiv

f. 418, o. 308, del. 1020: Semyon Frank, university file.
f. 418, o. 312, del. 972: Mikhail Frank, university file.
f. 2244, o. 1, del. 2808: letter, Frank to A. Chuprov, 25 Apr. 1899.

Gosudarstvennyi Arkhiv Rossiiskoi Federatsii (GARF)

f. 63, o. 1898, ed.khr. 111 (1–4): on student gathering, 2 Feb. 1898.
f. 63, o. 1896, ed.khr. 1510 (1, 2): G. A. Liven.
f. 102, d7, 1899, ed.khr. 145: G. A. Liven.
f. 102, oo., 1898, ed.khr. 163: V. S. Elpat'evskii.
f. 102, d3, 1899, ed.khr. 415: S. L. Frank.
f. 102, oo., 1898, ed.khr. 451: S. L. Frank.
f. 102, oo., 1898, ed.khr. 2, ch. 1, t. 2: "Svedeniia po gub. Mosk."
f. 102, oo., 1898, 3 ch. 10: on student gathering, 2 Feb. 1898.
f. 523, o. 1, ed.khr. 40: Kadet Party, delegates to First Congress, Oct. 1905.
f. 523, o. 1, ed.khr. 41: Ballot papers at Congress, Oct. 1905.
f. 523, o. 1, ed.khr. 62: Delegates to Second Congress, Jan. 1906.
f. 5912, o. 2, delo 110, 127: sixteen letters and cards from Frank to the Struves, 1922–25 (see Published Letters).

Rossiiskii Tsentr Khraneniia i Izucheniia Dokumentov Noveishei Istorii

f. 279, o. 1, delo 67: 34 letters from Frank to Struve, 1901–5 (see Published Letters).

Tsentral'nyi Gosudarstvennyi Istoricheskii Arkhiv Rossiiskoi Federatsii

f. 733, o. 155, delo 352/388: Department narodnogo prosvescheniia.

Rossiiskii Gosudarstvennyi Istoricheskii Arkhiv—"Sankt-Peterburg"
(RGIA-St.P.)

f. 14, o. 1, ed.khr. 10625: Frank becomes private docent at university.
f. 14, o. 3, t. 4, delo 16181–197, 16217: university courses.
f. 19, delo 8, sv. 4275: K. M. Aggeev.
f. 19, o. 127, ed.khr. 2674: Tserkov' Larinskoi Gimnazii.
f. 148, delo 256, sv. 11: Evening courses at Mme Stoiunina's gymnasium.
f. 253, o. 10, delo 266, ll. 152–73: Frank removed from police suspicion.
f. 478, o. 23, ed.khr. 312: Frank, St.P. Polytechnical Institute.
f. 556: Froebel Courses.

Columbia University: Bakhmeteff Archive (BA)

Semyon Frank Papers
This is the main archive on Semyon Frank's life and work. It contains a large
quantity of letters to and from him, his surviving manuscripts, and other
related materials. The following are items I refer to in the text:

Box 1
A. Einstein to Frank, nine letters, 1929–30.
Frank to Berdiaev, copies of letters, 1926–46, written out by E. Iu. Rapp (origi-
nals in RGALI).
Frank to V. Ivanov, two letters, 1947 (see Published Letters).

Box 2
Letters from Frank to M. I. Lot-Borodina, 1945–48.

Box 3
Three typed letters from Frank to P. B. Struve, 1927(1), 1943(2) (originals in
HI).
Two letters from O. Tompkins (WCC) to Frank, 1946, 1948.

Box 4
Letters from Frank to Viktor, 1939–45.
Letter, Frank to Natalia, Aug. 1940.

Box 5
Letters from Frank to Viktor, 1946–50. (Total correspondence in boxes 4 & 5
with Viktor 1939–50 includes 92 letters.)
Letter from Frank to Bishop of Chichester, 1947.

Box 9
Letter, Viktor to William Paton, July 1942.
Address from students, Sept. 1922.

Box 11 Manuscripts
The Christian Conscience and Politics.
The Christian Idea.
Deutschland zwischen West und Ost.

Eine französische Existentialphilosophie.
On Jewish conversion to Christianity.

Box 12 Manuscripts
Die Orthodoxe Kirche in Russland.
Paskha.
Predsmertnye vospominaniia i mysli.
Real'nyi smyl bor'by.
Religioznyi smysl ili nravstvennaia osnova demokratii.
Die russische Geistesart in ihrer Beziehung zur deutchen.
Ein russischer christlicher Humanist.
Ein russischer christlicher Sozialist.
Sovetskii imperializm.
Speech at Russian Academic Union.

Box 13
Course outlines.

Box 15
"Mysli v strashnye dni, nachato 19/11/43," itemized notebooks, 1942–43.
Diaries.

Box 16
Lev Zak, "Vospominaniia o Semene Franke," in folder "Manuscripts about Semyon Liudvigovich Frank."
Personal documents on finance.
Notes on Brotherhood of Holy Sophia.

N. A. Berdiaev Papers
Thirty-six letters and cards from Frank to Berdiaev, 1923–47.

G. P. Fedotov Papers,
Letter, Frank to Fedotov, 27 June 1949.

Archive of Aleksandr Solzhenitsyn (SA)

One box of materials relating to S. L. Frank, including
Tatiana Frank, private memoir.
Letter, Frank to A. S. Braude, Aug. 1924.
Letter, Frank to Sofiia Zhivotovskaia, Aug. 1935.
Interwar letters and cards from Frank to Tatiana Frank, 1923 ff.
Tatiana Frank's war notes, pp. 12–21.
Notes from Frank's illness, (1946)–50.
Conversation with Viktor, 3 Aug. 1950.

Hoover Institution: Boris Nikolaevskii Collection (HI)

Nineteen letters from Frank to Struve, 1926–43, Peter Struve Papers, box 6, folder 1.

Seventy-three letters and cards written by Struve, almost all to Frank, 1922–44, typed version, Peter Struve Papers, box 6, folder 2.

Twenty-six letters from Frank to Gleb Struve, 1924–50, Gleb Struve Papers, box 28, folder 10.

Notes from an interview between Boris Nikolaevskii and Semyon Frank, Boris Nikolaevskii Collection, box 525, folder 1.

British Library

H. Williams Papers

Two letters from Frank to A. Tyrkova-Williams, add. 5443, l. 72; add. 54444, l. 11.

Possession of Vasilii Frank

Draft memoirs.

Notebook of quotations as personal advice, 1 May 1948.

Notebook of 1950.

Possession of Natalia Norman (NN)

Edited correspondence between Frank and L.Binswanger, 1934–50, other related letters. Two bound and typed volumes, 541 items (4 items published in *Logos;* see Published Letters).

Fifty-nine photocopied letters from Frank to V. B. El'iashevich, 1922–50 (also in SA).

Tatiana Frank, Vasiute, pamiat' serdtsa (also in SA).

Tatiana Frank, private memoir (also in SA).

Extract from undated letter, probably to Viktor.

Letter, Frank to Natalia, 9 Jan. 1945.

Possession of Peter Scorer

Frank's Greek New Testament.

Possession of Nikita Struve (NS)

Sixty-seven letters from Frank to Aleksei Struve, 1927–50.

P. P. Suvchinskii Archive, (Vadim Kozevoi) Paris

Nine letters and cards from Frank to Suvchinskii, 1924–27

British Foreign Office

Russia Correspondance 1781–1945, F.O. 371, 1922, vol. 8205, despatch 681, pp. 68–71.

WORKS BY S. L. FRANK

This is not a complete bibliography of Frank's published works. Starred items are those not referred to in the *Bibliographie des Ouevres de Simon Frank*, Paris: Institut d'Études Slaves, 1980.
This section is ordered as follows: (1) published books and articles; (2) published reviews; (3) published letters.

Published books and articles

*"Apostol chelovechnosti." *Rossiia i slav'ianstvo*, 21 Feb. 1931, p. 3.
Biografiia P. B. Struve. New York: Izd. imeni Chekhova, 1956.
La Connaissance et L'Être. Paris: Aubier, 1937.
"De profundis." *Iz glubiny*, Paris: YMCA Press, 1967, pp. 311–30.
"Demokratiia v rasput'e." *Russkaia svoboda*, Mar. 1917, no. 1, pp. 13–17.
"Dukhovnoe nasledie Vladimira Solov'eva." *Vestnik RSKhD*, 1977, no. 121, pp. 173–81.
"Duma i obshchestvo." *Svoboda i kul'tura*, 7 May 1906, no. 6, pp. 371–77.
"Die eine heilige Kirche im Urteile eines russischen Christen." *Liebet Einander*, Feb. 1935, no. 2, pp. 21–25.
"Die Einheit der Kirche in Vergangenheit und Gegenwart." *Liebet Einander*, Mar. 1935, no. 3, pp. 43–47.
"Eres' utopizma." *Po tu storonu pravogo i levogo*, Paris: YMCA Press, 1972, pp. 83–106.
"Erkenntnis und Sein." *Logos*, 17, 1928, no. 1, pp. 165–95; 18, 1929, no. 1, pp. 231–61.
"Ethische, rechts- und sozialphilosophische Strömungen in der modernen russischen Philosophie ausserhalb USSR." *Archiv für Rechts und Sozialphilosophie*, 1936, no. 29, pp. 64–81.
"The Ethic of Nihilism." *Landmarks*, ed. B. Shragin, A. Todd, trans. Marian Schwartz. New York: Karz Howard, 1977.
"Filosofiia Gegelia." *Put'*, July 1932, no. 34, pp. 39–51.
"Filosofiia i religiia." *Sofiia*. Berlin, 1923, pp. 5–20.
Filosofiia i zhizn'. St.P.: Zemlia, 1910.
"Filosofiia religii V. Dzhemsa." *Zhivoe znanie*. Berlin: Obelisk, 1923, pp. 9–24.
"Filosofskie otkliki: Novaia kniga Berdiaeva." *Russkaia mysl'*, 1910, no. 4, pp. 137–45.
"Filosofskie predposylki despotizma." *Filosofiia i zhizn'*. St.P.: Zemlia, 1910, pp. 135–63.
"Fr. Nitsshe i etika 'liubvi k dal'nemu.'" *Problemy idealizma*, Moscow, 1902, pp. 137–95.
"Die gegenwärtige geistige Lage und die Idee der negativen Theologie." *Congrès International de Philosophie*, 1934, 8, pp. 444–48 (offprint, pp. 1–5).
"Ein geistiger Führer des alten Russlands." *Liebet Einander*, Sept. 1935, no. 9, p. 130–33.
"Gete i problema dukhovnoi kul'tury." *Put'*, Sept. 1932, no. 35, pp. 83–90.
"Gnoseologiia Göte." *Zhivoe znanie*. Berlin: Obelisk, 1923, pp. 27–70.

God with Us. Trans. Natalie Duddington. London: Jonathon Cape, 1946.

"Gosudarstvo i lichnost'." *Novyi put'*, Nov 1904, pp. 308–17.

"Ia i my." *Sbornik statei posviashchennykh Petru Berngardovichu Struve.* Prague: Plamia, 1925.

(N. K.) "Inostrannaia pechat' o voine." *Osvobozhdenie,* 5–18 Feb 1904, no. 41, pp. 302–6.

"Intelligentsia i osvoboditel'noe dvizhenie." *Poliarnaia zvezda,* 10 Feb 1906, no. 9, pp. 643–54.

Introduction to *Filosofskie issledovaniia i ocherki,* by A. V. Gurevich. Trud, 1914, pp. iii–vi.

"L'Intuition Fondamentale de Bergson." *Henri Bergson: essais et témoignages* (Les Cahiers du Rhone. Hors Serie), ed. A. Béguin et P. Thévenaz. Neuchâtel, 1943.

[Ed.] *Iz istorii russkoi filosofskoi mysli.* Washington: Inter-Language Literary Associates, 1965.

"Iz razmyshlenii o Russkoi revoliutsii." *Russkaia mysl',* 1923, no. 6–8, pp. 238–70.

"Eine Jüngerin Jesu im alten Russland." *Liebet Einander,* Jan 1935, no. 1, pp. 2–5.

"K kharakteristike Gete." *Filosofiia i zhizn',* pp. 355–66.

"K voprosu o sushchnosti morali." *Filosofiia i zhizn',* 1910, pp. 125–34; originally published in 1906 as introduction to M. Beme, *Dnevnik padshei.*

*"Kapitalizm i kul'tura." *Moskovskii ezhenedel'nik,* 5, 1910, no. 16, pp. 37–42.

"Kniga Dil'teia po istorii filosofii." *Russkaia mysl',* 1914, no. 4, pp. 37–40.

"Konstantin Leontjew, ein russischer Nietzsche." *Hochland,* 1928–29, no. 6, Oct.–Mar. pp. 613–32.

"Kosmicheskoe chuvstvo v poezii Tiutcheva." *Zhivoe znanie,* Berlin, 1923, pp. 201–49.

"Krizis sovremennoi filosofii." *Russkaia mysl',* 1916, no. 9, pp. 33–40.

*"Krizis zapadnoi kul'tury." *Osval'd Shpengler i zakat Evropy.* Moscow: Bereg, 1922.

Krushenie kumirov. Berlin: YMCA Press, 1924.

"Krushenie sotsializma kak religii." *Ideinye gorizonty mirovoi voiny,* ed. P. Kudriashov. Moscow: Trud, 1915, pp. 183–85.

"Kul'tura i religiia." *Russkaia mysl',* 1909, no. 7, pp. 147–61.

"Legenda o velikom inkvizitore." *Vestnik RSKhD,* 117, 1976, no. 1, pp. 102–11.

"Lev Tolstoi i Russkaia intelligentsia." *Filosofiia i zhizn',* pp. 303–11.

Lichnaia zhizn' i sotsial'noe stroitel'stvo. Paris: YMCA Press, n.d.

"Lichnost' i mirovozrenie Fr. Shleermakhera." *Rechi o religii,* by Fr.Schleiermacher, trans. S. L. Frank. Moscow, 1911, pp. iii–xlix; includes a preface by Frank, pp. l–lii; *Russkaia mysl',* 1911, no. 9, pp. 1–28.

"Lichnost' i veshch'." *Filosofiia i zhizn',* pp. 164–217.

The Light Shineth in Darkness. Trans. B. Jakim. Athens: Ohio University Press, 1989.

"Maks Sheller." *Put',* Oct. 1928, no. 13, pp. 83–86.

Man's Soul. Trans. B. Jakim. Athens: Ohio University Press, 1993.

"Maxim Gorki." *Hochland,* 1936, 33, no. 2, Apr.–Sept. pp. 566–69.

"Merezhkovskii o 'Vekhakh'." *Slovo*, 28 Apr. 1909, no. 779, p. 2.

"Mertvye molchat." *Russkaia svoboda*, June 1917, no. 7, pp. 13–18.

"Mirosozertsanie Konstantina Leont'eva." *Filosofiia i zhizn'*, pp. 382–89.

"Mistika Reinera Marii Ril'ke." *Put'*, Aug. 1928, no. 12, pp. 47–75; Oct. 1928, no. 13, pp. 37–52.

"Mobilizatsiia mysli v Germanii." *Russkaia mysl'*, 1916, no. 9, pp. 20–27.

"Molodaia demokratiia." *Svoboda i kul'tura*, 10 Apr. 1906, no. 2, pp. 67–82.

"Na iuridicheskom fakul'tete v 90-kh godakh." *Rossiia i slav'ianstvo*, 25 Jan. 1930, no. 61, p. 4.

"Nemetskaia literatura po filosofskoi antropologii." *Put'*, 1929, no. 15, pp. 127–34.

"Nepostizhimoe." *Sochineniia*, ed. Iu. Senokosov. Moscow: Izd Pravda, 1990, pp. 181–603.

Nepostizhimoe. Munich: Wilhelm Fink Verlag, 1971.

*"Novye dannye k kharakteristike kul'turno-istoricheskikh, sotsiologicheskikh i filosofskikh vzgliadov Lassalia." *Voprosy filosofii i psikhologii*, Nov.–Dec. 1902, no. 65, pp. 952–76.

"Nravstvennoe uchenie L. N. Tolstogo." *Filosofiia i zhizn'*, pp. 289–302.

Nravstvennyi vodorazdel v Russkoi revoliutsii. Izd G. A. Lemana i S.I.Sakharova, Biblioteka "Svoboda i pravo," no. 15, April 1917, 14 pp.; also in *Russkaia svoboda*, April 1917, no. 2, pp. 34–39.

"O blagorodstve i nizosti v politike." *Russkaia svoboda*, 25 Apr. 1917, no. 2, pp. 26–31.

"O dukhovnoi sushchnosti Germanii." *Russkaia mysl'*, 1915, no. 10, pp. 1–18.

"O filosofskoi intuitsii." *Russkaia mysl'*, 1912, no. 3, pp. 31–35.

"O kriticheskom idealisme." *Mir bozhii*, 1904, no. 12, pp. 224–64.

"O natsionalizme v filosofii." *Russkaia mysl'*, 1910, no. 9, pp. 162–71.

"O poiskakh smysla voiny." *Russkaia mysl'*, 1914, no. 12, pp. 125–32.

"O svobodnoi sovesti." *Poliarnaia zvezda*, 17 Jan. 1906, no. 6, pp. 413–19.

"O t–naz. 'novom religioznom soznanii'." *Filosofiia i zhizn'*, pp. 338–46.

Ocherk metodologii obshchestvennykh nauk. Moscow: Bereg, 1922.

[With Struve]. "Ocherki filosofii kul'tury: Chto takoe kul'tura." *Poliarnaia zvezda*, 22 Dec 1905, no. 2, pp. 170–84.

[With Struve]. "Ocherki filosofii kul'tury: Kul'tura i lichnost'." *Poliarnaia zvezda*, 30 Dec 1905, no. 3, pp. 104–17.

"Odnostoronnee samopoznanie." *Poliarnaia zvezda*, 1905, no. 2, pp. 128–35.

Osnovy Marksizma. Berlin: Evraziiskoe izd., 1926.

[N.Ch.]. "Pamiati Chekhova." *Osvobozhdenie*, 19 July–1 Aug. 1904, no. 52, pp. 42–43.

"Pamiati Iu. I. Aikhenval'da." *Put'*, Feb. 1929, no. 15, pp. 125–26.

"Pamiati L.M.Lopatina." *Put'*, Oct. 1930, no. 24, pp. 111–14.

"Pamiati L'va Tolstogo." *Russkaia mysl'*, 1910, no. 12, pp. 139–50.

"Pis'ma A. I. Ertelia." *Filosofiia i zhizn'*, pp. 328–37.

[N. K.]. "Po serbski ili po nemetski?" *Osvobozhdenie*, 2–15 Aug 1903, no. 28, pp. 55–57.

Po tu storonu pravogo i levogo. Sbornik statei, ed. V. S. Frank. Paris: YMCA Press, 1972.

"Politika i idei." *Poliarnaia zvezda*, 1905, no. 1, pp. 18–31.
"Pragmatizm kak filosofskoe uchenie." *Russkaia mysl'*, 1910, no. 5, pp. 90–120.
*"Pred istoricheskimi dniami." *Duma*, 25 Apr.–10 May 1906, no. 1, p. 2.
*"Predislovie" to *Logicheskie issledovaniia*. St.P., 1909, p. v–vii.
Predmet znaniia. Petrograd, 1915 (reprinted in Belgium, with an introduction by D. Chizhevskii, 1973).
"Predsmertnoe." *Vestnik RSKhD*, 146, 1986, no. 1, p. 103–26.
"Priroda i kul'tura." *Logos*, 1910, no. 2, p. 50–89.
"Problema 'Khristianskogo sotsializma'." *Po tu storonu pravogo i levogo*, Paris: YMCA Press, 1972, pp. 61–82.
"Problema vlasti." *Filosofiia i zhizn'*, pp. 72–124; originally in *Voprosy zhizni*, 1905, no. 3, pp. 205–50.
"Proekt deklaratsii prav." *Poliarnaia zvezda*, 1905, no. 3, pp. 243–54.
*[With A. F. Lazurskii]. "Programma izsledovaniia lichnosti v ee otnosheniiakh k srede." *Russkaia shkola*, Jan. 1912, no. 1, ot. 2, pp. 1–24; Feb 1912, no. 2, ot. 2, pp. 1–17.
"Psikhoanaliz kak mirosozertsanie." *Put'*, Dec. 1930, no. 25, pp. 22–50.
"Psikhologicheskoe napravlenie v teorii tsennosti." *Russkoe bogatstvo*, Aug. 1898, no. 8, pp. 60–110.
"Pushkin kak politicheskii myslitel'." *Etiudy o Pushkine*. Paris: YMCA Press, 1987, pp. 28–57.
"Pushkin ob otnosheniiakh mezhdu Rossiei i Evropoi." *Etiudy o Pushkine*. Paris: YMCA Press, 1987, pp. 93–107.
Real'nost' i chelovek. Paris: YMCA Press, 1956.
Reality and Man. Trans. N. Duddington, preface A. M. Allchin. London: Faber and Faber, 1965; foreword by G. Florovskii, New York: Taplinger, 1965.
"Religiia i kul'tura." *Poliarnaia zvezda*, 1906, no. 12, pp. 46–54.
Religiia i nauka. Brussels, 1953.
"Religiia i nauka v sovremennom soznanii." *Put'*, June–July 1926, no. 4, pp. 145–56 (speech at the Religious-Philosophical Academy in Paris, Feb. 1926).
"Die religiöse Tragödie des Judentums." *Eine heilige Kirche*, Apr.–June 1934, pp. 128–33.
"Religioznaia filosofiia Kogena." *Russkaia mysl'*, 1915, no. 12, pp. 29–31.
"Religiozno-istoricheskii smysl russkoi revoliutsii." *Po tu storonu pravogo i levogo*, pp. 11–38.
"Religioznye osnovy obshchestvennosti." *Put'*, Sept 1925, no. 1, pp. 9–30.
Die russische Weltanshauung. Charlottenburg: Pan-Verlag Rolf Heise, 1926.
"Die russische Philosophie der letzten fünfzehn Jahre." *Kantstudien*, 31, 1926, pp. 89–104.
[Drug Italii], "Russkoe samoderzhavie i ital'ianskoe obshchestvennoe mnenie." *Osvobozhdenie*, 2–15 June 1903, no. 24, pp. 430–31.
"Rytsar' dukha." *Rul'*, 19 Dec. 1928, no. 2453, p. 2.
S nami Bog. Paris: YMCA Press, 1964.
"Sila i pravo." *Russkaia mysl'*, 1916, no. 1, pp. 12–17.
Smysl zhizni. Paris: YMCA Press, 1926.
Sochineniia. Edited by Iu. Senokosov. Moscow: Pravda, 1990.
A Solovyov Anthology. London: SCM, 1950.

"Sotsializm i kantiantstvo." *Filosofiia i zhizn'*, pp. 347–54.

"The Soul of Man," unpublished draft translation by B. Jakim.

The Spiritual Foundations of Society. Trans. B. Jakim. Athens: Ohio University Press, 1987.

Svet vo t'me. Paris: YMCA Press, 1949.

"Svetlaia pechal'." *Etiudy o Pushkine.* Paris: YMCA Press, 1987.

Talks for BBC on V. Solov'ev. *The Listener,* 28 Apr. 1949, pp. 709–10; 5 May 1949, pp. 766–67; 12 May 1949, pp. 804–5.

Teoriia tsennosti Marksa i eia znachenie: Kriticheskii etiud. St.P.: M. I. Vodovozova, 1900.

[On G. N. Trubetskoi]. *Pamiati Kn. G.N.Trubetskogo: sbornik statei.* Paris, 1930, pp. 34–36.

*"Tsarit bessmyslennaia lozh'." *Osvobozhdenie,* 19 Feb. 1904, no. 18 (42), pp. 316–19.

*"Uchenie o pereselenii dush." *Pereselenie dush.* Sbornik statei. Paris: YMCA Press, 1935, pp. 7–33.

"Uchenie Spinozy ob attributakh." *Voprosy filosofii i psikhologii,* 1912, no. 114, pp. 523–67.

The Unknowable. Trans. B. Jakim, Athens: Ohio University Press, 1983.

"Vil'hel'm Dil'tei." *Russkaia mysl',* 1911, no. 11, pp. 37–40.

"Vil'hel'm Shuppe." *Russkaia mysl',* 1913, no. 5, pp. 42–45.

"Vil'hel'm Vindel'band." *Russkaia mysl',* 1915, no. 11, pp. 20–23.

*"Vostochnoe umozrenie i zapadnaia filosofiia." *Rossiia i slav'ianstvo,* 17 Sept. 1932, p. 3.

Vvedenie v filosofiiu. Berlin: Obelisk, 1923.

"Wesen und Richtlinien der russischen Philosophie." *Der Gral,* 14 May 1925, pp. 384–94.

Zhivoe znanie. Berlin: Obelisk, 1923.

"Zur Problematik des sozialen Rechts." *Neue Zürcher Zeitung,* 16 Jan. 1938.

FRANK: SELECTED BOOK REVIEWS
(*Chronological Order*)

*Sobelev, M. N., *Ocherki iz istorii vsemirnoi torgovli v sviazi s razvitiem ekonomicheskoi zhizni,* Moscow, 1899. *Nachalo,* 1899, no. 4, ot. 2, pp. 161–63.

*Khodskii, L. V., *Politicheskaia ekonomiia v sviazi s finansami,* St.P., 1899. *Nachalo,* 1899, no. 5, ot. 2, pp. 123–28.

*Manuilov, A. A., *Poniatie tsennosti po ucheniiu ekonomistov klassicheskoi shkoly,* Moscow, 1901. *Mir bozhii,* 10, 1901, no. 7, pt. 2, pp. 108–13.

*Zheleznov, V., *Ocherki politicheskoi ekonomii,* Moscow, 1902. *Mir bozhii,* 1902, no. 11, pt. 2, pp. 113–16.

*Pogozhev, A. V., ed., *Promyshlennost' i zdorov'e,* pts. 1, 2. *Mir bozhii,* 1902, no. 12, pt. 2, pp. 122–24.

[N. K.]. "Mysli redkogo administratora," review of *Filosofskie i politicheskie razmyshleniia starogo administratora,* Stuttgart, 1904. *Osvobozhdenie,* 19 Mar.–1 Apr. 1904, no. 44, pp. 350–51; *Osvobozhdenie,* 2–15 Apr., no. 45, pp. 363–65.

Schiller als Philosoph und seine Beziehung zu Kant, Berlin, 1905. *Voprosy zhizni,* 1905, no. 6, pp. 268–72.
Höffding, H., *Moderne Philosophen,* Leipzig, 1905. *Voprosy zhizni,* 1905, no. 8, pp. 180–82.
Joel, J., *Nietzche und die Romantik,* Leipzig und Jena, 1905. *Voprosy zhizni,* no. 9, pp. 277–79.
Medicus, F., *I.G.Fichte,* Berlin, 1905. *Voprosy zhizni,* 1905, no. 9, pp. 273–77.
[N. K.]. *Obshchestvennoe dvizhenie pri Aleksandre II (1855–1881),* Paris 1905. *Osvobozhdenie,* 8–12 June 1905, no. 72, p. 366.
Ivanov-Razumnik, R. V., *O smysle zhizni. Kriticheskoe obozrenie,* 1907, no. 7 (12), pp. 34–38.
Simmel, G., *Goethe,* Leipzig, 1913. *Russkaia mysl',* 1913, no. 3, pp. 32–36.
Dilthey, W., *Schriften,* 1914. *Russkaia mysl',* 1914, no. 54, pp. 37–40.
Vysheslavtsev, B., *Etika Fikhte,* Moscow, 1914. *Russkaia mysl',* 1915, no. 5, pp. 31–35.

PUBLISHED LETTERS OF S. L. FRANK

Four letters from Frank-Binswanger correspondence. L. B. to S. F, Nov. 1934, 21 Jan. 1935; S. F. to L. B., 30 Nov. 1934, 10 Aug. 1950 (on Heidegger). *Logos* (Moscow) (1) 1992, no. 3, pp. 264–68.
Letter to the Editor. *The Tablet,* 27 Apr. 1946, p. 212.
Extracts from a letter to V. Fedorovskii. *Vestnik RSKhD,* 121, 1977, no. 2, pp. 171–72.
Letter to G. P. Fedotov. *Novyi zhurnal,* 1952, no. 28, pp. 288–89.
Letter to a friend, 13 Aug. 1944, "O nevozmozhnosti filosofii." *Vestnik RSKhD,* 1977, no. 121, pp. 162–70.
Correspondence with Gershenzon, "K istorii sozdaniia 'Vekh.'" *Minuvshee,* 11, 1991, pp. 252–59.
Correspondence with Viacheslav Ivanov, 2 letters by Frank, 1 by Ivanov. *Mosty,* 1963, no. 10, pp. 357–69.
[With Struve]. "Pis'mo v redaktsiiu." *Rech',* 23 June 1906, no. 107, p. 3.
Letters to P. B. and N. A. Struve, with an introduction by M. A. Kolerov and N. S. Plotnikov, 1901–5. *Put'*(Moscow), 1992, no. 1, pp. 263–311.
Correspondence with P. B. Struve and N. A. Struve, 1922–25, with an introduction by N. S. Plotnikov. *Voprosy filosofii,* 1993, no. 2, pp. 115–39.
Three letters to G. N. Trubetskoi. *Vestnik RSKhD,* 159, 1990, no. 2, pp. 242–51.

OTHER WORKS

Aggeev, K. M., *Istoricheskii grekh.* St.P., 1907.
Allen, G. W., *William James,* London: Rupert Hart-Davis, 1967.
Anderson, P. B. *No East or West.* Paris: YMCA Press, 1985.
Anderson, T. *Russian Political Thought.* Ithaca, N.Y.: Cornell University Press, 1967.

Angarskii, N. *Legal'nyi Marksizm: Populiarnyi ocherk*, vyp 1. Moscow: Nedra, 1925.

Antonii, Arkh. "Otkrytoe pis'mo avtoram sbornika 'Vekhi'." *Slovo*, 10 May 1909, p. 3.

Arsen'ev, N. S. "Raskryvaiushchiesia glubiny." *Sbornik pamiati Semeno Liudvigovicha Franka*. Munich, 1954, pp. 73–75.

Bazarov, V. *Krasnaia nov'*, 1922, kn. 2, pp. 230–31.

Berdiaev, N. A. *Dream and Reality: An Essay in Autobiography*. Trans. K. Lampert. London: Geoffrey Bles, 1950.

_____. "Dva tipa mirovozzreniia." *Tipy religioznoi mysli v Rossii*. Paris: YMCA Press, 1989, pp. 635–49.

_____. "Eticheskaia problema v svete filosofskago idealizma." *Problemy idealizma*, 1902, pp. 91–136.

_____. "O knige S.L.Franka 'Nepostizhimoe.'" *Tipy religioznoi mysli v Rossii*. Paris: YMCA Press, 1989, pp. 650–54.

_____. "O novom russkom idealizme." *Sub specie aeternitatis*. St.P.: M. V. Pirozhkova, 1907, pp. 152–90.

_____. "Philosophic Truth and the Moral Truth of the Intelligentsia." *Landmarks*, pp. 3–22.

_____. "Socialism as Religion." *A Revolution of the Spirit: Crisis of Value in Russia 1890–1918*, ed. M.Bohachevsky-Chomiak, B.G.Rosenthal. Newtonville, Mass.: Oriental Research Associates, 1982.

_____. ed. *Sofiia: Problemy dukhovnoi kul'tury i religioznoi filosofii*. Berlin, 1923.

Berlin, I. *Four Essays on Liberty*. Oxford: Oxford University Press, 1969.

_____. *Russian Thinkers*. London: Hogarth Press, 1978.

Beyssac, M. *La Vie Culturelle de l'Émigration Russe en France*, (chronique, 1920–1930). Presses Universitaires de France, 1971.

Billington, J. *Mikhailovsky and Russian Populism*. New York: Oxford University Press, 1958.

Binswanger, L. "Vospominaniia o Semene Liudvigoviche Franke." *Sbornik*, 1954, pp. 25–39.

Bohachevsky-Chomiak, M. *S. N. Trubetskoi*. Belmont, Mass: Nordland, 1976.

Böhm-Bawerk, E. Von. *Capital and Interest*. Vol. 2. Trans. G. D. Huncke. South Holland, Ill.: Libertarian Press, 1959.

Boll, M. M. "The Political and Social Philosophy of Semen Liudvigovich Frank." Ph.D., diss., University of Wisconsin, 1970.

Boobbyer, P. C. "Liberal Conservatism: the Political Philosophy of Semen L.Frank." M.A. thesis, Georgetown University, 1988.

_____. "The Two Democracies: Semen Frank's Interpretation of the Russian Revolutions of 1917," *Revolutionary Russia*, vol. 6, Dec. 1993, no. 2, pp. 195–209.

Borne, E. Review of *Connaissance et l'Être*, *Revue Thomiste*, 1937, no. 3, pp. 501–3.

Bourret, J.-F. *Les Allemands de la Volga*. Presses Universitaires de Lyon, 1986.

Bradley, J. "Moscow: From Big Village to Metropolis." *The City in Late Imperial Russia*. Bloomington: Indiana University Press, 1986, pp. 9–41.

Buber, M. *I and Thou*. Trans. R. G. Smith. New York: Scribner's, 1958.
Bugaenko, P. A., et al. *Saratovskii Universitet 1909–59*. Saratov, 1959.
Bulgakov, S. N. *Avtobiograficheskie zametki*. Paris: YMCA Press, 1946.
———. "Heroism and Asceticism." *Landmarks*, pp. 23–63.
———. "Ivan Karamazov kak filosofskii tip." *Ot Marksizma k idealizmu*. St.P., 1903, pp. 83–112; first published in *Voprosy filosofii i psikhologii*, 1902, no. 1.
———. "O zakonomernosti sotsial'nykh iavlenii." *Voprosy filosofii i psikhologii*, no. 5, 35, 1896, pp. 575–611; reprinted in Sergei Bulgakov, *Ot Marksizma k idealizmu*, St.P., 1903, pp. 1–34.
———. "Russkye dumy." *Russkaia mysl'*, 1914, no. 12, pp. 108–15.
Burbank, J. *Intelligentsia and Revolution*. New York: Oxford University Press, 1989.
Carlson, M. *"No Religion Higher than Truth": A History of the Theosophical Movement in Russia, 1875–1922*, Princeton, NJ: Princeton University Press, 1993.
Carter, S. *The Politics of Solzhenitsyn*. Macmillan, 1977.
Chicherin, B. N., *Neskol'ko sovremennykh voprosov*, Moscow, 1862.
Chizhevskii, D. *Gegel' v Rossii*. Paris, 1939.
———. "S. L. Frank, kak istorik filosofii i literatury." *Sbornik*, 1954, pp. 157–74.
Chueva, I. P. *Kritika idei intuitivizma v Rossii*. Moscow: Izd Akadem. Nauk, 1963.
Clément, O. *Berdiaev*. Desclée de Brouwer, 1991.
Copleston, F. C. *Philosophy in Russia*. Notre Dame, Ind.: University of Notre Dame Press, 1986.
———. *Russian Religious Philosophy*. University of Notre Dame, Search Press, 1988.
Curtis, J. M. "Michael Bakhtin, Nietzsche and Russian Revolutionary Thought." *Nietzsche in Russia*, ed. B. G. Rosenthal. Princeton University Press, 1986, pp. 331–54.
Darlington, J. "Education in Russia." *Special Reports on Educational Subjects*, vol. 23. London: Board of Education, 1909.
Ddoratskii, B. Review of S. L. Frank, *Ocherk metodologii obshchestvennykh nauk*. *Pechat' i revoliutsiia*, 1922, no. 6, pp. 238–40.
Dubbink, J. H. *Coëxistentie in de Metafysika*, (speech on 17 Feb 1967). Universitaire pers Leiden.
Dubnow, S. M. *History of the Jews in Russia and Poland*, 3 vols. Philadelphia: The Jewish Publication Society of America, 1916–1919.
Elkin, B. "The Russian Intelligentsia on the Eve of Revolution." *The Russian Intelligentsia*, ed. Richard Pipes. New York: Columbia University Press, 1961, pp. 32–46.
Elpat'evskii, S. Ia. *Vospominaniia za 50 let*. Priboi, 1929.
Emmons, T. *The Formation of Political Parties and the First National Elections in Russia*. Cambridge, Mass.: Harvard University Press, 1983.
Entsiklopedicheskii slovar'. Edited by F. A. Brokgauz, I. A. Efron. St.P., 1896.
Ern, V. F. "Ot Kanta do Kruppa." *Russkaia mysl'*, 1914, no. 12, pp. 116–24.
Evreiskaia entsiklopediia, Edited by A. Gargavi, L. Kantsel'son. St.P., n.d.
Feishman, L., et al. *Russkii Berlin, 1921–1923*. Paris: YMCA Press, 1983.

Figes, O. *Peasant Russia, Civil War.* Oxford: Clarendon Press, 1989.

Fioletova, N. Iu. "Istoriia odnoi zhizni." *Minuvshee,* 9, 1990, pp. 7–105.

Fischer, G. *Russian Liberalism.* Cambridge, Mass.: Harvard University Press, 1958.

Fletcher, W. C. *The Russian Orthodox Church Underground, 1917–1970.* London: Oxford University Press, 1971.

Flikke, G., "Democracy or Theocracy—Four Idealist Philosophers and the 1905 Revolution," (MA level thesis). The University of Oslo, Autumn 1993.

Florovskii, G. V. "Religioznaia metafizika S. L. Franka." *Sbornik,* 1954, pp. 145–56.

Frank, I. M. "Mikhail Liudvigovich Frank." *Istoriko-matematicheskie issledovaniia,* vyp 26. Moscow, 1982, pp. 266–93.

Frank, Vasilii. *Pamiati Viktora Franka.* 1974.

Frank, Viktor. "Crisis among the Orthodox." *The Tablet,* 14 Sept 1946, p. 134.

_____. "The Late Metropolitan Eulogius." *The Tablet,* 17 Aug 1946, p. 84.

_____. *Po suti dela.* 1977.

_____. "Semen Liudvigovich Frank." *Sbornik,* 1954, pp. 1–16.

Frenkel, J. *Prophecy and Politics: Socialism, Nationalism and the Russian Jews, 1862–1917.* Cambridge: Cambridge University Press, 1981.

Galai, S. *The Liberation Movement in Russia, 1900–1905.* Cambridge: Cambridge University Press, 1973.

Geller, M. "'Pervoe predosterzhenie'—udar khlystom." *Vestnik RSKhD,* 1978, no. 127, pp. 187–232.

Gershenzon, M. O. "Preface to the First Edition." *Landmarks,* pp. 1–2.

_____. "Creative Self-Cognition." *Landmarks,* pp. 64–87.

Gessen, I. V. *V dvukh vekakh.* Berlin, 1937.

Gläser, Rupert. *Die Frage nach Gott in der Philosophie S. L. Franks.* Würzburg, 1975.

Great Soviet Encyclopedia. Translation of 3d ed. Edited by A. M. Prokhorov. New York: Macmillan, 1975.

Greenberg, L., *The Jews in Russia.* New York: Schocken, 1976.

Grigor'ev, M. G. "Marksisty v Nizhnom v 1881–94." *Proletarskaia revoliutsiia,* 4, no. 27, pp. 89–117.

Grot, N. Ia. "O zhizni i lichnosti Dekarta." *Voprosy filosofii i psikhologii,* 1896, no. 5, pp. 645–59.

Gul', R. *Ia unes Rossiiu.* Vols. 1, 2. New York: Most, 1981, 1984.

Haimson, L. *The Russian Marxists and the Origins of Bolshevism.* Boston: Beacon Press, 1966.

Hamburg, G. M., *Boris Chicherin and Early Russian Liberalism,* Stanford, Stanford University Press, 1993.

Harding, N. *Lenin's Political Thought.* Vol 1. Macmillan, 1987.

_____, ed. *Marxism in Russia: Key Documents 1879–1906.* Trans. R. Taylor. Cambridge: Cambridge University Press, 1973.

Hosking, G. *The Russian Constitutional Experiment, 1907–1914.* Cambridge: Cambridge University Press, 1973.

Istoriia Moskvy. Vol. 4. Moscow: Izd. Akadem. Nauk SSSR, 1954.

Il'in, B. N. "Nikolai Kuzanskii i S. L. Frank." *Sbornik,* 1954, pp. 85–116.

Illarionov, V. T., ed. *Materialy po istorii revoliutsionnogo dvizheniia*, t. 11, Nizhnii Novgorod: Gos. izd., 1922, vol 2.

Ivanov-Razumnik, R. V. *Istoriia russkoi obshchestvennoi mysli*. St.P., 1911, vol. 2.

Izgoev, A. "On Educated Youth." *Landmarks*, pp. 88–111.

Izvestiia Saratovskogo Universiteta: Istoriko-filologicheskii fakul'tet. vyp. 1. Saratov, 1918.

Johnston, R. M. *New Mecca, New Babylon*. Kingston, Ontario: McGill-Queen's University Press, 1988.

"K istorii sozdaniia 'Vekh.'" *Minuvshee*, 11, 1991, pp. 249–91.

Kananova, G. I., *Semidesiatipiatiletie Lazarevskogo Instituta*. Moscow, 1891.

Kartashev, A. V. "Ideologicheskii i tserkovnyi put' Franka." *Sbornik pamiati S. L. Franka*, 1954, pp. 67–70.

Kassow, S. D. *Students, Professors, and the State in Tsarist Russia*. Berkeley: University of California Press, 1989.

Kaufman, A. A. "Poznai samogo sebia." *Poliarnaia zvezda*, Dec. 1905, no. 2, pp. 136–45.

———. "Eshche o samopoznanii." *Poliarnaia zvezda*, Jan. 1906, no. 6, pp. 397–407.

Keep, J. *The Rise of Social Democracy in Russia*. Oxford: Clarendon Press, 1963.

Kelly, A. A. "Attitudes to the Individual in Russian Thought and Literature with Special Reference to the 'Vekhi' Controversy." Ph.D. diss., Oxford University, 1970.

Kiel, M. "The Jewish Narodnik." *Judaism*, 19, no. 3, Summer 1970, pp. 295–310.

Kindersley, R. *The First Russian Revisionists*. Oxford: Clarendon Press, 1962.

Kistiakovskii, B. "In Defense of Law." *Landmarks*, pp. 112–37.

Kizevetter, A. A. *Na rubezhe dvukh stoletii*. Prague, 1929.

Kline, G., "The Hegelian Roots of S. L. Frank's Ethics and Social Philosophy," *The Owl of Minerva*, 25, 2 (Spring 1994), pp. 195–208.

Kline, G. *Religious and Anti-Religious Thought in Russia*. Chicago: University of Chicago Press, 1968.

———. *Spinoza in Soviet Philosophy*. London: Routledge and Kegan Paul, 1952.

Koch, F. C. *The Volga Germans in Russia and the Americas from 1763 to the Present*. University Park: Pennsylvania State University Press, 1977.

Kolerov, M. A. "'Voprosy zhizni': Istoriia i soderzhanie (1905)." *Logos*, 1991, no. 2, pp. 264–83.

Konstitutsionnoe gosudarstvo. Izd. I. V. Gessena i priv. dots. A. I. Kamkina. St.P., 1905?.

Kolakowski, L. *Bergson*. Oxford: Oxford University Press, 1985.

———. "Politics and the Devil." *Encounter*, Dec. 1987, pp. 59–67.

Kremer, A., and Iu. Martov. "On Agitation." *Marxism in Russia: Key Documents, 1879–1906*, ed. N. Harding, trans. R. Taylor. Cambridge: Cambridge University Press, 1983, pp. 192–205.

Krotov, M. A. *Iakutskaia ssylka 70-80-kh godov*. Introduction by V. Vilenskii-Sibiriakov, 1925.

Krymskii, A. "Lazarevskii Institut Vostochnykh Iazykov v Moskve." *Entsiklopedicheskii slovar',* t. 17. St.P., 1896, pp. 247–48.

Kudrinskii, M. A. "Arkhivnaia istoriia sbornika 'Problemy idealizma' (1902). *Voprosy filosofii,* 1993, no. 4, pp. 157–65.

Landmarks. Edited by B. Shragin, A. Todd; trans. M. Schwartz. New York: Karz Howard, 1977.

Lapshin, I. I. "Misticheskii ratsionalizm Prof. S. L. Franka." *Mysl',* 1922, no. 3, pp. 140–53.

Leontovich, V. V. *Istoriia liberalizma v Rossii, 1762–1914,* Paris: YMCA Press, 1980.

Levitskii, S. A. "Etika Franka." *Sbornik,* 1954, pp. 117–32.

Libanova, G. *Studencheskoe dvizhenie, 1899–1901,* London: Russian Free Press, 1901.

Lieven, D. C. B. *Russia and the Origins of the First World War.* Macmillan, 1983.

_____. *Russia's Rulers.* New Haven, Conn.: Yale University Press, 1989.

Losskii, B. N. "Nasha sem'ia v poru likholet'ia 1914–1922." *Minuvshee,* 11, 1991, pp. 119–98.

Losskii, N. O. *History of Russian Philosophy.* London: George, Allen and Unwin, 1952.

_____. "Teoriia znaniia S. L. Franka." *Sbornik,* 1954, pp. 133–44.

_____. *Vospominaniia.* Munich, 1968.

Losskii, V. *The Mystical Theology of the Eastern Church.* Crestwood, N.Y.: St. Vladimir's Seminary Press, 1976.

Lot-Borodina, M. "In Memoriam." *Sbornik,* 1954, pp. 43–48.

Lowrie, D. A. *Rebellious Prophet.* London: Victor Gollancz, 1960.

Lur'e, S. V. "O sbornike 'Vekhi'." *Russkaia mysl',* 1909, no. 5, pp. 137–46.

McClelland, James C. "The Professoriate in the Russian Civil War." *Party, State and Society in the Russian Civil War,* ed. D. P. Koenker, et al. Bloomington: Indiana University Press, 1989, pp. 243–66.

Maslennikov, V. I. "Stranichki proshlogo." *Na zare rabochego dvizheniia v Moskve: Vospominaniia uchastnikov Moskovskogo Rabochego Soiuza 1893–5, i dukumenty,* ed. S. I. Mitskevich. Moscow: Izd. Vsesoiuznogo Obshchestva Politkatorzhan i Ssyl'no-Poselentsev, 1932.

Mendel, A. P. *Dilemmas of Progress in Tsarist Russia.* Cambridge: Cambridge University Press, 1961.

Menshchikov, L. P. *Okhrana i revoliutsiia.* 3 vols. Moscow, 1925.

Mihajlov, M. "The Great Catalyzer: Nietzsche and Russian Neo-Idealism." *Nietzsche in Russia,* ed. B. G. Rosenthal. Princeton, NJ: Princeton University Press, 1986, pp. 127–45.

Miliukov, P. "Intelligentsiia i istoricheskaia traditsiia." *Intelligentsiia v Rossii.* St.P.: Zemlia, 1910, pp. 89–191.

_____. *Vospominaniia, 1859–1917.* Vol. 1. New York: Izd imeni Chekhova, 1955.

Milosz, C. *The Captive Mind.* Trans. T. Zielonko. New York: Vintage Books, 1981.

Mitskevich, S. I. *Na grani dvukh epokh: Ot narodnichestva k Marksizmu.* Moscow: Gosudarstvennoe sotsial'no-ekonomicheskoe izd., 1937.
_____. *Revoliutsionnaia Moskva, 1888–1905.* Moscow: Gos. izd., 1940.
Mogilianskaia, M. N., and M. B. Pirozhkov. "Pis'mo v redaktsiiu." *Rech',* 24 June 1906, no. 108, p. 2
"Moskovskii soiuz bor'by." *Bor'ba sozdaniia Marksistskoi partii v Rossii: Obrazovanie RSDRP: Vozniknovenie Bol'shevizma 1894–1904: Dokumenty i materialy.* Moscow: Gos. izd. politicheskoi literatury, 1965, pp. 78–94.
Nabokov, V. D. *The Provisional Government.* Edited by A. Field, University of Queensland Press, 1970.
Nasha dan' Bestuzhevskim kursam. Izd ob'edineniia B.Bestuzhevok za rubezhom. Paris, 1971.
Naimark, N. M. *Terrorists and Social Democrats: The Russian Revolutionary Movement under Alexander III.* Cambridge, Mass.: Harvard University Press, 1983.
Newman, J. H. *Apologia pro Vita Sua.* London: J. M. Dent, 1946.
Nietzsche in Russia. Edited by B. G. Rosenthal. Princeton, NJ: Princeton University Press, 1986.
Nogin, V. *Na poliuse kholoda.* Moscow: Gos. izd., 1923.
Novgorodtsev, P. I. "Russian Universities and Higher Technical Schools during the War." *Russian Schools and Universities in the World War,* ed. P. N. Ignatiev et al. New Haven, Conn.: Yale University Press, 1929.
Oberlander, G. "Die Vechi-Discussione." Ph.D. diss., University of Cologne, 1965.
Offord, D. *The Russian Revolutionary Movement in the 1880's.* Cambridge: Cambridge University, 1986.
Oldenburg, S. S. "Pokhod na tserkov'." "Politicheskii obzor," *Russkaia mysl',* Prague, June–July 1922, pp. 343–46.
Orlov, V. I. *Studencheskoe dvizhenie Moskovskogo universiteta v XIX stoletii.* Moscow: Izd. Vsesoiuznogo Obshchestva Politkatorzhan i Ssyl'no-Poselentsev, 1934.
Pamiat'. Istoricheskii sbornik, Paris.
Petrunkevich, I. I. "Intelligentsiia i 'Vekhi.'" *Intelligentsiia v Rossii.* St.P.: Zemlia, 1910, pp. iii–xv.
Pipes, R. *The Russian Revolution, 1899–1919.* London: Collins Harvill, 1990.
_____. *Social Democracy and the St. Petersburg Labour Movement, 1885–1897.* Cambridge, Mass.: Harvard University Press, 1963.
_____. *Struve: Liberal on the Left: 1870–1905.* Cambridge, Mass.: Harvard University Press, 1970.
_____. *Struve, Liberal on the Right, 1905–1944.* Cambridge, Mass.: Harvard University Press, 1980.
Plekhanov, G. Review of Frank, *Teoriia tsennosti Marksa i eia znachenie. Sochineniia,* 24 vols. Moscow: Gos. izd., 1923–27, vol. 11, pp. 348–57.
Plotnikov, N. "Heidegger-Rezeption in Russland: Semen L. Frank und Ludwig Binswanger." *Daseinsnalyse,* Feb. 1994, pp. 113–131.
Poltoratskii, N. P. *Ivan Aleksandrovich Il'in.* Tenafly, N.J.: Hermitage, 1989.

———. *Rossiia i revoliutsiia: Russkaia religiozno-filosofskaia i natsional'no-politicheskaia mysl' XX veka.* Tenafly, N.J.: Hermitage, 1988.
Putnam, G. F. "P. B. Struve's View of the Russian Revolution of 1905." *Slavonic and East European Review,* 45, July 1967, no. 105, pp. 457–73.
———. *Russian Alternatives to Marxism.* Knoxville: The University of Tennessee Press, 1977.
Raeff, M. *Russia Abroad.* New York: Oxford University Press, 1990.
Raleigh, D. J. *Revolution on the Volga: 1917 in Saratov.* Ithaca, N.Y.: Cornell University Press, 1986.
———, ed. *A Russian Civil War Diary: Alexis Babine in Saratov, 1917–22.* Durham, N.C.: Duke University Press, 1988.
Read, C. *Religion, Revolution and the Russian Intelligentsia: The Vekhi Debate and Its Intellectual Background.* Totowa, N.J.: Barnes and Noble, 1979.
Redlikh, R. *Sotsial'naia filosofiia S. L. Franka.* Frankfurt/Main: Posev, 1972.
Riha, T. *A Russian European: Paul Miliukov in Russian Politics.* Notre Dame, Ind.: Notre Dame University Press, 1968
Rice, C. *The Russian Workers and the Socialist-Revolutionary Party through the Revolution of 1905–07,* Macmillan, 1988.
Robbins, R. G., Jr. *Famine in Russia.* New York: Columbia University Press, 1975.
Rosenberg, W. C. *Liberals in the Russian Revolution.* Princeton, N.J.: Princeton University Press, 1974.
Rosenthal, B. G. "The Search for a Russian Orthodox Work Ethic." *Between Tsar and People,* ed. E. W. Clowes, et al., Princeton, NJ: Princeton University Press, 1991, pp. 57–74.
Russell, B. *The Problems of Philosophy.* Oxford: Oxford University Press, 1983.
Sakwa, R. *Soviet Communists in Power.* Macmillan, 1988.
Sanburov, V. I. "K istorii cozdanii i deiatel'nosti Moskovskogo 'Rabochego Soiuza.'" *Voprosy istorii KPSS,* 1969, no. 1, pp. 68–77.
Savinov, A. I. *Pis'ma, dokumenty, vospominaniia.* Leningrad: Khudozhnik RSFSR, 1983.
Sbornik pamiati Semena Liudvigovicha Franka. Edited by V. V. Zen'kovskii. Munich, 1954.
Shakhovskoi, D. I. "Soiuz Osvobozhdeniia." *Zarnitsy,* 1909, pt. 2, pp. 81–171.
Schapiro, L. *1917.* Maurice Temple Smith, 1984.
———. "The Political Thought of the First Provisional Government." *Revolutionary Russia,* ed. R. Pipes. Cambridge, Mass.: Harvard University Press, 1968.
———. *Rationalism and Nationalism in Russian Nineteenth Century Political Thought.* New Haven, Conn.: Yale University Press, 1976.
———. "The 'Vekhi' group and the Mystique of Revolution." *Russian Studies,* ed. E. Dahrendorf. London: Collins Harvill, 1986, pp. 68–92.
Scherrer, J. "Die Petersburger religiös-philosophischen Vereinigungen: Die Entwicklung des religiösen Selbstverständnisses ihrer Intelligencija Mitglieder 1901-1917." *Forschungen zur osteuropäischen Geschichte,* no. 19. Berlin, Wiesbaden, 1973.

Schlögel, K. *Jenseits des großen Oktober: Das Laboratorium der moderne Petersburg 1909–1921.* Berlin: Siedler, 1988.

Scruton, R. *Spinoza.* Oxford: Oxford University Press, 1986.

Shatsillo, K. F. *Russkii liberalizm nakanune revoliutsii, 1905–1907 gg.* Moscow: Nauka, 1985.

Shein, L. J. "The Concept of the Unfathomable in S. L. Frank's Epistemology." *Canadian Slavic Studies,* 2, no. 1, Spring 1968, pp. 14–27.

———. "El concepto de hombre y sociedad en S. L. Frank." *Folia Humanistica,* 13, 1975, no. 156, pt. 1, pp. 765–74; pt. 2, pp. 843–51.

———, ed. *Readings in Russian Philosophical Thought.* The Hague: Mouton, 1968.

———, ed. *Readings in Russian Philosophical Thought: Logic and Aesthetics.* Mouton, 1973.

Silvin, M. A. *Lenin v periode zarozhdeniia partii.* Lenizdat, 1958.

Solzhenitsyn A. I. "Repentance and Self-Limitation in the Life of Nations." *From under the Rubble,* trans. M. Scammell et al., Washington, D.C., Regnery Gateway, 1981, pp. 105–43.

———. "The Smatterers." *From under the Rubble,* pp. 229–78.

Spravochnaia knizhka dlia slushitel'nits S.Peterburgskikh Vysshikh Zhenskikh Kursov. St.P., 1908–9, 1909–10, 1910–11, 1911–12, 1912–13, 1913–14, 1914–15, 1915–16, 1916–17.

Starchenko, N. N. "Filosofiia intuitivizma v Rossii i sovremennost'." Kand diss, Moscow, 1981.

Stepun, F. "Vera i znanie v filosofii S. L. Franka." *Novyi zhurnal,* 1965, no. 81, pp. 227–30.

———. *Vergangenes und Unvergängliches.* Kösel Verlag zu München, 1950.

Struve, G. P. "S. L. Frank i P. B. Struve: Glavnye etapy ikh druzhby." *Sbornik,* 1954, pp. 49–66.

Struve, K. "Tserkovnaia smuta v Berline: Beseda s Prof. S. L. Frankom." *Vozrozhdenie,* 27 Oct. 1926, no. 512, p. 2.

Struve, P. B. "The Intelligentsia and Revolution." *Landmarks,* pp. 138–54.

———. "Gete i Pushkin." *Dukh i slovo.* Paris: YMCA Press, 1967, pp. 136–47.

———. Introduction to Berdiaev. *Sub'ektivizm i individualizm v obshchestvennom filosofii. Collected Works in Fifteen Volumes,* vol. 4. Ann Arbor, Mich.: University Microfilms, 1970, pp. i–lxxxiv.

———. *Kriticheskie zametki po voprosu ob ekonomicheskom razvitii Rossii.* St.P., 1894.

———. "Krushenie dela Bismarka." *Russkaia mysl',* 1915, no. 4, sec. "V Rossii i za granitsy," pp. 5–7.

———. "Liga Russkoi kul'tury." *Russkaia svoboda,* 12 May 1917, no. 3, pp. 3–5.

———. "'Neiz'iasnimyi' i 'nepostizhnyi.'" *Dukh i slovo.* Paris, YMCA Press, 1981, pp. 23–31.

———. "Neskol'ko slov o Lige Russkoi kul'tury." *Russkaia svoboda,* 21 June 1917, no. 9, pp. 24–26.

———. "Neskol'ko slov po povodu stat'i S. N. Bulgakova." *Poliarnaia zvezda,* no. 13, pp. 128–30.

————. "Osnovnaia antinomiia teorii trudovoi tsennosti Marksa." *Zhizn',* 4, 1900, no. 2, pp. 297–306.

————. "Ot redaktora." *Osvobozhdenie,* 18 June–1 July 1902, no. 1, pp. 1–7.

————. "Ot redaktsii." *Poliarnaia zvezda,* 1905, no. 1, pp. 3–4.

————. "Pis'ma v redaktsiiu." *Rech',* 25 June 1906, no. 109, p. 2.

————. "Poznanie revoliutsii i vozrozhdenie dukha." *Russkaia mysl',* 1923, nos. 6–8, p. 303.

————. "Svoboda i istoricheskaia neobkhodimost'." *Voprosy filosofii i psikhologii,* 3, Jan.–Feb. 1897, no. 1 (36), pp. 120–39.

————. Review of Frank, *Teoriia tsennosti Marksa i eia znachenie. Mir bozhii,* 10, Aug 1901, no. 8, pt. 2, pp. 113–17.

————. "Velikaia Rossiia i Sviataia Rus'." *Russkaia mysl',* 1914, no. 12, pp. 176–80.

Sukhorukov, V. V. S. Frank: Zhiznennyi put' i sotsial'no-filosofskaia orientatsiia." Moscow: Institute of Sociological Research, 1985.

Sutton, J. *The Religious Philosophy of Vladimir Soloviev.* Macmillan, 1988.

Swoboda, P. J. Foreword to *Man's Soul.* Trans. B. Jakim. Athens: Ohio University Press, 1993, pp. xi–xxx.

————. "The Philosophical Thought of S. L. Frank, 1902–1915: A Study of the Metaphysical Impulse in Early Twentieth-Century Russia." Ph.D. diss., Columbia Univeristy, 1992.

Tannert, R. *Zur Theorie des Wissens: Ein Neuansatz nach S. L. Frank, 1877–1950.* Bern, Frankfurt/Main: Herbert Lang 1973.

Tkachenko, P. S. *Moskovskoe studenchestvo v obshchestvenno-politicheskoi zhizni Rossii vtoroi poloviny XIX veka.* Moscow: Izd. Moskovskogo Universiteta, 1958.

Trubetskoi, Kn. E. N. "Voina i mirovaia zadacha Rossii." *Russkaia mysl',* 1914, no. 12, pp. 88–96.

Trubetskoi, Kn. S. E. *Minuvshee.* Vserossiiskaia memuarnaia biblioteka. Paris: YMCA Press, 1989.

Tyrkova-Williams, A. *Na putiakh k svobode.* New York, 1952.

Ul'ianova, A. "Vospominaniia." *Bor'ba sozdaniia Marksistkoi partii v Rossii: Obrazovanie RSDRP: Vozniknovenie Bol'shevizma 1894–1904: Dokumenty i materialy.* Moscow: Gos. izd. politicheskoi literatury, 1965, pp. 94–97.

Vadimov, A. *Zhizn' Berdiaeva,* Berkeley Slavic Specialists, 1993.

Vaganian, V. "Nashi Russkie shpengleristy." *Pod znamenem Marksizma,* 1922, nos. 1–2, pp. 28–33.

Vallon, M. A. *An Apostle of Freedom: The Life and Teachings of Nicholas Berdiaev.* New York: Philosophical Library, 1960.

Vekhi. Moscow, 1909; reprint Frankfurt/Main: Posev, 1967.

Venturi, F. *Roots of Revolution.* Trans. F. Haskell. Introduction Isaiah Berlin. London: Weidenfeld and Nicolson, 1960.

Vertel', S. "Statisticheskie dannye o dvizhenii Evreiskago naseleniia v Moskve za poslednie gody." *Voskhod,* 1893, no. 6, pt. 2, pp. 34–37.

Ves' Peterburg. 1905–17.

Vilenskii-Sibiriakov, V., et al. *Deiateli revoliutsionnogo dvizheniia v Rossii: Bio-bibliograficheskii slovar',* 1870s. t. 2, vyp 2–4, 1929.

Villiers, M. *Charles Péguy.* London: Collins, 1965.
Vladimirskii M. "Iz istorii Moskovskoi sotsial-demokraticheskoi organizatsii." *Bor'ba sozdaniia Marksistskoi partii v Rossii: Obrazovanie RSDRP: Vozniknovenie Bol'shevizma 1894–1904: Dokumenty i materialy.* Moscow: Gos. izd. politicheskoi literatury, 1965, pp. 97–99.
——. *Ocherki rabochego i sotsial'no-demokraticheskogo dvizheniia v Nizhnom Novgorode i Sormove.* Moscow: Gos. izd. politicheskoi literatury, 1957.
Voden, A. "Na zare legal'nogo Marksizma." *Letopisi Marksizma,* 1927, no. 3, pp. 67–82.
Vodovozov, V. "Osvobozhdeniia Soiuz." *Entsiklopedicheskii slovar',* dopol'nitel'nyi tom, vol. 3, p. 154.
——. "Poliarnaia zvezda." *Entsiklopedicheskii slovar',* dopol'nitel'nyi tom, vol. 3, pp. 439–40.
"Vol'naia Akademiia Dukhovnoi Kul'tury v Moskve." *Sofiia,* vol. 1, ed. N. A. Berdiaev. Berlin: Obelisk, 1923, pp. 135–36.
Vrangel', Bar. Liudmila. *Vospominaniia i starodavnye vremena.* Washington: Victor Kamkin, 1964, p. 27.
Vsia Moskva. 1878–92.
Vuccinich, A. *Darwin in Russia.* Berkeley: University of California Press, 1988.
——. *Social Thought in Tsarist Russia.* Chicago: University of Chicago Press, 1976.
Vysheslavtsev, B. P. "Pamiati filosofa-druga." *Sbornik,* 1954, pp. 40–42
Walicki, A. *A History of Russian Thought from the Enlightenment to Marxism.* Trans. H. Andrews-Rusiecka. Oxford, 1989.
——. *Legal Philosophies of Russian Liberalism.* Oxford: Clarendon Press, 1987.
——. *The Slavophile Controversy.* Oxford: Clarendon Press, 1975.
Walters, P. M. "The Development of the Political and Religious Philosophy of Sergei Bulgakov, 1895–1922: A Struggle for Transcendence." Ph.D. diss., London, 1978.
Williams, R. C. *Culture in Exile: Russian Emigrés in Germany, 1881–1941.* Ithaca, N.Y.: Cornell University Press, 1972.
Wortman, R. *The Crisis of Russian Populism.* Cambridge: Cambridge University Press, 1967.
Yanovsky, V. S. *Elysian Fields.* Trans. I. & V. S. Yanovsky, foreword by Marc Raeff. Dekalb, Ill.: Northern Illinois University Press, 1987.
Zak, L. V. "Semen Liudvigovich Frank—moi brat." *Sbornik,* 1954, pp. 17–24.
Zaionchkovskii, P. A., ed. *Istoriia dorevoliutsionnoi Rossii v dnevnikakh i vospominaniiakh.* T. 3, pts. 1–4, t. 4, pts. 1–4, Moscow: Kniga, 1979–86.
Zapiski S-Peterburgskogo religiozno-filosofskogo obshchestva, vyp. 1. St.P., 1908.
Zen'kovskii, V. V. *A History of Russian Philosophy.* Trans. G. Kline, 2 vols. London, Routledge and Kegan Paul, 1953.
——. "Uchenie S. L. Franka o cheloveke." *Sbornik,* 1954, pp. 76–84.
——. "Zarozhdenie R. Kh. D. v emigratsii." *Vestnik RkhD,* no. 168, 1993, II–III, pp. 5–40.

Zernov N. M. *The Russian Religious Renaissance of the Twentieth Century.* London: Darton, Longman, and Todd, 1963.

Zhirmunskii, N. A., et al., eds. "Perepiska B. M. Eikhenbauma i V. M. Zhirmunskogo." *Tynianovskii sbornik,* tret'i tynianovskie chteniia. Riga: Zinatne, 1988.

Zimmerman, J. E. "The Political Views of the 'Vekhi' Authors." *Canadian-American Slavic Studies,* 10, no. 3, fall 1976, pp. 307–27.

Index